A Mathematics and Physical Sciences Textbook

Published under the auspices of

DMK Deutschschweizerische Mathematikkommission des VSMP
(German-Swiss Mathematics Commission of the Swiss Society of Mathematics and Physics Teachers)

DPK Deutschschweizerische Physikkommission des VSMP
(German-Swiss Physics Commission of the Swiss Society of Mathematics and Physics Teachers)

DCK Deutschschweizerische Chemiekommission des VSN
(German-Swiss Chemistry Commission of the Swiss Society of Natural Sciences Teachers)

Formulae, Tables and Concepts
A Concise Handbook of
Mathematics – Physics – Chemistry

DMK | DPK | DCK

Formulae
Tables
and Concepts

A Concise Handbook of
Mathematics – Physics – Chemistry

translated from the German edition
under the editorship of Andrew S. Glass

orell füssli Verlag

Authors

Mathematics:	Werner Durandi, Baoswan Dzung Wong, Markus Kriener, Hansruedi Künsch, Alfred Vogelsanger, Jörg Waldvogel
Physics:	Samuel Byland
Chemistry:	Klemens Koch, Andreas Bartlome, Michael Bleichenbacher
Astronomy:	Hans Roth
Editor:	Werner Durandi

The authors and the publisher are indebted to the following persons for critical reviews of various sections of the book.

Mathematics:	Christian Blatter, Patrick Ghanaat, Jürg Hüsler, Andreas Ruckstuhl, Hansklaus Rummler, Hansruedi Schneebeli, Urs Stammbach, Hans Heiner Storrer, Peter Thurnheer
Physics:	Martin Lieberherr, Manfred Sigrist, Christian Stulz
Chemistry:	Bernhard Erni, Hans Galliker, Jürg Hulliger
Astronomy:	Ralf Vanscheidt

1st edition 2014

© 2009, 2014 Orell Füssli Verlag, Zürich
www.ofv.ch
All rights reserved

This work is protected by copyright. All rights are reserved, including the rights of translation, reprinting, incorporation in lectures, use of illustrations and tables, use in broadcast media, microfilming or other forms of duplication, and storage in electronic data-processing systems, whether in whole or part. This applies likewise to extracts from this work. In individual cases this work or its parts may only be reproduced to the extent permitted by law, and is subject to charge.

Translation:	Andrew S. Glass (principal translator), Klemens Koch (Chemistry)
Note on the translation:	This edition makes use of British and World English incorporating Oxford Dictionaries preferred spellings.
Cover design:	Orell Füssli Verlag, Zürich
Typesetting:	Werner Durandi (LaTeX technical support: Daniel Baumgartner)
Graphics:	Werner Durandi, Wolfgang Gehrig
Printing:	fgb • freiburger graphische Betriebe, Freiburg

ISBN 978-3-280-04084-3

Catalogue information in the German National Library (Deutsche Nationalbibliothek): This publication is catalogued in the German National Library; detailed bibliographic information can be accessed on the Internet: www.dnb.de

Contents

MATHEMATICS

- **1 General** — 9
  - 1.1 Mathematical logic and methods of proof — 9
  - 1.2 Sets — 11
  - 1.3 Relations — 12
  - 1.4 Functions — 13
  - 1.5 Numbers — 14
- **2 Algebra** — 20
  - 2.1 Binomial expansions and factorizations — 20
  - 2.2 Polynomial functions — 21
  - 2.3 Polynomial equations of higher degree in one variable — 22
  - 2.4 Algebraic Structures — 25
  - 2.5 Linear Algebra — 27
  - 2.6 Systems of linear equations — 33
- **3 Discrete Mathematics** — 35
  - 3.1 Elementary number theory — 35
  - 3.2 Sequences — 38
  - 3.3 Factorials and binomial coefficients — 42
  - 3.4 Combinatorics (counting problems) — 44
  - 3.5 Graph theory — 46
- **4 Calculus** — 51
  - 4.1 Sequences of real numbers — 51
  - 4.2 Real functions — 54
  - 4.3 Limits of functions, continuity — 61
  - 4.4 Differentiation — 62
  - 4.5 Integration — 70
  - 4.6 Series expansions — 77
  - 4.7 Special inequalities and approximations — 81
  - 4.8 Differential equations — 81
- **5 Geometry** — 83
  - 5.1 Plane geometry — 83
  - 5.2 Solid geometry — 92
  - 5.3 Trigonometry — 97
  - 5.4 Spherical trigonometry — 100
  - 5.5 Analytical geometry and vectors — 101
  - 5.6 Affine maps — 111
  - 5.7 Coordinate transformations — 113

6		Probability and Statistics	115
	6.1	Descriptive Statistics	115
	6.2	Probability	117
	6.3	Statistical inference	124
	6.4	Important statistical tests and confidence intervals	126
7		Numerical Analysis	133
	7.1	Polynomials	133
	7.2	Interpolation	134
	7.3	Systems of linear equations	135
	7.4	Least squares approximations	136
	7.5	Numerical solution of equations in one unknown	138
	7.6	Numerical integration	139
	7.7	Numerical differentiation	141
	7.8	Numerical solution of differential equations	142
	7.9	Discrete Fourier transform (DFT)	143
	7.10	Random number generation	144
8		Mathematical Tables	146

PHYSICS

1		Classical Mechanics	155
	1.1	Kinematics	155
	1.2	Dynamics of a point mass	157
	1.3	Rigid bodies	162
	1.4	Continuous media	164
2		Waves, Optics and Acoustics	166
3		Thermodynamics	170
4		Electricity and Magnetism	173
	4.1	Electrostatics	173
	4.2	Direct current	175
	4.3	Magnetism	177
	4.4	Alternating current	179
5		Special Relativity	181
6		Atomic Physics	182
7		Nuclear Physics	183
8		Measurement Errors	184

9	Physical Data	185
9.1	Units	185
9.2	Mechanics	187
9.3	Thermodynamics	190
9.4	Optics	193
9.5	Electricity and Magnetism	194
9.6	Atomic and nuclear Physics	195
9.7	Geophysical data of Switzerland	204

ASTRONOMY

1	General	205
2	Earth and Its Satellites	209
3	Sun	211
4	Solar System	212
5	Stars	214
6	Galaxies	216
7	Cosmos	217

CHEMISTRY

1	Definitions and Formulae	218
2	Chemical Thermodynamics	222
3	Atomic Structure	226
4	Elements	228
5	Inorganic Chemistry	231
6	Organic Chemistry	233
7	Biochemistry	237
8	Instrumental Analysis	244
9	Acids and Bases	248
10	Redox Reactions	249

Index   251

Preface to the English edition

There has been an ever-increasing number of bilingual programmes at Swiss "Gymnasien" in the past decade. While in 2007 40% of all "Gymnasien" offered a bilingual course (Elmiger, 2008)[1] in 2012 this number has risen to 70% (Bildungsbericht Schweiz, 2014)[2]. Among all bilingual programmes the combination German-English is the most common. What is of particular interest in this context is the fact that mathematics and physics are among the top 3 subjects taught in those bilingual programmes. Therefore the publication of an English version of the concise handbook "Formeln, Tabellen, Begriffe" seemed a very logical step indeed.

The aim of this translation is to give the teacher an English version which is an equivalent of the German book, not only in content but also in design, and hence enables teachers to work with both language versions side by side. As "Formeln, Tabellen, Begriffe" is an accepted aid at Swiss Universities too, we hope to satisfy a demand at this level due to the increasing number of lectures held in English.

This first edition of the English "Formulae, Tables, Concepts" already includes changes that will only be implemented in the 5th edition of the German "Formeln, Tabellen, Begriffe". The main difference compared to the 4th German edition is the expansion of the chemistry part, which takes into account the large number of students choosing chemistry/biology as their core subject.

My special thanks go to the retired lecturer and teacher of maths and physics, Andrew Glass, who has not only done an awesome job translating the text into English but also suggested changes to the content. My thanks are extended to all the experts from Universities and "Gymnasien" who spent many hours of meticulous proof-reading and, last but not least, to the project leader, Werner Durandi, who not only typeset the book but also organized and coordinated the whole process with enormous energy and expertise.

Schwyz, 23rd March 2014

Daniela Grawehr
President DMK

Deutschschweizerische Mathematikkommission
Deutschschweizerische Physikkommission
Deutschschweizerische Chemiekommission

---

[1] D. Elmiger (2008). Die zweisprachige Maturität in der Schweiz. Die variantenreiche Umsetzung einer bildungspolitischen Innovation. Staatssekretariat für Bildung und Forschung SBF

[2] SKBF (2014). Bildungsbericht Schweiz 2014. Schweizerische Koordinationsstelle für Bildungsforschung

MATHEMATICS

1 General

1.1 Mathematical logic and methods of proof

proposition
Propositions will be denoted by $A, B, \ldots$.
A proposition is always either true (t) or false (f).

Propositional logic

truth table of the negation of a proposition A

A	not A $\neg A$
t	f
f	t

truth tables for binary operators connecting A and B

A	B	conjunction A and B $A \wedge B$	disjunction A or B $A \vee B$	material conditional if A then B $A \to B$	biconditional A if and only if B $A \leftrightarrow B$
t	t	t	t	t	t
t	f	f	t	f	f
f	t	f	t	t	f
f	f	f	f	t	t

implication
A valid material conditional statement is called implication, using the notation $A \Rightarrow B$.

equivalence
A valid biconditional statement is called equivalence, using the notation $A \Leftrightarrow B$.

converse of a material conditional statement
$B \to A$ is the converse of $A \to B$.

contrapositive of a material conditional statement
$\neg B \to \neg A$ is the contrapositive of $A \to B$.

Rules of propositional logic

commutativity $\qquad A \wedge B \Leftrightarrow B \wedge A \qquad\qquad A \vee B \Leftrightarrow B \vee A$

associativity $\qquad (A \wedge B) \wedge C \Leftrightarrow A \wedge (B \wedge C) \qquad (A \vee B) \vee C \Leftrightarrow A \vee (B \vee C)$

distributivity $\qquad (A \vee B) \wedge C \Leftrightarrow (A \wedge C) \vee (B \wedge C) \qquad (A \wedge B) \vee C \Leftrightarrow (A \vee C) \wedge (B \vee C)$

DE MORGAN's theorems $\qquad \neg(A \wedge B) \Leftrightarrow \neg A \vee \neg B \qquad \neg(A \vee B) \Leftrightarrow \neg A \wedge \neg B$

elimination of the material conditional operator	$A \to B \iff \neg A \vee B$
rule of contraposition	$A \to B \iff \neg B \to \neg A$
elimination of the biconditional operator	$A \leftrightarrow B \iff (A \to B) \wedge (B \to A)$
modus ponens (conditional elimination)	$A \wedge (A \to B) \Rightarrow B$
modus tollens	$\neg B \wedge (A \to B) \Rightarrow \neg A$
transitivity	$(A \to B) \wedge (B \to C) \Rightarrow (A \to C)$

Quantifiers

Let $R(x)$ and $S(x)$ denote predicates, where x is an element of a non-empty set M.

universal quantifier	The proposition $\forall x\, R(x)$ is true if and only if $R(x)$ is true for all values $x \in M$.
existential quantifier	The proposition $\exists x\, R(x)$ is true if and only if $R(x)$ is true for at least one value $x \in M$.

Properties

$\neg\bigl(\forall x\, R(x)\bigr) \iff \exists x\, (\neg R(x))$ $\qquad$ $\neg\bigl(\forall x\, (R(x) \to S(x))\bigr) \iff \exists x\, (R(x) \wedge \neg S(x))$

$\neg\bigl(\exists x\, R(x)\bigr) \iff \forall x\, (\neg R(x))$ $\qquad$ $\neg\bigl(\exists x\, (R(x) \wedge S(x))\bigr) \iff \forall x\, (\neg R(x) \vee \neg S(x))$

Methods of proof

direct proof	Starting from propositions which have already been proven, the required proposition is derived in a finite sequence of logically correct inferences.
proof by contradiction (reductio ad absurdum)	Suppose proposition B is to be proven. • Assume $\neg B$. • Starting with $\neg B$ and other proven propositions derive the negation $\neg A$ of a proposition A that can otherwise be proven to be true. • Resolve the contradiction $A \wedge \neg A$ by rejecting the assumption $\neg B$ and accepting the original proposition B.
proof by induction	mathematical induction ▶ p. 14

1.2 Sets

Let A, B, C be subsets of a given universal set U.

Inclusion (subsets)

special cases	$A \subset A, \quad \emptyset \subset A \ $ for all A
equality	$(A \subset B \ $ and $ \ B \subset A) \Leftrightarrow A = B$
transitivity	$(A \subset B \ $ and $ \ B \subset C) \Rightarrow A \subset C$

Binary operations on sets

Basic operations

union	$A \cup B = \{x \,|\, x \in A \ $ or $ \ x \in B\}$
intersection	$A \cap B = \{x \,|\, x \in A \ $ and $ \ x \in B\}$
	A, B disjoint $\Leftrightarrow A \cap B = \emptyset$
complement with respect to U	$\overline{U} = \{x \,|\, x \notin U\}$

Derived operations

set difference	$A \setminus B = A \cap \overline{B}$
symmetric difference	$A \triangle B = (A \cup B) \setminus (A \cap B)$

Laws

commutativity	$A \cup B = B \cup A$	$A \cap B = B \cap A$
associativity	$(A \cup B) \cup C = A \cup (B \cup C)$	$(A \cap B) \cap C = A \cap (B \cap C)$
distributivity	$A \cup (B \cap C) = (A \cup B) \cap (A \cup C)$	$A \cap (B \cup C) = (A \cap B) \cup (A \cap C)$
DE MORGAN's theorems	$\overline{A \cup B} = \overline{A} \cap \overline{B}$	$\overline{A \cap B} = \overline{A} \cup \overline{B}$
absorption	$A \cup (B \cap A) = A$	$A \cap (B \cup A) = A$
idempotence	$A \cup A = A$	$A \cap A = A$
special cases	$A \cup \emptyset = A$	$A \cap \emptyset = \emptyset$
	$A \cup U = U$	$A \cap U = A$
operations on sets and subsets	$A \subset B \Leftrightarrow A \cap B = A \Leftrightarrow A \cup B = B \Leftrightarrow A \cap \overline{B} = \emptyset$ $\Leftrightarrow A \setminus B = \emptyset$	

Power set, Cartesian product, partition

power set	The power set $P(M)$ of the set M is the set of all distinct subsets of M: $P(M) = \{T \mid T \subset M\}$
Cartesian product (product set)	The product set $A \times B$ of the sets A and B is the set of all ordered pairs (x, y) such that the first component is an element of A and the second an element of B: $A \times B = \{(x, y) \mid x \in A \text{ and } y \in B\}$ $A^2 = A \times A$
partition	A partition of a set M is a set of non-empty, pairwise disjoint subsets A_k ($k \in I$) whose union is equal to M: $M = \bigcup_{k \in I} A_k, \quad A_k \neq \emptyset \quad \text{and} \quad A_i \cap A_j = \emptyset \text{ for } i \neq j$

Cardinality

cardinality of a set	In the case of finite sets, the cardinality $|A|$ of the set A is understood to be the number of elements it contains. The definition of cardinality can be extended to infinite sets, but is more detailed. For finite sets A and B: $|A \cup B| = |A| + |B| - |A \cap B|$

1.3 Relations

relation	A binary relation R on a set M is a subset of $M \times M$. xRy: "x is R-related to y"

Properties of relations

R is reflexive	if for all x	xRx
R is symmetric	if for all x, y	$xRy \Rightarrow yRx$
R is transitive	if for all x, y, z	$(xRy \text{ and } yRz) \Rightarrow xRz$
R is antisymmetric	if for all x, y	$(xRy \text{ and } yRx) \Rightarrow x = y$

Special relations

equivalence relation	A relation that is reflexive, symmetric and transitive is called an equivalence relation. Every equivalence relation generates a partition of M (decomposition into equivalence classes).

partial order	A reflexive, transitive and antisymmetric relation is a partial ordering.
order	If every pair of elements x, y in M are related by a partial order (xRy or yRx), then R is an ordering.

1.4 Functions

A function (mapping) f of the set X to the set Y assigns to each element x of X a unique element y of Y. In this context x is called the independent variable and y the dependent variable.

$$f\colon X \to Y$$
$$x \mapsto f(x) \quad \text{or} \quad x \mapsto y \quad \text{or} \quad x \mapsto y = f(x)$$

Terminology

X	domain of definition or domain of f
Y	range or codomain of f
x	argument
$f(x)$	image of x under f, functional value of x
$f(A)$	image of the subset $A \subseteq X$ under f, $f(A) = \{f(x) \mid x \in A\}$
$f(X)$	image of the domain under f, range of f
$f^{-1}(B)$	inverse image of the subset $B \subseteq Y$, $f^{-1}(B) = \{x \in X \mid f(x) \in B\}$
id_X	identity mapping $X \to X$, $x \mapsto x$

Equality of functions

$f\colon X_1 \to Y_1$, $g\colon X_2 \to Y_2$

$f = g \iff (X_1 = X_2 \text{ and } Y_1 = Y_2 \text{ and } f(x) = g(x) \text{ for all } x \in X_1)$

Special properties of functions

f is injective	$x_1 \neq x_2 \Rightarrow f(x_1) \neq f(x_2)$ or $f(x_1) = f(x_2) \Rightarrow x_1 = x_2$
f is surjective (onto)	$f(X) = Y$
f is bijective (one-to-one correspondence)	f is injective and surjective

Functional composition

composition of f and g	Given $f\colon X \to Y$ and $g\colon Y \to Z$, the composite function $g \circ f\colon X \to Z$ is defined by $x \mapsto (g \circ f)(x) = g(f(x))$
composition is associative	$h \circ (g \circ f) = (h \circ g) \circ f$

Inverse function

If the function $f\colon X \to Y$ is bijective, there exists a corresponding inverse function f^{-1}.

$$f^{-1}\colon Y \to X$$
$$y \mapsto x = f^{-1}(y) \quad \text{where} \quad f(x) = y$$

properties
$$(f^{-1})^{-1} = f$$
$$f^{-1} \circ f = \mathrm{id}_X$$
$$f \circ f^{-1} = \mathrm{id}_Y$$

1.5 Numbers

$\mathbb{N} = \{1, 2, 3, 4, \ldots\}$ set of natural numbers (denoted by $\mathbb{N}^*$ in DIN 5473)

$\mathbb{N}_0 = \mathbb{N} \cup \{0\}$ set of natural numbers including zero (denoted by $\mathbb{N}$ in DIN 5473)

The principle of mathematical induction

If $\left\{\begin{array}{l} \bullet\ M \subset \mathbb{N} \\ \bullet\ 1 \in M \\ \bullet\ \forall n \in \mathbb{N}\colon n \in M \Rightarrow (n+1) \in M \end{array}\right\}$, then it follows that $M = \mathbb{N}$

Proof by mathematical induction

Suppose a property symbolized by the predicate $E(n)$ is to be proved to hold for all natural numbers $n \in \mathbb{N}$. One shows that:

- $E(1)$ holds for the first natural number.   (base case)
- If $E(n)$ holds for $n \in \mathbb{N}$, then $E(n+1)$ must also hold.   (inductive step)

Algebraic properties

number system	symbol		algebraic entity
natural numbers	$\mathbb{N}$	$\{1, 2, 3, \ldots\}$	
integers	$\mathbb{Z}$	$\{\ldots, -2, -1, 0, 1, 2, \ldots\}$	
rational numbers	$\mathbb{Q}$	$\left\{\frac{p}{q} \,\middle|\, p \in \mathbb{Z},\ q \in \mathbb{N}\right\}$	$(\mathbb{Q}, +, \cdot)$ is a field
real numbers	$\mathbb{R}$		$(\mathbb{R}, +, \cdot)$ is a field
complex numbers	$\mathbb{C}$	$\{a + ib \,|\, a \in \mathbb{R},\ b \in \mathbb{R}\}$	$(\mathbb{C}, +, \cdot)$ is a field

i ▶ p. 18

$\mathbb{N} \subset \mathbb{Z} \subset \mathbb{Q} \subset \mathbb{R} \subset \mathbb{C}$

The following relations hold among the respective cardinalities: $|\mathbb{N}| = |\mathbb{Z}| = |\mathbb{Q}| < |\mathbb{R}| = |\mathbb{C}|$

field ▶ p. 25

General
MATHEMATICS · PHYSICS · ASTRONOMY · CHEMISTRY

Real numbers

absence of zero divisors	$xy = 0 \Leftrightarrow (x = 0 \text{ or } y = 0)$ $x^2 + y^2 = 0 \Leftrightarrow (x = 0 \text{ and } y = 0)$
square root	For $a \geqslant 0$: $\sqrt{a} = x \Leftrightarrow (x^2 = a \text{ and } x \geqslant 0)$ $\sqrt{ab} = \sqrt{a}\sqrt{b},\ a,b \geqslant 0 \qquad \sqrt{\dfrac{a}{b}} = \dfrac{\sqrt{a}}{\sqrt{b}},\ a \geqslant 0,\ b > 0$
absolute value (modulus)	$\|a\| = \begin{cases} a, & \text{if } a \geqslant 0 \\ -a, & \text{if } a < 0 \end{cases}$ $\|a\| = \sqrt{a^2}$ $\|ab\| = \|a\|\|b\| \qquad \left\|\dfrac{a}{b}\right\| = \dfrac{\|a\|}{\|b\|}$ $\|a + b\| \leqslant \|a\| + \|b\|$ (triangle inequality)
sign function (or signum function)	$\operatorname{sgn} a = \begin{cases} 1, & \text{if } a > 0 \\ 0, & \text{if } a = 0 \\ -1, & \text{if } a < 0 \end{cases}$
floor function	$\lfloor a \rfloor = \max\{z \in \mathbb{Z} \mid z \leqslant a\}$ (largest integer less than or equal to a)
ceiling function	$\lceil a \rceil = \min\{z \in \mathbb{Z} \mid z \geqslant a\}$ (smallest integer greater than or equal to a)
remainder (modulo) of division by y	$x \bmod y = \operatorname{mod}(x, y) = x - y \left\lfloor \dfrac{x}{y} \right\rfloor,\ y \neq 0$
properties of inequalities	$a < b \Rightarrow \begin{cases} a + c < b + c \\ ac < bc \text{ for } c > 0 \\ ac > bc \text{ for } c < 0 \end{cases}$

Proportionality

direct proportionality $x \sim y$ $x \propto y$	If every multiple λx of a quantity x corresponds to the same multiple λy of a corresponding quantity y, the two quantities are said to be directly proportional. For directly proportional quantities x and y: $y = \lambda \cdot x \Leftrightarrow \dfrac{y}{x} = \lambda$, where λ is the proportionality constant.
inverse proportionality	If every non-zero multiple λx of a quantity x corresponds to the inverse multiple $\dfrac{1}{\lambda} y$ of a corresponding quantity y, the two quantities are said to be inversely proportional. For inversely proportional quantities x and y: $y = \lambda \cdot \dfrac{1}{x} \Leftrightarrow x \cdot y = \lambda$, where λ is the proportionality constant.

General
MATHEMATICS PHYSICS ASTRONOMY CHEMISTRY

Means

arithmetic mean	$A_2 = \dfrac{a_1 + a_2}{2}$	$A_n = \dfrac{a_1 + a_2 + ... + a_n}{n}$
weighted arithmetic mean	$M_2 = \dfrac{k_1 a_1 + k_2 a_2}{k_1 + k_2}$	$M_n = \dfrac{k_1 a_1 + k_2 a_2 + ... + k_n a_n}{k_1 + k_2 + ... + k_n}$
geometric mean	$G_2 = \sqrt{a_1 \cdot a_2}$ $\quad a_1, a_2 \geqslant 0$	$G_n = \sqrt[n]{a_1 \cdot a_2 \cdot ... \cdot a_n}$ $\quad a_1, a_2, ..., a_n \geqslant 0$
harmonic mean	$H_2 = \dfrac{2 a_1 a_2}{a_1 + a_2} = \dfrac{G_2^2}{A_2}$	$H_n = \dfrac{n}{\dfrac{1}{a_1} + \dfrac{1}{a_2} + ... + \dfrac{1}{a_n}}$
quadratic mean	$Q_2 = \sqrt{\dfrac{a_1^2 + a_2^2}{2}}$	$Q_n = \sqrt{\dfrac{a_1^2 + a_2^2 + ... + a_n^2}{n}}$
inequalities among AM, GM, HM and QM	$H_2 \leqslant G_2 \leqslant A_2 \leqslant Q_2$	$H_n \leqslant G_n \leqslant A_n \leqslant Q_n$ ▶ p. 81
• equality holds if and only if	$a_1 = a_2$	$a_1 = a_2 = ... = a_n$

Powers and roots

powers with non-negative integral exponents	$a^n = a \cdot a \cdot a \cdot a \cdot ... \cdot a \quad$ n factors a, $a \in \mathbb{R}$ $a^1 = a \quad\quad a^0 = 1,\ a \neq 0 \quad\quad$ (0^0 is undefined.)
powers with negative integral exponents	$a^{-n} = \dfrac{1}{a^n} = \left(\dfrac{1}{a}\right)^n,\ a \neq 0,\ n \in \mathbb{N}$
roots	Given $n \in \mathbb{N}$ the n-th root $\sqrt[n]{a}$ of a non-negative real number a is the non-negative solution of the equation $x^n = a$. For $a \geqslant 0$: $\quad x = \sqrt[n]{a} \iff (x^n = a \text{ and } x \geqslant 0)$ For roots of odd order, the definition can also be extended to negative real numbers: given $a < 0$, its n-th root is the real solution of the equation $x^n = a$. Thus, for odd n: $\quad \sqrt[n]{-a} = -\sqrt[n]{a},\ a \geqslant 0$
powers with rational exponents	$a^{\frac{1}{n}} = \sqrt[n]{a},\ a \geqslant 0,\ n \in \mathbb{N}$ $a^{\frac{m}{n}} = \sqrt[n]{a^m},\ a > 0,\ n \in \mathbb{N}\text{ and }m \in \mathbb{Z}$
powers with real exponents	$a^x = e^{x \cdot \ln a},\ a > 0,\ x \in \mathbb{R}$ $\quad\quad$ e ▶ p. 52

assumptions	$a, b \in \mathbb{R}^+,\ m, n \in \mathbb{R}$	$a, b \in \mathbb{R}^+,\ k, n \in \mathbb{N},\ m \in \mathbb{Z}$
identities (laws of exponents and roots)	$a^m a^n = a^{m+n}$	$\sqrt[n]{a^m} = \sqrt[kn]{a^{km}}$
	$\dfrac{a^m}{a^n} = a^{m-n}$	$\sqrt[n]{\sqrt[k]{a}} = \sqrt[nk]{a}$
	$(a^m)^n = a^{mn}$	
	$a^n b^n = (ab)^n$	$\sqrt[n]{a}\,\sqrt[n]{b} = \sqrt[n]{ab}$
	$\dfrac{a^n}{b^n} = \left(\dfrac{a}{b}\right)^n$	$\dfrac{\sqrt[n]{a}}{\sqrt[n]{b}} = \sqrt[n]{\dfrac{a}{b}}$
special cases	$a^1 = a$	$\sqrt[n]{0} = 0$
	$a^0 = 1,\ a \neq 0$	$\sqrt{a} = \sqrt[2]{a}$
	$a a^n = a^{n+1}$	$\sqrt[1]{a} = a$
	$1^n = 1$	
	$0^n = 0,\ n > 0$	$\sqrt[n]{a^n} = |a|,\ a \in \mathbb{R},\ n$ even
	$a^{-n} = \dfrac{1}{a^n}$	$\sqrt[n]{a^{-m}} = \dfrac{1}{\sqrt[n]{a^m}}$

Logarithms

definition	$y = \log_a x \iff a^y = x,\ a, x \in \mathbb{R}^+$ and $a \neq 1$	
• consequences	$a^{\log_a x} = x,\ x \in \mathbb{R}^+$ and $\log_a a^x = x,\ x \in \mathbb{R}$	
	$\log_a a = 1$ and $\log_a 1 = 0$	
• special cases (ISO notation)	$\lg x = \log_{10} x = \log x$ (common logarithm)	e ▶ p. 52
	$\ln x = \log_e x$ (natural logarithm)	
	$\operatorname{lb} x = \log_2 x$ (binary logarithm)	
identities (laws of logarithms)	$\log(uv) = \log u + \log v$	
	$\log\left(\dfrac{u}{v}\right) = \log u - \log v$	these identities hold for arbitrary admissible bases a.
	$\log\left(\dfrac{1}{v}\right) = -\log v$	
	$\log(u^r) = r \log u$	
change of base	$\log_a x = \dfrac{\log_b x}{\log_b a}$	
• special cases	$\log_a x = \dfrac{\ln x}{\ln a} = \dfrac{\lg x}{\lg a} = \dfrac{\operatorname{lb} x}{\operatorname{lb} a},\quad \lg x = \dfrac{\ln x}{\ln 10},\quad \operatorname{lb} x = \dfrac{\lg x}{\lg 2}$	

General
MATHEMATICS PHYSICS ASTRONOMY CHEMISTRY

Complex numbers

standard form (Cartesian form)	$z = x + \mathrm{i}y, \ x, y \in \mathbb{R}$
	$x = \operatorname{Re} z$ (real part), $y = \operatorname{Im} z$ (imaginary part)
	i: imaginary unit where $\mathrm{i}^2 = -1$
polar form	$z = r(\cos\varphi + \mathrm{i}\sin\varphi) = r\operatorname{cis}\varphi, \ r \in \mathbb{R}_0^+, \ \varphi \in \mathbb{R}$
exponential form	$z = r\mathrm{e}^{\mathrm{i}\varphi}$ (φ in radians) radian measure ▶ p. 91
	$\mathrm{e}^{\mathrm{i}\varphi} = \cos\varphi + \mathrm{i}\sin\varphi$ (EULER's formula) e ▶ p. 52
EULER's identity	$\mathrm{e}^{\mathrm{i}\pi} + 1 = 0$
complex plane	Each complex number is represented by a unique point on the plane.

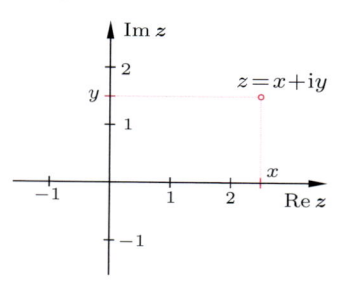

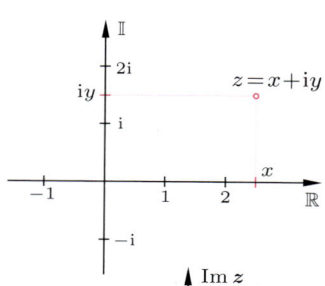

imaginary numbers	$\mathbb{I} = \{\mathrm{i}y \mid y \in \mathbb{R}\} = \mathrm{i}\mathbb{R}$

Transformation formulae

standard form → polar form	$r = \sqrt{x^2 + y^2}$
	$\cos\varphi = \dfrac{x}{r}$ and $\sin\varphi = \dfrac{y}{r}$
polar form → standard form	$x = r\cos\varphi, \quad y = r\sin\varphi$

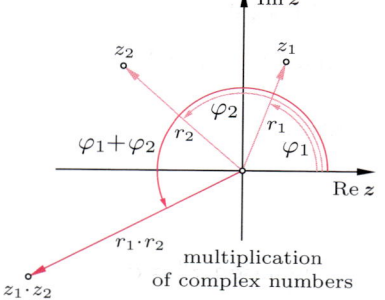

Arithmetical operations

	standard form	polar form
$z_1 + z_2$	$(x_1 + x_2) + \mathrm{i}(y_1 + y_2)$	
$z_1 z_2$	$(x_1 x_2 - y_1 y_2) + \mathrm{i}(x_1 y_2 + x_2 y_1)$	$r_1 r_2 \operatorname{cis}(\varphi_1 + \varphi_2) = r_1 r_2 \mathrm{e}^{\mathrm{i}(\varphi_1 + \varphi_2)}$
$z^{-1} = \dfrac{1}{z}$	$\dfrac{x}{x^2 + y^2} - \mathrm{i}\dfrac{y}{x^2 + y^2}$	$r^{-1}\operatorname{cis}(-\varphi) = r^{-1}\mathrm{e}^{-\mathrm{i}\varphi}$
$\dfrac{z_1}{z_2}$	$\dfrac{x_1 x_2 + y_1 y_2}{x_2^2 + y_2^2} + \mathrm{i}\dfrac{x_2 y_1 - x_1 y_2}{x_2^2 + y_2^2}$	$\dfrac{r_1}{r_2}\operatorname{cis}(\varphi_1 - \varphi_2) = \dfrac{r_1}{r_2}\mathrm{e}^{\mathrm{i}(\varphi_1 - \varphi_2)}$
$z^n, \ n \in \mathbb{Z}$		$r^n \operatorname{cis}(n\varphi) = r^n \mathrm{e}^{\mathrm{i}n\varphi}$ (DE MOIVRE)

General
MATHEMATICS   PHYSICS   ASTRONOMY   CHEMISTRY

Conjugation, real and imaginary parts

complex conjugate

$$\overline{z} = x - \mathrm{i}y \qquad \text{if } z = x + \mathrm{i}y$$
$$\overline{z} = r\operatorname{cis}(-\varphi) = r\mathrm{e}^{-\mathrm{i}\varphi} \qquad \text{if } z = r\operatorname{cis}\varphi$$

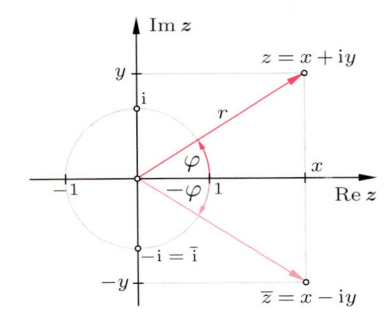

identities

$$\overline{z + w} = \overline{z} + \overline{w}$$
$$\overline{z - w} = \overline{z} - \overline{w}$$
$$\overline{zw} = \overline{z} \cdot \overline{w}$$
$$\overline{\left(\frac{z}{w}\right)} = \frac{\overline{z}}{\overline{w}}$$

$$\operatorname{Re} z = \frac{z + \overline{z}}{2}$$
$$\operatorname{Im} z = \frac{z - \overline{z}}{2\mathrm{i}}$$
$$z\overline{z} = \operatorname{Re}^2(z) + \operatorname{Im}^2(z) = r^2$$
$$\overline{\overline{z}} = z$$

Absolute value

absolute value (modulus)

$$r = |z| = \sqrt{z\overline{z}} \geqslant 0 \qquad |z| = \sqrt{x^2 + y^2}$$

identities

$$|zw| = |z||w| \qquad \left|\frac{z}{w}\right| = \frac{|z|}{|w|}$$

$$|z + w| \leqslant |z| + |w| \qquad \text{(triangle inequality)}$$

The equation $z^n = a$

Given $a = |a|\operatorname{cis}\varphi$, the equation $z^n = a$ has n solutions

$$z_k = \sqrt[n]{|a|}\operatorname{cis}\left(\frac{\varphi + 2k\pi}{n}\right),$$
$$k = 0, 1, \ldots, n-1$$

- special case $z^n = 1$ (roots of unity)

$$z_k = \varepsilon_k = \operatorname{cis}\frac{2k\pi}{n},$$
$$k = 0, 1, \ldots, n-1$$

(z_k is an n-th root of unity)

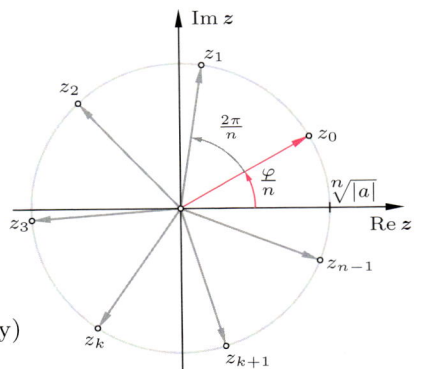

2 Algebra

2.1 Binomial expansions and factorizations

Binomial products

$$(a+b)^2 = a^2 + 2ab + b^2$$
$$(a-b)^2 = a^2 - 2ab + b^2$$
$$(a+b)(a-b) = a^2 - b^2$$

Powers of binomials

$$(a+b)^0 = 1$$
$$(a+b)^1 = a+b$$
$$(a+b)^2 = a^2 + 2ab + b^2$$
$$(a+b)^3 = a^3 + 3a^2b + 3ab^2 + b^3$$
$$(a+b)^4 = a^4 + 4a^3b + 6a^2b^2 + 4ab^3 + b^4$$
$$\vdots$$
$$(a+b)^n = \binom{n}{0}a^n + \binom{n}{1}a^{n-1}b + \ldots + \binom{n}{k}a^{n-k}b^k + \ldots + \binom{n}{n}b^n = \sum_{k=0}^{n}\binom{n}{k}a^{n-k}b^k$$

binomial coefficients $\binom{n}{k}$ ▶ p. 42

multinomials ▶ p. 43

Factorizations

$$a^2 - b^2 = (a+b)(a-b)$$
$$a^3 - b^3 = (a-b)(a^2 + ab + b^2)$$
$$a^3 + b^3 = (a+b)(a^2 - ab + b^2)$$
$$a^4 - b^4 = (a-b)(a^3 + a^2b + ab^2 + b^3) = (a+b)(a^3 - a^2b + ab^2 - b^3) = (a^2 - b^2)(a^2 + b^2)$$
$$\vdots$$
$$a^n - b^n = (a-b)(a^{n-1} + a^{n-2}b + \ldots + ab^{n-2} + b^{n-1}), \ n \text{ arbitrary}$$
$$a^n - b^n = (a+b)(a^{n-1} - a^{n-2}b + - \ldots + ab^{n-2} - b^{n-1}), \ n \text{ even}$$
$$a^n + b^n = (a+b)(a^{n-1} - a^{n-2}b + - \ldots - ab^{n-2} + b^{n-1}), \ n \text{ odd}$$

Examples of factorizations with non-real or non-integer coefficients

$$a^2 + b^2 = (a+ib)(a-ib)$$
$$a^4 + b^4 = (a^2 + \sqrt{2}\,ab + b^2)(a^2 - \sqrt{2}\,ab + b^2)$$

p. 18 ◀ i

Algebra
MATHEMATICS   PHYSICS   ASTRONOMY   CHEMISTRY

2.2 Polynomial functions

Terms and definitions

polynomial (polynomial function) of degree n over $\mathbb{R}$ or $\mathbb{C}$	$f(x) = a_n x^n + a_{n-1} x^{n-1} + \ldots + a_1 x + a_0$ with coefficients $a_i \in \mathbb{R}$ or $a_i \in \mathbb{C}$, $a_n \neq 0$, $n \in \mathbb{N}$	▶ p. 57
root (zero)	x_0 is a root of the polynomial f if $f(x_0) = 0$.	
multiple root	x_0 is a root of multiplicity k of the polynomial f if there exists a polynomial g of degree $n-k$ such that $f(x) = (x - x_0)^k \cdot g(x)$ and $g(x_0) \neq 0$.	

Theorems

identity theorem

If two polynomials of at most degree n take equal values for more than n distinct values of x, then the polynomials are identical – i.e. their respective coefficients are equal.

factor theorem

(DESCARTES factor theorem)
If x_0 is a root of a nonzero polynomial f, then there exists a polynomial g such that $f(x) = (x - x_0) \cdot g(x)$.

fundamental theorem of algebra

(GAUSS) Every polynomial of degree $n > 0$ over $\mathbb{C}$ has a complex root.

It follows that every polynomial of degree $n > 0$ over $\mathbb{C}$ can be expressed as the product of n linear factors:
$f_n(x) = a_n \cdot (x - x_1) \cdot (x - x_2) \cdot \ldots \cdot (x - x_n)$, $a_n, x_i \in \mathbb{C}$.

Further consequences: The roots x_i of polynomials with real coefficients are either real or occur in complex conjugate pairs. The polynomial can be expressed as a product of real linear and quadratic factors.

rational root theorem (rational root test)

Suppose a polynomial $a_n x^n + a_{n-1} x^{n-1} + \ldots + a_1 x + a_0$ has integral coefficients $a_0, a_1, \ldots, a_n$.
If $x_0 = \frac{p}{q}$ is a rational root expressed in simplest form (p, q relatively prime), then p must be a factor of a_0 and q must be a factor of a_n.

- special case integral roots

If the polynomial is monic ($a_n = 1$), then x_0 must be an integer such that x_0 is divisible by a_0.

bounds on the moduli of roots

Let f be a polynomial of degree $n > 0$. The moduli (absolute values) of its roots lie within the

interval $\left[\dfrac{|a_0|}{m + |a_0|}, \dfrac{M + |a_n|}{|a_n|} \right]$,

where $m = \max\limits_{1 \leqslant i \leqslant n} |a_i|$ and $M = \max\limits_{0 \leqslant i \leqslant n-1} |a_i|$.

Algebra

Linear and quadratic functions

linear function
(polynomial of degree 1,
affine linear function)

$f(x) = mx + q, \ m \neq 0$

The graph of the function f is a straight line with slope m and y-intercept q. The function has exactly one root (zero) at $x = -\frac{q}{m}$.

▶ p. 101

quadratic function
(polynomial function of degree 2)

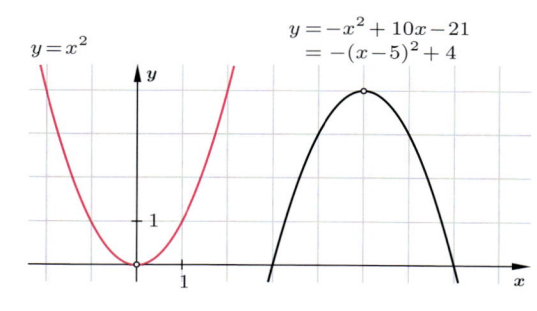

$f(x) = ax^2 + bx + c, \ a \neq 0$

An arbitrary quadratic function can always be expressed in vertex form:
$f(x) = a(x-u)^2 + v.$

Its graph is a parabola with vertex (u, v), where
$$u = -\frac{b}{2a} \text{ and } v = \frac{-b^2 + 4ac}{4a}.$$

$a > 0$: parabola open upward
$a < 0$: parabola open downward

2.3 Polynomial equations of higher degree in one variable

equation of degree n over $\mathbb{R}$ or $\mathbb{C}$

$a_n x^n + a_{n-1} x^{n-1} + \ldots + a_1 x + a_0 = 0,$
$a_i \in \mathbb{R}$ or $a_i \in \mathbb{C}, \ a_n \neq 0$

Quadratic equations (polynomial equations of 2nd degree)

General quadratic equations with real coefficients

standard form
$ax^2 + bx + c = 0, \ a, b, c \in \mathbb{R}, \ a \neq 0$

$$x_{1,2} = \frac{-b \pm \sqrt{b^2 - 4ac}}{2a}$$

The discriminant $D = b^2 - 4ac$ determines the number and type of solutions.

- $D > 0$: two distinct solutions in $\mathbb{R}$

$$x_{1,2} = \frac{-b \pm \sqrt{D}}{2a}$$

- $D = 0$: one (double) solution in $\mathbb{R}$

$$x_1 = x_2 = -\frac{b}{2a}$$

- $D < 0$: no solution in $\mathbb{R}$, two complex conjugate solutions in $\mathbb{C}$

$$x_{1,2} = \frac{-b \pm i\sqrt{-D}}{2a}$$

monic form
$x^2 + px + q = 0, \ p, q \in \mathbb{R}$

$$x_{1,2} = -\frac{p}{2} \pm \sqrt{\frac{p^2}{4} - q}$$

Algebra

MATHEMATICS

Square roots of complex numbers

$z^2 = c = p + iq, \ c \in \mathbb{C}, \ p, q \in \mathbb{R}$
$$z_{1,2} = \pm\left(\sqrt{\frac{\sqrt{p^2+q^2}+p}{2}} + i\operatorname{sgn} q \cdot \sqrt{\frac{\sqrt{p^2+q^2}-p}{2}}\right)$$

p. 15 ◀ sgn (sign function)

General quadratic equations with complex coefficients

$ax^2 + bx + c = 0, \ a, b, c \in \mathbb{C}, \ a \neq 0$

$x_{1,2} = \dfrac{-b + d_{1,2}}{2a}$, where $d_{1,2}$ are the complex square roots of the discriminant $z^2 = b^2 - 4ac$

Vieta's formulae

If x_1 and x_2 are the solutions of $ax^2 + bx + c = 0$, it follows that

$$x_1 + x_2 = -\frac{b}{a} \quad \text{and} \quad x_1 x_2 = \frac{c}{a}$$

Cubic equations (polynomial equations of 3rd degree) with real coefficients

standard form
$ax^3 + bx^2 + cx + d = 0, \ a, b, c, d \in \mathbb{R}, \ a \neq 0$

monic form
$x^3 + rx^2 + sx + t = 0$
$\quad r = \dfrac{b}{a}, \ s = \dfrac{c}{a}, \ t = \dfrac{d}{a}$

reduced form (depressed cubic)
$y^3 + py + q = 0$
$\quad p = s - \dfrac{r^2}{3}, \ q = \dfrac{2r^3}{27} - \dfrac{rs}{3} + t$

The discriminant $D = \left(\dfrac{p}{3}\right)^3 + \left(\dfrac{q}{2}\right)^2$ determines the number and type of solutions.

- $D > 0$: one real solution and a pair of complex conjugate solutions, Cardano's formulae

  $u = \sqrt[3]{-\dfrac{q}{2} + \sqrt{D}}, \quad v = \sqrt[3]{-\dfrac{q}{2} - \sqrt{D}}$

  $y_1 = u + v, \quad y_{2,3} = -\dfrac{u+v}{2} \pm i \dfrac{u-v}{2}\sqrt{3}$

- $D = 0$: one or two real solutions

  $y_1 = -\sqrt[3]{4q}$ (simple solution)

  $y_2 = y_3 = \sqrt[3]{\dfrac{q}{2}}$ (double solution)

  $q = 0 \Rightarrow y_1 = y_2 = y_3 = 0$ (triple solution)

- $D < 0$: three distinct real solutions (casus irreducibilis)

  $\varrho = \sqrt{-\dfrac{p^3}{27}}, \quad \cos\varphi = -\dfrac{q}{2\varrho}$

  $y_1 = 2\sqrt[3]{\varrho}\cos\dfrac{\varphi}{3}, \ y_2 = 2\sqrt[3]{\varrho}\cos\left(\dfrac{\varphi}{3} + \dfrac{2\pi}{3}\right),$

  $y_3 = 2\sqrt[3]{\varrho}\cos\left(\dfrac{\varphi}{3} + \dfrac{4\pi}{3}\right)$

solutions x_1, x_2, x_3
$\quad x_i = y_i - \dfrac{r}{3}$

Algebra

Vieta's formulae

If x_1, x_2 and x_3 are the solutions of $ax^3 + bx^2 + cx + d = 0$, it follows that

$$x_1 + x_2 + x_3 = -\frac{b}{a}$$

$$x_1 x_2 + x_1 x_3 + x_2 x_3 = \frac{c}{a}$$

$$x_1 x_2 x_3 = -\frac{d}{a}$$

Equations of 4th and higher degree

The general equation of 4th degree

Quartic equations $ax^4 + bx^3 + cx^2 + dx + e = 0$, $a, b, c, d, e \in \mathbb{C}$, $a \neq 0$ can be solved by radicals using methods developed by Ferrari and Descartes.

Vieta's formulae

If $x_1, x_2, \ldots, x_n$ are the solutions of the equation $a_n x^n + a_{n-1} x^{n-1} + \ldots + a_1 x + a_0 = 0$, $a_n \neq 0$, it follows that

$$x_1 + x_2 + \ldots + x_n = \sum_{i=1}^{n} x_i = -\frac{a_{n-1}}{a_n}$$

$$x_1 x_2 + x_1 x_3 + \ldots + x_{n-1} x_n = \sum_{i<j} x_i x_j = \frac{a_{n-2}}{a_n}$$

$$x_1 x_2 x_3 + x_1 x_2 x_4 + \ldots + x_{n-2} x_{n-1} x_n = \sum_{i<j<k} x_i x_j x_k = -\frac{a_{n-3}}{a_n}$$

$$\vdots$$

$$x_1 \cdot x_2 \cdot \ldots \cdot x_n = \prod_{i=1}^{n} x_i = (-1)^n \frac{a_0}{a_n}$$

Theorem of Abel-Ruffini

The general polynomial equation of degree n cannot be solved by radicals for $n \geqslant 5$.

Algebra

2.4 Algebraic Structures

Groups

A group is an algebraic structure $(M, *)$ in which M is a set and $*$ a binary operation $M \times M \to M$, $(a, b) \mapsto a * b$ satisfying the following properties:

- associativity $\qquad (a * b) * c = a * (b * c)$ for all $a, b \in M$
- identity element $\qquad$ There exists an element $e \in M$ such that for all $a \in M$: $a * e = e * a = a$
- inverse element $\qquad$ For every element $a \in M$ there exists an inverse element $a' \in M$ such that: $a * a' = a' * a = e$

Special cases

- commutative group (ABELian group) $\qquad$ For all $a, b \in M$: $a * b = b * a$
- cyclic group $\qquad$ There exists an element $a \in M$ such that every element of M can be expressed as a power of a.
- finite group $\qquad$ M is a finite set. The number of elements is called the order of the group.

Fields

A field is an algebraic structure $(M, +, \cdot)$ which satisfies the following properties:

- addition $\qquad (M, +)$ is a commutative group with the additive identity element 0.
- multiplication $\qquad (M \setminus \{0\}, \cdot)$ is a commutative group with the multiplicative identity element 1.
- distributivity $\qquad$ For all $a, b, c \in M$: $a \cdot (b + c) = (a \cdot b) + (a \cdot c)$

Algebra

Real vector spaces

A real vector space is an algebraic structure consisting of a set V
and an operation $+\colon V \times V \to V$, $(x, y) \mapsto x + y$
and an operation $\cdot\colon \mathbb{R} \times V \to V$, $(\lambda, x) \mapsto \lambda \cdot x$ satisfying the following properties:

- $(V, +)$ is a commutative group.
- For arbitrary $x, y \in V$:
  - $\lambda(x + y) = \lambda x + \lambda y$
  - $(\lambda + \mu)x = \lambda x + \mu x$
  - $\lambda(\mu x) = (\lambda \mu)x$
  - $1x = x$

The elements of V are called vectors and the real numbers are called scalars. The binary operation $\cdot$ is called scalar multiplication.

linear combination	If $x_1, x_2, \ldots, x_k$ are vectors in V and $\lambda_1, \lambda_2, \ldots, \lambda_k$ are scalars in $\mathbb{R}$, the vector defined by $\lambda_1 x_1 + \lambda_2 x_2 + \ldots + \lambda_k x_k$ is called a linear combination of the vectors $x_1, x_2, \ldots, x_k$ with coefficients $\lambda_1, \lambda_2, \ldots, \lambda_k$.
linear span (linear hull)	The set of all linear combinations of the vectors $x_1, x_2, \ldots, x_k$ is called the linear span (or linear hull) of $x_1, x_2, \ldots, x_k$ and is denoted by $\mathrm{span}\{x_1, x_2, \ldots, x_k\}$. It constitutes a subspace of V.
subspace	$V' \subset V$ is a subspace of the vector space V, if V' itself constitutes a vector space with respect to the $+$ and $\cdot$ operations.
linear independence	The vectors $x_1, x_2, \ldots, x_k$ are linearly independent if the only solution of the equation $\lambda_1 x_1 + \lambda_2 x_2 + \ldots + \lambda_k x_k = 0$ for $(\lambda_1, \lambda_2, \ldots, \lambda_k)$ is the trivial solution $(0, 0, \ldots, 0)$.
linear dependence	The vectors $x_1, x_2, \ldots, x_k$ are linearly dependent if there exists a nontrivial solution $(\lambda_1, \lambda_2, \ldots, \lambda_k)$ of the equation $\lambda_1 x_1 + \lambda_2 x_2 + \ldots + \lambda_k x_k = 0$ i.e. $(\lambda_1, \lambda_2, \ldots, \lambda_k) \neq (0, 0, \ldots, 0)$.
basis	A set B of vectors in V is called a basis of V if • the vectors in B are linearly independent, and • B spans V – i.e. every $x \in V$ can be expressed as a unique linear combination of the vectors in B.
dimension	If B is a basis of V, the number of vectors in B is called the dimension of V, denoted by $\dim V$. Any two bases B and B' always have the same number of elements.

Algebra
MATHEMATICS PHYSICS ASTRONOMY CHEMISTRY

2.5 Linear Algebra

the vector space $\mathbb{R}^n$

scalar — $a \in \mathbb{R}$ is called a scalar.

vector — With respect to the standard basis (canonical basis)

$$\vec{e}_1 = \begin{pmatrix} 1 \\ 0 \\ \vdots \\ 0 \end{pmatrix}, \quad \vec{e}_2 = \begin{pmatrix} 0 \\ 1 \\ \vdots \\ 0 \end{pmatrix}, \quad \ldots, \vec{e}_n = \begin{pmatrix} 0 \\ 0 \\ \vdots \\ 1 \end{pmatrix}$$

a vector $\vec{a} \in \mathbb{R}^n$ can be written as

$$\vec{a} = a_1 \vec{e}_1 + a_2 \vec{e}_2 + \ldots + a_n \vec{e}_n = \begin{pmatrix} a_1 \\ a_2 \\ \vdots \\ a_n \end{pmatrix} \text{ with } a_1, a_2, \ldots, a_n \in \mathbb{R}$$

- **special case $\mathbb{R}^3$** — If $\vec{e}_1$, $\vec{e}_2$ and $\vec{e}_3$ are unit vectors in the directions of the x-, y- and z-axes respectively, every vector $\vec{a} \in \mathbb{R}^3$ can be written as

$$\vec{a} = a_1 \vec{e}_1 + a_2 \vec{e}_2 + a_3 \vec{e}_3 = \begin{pmatrix} a_1 \\ a_2 \\ a_3 \end{pmatrix}.$$

Vector arithmetic

vector addition — If $\vec{a}$ and $\vec{b}$ are two vectors in $\mathbb{R}^n$, their sum is given by

$$\vec{a} + \vec{b} = \begin{pmatrix} a_1 \\ a_2 \\ \vdots \\ a_n \end{pmatrix} + \begin{pmatrix} b_1 \\ b_2 \\ \vdots \\ b_n \end{pmatrix} = \begin{pmatrix} a_1 + b_1 \\ a_2 + b_2 \\ \vdots \\ a_n + b_n \end{pmatrix}$$

scalar multiplication — If λ is a scalar in $\mathbb{R}$ and $\vec{a}$ a vector in $\mathbb{R}^n$, their product is the vector given by

$$\lambda \vec{a} = \lambda \begin{pmatrix} a_1 \\ a_2 \\ \vdots \\ a_n \end{pmatrix} = \begin{pmatrix} \lambda a_1 \\ \lambda a_2 \\ \vdots \\ \lambda a_n \end{pmatrix}$$

linear combination of vectors — If $\lambda_1, \lambda_2, \ldots, \lambda_n$ are scalars in $\mathbb{R}$ and $\vec{a}_1, \vec{a}_2, \ldots, \vec{a}_n$ vectors $\in \mathbb{R}^n$, the expression

$$\lambda_1 \vec{a}_1 + \lambda_2 \vec{a}_2 + \ldots + \lambda_n \vec{a}_n$$

is called a linear combination of the vectors $\vec{a}_1, \vec{a}_2, \ldots, \vec{a}_n$ with coefficients $\lambda_1, \lambda_2, \ldots, \lambda_n$.

Matrices

matrix — An $m \times n$ matrix over $\mathbb{R}$, where $m, n \in \mathbb{N}$, is a rectangular array of real numbers arranged in m rows and n columns

$$A = \begin{pmatrix} a_{11} & a_{12} & \ldots & a_{1n} \\ a_{21} & a_{22} & \ldots & a_{2n} \\ \vdots & \vdots & \ddots & \vdots \\ a_{m1} & a_{m2} & \ldots & a_{mn} \end{pmatrix} = (a_{ij}) = (\vec{a}_1 \, \vec{a}_2 \ldots \vec{a}_n),$$

with $a_{ij} \in \mathbb{R}$ and $\vec{a}_i \in \mathbb{R}^m$
$i = 1, 2, \ldots, m, \; j = 1, 2, \ldots, n$

Algebra
MATHEMATICS   PHYSICS   ASTRONOMY   CHEMISTRY

	The integers m and n are called the dimensions of the matrix. The individual entries a_{ij} are called elements (or coefficients) of the matrix. The vectors $\vec{a}_1, \vec{a}_2, \ldots, \vec{a}_n$ are the column vectors of the matrix.
linear transformation	A mapping $f\colon \mathbb{R}^n \to \mathbb{R}^m$ from the vector space $\mathbb{R}^n$ to the vector space $\mathbb{R}^m$ is called a linear transformation, if it satisfies both the following properties: • additivity For all $\vec{a}, \vec{b} \in \mathbb{R}^n$: $f(\vec{a}+\vec{b}) = f(\vec{a}) + f(\vec{b})$, and • homogeneity For all $\vec{a} \in \mathbb{R}^n$ and for all $k \in \mathbb{R}$: $f(k \cdot \vec{a}) = k \cdot f(\vec{a})$
linear transformation matrix	If $f\colon \mathbb{R}^n \to \mathbb{R}^m$ is a linear transformation from the vector space $\mathbb{R}^n$ to the vector space $\mathbb{R}^m$, it can be described in terms of the respective standard bases of $\mathbb{R}^n$ and $\mathbb{R}^m$ by the matrix $A = (\vec{a}_1\, \vec{a}_2 \ldots \vec{a}_n)$ where the column vectors of the matrix are the images of the basis vectors: $f(\vec{e}_1) = \vec{a}_1,\ f(\vec{e}_2) = \vec{a}_2,\ \ldots,\ f(\vec{e}_n) = \vec{a}_n$ ▶ p. 112
matrix kernel (null space)	The vector space $\ker A$ of an $m \times n$ matrix A consists of all vectors $\vec{v}$ such that $A\vec{v} = \vec{0}$.
row vector column vector	A row vector [column vector] of A is an n-dimensional [m-dimensional] vector whose components are the elements of a particular row [column] of A.
row space column space	The row space [column space] of an $m \times n$ matrix A is the linear span (linear hull) of its row vectors [column vectors].

Matrix operations

matrix-vector multiplication	If A is an $m \times n$ matrix and $\vec{v}$ a vector in $\mathbb{R}^n$, the product $A\vec{v}$ is the vector

$$A\vec{v} = \begin{pmatrix} a_{11} & a_{12} & \cdots & a_{1n} \\ a_{21} & a_{22} & \cdots & a_{2n} \\ \vdots & \vdots & \ddots & \vdots \\ a_{m1} & a_{m2} & \cdots & a_{mn} \end{pmatrix} \begin{pmatrix} v_1 \\ v_2 \\ \vdots \\ v_n \end{pmatrix} = \begin{pmatrix} a_{11}v_1 + a_{12}v_2 + \ldots + a_{1n}v_n \\ a_{21}v_1 + a_{22}v_2 + \ldots + a_{2n}v_n \\ \vdots \\ a_{m1}v_1 + a_{m2}v_2 + \ldots + a_{mn}v_n \end{pmatrix}$$

$= v_1\vec{a}_1 + v_2\vec{a}_2 + \ldots + v_n\vec{a}_n$,

where $\vec{a}_i$ is the ith column vector of A ($i = 1, \ldots, n$).

If A represents a linear transformation $f\colon \mathbb{R}^n \to \mathbb{R}^m$ from the vector space $\mathbb{R}^n$ to the vector space $\mathbb{R}^m$ with respect to their respective standard bases, then

$f(\vec{v}) = A\vec{v}$

The ith column vector $\vec{a}_i$ of the matrix A is the image of the ith basis vector $\vec{e}_i$ of $\mathbb{R}^n$: $f(\vec{e}_i) = \vec{a}_i$

Algebra
MATHEMATICS

matrix addition	If A and B are two $m \times n$ matrices, their sum is the $m \times n$ matrix C each of whose components is the sum of the corresponding components of A and B: $$C = A + B \iff c_{ij} = a_{ij} + b_{ij}, \quad 1 \leqslant i \leqslant m \text{ and } 1 \leqslant j \leqslant n$$ If A and B represent a pair of linear transformations $g\colon \mathbb{R}^n \to \mathbb{R}^m$ and $f\colon \mathbb{R}^n \to \mathbb{R}^m$ from the vector space $\mathbb{R}^n$ to the vector space $\mathbb{R}^m$ with respect to their respective standard bases, then $A+B$ represents the linear transformation $g+f\colon \mathbb{R}^n \to \mathbb{R}^m$, $(g+f)(\vec{v}) = g(\vec{v}) + f(\vec{v})$
scalar multiplication	If λ is a scalar in $\mathbb{R}$ and A an $m \times n$ matrix, the product λA is the $m \times n$ matrix B, each of whose elements is λ times the corresponding element of A: $$B = \lambda A \iff b_{ij} = \lambda a_{ij}, \quad 1 \leqslant i \leqslant m \text{ and } 1 \leqslant j \leqslant n$$
matrix multiplication	If A is an $m \times n$ matrix and B an $n \times p$ matrix, their product $A \cdot B$ is the $m \times p$ matrix C, whose elements are given by $$c_{ij} = \sum_{k=1}^{n} a_{ik} \cdot b_{kj} = (i^{\text{th}} \text{ row of } A) \cdot (j^{\text{th}} \text{ column of } B),$$ $$1 \leqslant i \leqslant m \text{ and } 1 \leqslant j \leqslant p$$ If A represents a linear transformation $g\colon \mathbb{R}^n \to \mathbb{R}^m$ from the vector space $\mathbb{R}^n$ to the vector space $\mathbb{R}^m$ and B a linear transformation $f\colon \mathbb{R}^p \to \mathbb{R}^n$ from the vector space $\mathbb{R}^p$ to the vector space $\mathbb{R}^n$ with respect to their respective standard bases, then $A \cdot B$ represents the linear transformation $g \circ f\colon \mathbb{R}^p \to \mathbb{R}^m$, $(g \circ f)(\vec{v}) = g(f(\vec{v}))$
transpose	If $A = (a_{ij})$ is an $m \times n$ matrix, its transpose A^{T} is the $n \times m$ matrix, whose columns correspond to rows of A: $$A^{\text{T}} = (a_{ij})^{\text{T}} = (a_{ji})$$
• special case $n=1$	$$\begin{pmatrix} a_1 \\ a_2 \\ \vdots \\ a_m \end{pmatrix}^{\text{T}} = \begin{pmatrix} a_1 & a_2 & \dots & a_m \end{pmatrix}$$
trace	If $A = (a_{ij})$ is an $n \times n$ matrix, its trace $\operatorname{tr}(A)$ is the sum of the elements $a_{11}, a_{22}, \dots, a_{nn}$ on the main diagonal: $$\operatorname{tr} A = \sum_{i=1}^{n} a_{ii}$$

Algebra

Square matrices

The following definitions apply to $n \times n$ matrices. Such matrices are called square matrices.

identity matrix	The identity matrix E is the matrix whose elements on the main diagonal are 1 and whose off-diagonal elements are 0: $$E = \begin{pmatrix} 1 & 0 & 0 & \cdots & 0 \\ 0 & 1 & 0 & \cdots & 0 \\ 0 & 0 & 1 & \cdots & 0 \\ \vdots & \vdots & \vdots & \ddots & \vdots \\ 0 & 0 & 0 & \cdots & 1 \end{pmatrix} = (\delta_{ij}), \text{ where } \delta_{ij} = \begin{cases} 1, & \text{if } i = j \\ 0, & \text{if } i \neq j \end{cases}$$ With respect to the standard basis, E describes the identity transformation id: $\mathbb{R}^n \to \mathbb{R}^n$.
invertible matrix	A matrix A is called invertible if there exists a matrix B such that $AB = BA = E$.
inverse matrix	If $AB = BA = E$, B is called the inverse of A and is denoted by A^{-1}. ▶ p. 32
singular matrix	A matrix that is not invertible is called singular (or degenerate).
diagonal matrix	A matrix $A = (a_{ij})$ is called a diagonal matrix if all elements off the main diagonal are zero: $a_{ij} = 0$ for all $i \neq j$ ▶ p. 32
diagonalizable matrix	A matrix A is called diagonalizable if there exists an invertible matrix P such that the matrix $P^{-1}AP$ is diagonal.
similar matrices	Two matrices A and B are called similar if there exists an invertible matrix P such that $B = P^{-1}AP$.
symmetric matrix	A matrix A is called symmetric if $A = A^T$.
skew symmetric matrix	A matrix A is called skew-symmetric (or antisymmetric) if $A = -A^T$.

Row echelon form and matrix rank

row echelon form	Each row with non-zero elements has more leading zeros than the preceding rows. If any row consists entirely of zeros, all succeeding rows must consist entirely of zeros.
elementary row operations	• transposition of two rows • multiplication of a row by a factor $k \neq 0$ • addition of an arbitrary multiple of one row to another row
rank	The rank of an $n \times n$ matrix A is the number of rows containing non-zero elements in the row echelon form of A and is denoted by rank A. The respective vector spaces spanned by the row vectors of A and the column vectors of A have the same dimension, which is equal to the rank of A. p. 28 ◀ Elementary row operations do not change the rank.

Algebra

Determinants

determinant of a 2×2 matrix

For $A = \begin{pmatrix} a & b \\ c & d \end{pmatrix}$, $\det A = \begin{vmatrix} a & b \\ c & d \end{vmatrix} = ad - bc$

determinant of a 3×3 matrix

For $A = \begin{pmatrix} a & b & c \\ d & e & f \\ g & h & i \end{pmatrix}$,

$\det A = \begin{vmatrix} a & b & c \\ d & e & f \\ g & h & i \end{vmatrix} = a\begin{vmatrix} e & f \\ h & i \end{vmatrix} - b\begin{vmatrix} d & f \\ g & i \end{vmatrix} + c\begin{vmatrix} d & e \\ g & h \end{vmatrix}$

$= aei + bfg + cdh - afh - bdi - ceg$

SARRUS' rule for 3×3 matrices

One extends the 3×3 matrix by replicating its first and second columns in cyclic order. One then adds the three descending diagonal products and subtracts the three ascending diagonal products.

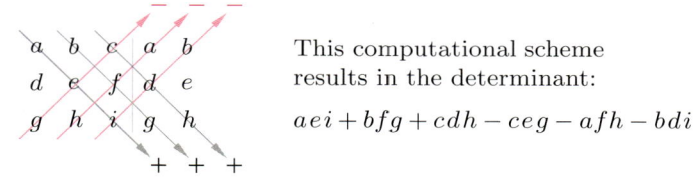

$\begin{matrix} a & b & c & a & b \\ d & e & f & d & e \\ g & h & i & g & h \end{matrix}$

This computational scheme results in the determinant:

$aei + bfg + cdh - ceg - afh - bdi$

submatrix A_{ij}

The submatrix A_{ij} is the $(n-1)\times(n-1)$ matrix, obtained by excluding the ith row and j^{th} column of A.

determinant of an $n \times n$ matrix $(n>2)$ in terms of an expansion of its ith row

$\det A = \begin{vmatrix} a_{11} & & \cdots & & a_{1n} \\ \vdots & & & & \vdots \\ a_{i1} & a_{i2} & \cdots & a_{i,n-1} & a_{in} \\ \vdots & & & & \vdots \\ a_{n1} & & \cdots & & a_{nn} \end{vmatrix} = \sum_{j=1}^{n} a_{ij} \cdot c_{ij}$

$= a_{i1} \cdot c_{i1} + a_{i2} \cdot c_{i2} + \ldots + a_{in} \cdot c_{in}$

cofactors c_{ij}

$c_{ij} = (-1)^{i+j} \det A_{ij}$ is the determinant of the submatrix A_{ij} multiplied by a factor ± 1 according to the scheme:

$\begin{pmatrix} + & - & + & \cdots \\ - & + & - & \cdots \\ + & - & + & \cdots \\ \vdots & \vdots & \vdots & \ddots \end{pmatrix}$

theorems

- $\det(AB) = \det A \cdot \det B$
- $\det A^{\text{T}} = \det A$
- A is invertible $\Leftrightarrow$ $\det A \neq 0$
- A is invertible $\Rightarrow$ $\det A^{-1} = \dfrac{1}{\det A}$

Algebra

Inverse of a matrix

inverse of an 2×2 matrix

For $A = \begin{pmatrix} a & b \\ c & d \end{pmatrix}$, $A^{-1} = \dfrac{1}{\det A} \begin{pmatrix} d & -b \\ -c & a \end{pmatrix}$, $\det A \neq 0$

inverse of a 3×3 matrix

For $A = \begin{pmatrix} a & b & c \\ d & e & f \\ g & h & i \end{pmatrix}$,

$$A^{-1} = \frac{1}{\det A} \begin{pmatrix} ei-fh & ch-bi & bf-ce \\ fg-di & ai-cg & cd-af \\ dh-eg & bg-ah & ae-bd \end{pmatrix}, \quad \det A \neq 0$$

inverse of a $n \times n$ matrix

$A^{-1} = \dfrac{1}{\det A} \cdot C^{\mathrm{T}}$, $\det A \neq 0$,

where C is the matrix of the cofactors of A.

inverse of the transpose

$\left(A^{\mathrm{T}}\right)^{-1} = \left(A^{-1}\right)^{\mathrm{T}}$

Eigenvalues, eigenvectors and eigenspace

eigenvalue, eigenvector

If A is an $n \times n$ matrix, a scalar λ is called an eigenvalue of A, if there exists a vector $\vec{v} \neq \vec{0}$ such that $A\vec{v} = \lambda \vec{v}$. Alternatively λ is an eigenvalue if $\vec{v} \neq \vec{0}$ is a solution of the equation $(A - \lambda E)\vec{v} = \vec{0}$.

Each such vector $\vec{v}$ is called an eigenvector corresponding to the eigenvalue λ.

eigenspace

If A is an $n \times n$ matrix and λ an eigenvalue, the eigenspace E_λ is the set of all eigenvectors corresponding to λ.
The following properties hold:

- E_λ is the space of solutions $\vec{x}$ of $(A - \lambda E)\vec{x} = \vec{0}$
- E_λ is the kernel of $A - \lambda E$

characteristic polynomial

If A is an $n \times n$ matrix, then the characteristic polynomial $p_A(\lambda)$ of A is given by $p_A(\lambda) = \det(A - \lambda E)$.

- special case

For a 2×2 matrix $A = \begin{pmatrix} a & b \\ c & d \end{pmatrix}$,

$p_A(\lambda) = \lambda^2 - \operatorname{tr} A \cdot \lambda + \det A = \lambda^2 - (a+d)\lambda + (ad - bc)$

theorems

- λ is an eigenvalue of A if and only if λ is a root of the characteristic polynomial of A.

- A is diagonalizable if and only if it has an eigenbasis – i.e. a basis of $\mathbb{R}^n$ consisting of eigenvectors of A. In the representation $A = PDP^{-1}$, where D is diagonal, the column vectors of P form an eigenbasis of A and the diagonal elements of D are the corresponding eigenvalues.

Algebra

2.6 Systems of linear equations

Two equations in two unknowns

$$\begin{vmatrix} a_1x + b_1y = k_1 \\ a_2x + b_2y = k_2 \end{vmatrix}$$

relevant determinants:
$$D = \det\begin{pmatrix} a_1 & b_1 \\ a_2 & b_2 \end{pmatrix}, \quad D_x = \det\begin{pmatrix} k_1 & b_1 \\ k_2 & b_2 \end{pmatrix}, \quad D_y = \det\begin{pmatrix} a_1 & k_1 \\ a_2 & k_2 \end{pmatrix}$$

D, D_x and D_y determine the solutions of the system of equations.

$D \neq 0$	unique solution: $x = \dfrac{D_x}{D},\ y = \dfrac{D_y}{D}$
$D = 0$ and $(D_x \neq 0$ or $D_y \neq 0)$	no solutions
$D = 0$ and $D_x = D_y = 0$	infinitely many or no solutions

Three equations in three unknowns

$$\begin{vmatrix} a_1x + b_1y + c_1z = k_1 \\ a_2x + b_2y + c_2z = k_2 \\ a_3x + b_3y + c_3z = k_3 \end{vmatrix}$$

relevant determinants:

$$D = \det\begin{pmatrix} a_1 & b_1 & c_1 \\ a_2 & b_2 & c_2 \\ a_3 & b_3 & c_3 \end{pmatrix},$$

$$D_x = \det\begin{pmatrix} k_1 & b_1 & c_1 \\ k_2 & b_2 & c_2 \\ k_3 & b_3 & c_3 \end{pmatrix}, \quad D_y = \det\begin{pmatrix} a_1 & k_1 & c_1 \\ a_2 & k_2 & c_2 \\ a_3 & k_3 & c_3 \end{pmatrix}, \quad D_z = \det\begin{pmatrix} a_1 & b_1 & k_1 \\ a_2 & b_2 & k_2 \\ a_3 & b_3 & k_3 \end{pmatrix}$$

$D \neq 0$	unique solution: $x = \dfrac{D_x}{D},\ y = \dfrac{D_y}{D},\ z = \dfrac{D_z}{D}$
$D = 0$ and at least one of the determinants $D_x, D_y, D_z \neq 0$	no solutions
$D = 0$ and $D_x = D_y = D_z = 0$	infinitely many or no solutions

The above formulae, known as CRAMER's rule, can be extended by analogy to the case of n equations in n unknowns.

Algebra
MATHEMATICS PHYSICS ASTRONOMY CHEMISTRY

Systems of linear equations in n unknowns

Numerical Analysis ▶ p. 135

system of n linear equations in n unknowns	$\begin{vmatrix} a_{11}x_1 + a_{12}x_2 + \ldots + a_{1n}x_n = b_1 \\ a_{21}x_1 + a_{22}x_2 + \ldots + a_{2n}x_n = b_2 \\ \vdots \\ a_{n1}x_1 + a_{n2}x_2 + \ldots + a_{nn}x_n = b_n \end{vmatrix}$
coefficient matrix	$A = \begin{pmatrix} a_{11} & a_{12} & \ldots & a_{1n} \\ a_{21} & a_{22} & \ldots & a_{2n} \\ \vdots & \vdots & \ddots & \vdots \\ a_{n1} & a_{n2} & \ldots & a_{nn} \end{pmatrix}$
vector of unknowns	$\vec{x} = \begin{pmatrix} x_1 \\ x_2 \\ \vdots \\ x_n \end{pmatrix}$
vector of constants	$\vec{b} = \begin{pmatrix} b_1 \\ b_2 \\ \vdots \\ b_n \end{pmatrix}$

Homogeneous system $A\vec{x} = \vec{0}$

solutions	• $\vec{x} = \vec{0}$ is always a solution. • If $\det A = 0$ i.e. rank $A < n$, then there exist infinitely many solutions. p. 30 ◀ rank • The set of solutions form a subspace L of $\mathbb{R}^n$: $L = \ker A$ p. 28 ◀ kernel
rank-nullity theorem	rank A + dim $L = n$

Inhomogeneous System $A\vec{x} = \vec{b},\ \vec{b} \neq \vec{0}$

solutions	• If $\det A \neq 0$, then there exists a unique solution: $\vec{x} = A^{-1}\vec{b}$ • If $\det A = 0$ i.e. rank $A < n$, then there exist infinitely many or no solutions.
superposition principle	If $\vec{x}_1$ is an arbitrary solution of an inhomogeneous system $A\vec{x} = \vec{b}$ and $\vec{x}_0$ of the corresponding homogeneous system $A\vec{x} = \vec{0}$, then $\vec{x} = \vec{x}_1 + \vec{x}_0$ is also a solution of the inhomogeneous system.

3 Discrete Mathematics

3.1 Elementary number theory (the underlying set is assumed to be $\mathbb{Z}$)

Divisibility relation

$a\,|\,b$ (a divides b) $\qquad\qquad a\,|\,b \Leftrightarrow$ there exists a $q \in \mathbb{Z}$ such that $qa = b$

theorems
$\qquad$ For all a: $\quad a\,|\,a, \quad 1\,|\,a, \quad a\,|\,0$
$\qquad (a\,|\,b$ and $b\,|\,c) \Rightarrow a\,|\,c$
$\qquad (a\,|\,b$ and $b\,|\,a) \Rightarrow a = b$ or $a = -b$
$\qquad (a\,|\,c$ and $b\,|\,d) \Rightarrow ab\,|\,cd$
$\qquad$ For all x, y: $(t\,|\,a$ and $t\,|\,b) \Rightarrow t\,|\,(xa + yb)$

Greatest common divisor, least common multiple

t common divisor of a, b	$t\,|\,a$ and $t\,|\,b$
w common multiple of a, b	$a\,|\,w$ and $b\,|\,w$
d greatest common divisor of a, b, where $a \neq 0$ or $b \neq 0$: $d = \gcd(a, b)$ (alternative notation: $d = (a, b)$)	the largest positive common divisor of a and b
v least common multiple of a, b, where $a \neq 0$ and $b \neq 0$: $v = \operatorname{lcm}(a, b)$ (alternative notation: $d = [a, b]$)	the smallest positive common multiple of a and b
a, b relatively prime	$\gcd(a, b) = 1$

Theorems

- $t\,|\,a$ and $t\,|\,b \Rightarrow t\,|\gcd(a, b)$
  Every common divisor of a and b divides $\gcd(a, b)$.
- $a\,|\,t$ and $b\,|\,t \Rightarrow \operatorname{lcm}(a, b)\,|\,t$
  Every common multiple of a and b is also a multiple of $\operatorname{lcm}(a, b)$.
- $\gcd(a, b) = \gcd(b, a)$
- $c\,|\,ab$ and $\gcd(c, a) = 1 \Rightarrow c\,|\,b$
- $a\,|\,c$, $b\,|\,c$ and $\gcd(a, b) = 1 \Rightarrow ab\,|\,c$
- $(a = qb + r$ and $0 \leqslant r < b) \Rightarrow \gcd(a, b) = \gcd(b, r)$
  or, alternatively: $\gcd(a, b) = \gcd(a, b + ka)$ for $k \in \mathbb{Z}$ $\Big\}$ basis of EUCLID's algorithm ▶ p. 36
- The gcd of a pair of numbers can be expressed as a linear combination of the numbers
  – i.e. there exist numbers $x, y \in \mathbb{Z}$ such that $\gcd(a, b) = xa + yb$.
  special case: a, b are relatively prime $\Leftrightarrow$ there exist $x, y \in \mathbb{Z}$ such that $1 = xa + yb$
- $\gcd(a, b) \cdot \operatorname{lcm}(a, b) = ab$
- $d = \gcd(a, b) \Rightarrow$ there exist $x, y \in \mathbb{Z}$ such that $\gcd(x, y) = 1$, $a = xd$, $b = yd$, $\operatorname{lcm}(a, b) = xyd$

Discrete Mathematics

Euclid's algorithm

If $a, b \in \mathbb{N}$, $b \leqslant a$, then $\gcd(a, b)$ can be calculated as shown opposite

Starting with a, b, the sequence of non-zero remainders $r_1, r_2, \ldots, r_n$ are computed until a remainder 0 is obtained:

$$\begin{aligned}
a &= q_1 b + r_1 & (0 \leqslant r_1 < b) \\
b &= q_2 r_1 + r_2 & (0 \leqslant r_2 < r_1) \\
r_1 &= q_3 r_2 + r_3 & (0 \leqslant r_3 < r_2) \\
&\vdots \\
r_{n-2} &= q_n r_{n-1} + r_n & (0 \leqslant r_n < r_{n-1}) \\
r_{n-1} &= q_{n+1} r_n + 0
\end{aligned}$$

Then $\gcd(a, b) = r_n$

Prime numbers

p is a prime number (or prime) $\quad p \in \mathbb{N}$, $p \neq 1$ and p and 1 are the only positive divisors of p.

the first few primes $\quad 2, 3, 5, 7, 11, 13, 17, 19, 23, 29, \ldots$ ▶ p. 146

Theorems

- the fundamental theorem of arithmetic (unique factorization theorem)

  Each integer $n > 1$ can be expressed uniquely as a product of prime factors:

  $$n = p_1^{\alpha_1} \cdot p_2^{\alpha_2} \cdot \ldots \cdot p_k^{\alpha_k} = \prod_{i=1}^{k} p_i^{\alpha_i}, \quad \alpha_i \in \mathbb{N} \text{ and } p_i \text{ prime}, \ p_1 < p_2 < \ldots < p_k$$

- $\left\{\begin{array}{l}\text{For each } n \in \mathbb{N} \ n! + 1 \text{ has a prime factor } p > n. \\ \text{If } p_1, p_2, \ldots, p_n \text{ are prime, then every prime factor} \\ \text{of } p_1 \cdot p_2 \cdot \ldots \cdot p_n + 1 \text{ differs from } p_1, p_2, \ldots, p_n.\end{array}\right\}$ There exist infinitely many prime numbers (Euclid).

- For every $n \geqslant 2$ there exists a sequence of n consecutive numbers which are not prime.

- If $\gcd(a, b) = 1$, then the arithmetic sequence of numbers $(an + b)$ $(n \in \mathbb{N})$ contains infinitely many primes (Dirichlet).

- The number of primes $\pi(x)$ between 2 and x can be approximated by $\pi(x) \approx \dfrac{x}{\ln x}$ (Gauss-Hadamard-de la Vallée Poussin).

Distribution of prime numbers

x	10^2	10^3	10^4	10^5	10^6	10^7	10^8	10^9	10^{10}
$\pi(x)$	25	168	1229	9592	78498	664579	5761455	50847534	455052511
$\left\lfloor \dfrac{x}{\ln x} \right\rfloor$	21	144	1085	8685	72382	620420	5428681	48254942	434294481

Greatest common divisor (gcd) and least common multiple (lcm)

$$\left\{\begin{array}{l} a = \prod_{i=1}^{k} p_i^{\alpha_i}, \ b = \prod_{i=1}^{k} p_i^{\beta_i} \\ \text{where } \alpha_i, \beta_i \in \mathbb{N}_0, \ p_i \text{ prime} \end{array}\right\} \Rightarrow \left\{\begin{array}{l} \gcd(a, b) = \prod_{i=1}^{k} p_i^{m_i}, \ \text{where } m_i = \min(\alpha_i, \beta_i) \\ \operatorname{lcm}(a, b) = \prod_{i=1}^{k} p_i^{M_i}, \ \text{where } M_i = \max(\alpha_i, \beta_i) \end{array}\right\}$$

Discrete Mathematics

Congruences

a and b are congruent modulo m m is a divisor of $a-b$, i.e. the respective remainders resulting from division of a and b by m are identical.

- notation $a \equiv b \pmod{m}$ or $a \equiv b \,(m)$ p. 15 ◀ mod

Theorems

- $\left\{ \begin{array}{l} a \equiv b \pmod{m} \\ c \equiv d \pmod{m} \end{array} \right\} \Rightarrow \left\{ \begin{array}{rcll} a \pm c & \equiv & b \pm d & \pmod{m} \\ ac & \equiv & bd & \pmod{m} \\ a^k & \equiv & b^k & \pmod{m} \text{ for } k \in \mathbb{N} \end{array} \right\}$

- $ca \equiv cb \pmod{m}$ and $\gcd(c, m) = d \Rightarrow a \equiv b \pmod{m/d}$
- $ax \equiv b \pmod{m}$ has a solution $x \in \mathbb{Z} \Leftrightarrow \gcd(a, m) \,|\, b$

The Chinese remainder theorem

If $m_1, m_2, \ldots, m_r \in \mathbb{N}$ are mutually relatively prime (i.e. $\gcd(m_1, m_2, \ldots, m_r) = 1$) and $a_1, a_2, \ldots, a_r \in \mathbb{Z}$, then the system of congruences

$$\begin{vmatrix} x \equiv a_1 \pmod{m_1} \\ x \equiv a_2 \pmod{m_2} \\ \vdots \\ x \equiv a_r \pmod{m_r} \end{vmatrix}$$

has an integer solution x which is uniquely determined modulo $m_1 \cdot m_2 \cdot \ldots \cdot m_r$.

Euler's totient function

Given $n \in \mathbb{N}$, $\varphi(n)$ is defined as the number of positive integers $m < n$ which are relatively prime to n.

Theorems

- $\gcd(m, n) = 1 \Rightarrow \varphi(mn) = \varphi(m)\varphi(n)$
- $\sum_{d \mid n} \varphi(d) = n$ for all $n \in \mathbb{N}$
- If $p_1^{n_1} \cdot p_2^{n_2} \cdot p_3^{n_3} \cdot \ldots \cdot p_r^{n_r}$ is the prime factorization of m, then

$$\varphi(m) = m\left(1 - \frac{1}{p_1}\right) \cdot \ldots \cdot \left(1 - \frac{1}{p_r}\right) = p_1^{n_1-1} \cdot \ldots \cdot p_r^{n_r-1} \cdot (p_1 - 1) \cdot \ldots \cdot (p_r - 1)$$

- p prime $\Rightarrow \varphi(p^k) = p^{k-1}(p-1)$
- $\gcd(a, m) = 1 \Rightarrow a^{\varphi(m)} \equiv 1 \pmod{m}$ (EULER-FERMAT theorem, or EULER's totient theorem)
- special case: p prime and $\gcd(a, p) = 1 \Rightarrow a^{p-1} \equiv 1 \pmod{p}$ (FERMAT's little theorem)

Discrete Mathematics

Residue classes

$\bar{a}$ residue class modulo m $\quad \bar{a} = [a] = a + m\mathbb{Z} = \{a + mk \mid k \in \mathbb{Z}\}$

set of residue classes
(mod m) $\quad \mathbb{Z}_m = \mathbb{Z}/m\mathbb{Z} = \{\bar{0}, \bar{1}, \bar{2}, \ldots, \overline{m-1}\}$

binary operations $\quad \bar{a} + \bar{b} = \overline{a+b}$ and $\bar{a} \cdot \bar{b} = \overline{a \cdot b}$

Theorems

- $\bar{a} = \bar{b} \iff a \equiv b \pmod{m}$
- $\left\{ \begin{array}{c} \bar{a} = \bar{b} \\ \bar{c} = \bar{d} \end{array} \right\} \Rightarrow \left\{ \begin{array}{c} \bar{a} + \bar{c} = \bar{b} + \bar{d} \\ \bar{a} \cdot \bar{c} = \bar{b} \cdot \bar{d} \end{array} \right\}$
- $(\mathbb{Z}_m, +)$ is a cyclic group.
- $\bar{a} \cdot \bar{x} = \bar{1}$ is solvable for $\bar{x}$ if and only if $\gcd(a, m) = 1$.
- $(\mathbb{Z}_m \setminus \{0\}, \cdot)$ is a cyclic group if and only if m is prime.
- $(\mathbb{Z}_m, +, \cdot)$ is a field if and only if m is prime.

3.2 Sequences

General
sequences of real numbers ▶ p. 51

sequence (a_n) — A sequence of numbers is a function assigning to each integer $n \in \mathbb{N}$ ($\mathbb{N}_0$) a real number a_n.
- $a \colon \mathbb{N} \to \mathbb{R}, \ n \mapsto a_n$ (explicit definition)
- $a_1, a_2, a_3, \ldots, a_n, \ldots, \ a_n \in \mathbb{R}$

A sequence may be specified by recursion, in which the kth element of the sequence is defined in terms of one or more preceding elements.
- $a_1 = c_0 \in \mathbb{R}$ (initial element)
- $a_{n+1} = f(a_1, \ldots, a_n)$ for $n \geqslant 1$ (recursion formula)

The initial index of a sequence can also be 0 or any other integer.

difference sequence (d_n) — Given a sequence (a_n), its difference sequence (d_n) (also denoted by (Δa_n)) is defined by the respective differences between successive elements of (a_n):

$d_n = a_{n+1} - a_n$

k^{th} difference sequence — Given a sequence (a_n), its kth difference sequence $(\Delta^k a_n)$ is defined by the respective differences between successive elements of the $(k-1)^{\text{th}}$ difference sequence $(\Delta^{k-1} a_n)$.

quotient sequence (q_n) — Given a sequence (a_n), none of whose elements is zero, its quotient sequence (q_n) is defined by the respective quotients of successive elements of (a_n):

$q_n = \dfrac{a_{n+1}}{a_n}$

Discrete Mathematics

sum sequence (s_n) (sequence of partial sums, series)	Given a sequence (a_n), its sum sequence (s_n) is defined by the respective sums of the first n elements of (a_n):

$$s_1 = a_1,\ s_2 = a_1 + a_2,\ s_3 = a_1 + a_2 + a_3,\ \dots,$$

$$s_n = a_1 + a_2 + \dots + a_n = \sum_{i=1}^{n} a_i,\ \dots \quad \text{or}$$

$$s_1 = a_1,\ s_2 = s_1 + a_2,\ s_3 = s_2 + a_3,\ \dots,\ s_n = s_{n-1} + a_n,\ \dots$$

Arithmetic progressions

arithmetic progression of order k (arithmetic sequence)

A sequence (a_n) is an arithmetic progression of order k, if k is the smallest number such that the kth difference sequence is a constant different from zero.

properties of arithmetic progressions

An arithmetic progression (a_n) of order k can be specified by a polynomial of degree k:
(a_n) is a kth-order arithmetic progression if and only if

$$a_n = c_k n^k + c_{k-1} n^{k-1} + \dots + c_2 n^2 + c_1 n + c_0 = \sum_{i=0}^{k} c_i n^i$$

The sum sequence of a kth-order arithmetic progression can be specified by a polynomial of degree $k+1$.

arithmetic progression of first order (arithmetic sequence)

- If $d = a_{n+1} - a_n$ is the constant of the first difference sequence, it follows that
$$a_n = a_1 + (n-1)d$$
- $s_n = \sum_{k=1}^{n} a_k = na_1 + \dfrac{n(n-1)}{2} d = n \dfrac{a_1 + a_n}{2}$
- Every element of the sequence except for the first is equal to the arithmetic mean of the two neighbouring elements:
$$a_n = \dfrac{a_{n+1} + a_{n-1}}{2}$$

- **special case**

the sequence of natural numbers: $a_n = n$

$$s_n = 1 + 2 + 3 + \dots + n = \dfrac{n(n+1)}{2}$$

arithmetic progression of second order

If d_1 and d_2 are the first two elements of the first difference sequence, it follows that

$$a_n = a_1 + (n-1)d_1 + \binom{n-1}{2}(d_2 - d_1)$$

$$s_n = \sum_{k=1}^{n} a_k = \binom{n}{1} a_1 + \binom{n}{2} d_1 + \binom{n}{3}(d_2 - d_1)$$

- **special case**

the sequence of squared natural numbers: $a_n = n^2$

$$s_n = 1^2 + 2^2 + 3^2 + \dots + n^2 = \dfrac{n(n+1)(2n+1)}{6}$$

Discrete Mathematics

Geometric progressions

geometric progression (geometric sequence)

A sequence (a_n) is a geometric progression if the quotient sequence is a constant differing from 0 and 1.

properties of geometric progressions

If $q = \dfrac{a_{n+1}}{a_n}$ ($q \neq 0$ and $q \neq 1$) is the constant of the quotient sequence, it follows that

- $a_n = a_1 q^{n-1}$
- $s_n = \sum\limits_{k=1}^{n} a_k = a_1 \dfrac{1-q^n}{1-q}$
- The absolute value of every element of the sequence except for the first is equal to the geometric mean of the two neighbouring elements:
  $|a_n| = \sqrt{a_{n+1} a_{n-1}}$
- The first difference sequence of a geometric progression is directly proportional to the sequence:
  $a_{n+1} - a_n = (q-1) \cdot a_n$

- **geometric series**

$s_n = \sum\limits_{k=1}^{n} a_k = a_1 \dfrac{1-q^n}{1-q}, \quad q \neq 1$

- **sum of an infinite geometric series**

$s = \lim\limits_{n \to \infty} s_n = \dfrac{a_1}{1-q}, \quad |q| < 1$ ▶ p. 53

Special sums

$\sum\limits_{k=1}^{n} k = 1 + 2 + \ldots + n = \dfrac{n(n+1)}{2}$

$\sum\limits_{k=1}^{n} k^2 = 1^2 + 2^2 + \ldots + n^2 = \dfrac{n(n+1)(2n+1)}{6}$

$\sum\limits_{k=1}^{n} k^3 = 1^3 + 2^3 + \ldots + n^3 = \left(\dfrac{n(n+1)}{2}\right)^2 = \left(\sum\limits_{k=1}^{n} k\right)^2$

$\sum\limits_{k=1}^{n} (2k-1) = 1 + 3 + 5 + \ldots + (2n-1) = n^2$

$\sum\limits_{k=1}^{n} (2k-1)^2 = 1^2 + 3^2 + 5^2 + \ldots + (2n-1)^2 = \dfrac{n(2n-1)(2n+1)}{3}$

$\sum\limits_{k=0}^{n-1} q^k = 1 + q + q^2 + \ldots + q^{n-1} = \dfrac{q^n - 1}{q - 1} = \dfrac{1 - q^n}{1 - q}, \quad q \neq 1,\ q \neq 0$

Discrete Mathematics

Second-order linear recurrence relations

A linear homogeneous recurrence relation of order 2 with constant coefficients A and B for the sequence (a_n) is an equation of the form: $a_k = A \cdot a_{k-1} + B \cdot a_{k-2}$

superposition principle	If a second-order linear homogeneous recurrence relation with constant coefficients is satisfied by both the sequences (p_n) and (q_n), then it is also satisfied by the linear combination $(\lambda p_n + \mu q_n)$ of the two sequences.
characteristic equation	Given the second-order linear homogeneous recurrence relation $a_k = A \cdot a_{k-1} + B \cdot a_{k-2}$, its characteristic equation in r is defined by $r^2 = A \cdot r + B$
solutions	Suppose the first two elements of a sequence (a_n) are given and the sequence satisfies a second-order linear homogeneous recurrence relation: $a_0 = c_0, \quad a_1 = c_1$ $a_k = A \cdot a_{k-1} + B \cdot a_{k-2}$ Then, if the characteristic equation has two distinct solutions α and β, it follows that $$a_n = \frac{c_0 \cdot \beta - c_1}{\beta - \alpha} \alpha^{n-1} + \frac{c_1 - c_0 \cdot \alpha}{\beta - \alpha} \beta^{n-1}$$ If the characteristic equation has a double solution α, it follows that $$a_n = \left(\left(\frac{c_1}{\alpha} - c_0\right) \cdot (n-1) + c_0\right) \alpha^{n-1}$$
FIBONACCI numbers (f_n)	$f_0 = 0, \ f_1 = 1, \ f_n = f_{n-1} + f_{n-2} \ (n \geqslant 2)$
LUCAS numbers (l_n)	$l_0 = 2, \ l_1 = 1, \ l_n = l_{n-1} + l_{n-2} \ (n \geqslant 2)$
Theorems	• $f_n = \dfrac{\Phi^n - (-\varphi)^n}{\Phi + \varphi} = \dfrac{\sqrt{5}}{5}\left(\left(\dfrac{1+\sqrt{5}}{2}\right)^n - \left(\dfrac{1-\sqrt{5}}{2}\right)^n\right)$
	• $l_n = \Phi^n + (-\varphi)^n$
	• $\lim\limits_{n \to \infty} \dfrac{f_{n+1}}{f_n} = \lim\limits_{n \to \infty} \dfrac{l_{n+1}}{l_n} = \Phi$ $\qquad$ golden ratio ▶ p. 83
	• $f_{2n} = f_n l_n, \qquad l_{2n} = l_n^2 - 2(-1)^n$
	• $l_n = f_{n-1} + f_{n+1}, \quad 5 f_n = l_{n-1} + l_{n+1}$
	• $f_{n+1} = \sum\limits_{k \geqslant 0} \binom{n-k}{k}$ $\qquad$ PASCAL's triangle ▶ p. 43
	• $\sum\limits_{k=0}^{n} f_k = f_{n+2} - 1, \quad \sum\limits_{k=0}^{n} l_k = l_{n+2} - 1$
	• $f_{m+n} = f_{m+1} f_n + f_m f_{n-1}$
	• $2 f_{m+n} = f_m l_n + f_n l_m \qquad 2 l_{m+n} = l_m l_n + 5 f_m f_n$
	• $m \mid n \Rightarrow f_m \mid f_n$
	• $\gcd(f_n, f_{n-1}) = 1, \quad \gcd(f_m, f_n) = f_{\gcd(m,n)}$

Discrete Mathematics

3.3 Factorials and binomial coefficients

Factorials

explicit definition
$$0! = 1$$
$$n! = 1 \cdot 2 \cdot 3 \cdot \ldots \cdot (n-1) \cdot n = \prod_{k=1}^{n} k, \quad n \in \mathbb{N}$$

recursive definition
$$0! = 1 \qquad \text{(initial value)}$$
$$n! = n \cdot (n-1)!, \quad n \in \mathbb{N} \qquad \text{(recurrence relation)}$$

$1!$	=	1	$20!$	$\approx$	$2.432902 \cdot 10^{18}$
$2!$	=	2	$30!$	$\approx$	$2.652529 \cdot 10^{32}$
$3!$	=	6	$40!$	$\approx$	$8.159153 \cdot 10^{47}$
$4!$	=	24	$50!$	$\approx$	$3.041409 \cdot 10^{64}$
$5!$	=	120	$100!$	$\approx$	$9.332622 \cdot 10^{157}$
$6!$	=	720	$1\,000!$	$\approx$	$4.023873 \cdot 10^{2\,567}$
$7!$	=	5 040	$10\,000!$	$\approx$	$2.846260 \cdot 10^{35\,659}$
$8!$	=	40 320	$100\,000!$	$\approx$	$2.824229 \cdot 10^{456\,573}$
$9!$	=	362 880	$1\,000\,000!$	$\approx$	$8.263932 \cdot 10^{5\,565\,708}$
$10!$	=	3 628 800	$10\,000\,000!$	$\approx$	$1.202423 \cdot 10^{65\,657\,059}$

STIRLING's approximation
$$n! \approx \sqrt{2\pi n} \left(\frac{n}{e}\right)^n, \quad n \in \mathbb{N}$$

with error bounds ▶ p. 81

Binomial coefficients

explicit definition
$$\binom{n}{k} = \frac{n!}{k!\,(n-k)!} = \frac{n \cdot (n-1) \cdot (n-2) \cdot \ldots \cdot (n-k+1)}{k \cdot (k-1) \cdot (k-2) \cdot \ldots \cdot 3 \cdot 2 \cdot 1}$$

$$k, n \in \mathbb{N}_0, \quad k \leqslant n \qquad \binom{n}{k} = 0, \quad k > n$$

recursive definition

$$\binom{0}{0} = 1 \qquad \binom{n}{0} = \binom{n}{n} = 1 \qquad \text{initial and boundary values}$$

$$\binom{n+1}{k+1} = \binom{n}{k} + \binom{n}{k+1}, \quad k < n \qquad \text{addition principle (recurrence relation)}$$

$$\binom{n+1}{k+1} = \frac{n+1}{k+1} \cdot \binom{n}{k} \qquad \text{(further recurrence relation)}$$

symmetry property
$$\binom{n}{k} = \binom{n}{n-k}$$

Discrete Mathematics
MATHEMATICS   PHYSICS   ASTRONOMY   CHEMISTRY

special sums

$$\sum_{k=0}^{n} \binom{n}{k} = \binom{n}{0} + \binom{n}{1} + \binom{n}{2} + \ldots + \binom{n}{n} = 2^n$$

$$\sum_{k=0}^{n} (-1)^k \binom{n}{k} = \binom{n}{0} - \binom{n}{1} + \binom{n}{2} - + \ldots = 0$$

$$\sum_{k=0}^{m} \binom{n+k}{n} = \binom{n}{n} + \binom{n+1}{n} + \ldots + \binom{n+m}{n} = \binom{n+m+1}{n+1}$$

PASCAL's triangle

```
                              1
                          1       1
                       1     2      1
                    1    3      3     1           k=3
                 1    4      6     4     1         k=4
              1    5     10    10    5     1        k=5
           1    6    15    20   15    6    1         k=6
        1    7   21    35   35   21    7    1
n=8 →  1   8   28    56   70    56   28    8    1          (8 6) = 28
      1   9   36    84   126  126   84   36    9    1
   1   10  45   120   210  252   210  120   45   10    1
 1   11   55  165   330  462   462  330  165   55   11   1
1  12   66   220  495  792   924  792  495  220   66   12   1
```

$\binom{n}{0}$ $\binom{n}{1}$ $\binom{n}{2}$ $\binom{n}{3}$ $\ldots$ $\ldots$ $\binom{n}{k}$ $\binom{n}{k+1}$ $\ldots$ $\binom{n}{n-1}$ $\binom{n}{n}$

$\binom{n+1}{k+1}$

Binomial theorem

$$(a+b)^n = \sum_{k=0}^{n} \binom{n}{k} a^{n-k} b^k = \binom{n}{0} a^n + \binom{n}{1} a^{n-1} b + \binom{n}{2} a^{n-2} b^2 + \ldots + \binom{n}{n-1} a b^{n-1} + \binom{n}{n} b^n$$

Generalization to trinomials

The coefficient of $a^p b^q c^r$ in $(a+b+c)^n$ is given by $\dfrac{n!}{p!\, q!\, r!} = \binom{n}{p}\binom{n-p}{q}$, $p+q+r = n$

Generalization to multinomials

The coefficient of $a_1^{p_1} \cdot a_2^{p_2} \cdot \ldots \cdot a_m^{p_m}$ in $(a_1 + a_2 + \ldots + a_m)^n$ is given by

$$\dfrac{n!}{p_1! \cdot p_2! \cdot \ldots \cdot p_m!} = \binom{n}{p_1} \cdot \binom{n-p_1}{p_2} \cdot \ldots \cdot \binom{n-p_1-\ldots-p_{m-2}}{p_{m-1}}, \quad p_1 + p_2 + \ldots + p_m = n$$

Discrete Mathematics

3.4 Combinatorics (counting problems)

Rule of product (multiplication principle)

Suppose a selection involves k consecutive steps. If in the ith step there are m_i possibilities to choose from $(i = 1, 2, \ldots, k)$, then there are
$$m_1 \cdot m_2 \cdot \ldots \cdot m_k$$
distinct possibilities for making the selection.

Selections

Suppose an urn contains n lots, which may be numbered or otherwise distinguished from one another. By drawing k lots from the urn one obtains a selection of size k, or k-selection. The number of possible distinct selections depends on whether the drawn lots are replaced in the urn before drawing the next, and whether the order in which the lots are drawn is taken into account.

	with replacement	without replacement
with regard to order	$\overline{P}(n,k) = n^k$	$P(n,k) = n \cdot (n-1) \cdot \ldots \cdot (n-k+1) = \dfrac{n!}{(n-k)!}$
without regard to order	$\overline{C}(n,k) = \binom{n+k-1}{k}$	$C(n,k) = \binom{n}{k}$

Many problems in combinatorics are equivalent to one of these four ways of selecting lots from an urn: e. g. placing k numbered balls in n different containers. The number of such assignments depends on whether a container may contain arbitrarily many balls or just one ball, and also on whether the individual numbers of the balls in each compartment are taken into account. If one identifies each container with a particular lot and the number on each ball with the sequence number of a particular draw from the urn, the following table holds:

	arbitrarily many balls in each container	at most one ball in each container
with regard to ball numbers	$\overline{P}(n,k) = n^k$	$P(n,k) = n \cdot (n-1) \cdot \ldots \cdot (n-k+1) = \dfrac{n!}{(n-k)!}$
without regard to ball numbers	$\overline{C}(n,k) = \binom{n+k-1}{k}$	$C(n,k) = \binom{n}{k}$

Consider selections made by drawing without replacement. If the order in which k objects are selected is taken into account, the selection is called a permutation (or k-permutation). The number of distinct permutations of k objects selected from a set of n objects is denoted by $P(n,k)$. Otherwise, if the order of selection is disregarded, the selection is called a combination. The number of distinct combinations of k objects selected from n objects is denoted by $C(n,k)$. Analogously, if the selections are made by drawing with replacement, the number of permutations and the number of combinations are denoted by $\overline{P}(n,k)$ and $\overline{C}(n,k)$ respectively.

Discrete Mathematics

Permutations

Let Ω be a set with n elements.

The number of distinct permutations (ordered selections) of k objects selected from Ω is given by

$$P(n,k) = n \cdot (n-1) \cdot \ldots \cdot (n-k+1) = \frac{n!}{(n-k)!}$$

For $k = n$ the permutations correspond to possible orderings of the objects in Ω. The number of such permutations is given by

$$P(n) = P(n,n) = n!$$

A rearrangement of a sequence of n objects such that no object is assigned to its original position is called a derangement. The number of distinct derangements of n objects is given by

$$A(n) = n! \left(\frac{1}{0!} - \frac{1}{1!} + \frac{1}{2!} - \frac{1}{3!} + - \ldots + \frac{(-1)^n}{n!} \right) = \left\lfloor \frac{n!}{e} + \frac{1}{2} \right\rfloor$$

e ▶ p. 52

Combinations

Let Ω be a set with n elements.

The number of distinct combinations (subsets of Ω) with k objects is given by

$$C(n,k) = \frac{P(n,k)}{k!} = \frac{n!}{k!(n-k)!} = \binom{n}{k}$$

The number of distinct partitions of Ω into r disjoint subsets with $k_1, k_2, \ldots, k_r$ elements respectively is given by

$$\frac{n!}{k_1! \cdot k_2! \cdot \ldots \cdot k_r!}, \quad k_1 + k_2 + \ldots + k_r = n$$

Inclusion-exclusion principle

Let $A_1, A_2, \ldots, A_n$ be finite sets, and let $M = A_1 \cup A_2 \cup \ldots \cup A_n = \bigcup_{k=1}^{n} A_k$.

Then it follows that

$$|M| = \sum_{i} |A_i| - \sum_{i,j} |A_i \cap A_j| + \sum_{i,j,k} |A_i \cap A_j \cap A_k| - + \ldots + (-1)^{n-1} |A_1 \cap A_2 \cap \ldots \cap A_n|$$

where the summations are understood to range over all distinct combinations of the indices.

special cases

- $n = 2$: $|A \cup B| = |A| + |B| - |A \cap B|$
- $n = 3$: $|A \cup B \cup C| = |A| + |B| + |C| - |A \cap B| - |A \cap C| - |B \cap C| + |A \cap B \cap C|$

Discrete Mathematics

3.5 Graph theory

Basic terms

graph vertices edges	A graph G is a diagram consisting of a finite set of points, some of which are connected by curve segments. The points are called vertices (or nodes) and the curve segments are called edges.

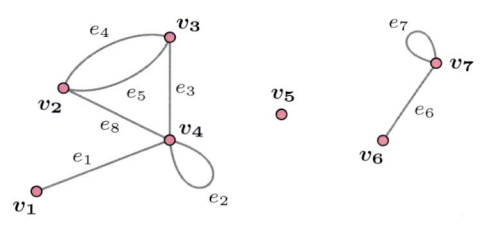

graph with vertices $v_1, v_2, \ldots, v_7$ and edges $e_1, e_2, \ldots, e_8$

loop	A loop is an edge connecting a vertex to itself. (e.g. edge e_2 connects vertex v_4 in the figure above)
incident	A vertex and an edge are said to be incident whenever the vertex is an end point of the edge.
isolated vertex	An isolated vertex is a vertex which is not incident to any edges.
adjacent	Two vertices incident to a common edge are said to be adjacent to one another. Likewise, two edges sharing a common end point are said to be adjacent.
walk	In a graph G with the vertices v_0 and v_n, a walk from v_0 to v_n is a finite alternating sequence of adjacent vertices and edges. It takes the form $v_0 e_1 v_1 e_2 v_2 \ldots v_{n-1} e_n v_n$.
trail	In a graph G with the vertices v_0 and v_n, a trail from v_0 to v_n is a walk in which no edge is repeated. It takes the form $v_0 e_1 v_1 e_2 v_2 \ldots v_{n-1} e_n v_n$, where all e_i are distinct.
path (simple path)	In a graph G with the vertices v_0 and v_n, a path from v_0 to v_n is a walk in which no vertex (and hence no edge) is repeated. It takes the form $v_0 e_1 v_1 e_2 v_2 \ldots v_{n-1} e_n v_n$, where all v_i and e_j are distinct.
circuit (tour)	A circuit is a closed trail. It takes the form $v_0 e_1 v_1 e_2 v_2 \ldots v_{n-1} e_n v_0$, where all e_i are distinct.
cycle (closed path)	A cycle is a circuit in which no vertex except the first (and hence no edge) is repeated – i.e. a closed path. It takes the form $v_0 e_1 v_1 e_2 v_2 \ldots v_{n-1} e_n v_0$ where all v_i and e_j are distinct.

Discrete Mathematics

Properties of graphs

isomorphic graphs
: Two graphs are isomorphic if and only if a bijection exists between their respective sets of vertices such that it preserves adjacent pairs – i.e. vertices in one graph are adjacent if and only if their isomorphic images in the other graph are adjacent.

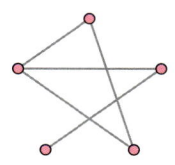

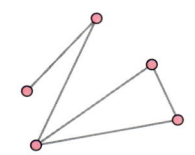

two isomorphic graphs (a plane graph at right)

plane graph
: A plane graph is a graph in which the vertices and edges lie in a plane and the edges intersect only at the vertices.

planar graph
: A planar graph is a graph which is isomorphic to a plane graph.

connected graph
: A graph is said to be connected if between every pair of vertices v_i and v_j there exists a trail.

tree
: A graph G is called a tree if it is connected and contains no circuits.

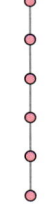

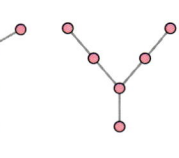

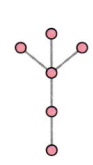

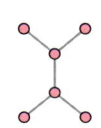

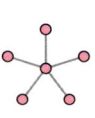

all possible trees with six vertices

- Let v_i and v_j be two distinct vertices of a tree T. Then there exists exactly one trail from v_i to v_j.
- Let G be a graph without any loops. If for every pair of distinct vertices v_i and v_j there exists exactly one trail from v_i to v_j, then G is a tree.
- If T is a tree with n vertices, then it has exactly $n-1$ edges.

complete graph
: A graph is said to be complete if every pair of distinct vertices is connected by a unique edge.

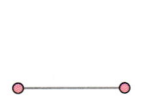

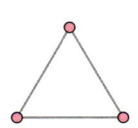

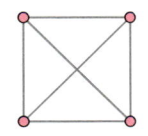

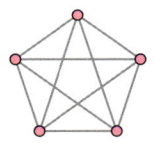

examples of complete graphs

Discrete Mathematics

vertex-labelled graph	A vertex-labelled graph is a graph in which a symbol – e. g. a number – is assigned to each vertex.. • Colours may be assigned to the vertices, in which case the graph is said to be a vertex-coloured graph.
edge-labelled graph (weighted graph)	An edge-labelled graph is a graph in which a symbol is assigned to each edge. In a weighted graph the edges are assigned real numbers. • Weighted graphs are frequently used in optimization problems, in which the weights usually represent costs (e. g. travel time or transport costs in a road network).
weight of a trail	In a weighted graph the weight of a trail is the sum of the weights of the edges encountered in the trail.

Theorems concerning graphs

degree (valency)	The degree $\deg(v)$ or the valency of a vertex v is the number of edges incident to the vertex, with any loops counted twice. • Isolated vertices have degree 0.
total degree of a graph	The total degree of a graph is the sum of the degrees of its vertices.
handshaking lemma	The total degree of the graph G with vertices $v_1, v_2, \ldots, v_n$ and edges $e_1, e_2, \ldots, e_m$ is equal to twice the number of edges: $\deg(G) = \deg(v_1) + \ldots + \deg(v_n) = 2 \cdot m$ Consequences • The total degree of a graph is even. • The number of vertices with odd degree is even.
EULERian circuit	An Eulerian circuit in a graph G is a circuit that includes every edge and every vertex of G.
EULER's theorem	A graph contains an Eulerian circuit if and only if it is connected and the degree of every vertex is even.

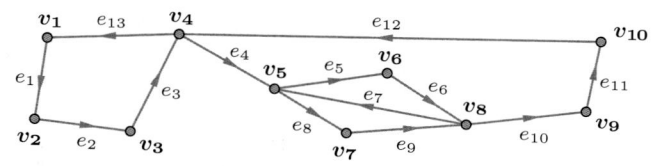

graph with an EULERian circuit (indicated by arrows)

Discrete Mathematics

Hamiltonian cycle	A Hamiltonian cycle in a graph G is a cycle that includes every vertex of G.

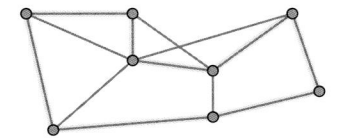

graph with a Hamiltonian cycle

Dirac's theorem	In a simple graph – i.e. one with no loops and just one edge between each pair of vertices – with n vertices $(n > 2)$, if the degree of every vertex is at least $\frac{n}{2}$, then the graph contains a Hamiltonian cycle.
adjacency matrix	Given a graph G with indexed vertex labels $v_1, v_2, \ldots, v_n$, its adjacency matrix is defined as $A = (a_{ij})$, $a_{ij} \in \mathbb{N}_0$, $i, j = 1, \ldots, n$, where a_{ij} is the number of edges which connect v_i, to v_j.

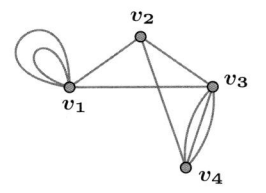

$$A = \begin{pmatrix} 2 & 1 & 1 & 0 \\ 1 & 0 & 1 & 1 \\ 1 & 1 & 0 & 3 \\ 0 & 1 & 3 & 0 \end{pmatrix}$$

graph with the corresponding adjacency matrix

theorem on adjacency matrices	If the graph G has the adjacency matrix A, then the ij^{th} element of A^n is equal to the number of walks from vertex v_i to vertex v_j consisting of n edges.
face	A plane graph G subdivides the plane into finitely many areas surrounded by edges. These areas are called faces of G. • Every plane graph has exactly one external (unbounded) face. Every other face is bounded by a cycle and is called an interior face. • Neighbouring faces have at least one common edge.
Euler's formula	If G is a connected plane graph with v vertices, e edges and f faces, it follows that $$v - e + f = 2 \qquad \blacktriangleright \text{p. 95}$$
dual graph	Let G be a plane graph. The graph G^* is called the dual of G if every face f of G corresponds to a vertex f^* of G^*, and every edge e of G corresponds to an edge e^* of G^* such that e^* connects adjacent vertices f^* and g^* of G^* if and only if e is on the boundary between neighbouring faces f and g of G.

Discrete Mathematics

p-partite graph	Let G be a graph. A partition of the vertex set V into p disjoint subsets $V_1, V_2, \ldots, V_p$ is called a p-partite graph, provided no adjacent vertices lie in the same subset. In other words, all edges run between subsets; none lies within a subset.
p-vertex colourable	A graph G is called p-vertex colourable if its vertices can be labelled with at most p colours such that adjacent vertices have different colours.
chromatic number	The chromatic number of a graph is the smallest number p for which it is p-vertex colourable.
four colour theorem	The chromatic number of every planar graph cannot exceed 4. By implication, every political map, which requires different colours either side of common borders, can be coloured with four or fewer colours.

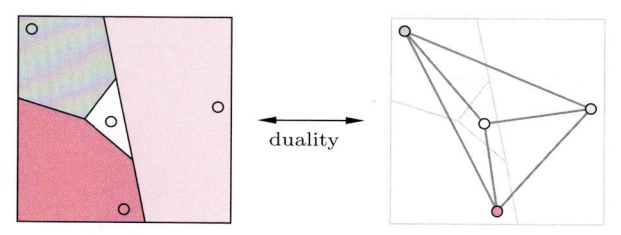

duality

Graph-theoretic problems

travelling salesman problem	This is the problem of finding a Hamiltonian cycle of minimal weight in a weighted graph. (Note, if the graph is not complete, it need not have a Hamiltonian cycle.)
Chinese postman problem	This is the problem of finding a walk in a weighted graph such that every edge is traversed at least once, the walk returns to its starting point and its weight is minimal among all such walks. (Note, if the degrees of all vertices are even, then the optimal walk will be an Eulerian cycle.)

4 Calculus

4.1 Sequences of real numbers

General

Sequence (a_n)	$a_1, a_2, a_3, \ldots$, where $a_n \in \mathbb{R}$ p. 38 ◂
• definition as a function	$a\colon \mathbb{N} \to \mathbb{R},\ n \mapsto a_n$
(a_n) is monotonically increasing or monotonically decreasing	$a_{n+1} \geqslant a_n$ or $a_{n+1} \leqslant a_n$ for all $n \in \mathbb{N}$
(a_n) is bounded	There exists a number $M \in \mathbb{R}^+$ such that $|a_n| \leqslant M$ for all $n \in \mathbb{N}$.
sequence of partial sums (s_n) (series)	$s_n = \sum_{k=1}^{n} a_k$
(a_n) converges to the limit a_*	For every $\varepsilon > 0$ there exists an integer $N(\varepsilon)$ such that for all $n > N(\varepsilon)$, $|a_n - a_*| < \varepsilon$.
• notation	$\lim\limits_{n \to \infty} a_n = a_*$ or $a_n \to a_*$ for $n \to \infty$
(a_n) is a null sequence	$\lim\limits_{n \to \infty} a_n = 0$
$\lim\limits_{n \to \infty} a_n = \infty$	For every $M \in \mathbb{R}$, $a_n > M$ for almost all n (i.e. for all but a finite number of $n \in \mathbb{N}$).

Theorems on limits of sequences

Let the sequences (a_n) and (b_n) be convergent. It follows that

$\lim\limits_{n \to \infty} (a_n \pm b_n) = \lim\limits_{n \to \infty} a_n \pm \lim\limits_{n \to \infty} b_n$

$\lim\limits_{n \to \infty} (a_n \cdot b_n) = \left(\lim\limits_{n \to \infty} a_n \right) \cdot \left(\lim\limits_{n \to \infty} b_n \right)$

$\lim\limits_{n \to \infty} (c \cdot a_n) = c \cdot \lim\limits_{n \to \infty} a_n$

$\lim\limits_{n \to \infty} \left(\dfrac{a_n}{b_n} \right) = \dfrac{\lim\limits_{n \to \infty} a_n}{\lim\limits_{n \to \infty} b_n}$, if $\lim\limits_{n \to \infty} b_n \neq 0$

convergence criterion for monotone sequences

If a sequence (a_n) is monotone and bounded, it converges.

Calculus

Limits of special sequences

$$\lim_{n \to \infty} a^n = 0, \ |a| < 1 \qquad \lim_{n \to \infty} \frac{a^n}{n!} = 0$$

$$\lim_{n \to \infty} \sqrt[n]{a} = \lim_{n \to \infty} \sqrt[n]{n^a} = 1, \ a > 0 \qquad \lim_{n \to \infty} \sqrt[n]{p(n)} = 1, \ p(n) \text{ polynomial}$$

$$\lim_{n \to \infty} \frac{\log_a(n)}{n} = 0, \ a > 1 \qquad \lim_{n \to \infty} n\left(\sqrt[n]{a} - 1\right) = \ln a$$

$$\lim_{n \to \infty} \frac{n^k}{a^n} = 0, \ a > 1, \text{ i.e. an exponential function grows faster than any given power function.}$$

$$\lim_{n \to \infty} \sum_{k=1}^{n} \frac{1}{k} = \lim_{n \to \infty} \left(1 + \frac{1}{2} + \frac{1}{3} + \ldots + \frac{1}{n}\right) = \sum_{k=1}^{\infty} \frac{1}{k} = \infty \qquad \text{harmonic series, divergent}$$

$$\lim_{n \to \infty} \left(\sum_{k=1}^{n} \frac{1}{k} - \ln(n)\right) = \lim_{n \to \infty} \left(1 + \frac{1}{2} + \frac{1}{3} + \ldots + \frac{1}{n} - \ln(n)\right) = C = 0.57721\,56649\,01532\ldots$$

EULER-MASCHERONI constant

EULER's number e

The sequence $\left(1 + \frac{1}{n}\right)^n$ is monotonically increasing and bounded, hence convergent. Its limit is the mathematical constant e, called EULER's number.

$$\lim_{n \to \infty} \left(1 + \frac{1}{n}\right)^n = e = 2.71828\,18284\,59045\,23536\,02874\,71352\,66249\,77572\,47093\,69995\,95749\,66967\,6$$

$$\lim_{n \to \infty} \left(1 - \frac{1}{n}\right)^n = \frac{1}{e} = 0.36787\,94411\ldots$$

$$\lim_{n \to \infty} \left(1 + \frac{x}{n}\right)^n = e^x$$

$$e = 2 + \cfrac{1}{1 + \cfrac{1}{2 + \cfrac{1}{1 + \cfrac{1}{1 + \cfrac{1}{4 + \cfrac{1}{1 + \cfrac{1}{1 + \cfrac{1}{6 + \cdots}}}}}}}}$$

(continued fraction)

Infinite series

$$\sum_{k=1}^{\infty} a_k = \lim_{n \to \infty} \sum_{k=1}^{n} a_k \qquad \text{stands for both the series (i.e. sequence of partial sums } (s_n)\text{) of the sequence } (a_n) \text{ and its sum, if the latter exists.}$$

$$\sum_{k=1}^{\infty} a_k \text{ is convergent} \qquad \text{The sequence of partial sums } (s_n) \text{ of the sequence } (a_n) \text{ is convergent.}$$

- notation

$$s = \lim_{n \to \infty} s_n = \sum_{k=1}^{\infty} a_k$$

$$\sum_{k=1}^{\infty} a_k \text{ is absolutely convergent} \qquad \sum_{k=1}^{\infty} |a_k| \text{ is convergent}$$

- Every absolutely convergent series is also convergent.

Calculus
MATHEMATICS PHYSICS ASTRONOMY CHEMISTRY

Convergence criteria for infinite series

necessary condition	If $\sum a_k$ is convergent, then (a_k) is a null sequence.
LEIBNIZ test	If (a_k) is alternating and $(|a_k|)$ is a monotone null sequence, then $\sum a_k$ is convergent and $|s - s_n| < |a_{n+1}|$.
comparison test	If $|a_k| \leqslant c_k$ for almost all k (i.e. for all but a finite number of $k \in \mathbb{N}$) and if $\sum c_k$ is convergent, then $\sum a_k$ is absolutely convergent.
ratio test	If $\left|\dfrac{a_{k+1}}{a_k}\right| \leqslant q$ with $0 < q < 1$ for almost all k, then $\sum a_k$ is absolutely convergent.
root test	If $\sqrt[k]{|a_k|} \leqslant q$ with $0 < q < 1$ for almost all k, then $\sum a_k$ is absolutely convergent.

Special infinite series

$$\sum_{k=0}^{\infty} aq^k = a + aq + aq^2 + aq^3 + \ldots = \frac{a}{1-q}, \quad 0 < |q| < 1 \qquad \text{geometric series} \qquad \text{p. 40} \blacktriangleleft$$

$$\sum_{k=0}^{\infty} (k+1)q^k = 1 + 2q + 3q^2 + 4q^3 + \ldots = \frac{1}{(1-q)^2}, \quad 0 < |q| < 1$$

$$\sum_{k=0}^{\infty} \frac{(-1)^k}{2k+1} = 1 - \frac{1}{3} + \frac{1}{5} - \frac{1}{7} + - \ldots = \frac{\pi}{4} \qquad \sum_{k=1}^{\infty} \frac{(-1)^{k+1}}{k} = 1 - \frac{1}{2} + \frac{1}{3} - \frac{1}{4} + - \ldots = \ln 2$$

$$\sum_{k=1}^{\infty} \frac{1}{k^2} = 1 + \frac{1}{2^2} + \frac{1}{3^2} + \frac{1}{4^2} + \ldots = \frac{\pi^2}{6} \qquad \sum_{k=1}^{\infty} \frac{(-1)^{k+1}}{k^2} = 1 - \frac{1}{2^2} + \frac{1}{3^2} - \frac{1}{4^2} + - \ldots = \frac{\pi^2}{12}$$

$$\sum_{k=1}^{\infty} \frac{1}{k^4} = 1 + \frac{1}{2^4} + \frac{1}{3^4} + \frac{1}{4^4} + \ldots = \frac{\pi^4}{90} \qquad \sum_{k=1}^{\infty} \frac{(-1)^{k+1}}{k^4} = 1 - \frac{1}{2^4} + \frac{1}{3^4} - \frac{1}{4^4} + - \ldots = \frac{7\pi^4}{720}$$

$$\sum_{k=1}^{\infty} \frac{1}{k^a} \text{ is convergent} \Leftrightarrow a > 1$$

$$\sum_{k=0}^{\infty} \frac{1}{k!} = 1 + \frac{1}{1!} + \frac{1}{2!} + \frac{1}{3!} + \ldots = e \qquad \sum_{k=0}^{\infty} \frac{(-1)^k}{k!} = 1 - \frac{1}{1!} + \frac{1}{2!} - \frac{1}{3!} + - \ldots = \frac{1}{e}$$

4.2 Real functions

General

real function f (referred to below simply as function f)	$f\colon D_f \to \mathbb{R}$, $x \mapsto f(x)$ with $D_f \subset \mathbb{R}$
• alternative notation	$f\colon x \mapsto f(x)$, $x \in D_f \subset \mathbb{R}$, $f(x) \in \mathbb{R}$
function value at x	$f(x)$
domain of f	D_f, or D for short
range, (image) of f	$R_f = f(D_f) = \{f(x) \mid x \in D_f\}$, or R for short
graph of f	$G_f = \{(x,y) \mid x \in D_f,\ y = f(x)\}$
equality of functions	$f = g \iff \begin{cases} D_f = D_g \text{ and} \\ f(x) = g(x) \text{ for all } x \in D_f \end{cases}$
f is even	G_f is symmetric with respect to reflection about the y-axis: $f(x) = f(-x)$ for all $x \in D_f$
f is odd	G_f is symmetric with respect to inversion through the origin: $f(x) = -f(-x)$ for all $x \in D_f$
f is bounded	There exists $M \in \mathbb{R}^+$ such that $\lvert f(x) \rvert \leqslant M$ for all $x \in D_f$
f is periodic with period $p \neq 0$	$f(x+p) = f(x)$ for all $x \in \mathbb{R}$, hence: $f(x+kp) = f(x)$ for all $k \in \mathbb{Z}$
f is monotonically increasing on $T \subset D_f$	$x_1 < x_2 \Rightarrow f(x_1) \leqslant f(x_2)$ for all $x_1, x_2 \in T$
f is monotonically decreasing on $T \subset D_f$	$x_1 < x_2 \Rightarrow f(x_1) \geqslant f(x_2)$ for all $x_1, x_2 \in T$
f is strictly monotonically increasing on $T \subset D_f$	$x_1 < x_2 \Rightarrow f(x_1) < f(x_2)$ for all $x_1, x_2 \in T$
f is strictly monotonically decreasing on $T \subset D_f$	$x_1 < x_2 \Rightarrow f(x_1) > f(x_2)$ for all $x_1, x_2 \in T$
composition of two functions f_1 and f_2	$f_1\colon D_1 \to \mathbb{R},\ x \mapsto f_1(x)$ $f_2\colon D_2 \to \mathbb{R},\ x \mapsto f_2(x),\ f_1(D_1) \subset D_2$ $f_2 \circ f_1\colon D_1 \to \mathbb{R},\ x \mapsto f_2\big(f_1(x)\big)$
f is invertible on $T \subset D_f$	f is injective on T p. 13 ◀ injective
inverse function f^{-1} of f, inverse mapping	$f^{-1}\colon f(T) \to T,\ y \mapsto x,\ f(x) = y$
identity function on D	$\mathrm{id}_D\colon D \to D,\ x \mapsto x$
composition of f and f^{-1}	$f^{-1} \circ f = \mathrm{id}_T$ and $f \circ f^{-1} = \mathrm{id}_{f(T)}$
geometric relationship between G_f and $G_{f^{-1}}$	$G_{f^{-1}}$ is obtained by reflecting G_f about the line $y = x$ and vice versa.

Calculus
MATHEMATICS   PHYSICS   ASTRONOMY   CHEMISTRY

Affine transformatons

Vertical translation

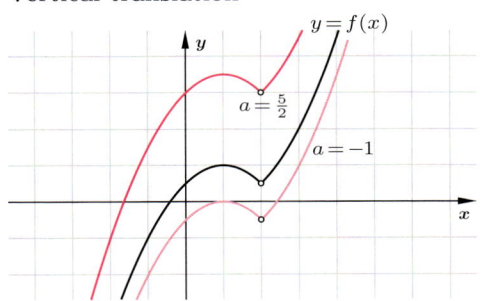

$\overline{f}(x) = f(x) + a$

Horizontal translation

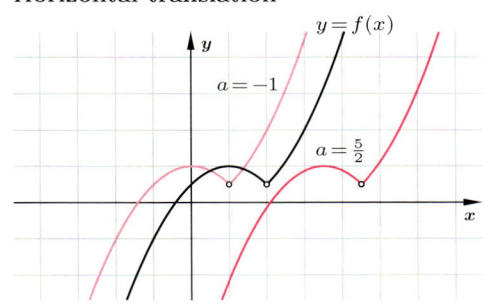

$\overline{f}(x) = f(x - a)$

Vertical scaling

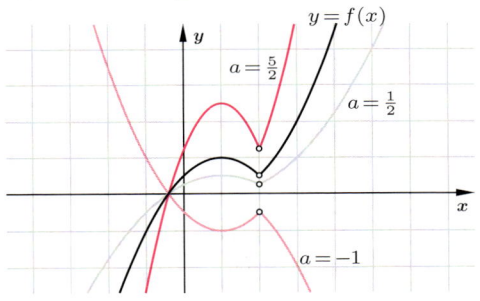

$\overline{f}(x) = a f(x)$

special case $a = -1$: $\overline{f}(x) = -f(x)$
reflection about the x-axis

Horizontal scaling

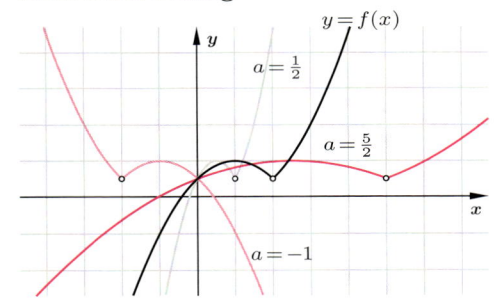

$\overline{f}(x) = f\left(\dfrac{x}{a}\right)$

special case $a = -1$: $\overline{f}(x) = f(-x)$
reflection about the y-axis

Homogeneous dilation

with respect to centre $Z = (u, v)$

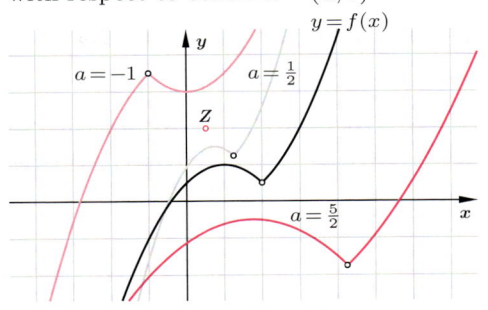

$\overline{f}(x) = a\left[f\left(\dfrac{x - u}{a} + u\right) - v\right] + v$

special case: centre at origin

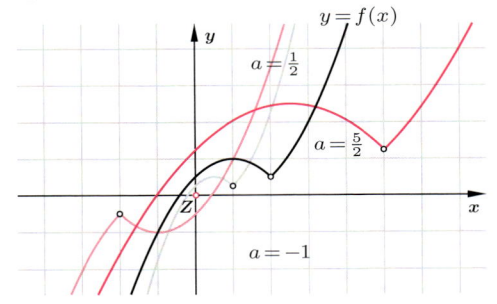

$\overline{f}(x) = a f\left(\dfrac{x}{a}\right)$

Calculus
MATHEMATICS PHYSICS ASTRONOMY CHEMISTRY

Power functions

Positive integer exponents

$x \mapsto x^n$, $n \in \mathbb{N}$, $D = \mathbb{R}$, $R = \begin{cases} \mathbb{R}_0^+ & \text{for even } n \\ \mathbb{R} & \text{for odd } n \end{cases}$

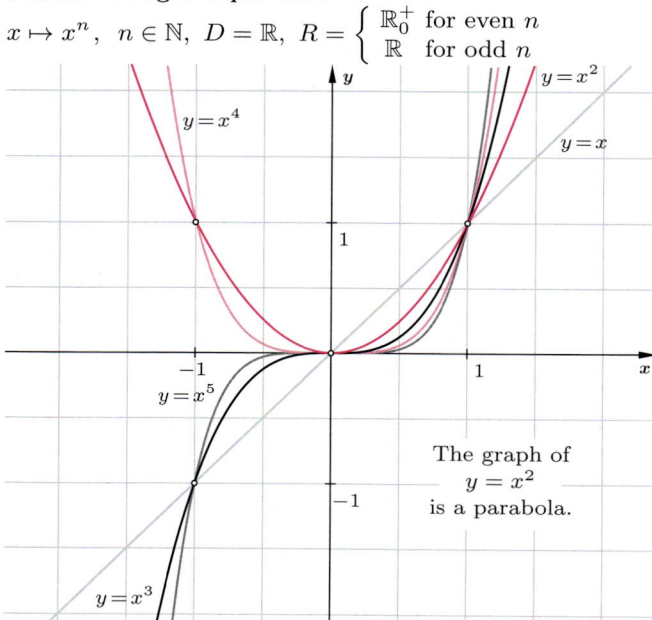

In the plots below, the function values are represented by the y coordinates of points on the graphs.

The graph of $y = x^2$ is a parabola.

Unit fractions as exponents (root functions)

$x \mapsto x^{\frac{1}{n}}$, $n \in \mathbb{N}$
$D = \mathbb{R}_0^+$, $R = \mathbb{R}_0^+$

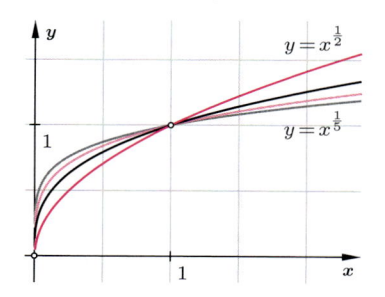

Negative integer exponents

$x \mapsto x^{-n}$, $n \in \mathbb{N}$, $D = \mathbb{R}\setminus\{0\}$, $R = \begin{cases} \mathbb{R}^+ & \text{for even } n \\ \mathbb{R}\setminus\{0\} & \text{for odd } n \end{cases}$

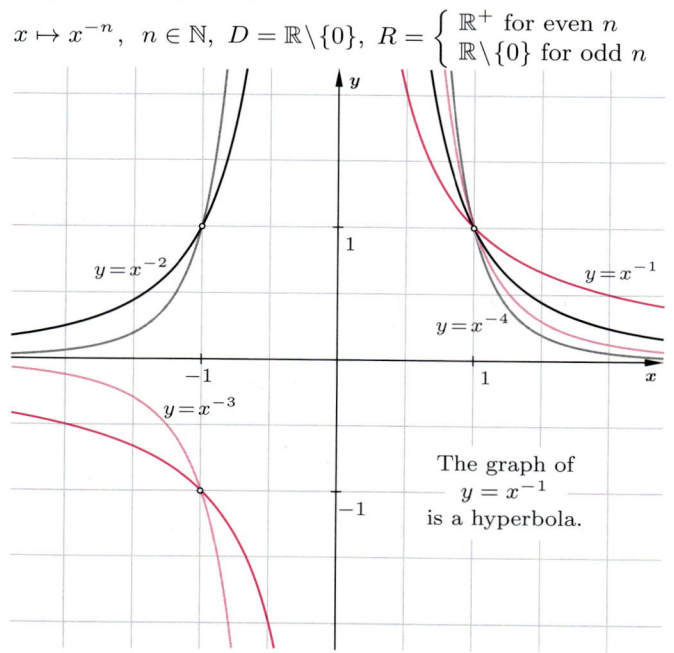

The graph of $y = x^{-1}$ is a hyperbola.

Arbitrary real exponents

$x \mapsto x^p$, $p \in \mathbb{R}$
$D = \mathbb{R}_0^+$ for $p > 0$
$D = \mathbb{R}^+$ for $p \leq 0$

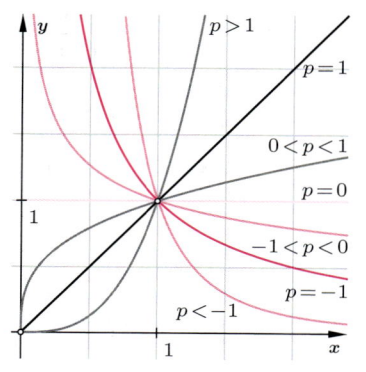

The function $x \mapsto x^{\frac{1}{p}}$ is the inverse function of $x \mapsto x^p$.

Calculus
MATHEMATICS   PHYSICS   ASTRONOMY   CHEMISTRY

Polynomial functions

$f\colon x \mapsto a_n x^n + a_{n-1} x^{n-1} + \ldots + a_2 x^2 + a_1 x + a_0$, f is of degree n, if $a_n \neq 0$

$y = x^2 + 14x + 51$

$y = \frac{1}{3} x^4 - 8x^3 + 72 x^2 - \frac{862}{3} x + 430$

$y = \frac{1}{4} x^3 + \frac{9}{2} x^2 + \frac{105}{4} x + 50$

$y = \frac{3}{10} x^3 - \frac{63}{10} x^2 + \frac{222}{5} x - 104$

$y = \frac{1}{50} x^5 + \frac{1}{10} x^4$

$y = -\frac{1}{20} x^4 + \frac{1}{20} x^3 + \frac{3}{5} x^2 - 2$

$y = -\frac{(x+1)(x-2)(x-3)(x-7)^3}{400}$

examples of polynomial functions with degrees between two and six

polynomial ◀ p. 21/22

Behaviour at infinity

	$\lim\limits_{x \to -\infty} f(x)$	$\lim\limits_{x \to \infty} f(x)$
$a_n < 0$	$\begin{cases} \infty \text{ for } n \text{ odd} \\ -\infty \text{ for } n \text{ even} \end{cases}$	$-\infty$
$a_n > 0$	$\begin{cases} -\infty \text{ for } n \text{ odd} \\ \infty \text{ for } n \text{ even} \end{cases}$	∞

Rational functions

$f\colon x \mapsto \dfrac{\text{polynomial function of degree } m}{\text{polynomial function of degree } n}$

For $m \geqslant n$, f is asymptotic to a polynomial function of degree $m - n$.   ▶ p. 66
For $m < n$, f has the horizontal asymptote $y = 0$ (x-axis).

$y = \dfrac{x^3 + 12x^2 + 48x + 64}{5x + 25}$

$y = \dfrac{x^2 - 7x + 13}{2x - 8}$

asymptotic polynomial $y = \frac{1}{5} x^2 + \frac{7}{5} x + \frac{13}{5}$

oblique asymptote $y = \frac{1}{2} x - \frac{3}{2}$

vertical asymptote $x = -5$

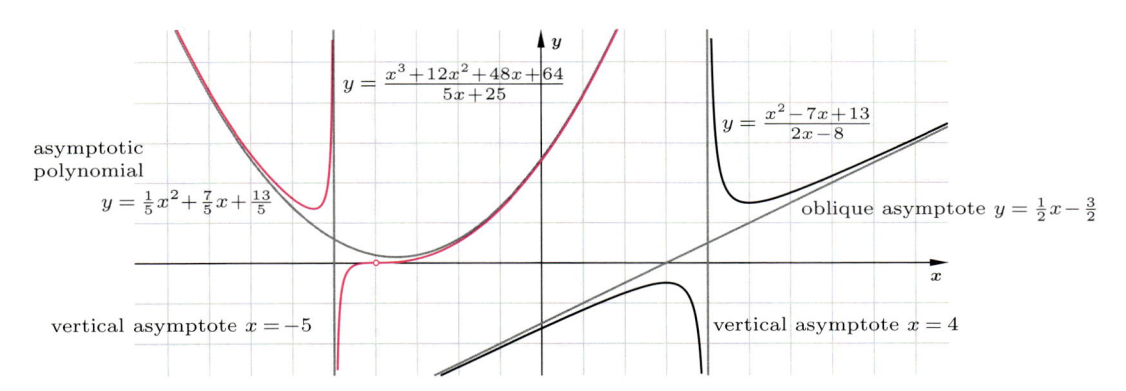

vertical asymptote $x = 4$

Calculus
MATHEMATICS PHYSICS ASTRONOMY CHEMISTRY

Exponential and logarithmic functions

Natural exponential function

$x \mapsto e^x = \exp(x)$
$D = \mathbb{R}, \ R = \mathbb{R}^+$

Exponential function to base a, $a > 0$, $a \neq 1$:

$x \mapsto a^x = e^{x \ln(a)}$
$D = \mathbb{R}, \ R = \mathbb{R}^+$

Natural logarithmic function

$x \mapsto \ln(x), \ D = \mathbb{R}^+, \ R = \mathbb{R}$

Logarithmic function to base a, $a > 0$, $a \neq 1$:

$x \mapsto \log_a(x) = \dfrac{\ln(x)}{\ln(a)}$

$D = \mathbb{R}^+, \ R = \mathbb{R}$

The functions $x \mapsto \ln x$ and $x \mapsto e^x$ are inverse to one another on the specified intervals.

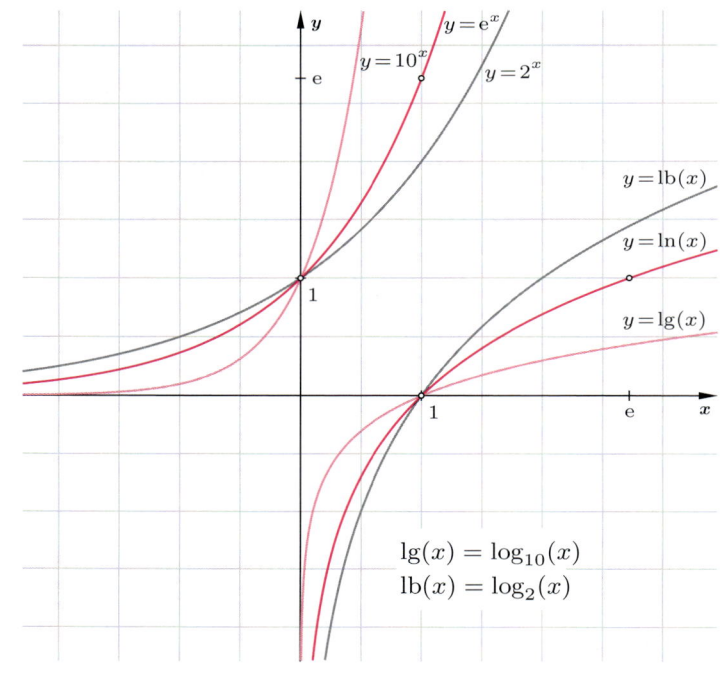

- $\ln(e^x) = x$
- $e^{\ln(x)} = x$
- $\log_a(a^x) = x, \ x \in \mathbb{R}$
- $a^{\log_a(x)} = x, \ x \in \mathbb{R}^+$

$\lg(x) = \log_{10}(x)$
$\text{lb}(x) = \log_2(x)$

◀ p. 17

Trigonometric functions and inverse trigonometric functions

Sine function

$x \mapsto \sin x$
$D = \mathbb{R}, \ R = [-1, 1]$
2π periodic

Arcsine function

$x \mapsto \arcsin x$
$D = [-1, 1], \ R = \left[-\dfrac{\pi}{2}, \dfrac{\pi}{2}\right]$

The functions $x \mapsto \sin x$ and $x \mapsto \arcsin x$ are inverse to one another on the specified intervals.

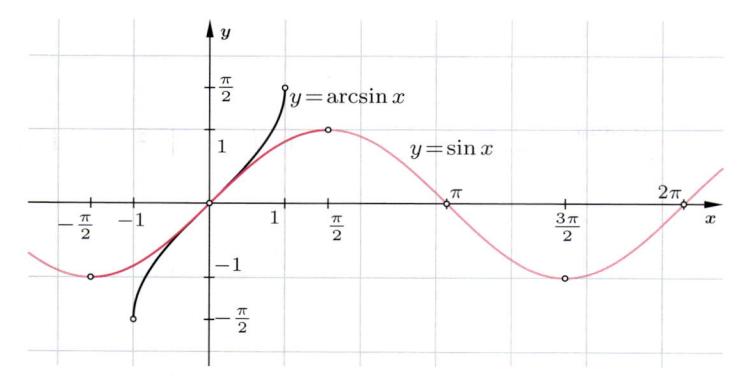

- $\arcsin(\sin x) = x, \ x \in \left[-\dfrac{\pi}{2}, \dfrac{\pi}{2}\right]$
- $\sin(\arcsin x) = x, \ x \in [-1, 1]$

▶ p. 97

Calculus
MATHEMATICS   PHYSICS   ASTRONOMY   CHEMISTRY

Cosine function

$x \mapsto \cos x$

$D = \mathbb{R},\ R = [-1, 1]$

2π periodic

Arccosine function

$x \mapsto \arccos x$

$D = [-1, 1],\ R = [0, \pi]$

The functions $x \mapsto \cos x$ and $x \mapsto \arccos x$ are inverse to one another on the specified intervals.

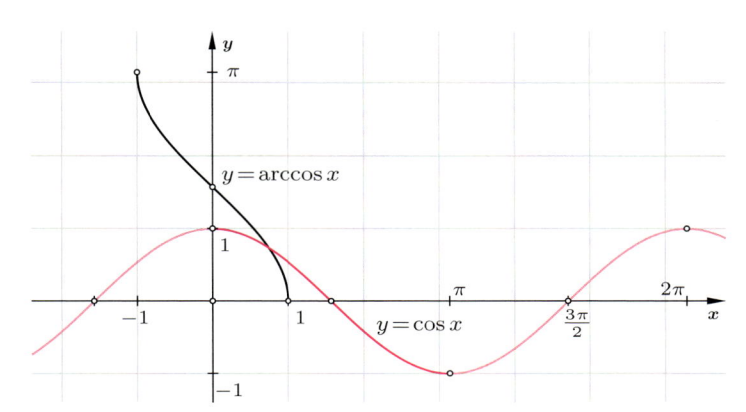

- $\arccos(\cos x) = x,\ x \in [0, \pi]$
- $\cos(\arccos x) = x,\ x \in [-1, 1]$

Tangent function

$x \mapsto \tan x$

$D = \mathbb{R} \setminus \left\{ \pm\dfrac{\pi}{2}, \pm\dfrac{3\pi}{2}, \pm\dfrac{5\pi}{2}, \ldots \right\}$

$R = \mathbb{R}$

π periodic

The lines
$x = \pm\dfrac{\pi}{2}, \pm\dfrac{3\pi}{2}, \pm\dfrac{5\pi}{2}, \ldots$
are asymptotes of the tangent curve.   ▶ p. 66

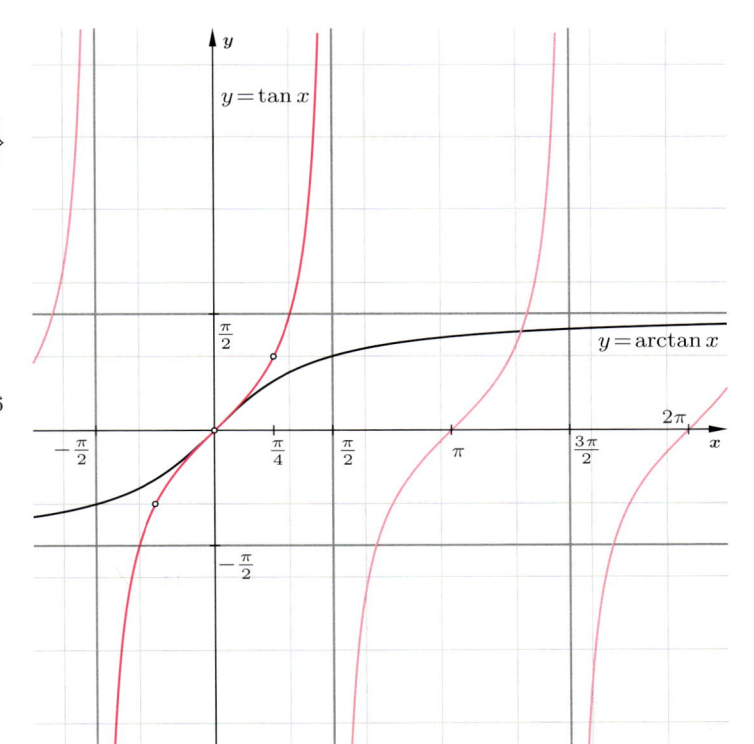

Arctangent function

$x \mapsto \arctan x$

$D = \mathbb{R},\ R = \left(-\dfrac{\pi}{2}, \dfrac{\pi}{2}\right)$

The lines
$y = \pm\dfrac{\pi}{2}$
are asymptotes of the arctangent curve.

The functions $x \mapsto \tan x$ and $x \mapsto \arctan x$ are inverse to one another on the specified intervals.

- $\arctan(\tan x) = x,\ x \in \left(-\dfrac{\pi}{2}, \dfrac{\pi}{2}\right)$
- $\tan(\arctan x) = x,\ x \in \mathbb{R}$

Calculus
MATHEMATICS   PHYSICS   ASTRONOMY   CHEMISTRY

Hyperbolic functions and inverse hyperbolic functions

Hyperbolic sine function
$x \mapsto \sinh x = \frac{1}{2}\left(e^x - e^{-x}\right)$
$D = \mathbb{R}, \ R = \mathbb{R}$

Inverse hyperbolic sine function
$x \mapsto \operatorname{arsinh} x = \ln\left(x + \sqrt{x^2 + 1}\right)$
$D = \mathbb{R}, \ R = \mathbb{R}$

Hyperbolic cosine function
$x \mapsto \cosh x = \frac{1}{2}\left(e^x + e^{-x}\right)$
$D = \mathbb{R}, \ R = [1, \infty)$

Inverse hyperbolic cosine function
$x \mapsto \operatorname{arcosh} x = \ln\left(x + \sqrt{x^2 - 1}\right)$
$D = [1, \infty), \ R = \mathbb{R}_0^+$

Hyperbolic tangent function
$x \mapsto \tanh x = \dfrac{\sinh x}{\cosh x} = \dfrac{e^x - e^{-x}}{e^x + e^{-x}}$
$D = \mathbb{R}, \ R = (-1, 1)$

Inverse hyperbolic tangent function
$x \mapsto \operatorname{artanh} x = \dfrac{1}{2} \ln \dfrac{1 + x}{1 - x}$
$D = (-1, 1), \ R = \mathbb{R}$

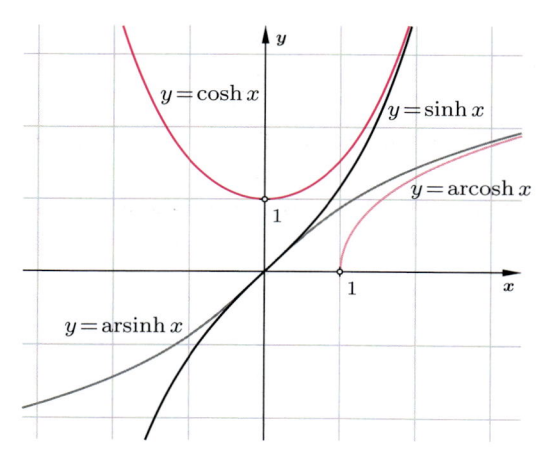

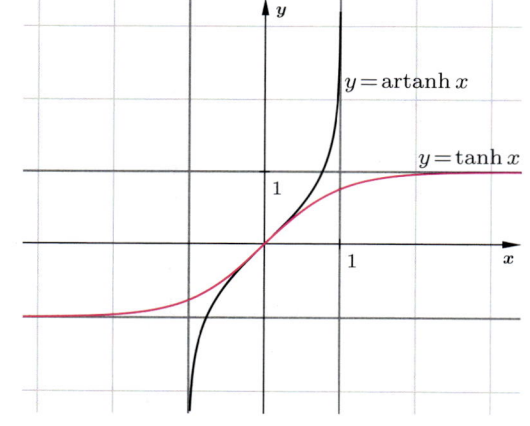

- $\operatorname{arsinh}(\sinh x) = x, \ x \in \mathbb{R}$
- $\operatorname{arcosh}(\cosh x) = x, \ x \in \mathbb{R}_0^+$
- $\operatorname{artanh}(\tanh x) = x, \ x \in \mathbb{R}$

- $\sinh(\operatorname{arsinh} x) = x, \ x \in \mathbb{R}$
- $\cosh(\operatorname{arcosh} x) = x, \ x \in [1, \infty)$
- $\tanh(\operatorname{artanh} x) = x, \ x \in (-1, 1)$

Hyperbolic function identities

$\cosh^2 x - \sinh^2 x = 1$

$\sinh(x_1 + x_2) = \sinh x_1 \cosh x_2 + \cosh x_1 \sinh x_2$

$\cosh(x_1 + x_2) = \cosh x_1 \cosh x_2 + \sinh x_1 \sinh x_2$

$\sin x = \dfrac{1}{2i}\left(e^{ix} - e^{-ix}\right) \qquad \cos x = \dfrac{1}{2}\left(e^{ix} + e^{-ix}\right) \qquad \sinh x = -i \sin ix$

$\sin x = -i \sinh ix \qquad\qquad\qquad \cos x = \cosh ix \qquad\qquad\qquad \cosh x = \cos ix$

p. 18 ◀

Calculus

4.3 Limits of functions, continuity

General

Consider a given function $f\colon D \to \mathbb{R}$.
In references to $f(x)$ below it will be assumed that $x \in D$.

f is continuous at the point $a \in D$	For every $\varepsilon > 0$ there exists a $\delta > 0$ such that $\bigl|f(x) - f(a)\bigr| < \varepsilon$ whenever $|x - a| < \delta$.
criterion for continuity at the point a	For every sequence (x_n) with $x_n \in D$ and $\lim\limits_{n \to \infty} x_n = a$ it follows that $\lim\limits_{n \to \infty} f(x_n) = f(a)$.
f is continuous on $T \subset D$	f is continuous at every point $a \in T$
a is a limit point of a set $D \subset \mathbb{R}$	For every $\varepsilon > 0$ there exists at least one point $x \in D$ such that $0 < |x - a| < \varepsilon$.
b is the limit of $f\colon D \to \mathbb{R}$ at the point a	a is a limit point of D and for every $\varepsilon > 0$ there exists a $\delta > 0$ such that $\bigl|f(x) - b\bigr| < \varepsilon$ whenever $0 < |x - a| < \delta$.
• notation	$\lim\limits_{x \to a} f(x) = b$ or $f(x) \to b$ for $x \to a$
relationship to continuity	f is continuous at a limit point $a \in D$ if and only if $\lim\limits_{x \to a} f(x) = f(a)$.
b is the limit of f as $x \to \infty$	For every $\varepsilon > 0$ there exists an $M > 0$ such that $\bigl|f(x) - b\bigr| < \varepsilon$ whenever $x > M$.
∞ is the limit of f at the point a	a is a limit point of D and for every $M > 0$ there exists a $\delta > 0$ such that $f(x) > M$ whenever $0 < |x - a| < \delta$.

Theorems on limits of functions

Suppose the limits $\lim\limits_{x \to a} f(x)$ and $\lim\limits_{x \to a} g(x)$ exist for $a \in \mathbb{R} \cup \{-\infty, \infty\}$.
The following rules apply:

sum	$\lim\limits_{x \to a} \bigl(f(x) \pm g(x)\bigr) = \lim\limits_{x \to a} f(x) \pm \lim\limits_{x \to a} g(x)$
constant multiple	$\lim\limits_{x \to a} c \cdot f(x) = c \cdot \lim\limits_{x \to a} f(x)$
product	$\lim\limits_{x \to a} \bigl(f(x) \cdot g(x)\bigr) = \bigl(\lim\limits_{x \to a} f(x)\bigr) \cdot \bigl(\lim\limits_{x \to a} g(x)\bigr)$
quotient	$\lim\limits_{x \to a} \dfrac{f(x)}{g(x)} = \dfrac{\lim\limits_{x \to a} f(x)}{\lim\limits_{x \to a} g(x)}$, where $\lim\limits_{x \to a} g(x) \neq 0$
composite function	If $\lim\limits_{x \to a} f(x) = u_0$ and $g(u)$ is continuous at u_0, then $\lim\limits_{x \to a} g\bigl(f(x)\bigr) = g\bigl(\lim\limits_{x \to a} f(x)\bigr) = g(u_0)$.
BERNOULLI-L'HÔPITAL rule	If f and g are differentiable and $g'(x) \neq 0$ on (a, b), $\lim\limits_{x \to a} f(x) = \lim\limits_{x \to a} g(x) = 0$ (or $\pm\infty$) and $\lim\limits_{x \to a} \dfrac{f'(x)}{g'(x)}$ exists, then $\lim\limits_{x \to a} \dfrac{f(x)}{g(x)} = \lim\limits_{x \to a} \dfrac{f'(x)}{g'(x)}$.

Calculus

Intermediate value theorem

If $f\colon [a,b] \to \mathbb{R}$ is continuous, then $f(x)$ assumes every value between $f(a)$ and $f(b)$ at some point $x \in [a,b]$.

Special limits of functions

$a \in \mathbb{R}^+$

$$\lim_{x \to 0} \frac{\sin x}{x} = 1 \qquad \lim_{x \to 0} \frac{e^x - 1}{x} = 1 \qquad \lim_{x \to 0} \frac{a^x - 1}{x} = \ln a$$

$$\lim_{x \to 1} \frac{\ln x}{x - 1} = 1 \qquad \lim_{x \to 0} \frac{\ln(1+x)}{x} = 1$$

$$\lim_{x \to \infty} \frac{x^m}{e^{ax}} = 0, \ m \in \mathbb{R} \qquad \lim_{x \to \infty} \frac{\ln x}{x^a} = 0 \qquad \lim_{x \to 0} (x^a \ln x) = 0$$

4.4 Differentiation

The derivative

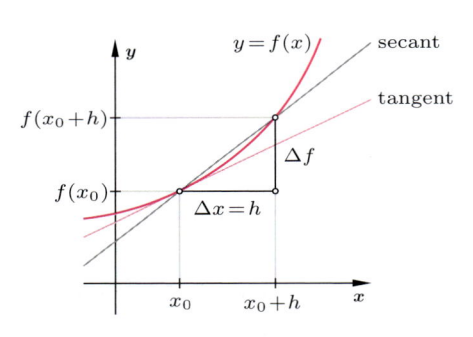

Difference quotient
(average rate of change, slope of the secant)

$$\frac{\Delta f}{\Delta x} = \frac{f(x) - f(x_0)}{x - x_0}, \quad \Delta x = x - x_0 \neq 0$$

• alternative notation

$$\frac{f(x_0 + h) - f(x_0)}{h}, \quad x_0, x_0 + h \in D, \ h \neq 0$$

$f\colon D \to \mathbb{R}$ is diffentiable at the point x_0

x_0 is a limit point of D and

$$\lim_{x \to x_0} \frac{f(x) - f(x_0)}{x - x_0} \ \text{exists}$$

f is differentiable on $T \subset D$

f is differentiable at every point $x \in T$

f is continuously differentiable on $T \subset D$

f is differentiable and f' is continuous on T

derivative of f at the point x_0
(local or instantaneous rate of change, slope of the tangent)

$$f'(x_0) = \lim_{x \to x_0} \frac{f(x) - f(x_0)}{x - x_0}$$

• alternative notations

$$f'(x_0) = \lim_{h \to 0} \frac{f(x_0 + h) - f(x_0)}{h} = \lim_{\Delta x \to 0} \frac{\Delta f}{\Delta x}\bigg|_{x = x_0} = \frac{df}{dx}\bigg|_{x = x_0}$$

Calculus

MATHEMATICS PHYSICS ASTRONOMY CHEMISTRY

Derivative function	$f': T \to \mathbb{R},\ x \mapsto f'(x)$
• alternative notations	$f' = \dfrac{\mathrm{d}}{\mathrm{d}x} f = \dfrac{\mathrm{d}f}{\mathrm{d}x}$ or $\dot{u} = \dfrac{\mathrm{d}}{\mathrm{d}t} u = \dfrac{\mathrm{d}u}{\mathrm{d}t}$
higher order derivatives	$f^{(n)} = \left(f^{(n-1)}\right)',\ n \in \mathbb{N},\ n > 1$
• alternative notations	$f'' = \dfrac{\mathrm{d}^2}{\mathrm{d}x^2} f = \dfrac{\mathrm{d}^2 f}{\mathrm{d}x^2}$ or $\ddot{u} = \dfrac{\mathrm{d}^2}{\mathrm{d}t^2} u = \dfrac{\mathrm{d}^2 u}{\mathrm{d}t^2}$
	$f^{(n)} = \dfrac{\mathrm{d}^n}{\mathrm{d}x^n} f$
partial derivatives of a function $f(x,y)$ in two variables	$\left.\dfrac{\partial f}{\partial x}\right|_{(a,b)} = f_x(a,b) = \lim\limits_{h \to 0} \dfrac{f(a+h,b) - f(a,b)}{h}$
	$\left.\dfrac{\partial f}{\partial y}\right|_{(a,b)} = f_y(a,b) = \lim\limits_{h \to 0} \dfrac{f(a,b+h) - f(a,b)}{h}$

Rules of differentiation

$u(x)$ and $v(x)$ are assumed to be differentiable functions, c a constant real factor.

function	derivative	notation without arguments
sum rule $f(x) = u(x) \pm v(x)$	$f'(x) = u'(x) \pm v'(x)$	$(u \pm v)' = u' \pm v'$
constant factor rule $f(x) = c \cdot u(x)$	$f'(x) = c \cdot u'(x)$	$(cu)' = cu'$
product rule $f(x) = u(x) \cdot v(x)$	$f'(x) = u'(x) \cdot v(x) + u(x) \cdot v'(x)$	$(uv)' = u'v + uv'$
quotient rule $f(x) = \dfrac{u(x)}{v(x)}$	$f'(x) = \dfrac{u'(x) \cdot v(x) - u(x) \cdot v'(x)}{v^2(x)}$	$\left(\dfrac{u}{v}\right)' = \dfrac{u'v - uv'}{v^2}$
chain rule $f(x) = u(v(x))$	$f'(x) = u'(v(x)) \cdot v'(x)$	$(u \circ v)' = (u' \circ v)\, v'$

special cases of the chain rule:

- $f(f^{-1}(x)) = x$ $\qquad (f^{-1})'(x) = \dfrac{1}{f'(f^{-1}(x))}$ $\qquad$ derivative of the inverse function

- $f(x) = u(ax+b)$ $\qquad f'(x) = a \cdot u'(ax+b)$

Calculus

Mean value theorem

If f is continuous on $[a,b]$ and differentiable on (a,b), then there exists $\xi \in (a,b)$ such that

$$f(b) - f(a) = (b-a) \cdot f'(\xi)$$

In terms of the graph of f over the interval, this means that there is at least one point in the interior of the interval at which the slope of the tangent at that point coincides with the slope of the secant between the end points of the graph.

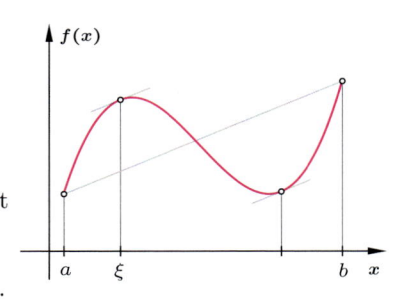

Approximation errors

Absolute and relative errors

Let a_0 be an approximation of a. One distinguishes two types of approximation error:

- absolute error $\varepsilon_a = a_0 - a$
- relative error $\dfrac{\varepsilon_a}{a}$ where $\dfrac{\varepsilon_a}{a} \approx \dfrac{\varepsilon_a}{a_0}$ for $a \approx a_0$

The following relations hold:

- $\varepsilon_{a+b} = \varepsilon_a + \varepsilon_b$
- $\varepsilon_{a-b} = \varepsilon_a - \varepsilon_b$

For sufficiently small ε_a and ε_b:

- $\dfrac{\varepsilon_{ab}}{ab} \approx \dfrac{\varepsilon_a}{a} + \dfrac{\varepsilon_b}{b}$
- $\dfrac{\varepsilon_{a/b}}{a/b} \approx \dfrac{\varepsilon_a}{a} - \dfrac{\varepsilon_b}{b}$
- $\varepsilon_{f(a)} \approx f'(a_0)\varepsilon_a$
- $\varepsilon_{f(a,b)} \approx f_x(a_0, b_0)\varepsilon_a + f_y(a_0, b_0)\varepsilon_b$

p. 63 ◀ f_x, f_y

Error bounds and propagation of errors

The notation $|x| \lesssim y$ is understood to mean that $|x| \leqslant y_0$ with $y_0 \approx y$. If error bounds Δ_a and Δ_b are specified for a and b respectively, where $|\varepsilon_a| \leqslant \Delta_a$ and $|\varepsilon_b| \leqslant \Delta_b$, then:

- $|\varepsilon_{a+b}| \leqslant \Delta_a + \Delta_b$
- $|\varepsilon_{a-b}| \leqslant \Delta_a + \Delta_b$

For sufficiently small ε_a and ε_b:

- $\left|\dfrac{\varepsilon_{ab}}{ab}\right| \lesssim \dfrac{\Delta_a}{|a|} + \dfrac{\Delta_b}{|b|}$
- $\left|\dfrac{\varepsilon_{a/b}}{a/b}\right| \lesssim \dfrac{\Delta_a}{|a|} + \dfrac{\Delta_b}{|b|}$
- $|\varepsilon_{f(a)}| \lesssim |f'(a_0)|\Delta_a$
- $|\varepsilon_{f(a,b)}| \lesssim |f_x(a_0, b_0)|\Delta_a + |f_y(a_0, b_0)|\Delta_b$

Analogous estimates apply to functions $f(x_1, x_2, \ldots, x_n)$ in several variables.

Calculus

MATHEMATICS PHYSICS ASTRONOMY CHEMISTRY

Derivatives of elementary functions

$(c)' = 0$, c constant $\qquad$ $(cx)' = c$, c constant

$(x^s)' = s x^{s-1}$ $\qquad$ $\left(\dfrac{1}{x}\right)' = -\dfrac{1}{x^2}$ $\qquad$ $(\sqrt{x})' = \dfrac{1}{2\sqrt{x}}$

$(\ln|x|)' = \dfrac{1}{x}$ $\qquad$ $(\log_a|x|)' = (\log_a e) \cdot \dfrac{1}{x} = \dfrac{1}{x \ln a}$

$(e^x)' = e^x$ $\qquad$ $(a^x)' = (\ln a)\, a^x$

$(\sin x)' = \cos x$ $\qquad$ $(\cos x)' = -\sin x$ $\qquad$ $(\tan x)' = \dfrac{1}{\cos^2 x} = 1 + \tan^2 x$

$(\arcsin x)' = \dfrac{1}{\sqrt{1-x^2}}$ $\qquad$ $(\arccos x)' = -\dfrac{1}{\sqrt{1-x^2}}$ $\qquad$ $(\arctan x)' = \dfrac{1}{1+x^2}$

$(\sinh x)' = \cosh x$ $\qquad$ $(\cosh x)' = \sinh x$ $\qquad$ $(\tanh x)' = \dfrac{1}{\cosh^2 x} = 1 - \tanh^2 x$

$(\operatorname{arsinh} x)' = \dfrac{1}{\sqrt{x^2+1}}$ $\qquad$ $(\operatorname{arcosh} x)' = \dfrac{1}{\sqrt{x^2-1}}$ $\qquad$ $(\operatorname{artanh} x)' = \dfrac{1}{1-x^2}$

Analysis of curves

Let $f\colon D \to \mathbb{R}$ be a function which is differentiable sufficiently many times in its domain, $P_0 = (x_0, f(x_0))$ a point in the graph G_f in a Cartesian coordinate system, $(a,b) \subset D$ an open interval and $\mathring{x}$ a singular point of f.

Roots (zeros)

x_0 is a root of f	$f(x_0) = 0$
x_0 is a root of multiplicity k of f	$f^{(i)}(x_0) = 0$, $i = 0, \dots, k-1$, $f^{(k)}(x_0) \neq 0$

Monotonicity, extrema

	sufficient condition
f is monotonically increasing in (a,b)	$f'(x) > 0$ in (a,b)
f is monotonically decreasing (a,b)	$f'(x) < 0$ in (a,b)
f has a critical point x_0	$f'(x_0) = 0$
f has a local maximum at x_0, P_0 is a local maximum of G_f	$f'(x_0) = 0$ and $f''(x_0) < 0$
f has a local minimum at x_0, P_0 is a local minimum of G_f	$f'(x_0) = 0$ and $f''(x_0) > 0$

Curvature, inflection points

	sufficient condition
G_f is concave up (convex) in (a,b)	$f''(x) > 0$ in (a,b)
G_f concave down (concave) in (a,b)	$f''(x) < 0$ in (a,b)
P_0 is an inflection point of G_f	$f''(x_0) = 0$ and $f'''(x_0) \neq 0$
P_0 is a saddle point of G_f	$f'(x_0) = f''(x_0) = 0$ and $f'''(x_0) \neq 0$

Calculus
MATHEMATICS PHYSICS ASTRONOMY CHEMISTRY

Removable discontinuity

$\mathring{x}$ is a removable discontinuity (removable singularity) of f

$\lim\limits_{x \to \mathring{x}} f(x)$ exists

f^* is the extension of f such that f^* is continuous at the point $\mathring{x}$

$$f^*(x) = \begin{cases} f(x) & \text{for } x \neq \mathring{x} \\ \lim\limits_{x \to \mathring{x}} f(x) & \text{for } x = \mathring{x} \end{cases}$$

Poles

x_P is a pole (of order k) of $f(x) = \dfrac{g(x)}{h(x)}$

$g(x_P) \neq 0$ and x_P is a root (of multiplicity k) of h

Asymptotes and asymptotic functions

If the distances between a point (x, y) on the graph of f and a line g tends to zero as x or y approaches ∞ or $-\infty$, the line g is called an asymptote of f. One distinguishes three types:

- vertical asymptote

  The line $x = x_0$, parallel to the y-axis, is an asymptote of f if and only if $|f(x)| \to \infty$ for $x \to x_0$.

- horizontal asymptote

  The line $y = y_0$, parallel to the x-axis, is an asymptote of f if and only if $y_0 = \lim\limits_{x \to \infty} f(x)$ or $y_0 = \lim\limits_{x \to -\infty} f(x)$.

- oblique asymptote

  The line $y = mx + q$ is an asymptote of f if and only if both the limits
  $$m = \lim_{x \to \infty} \frac{f(x)}{x} \quad \text{and} \quad q = \lim_{x \to \infty} \big(f(x) - mx\big)$$
  (or the corresp. limits as $x \to -\infty$) exist.

the approximation function g is asymptotic to f for $x \to \infty$

$\lim\limits_{x \to \infty} \big(f(x) - g(x)\big) = 0$

Plane curves

Curve defined by the equation $y = f(x)$ (Cartesian coordinates)

point on the curve

$P_0 = (x_0, f(x_0))$

slope of the tangent line through P_0

$f'(x_0)$

slope of the normal line through P_0

$-\dfrac{1}{f'(x_0)}$

radius of curvature at P_0

$\varrho = \dfrac{\left[1 + \big(f'(x_0)\big)^2\right]^{\frac{3}{2}}}{f''(x_0)}$

midpoint of the osculating circle at P_0

$u = x_0 - \dfrac{f'(x_0)}{f''(x_0)} \cdot \left[1 + \big(f'(x_0)\big)^2\right]$

$v = f(x_0) + \dfrac{1 + \big(f'(x_0)\big)^2}{f''(x_0)}$

Calculus
MATHEMATICS   PHYSICS   ASTRONOMY   CHEMISTRY

Curve defined by the parametric equation $\vec{r}(t) = \begin{pmatrix} x(t) \\ y(t) \end{pmatrix}$ (Cartesian coordinates)

In the expressions below, $x = x(t_0)$, $y = y(t_0)$, $\dot{x} = \dot{x}(t_0)$, etc.

point on the curve	$P_0 = (x(t_0), y(t_0)) = (x, y)$
direction vector of the tangent through P_0	$\dot{\vec{r}}(t_0) = \begin{pmatrix} \dot{x} \\ \dot{y} \end{pmatrix}$
direction vector of the normal through P_0	$\vec{n}(t_0) = \begin{pmatrix} \dot{y} \\ -\dot{x} \end{pmatrix}$
radius of curvature at P_0	$\varrho(t_0) = \dfrac{(\dot{x}^2 + \dot{y}^2)^{\frac{3}{2}}}{\dot{x}\ddot{y} - \ddot{x}\dot{y}}$
centre of the osculating circle at P_0	$\vec{r}_M(t_0) = \vec{r}_0 - \dfrac{\varrho}{|\vec{n}(t_0)|} \cdot \vec{n}(t_0)$

$$M = \left(x - \frac{\dot{x}^2 + \dot{y}^2}{\dot{x}\ddot{y} - \ddot{x}\dot{y}} \dot{y},\ y + \frac{\dot{x}^2 + \dot{y}^2}{\dot{x}\ddot{y} - \ddot{x}\dot{y}} \dot{x}\right)$$

Curve defined by the polar equation $r = f(\varphi)$

This case corresponds to the parameter representation given by
$$\vec{r}(\varphi) = \begin{pmatrix} f(\varphi)\cos\varphi \\ f(\varphi)\sin\varphi \end{pmatrix}$$

Consequently the formulae for parametric equations can be applied.

Special plane curves

conic sections ▶ p. 108

Growth functions

differential equations ▶ p. 81

- f is the quantity that grows or decays in the course of time.
- G is the saturation level (carrying capacity), $G > 0$.

exponential growth

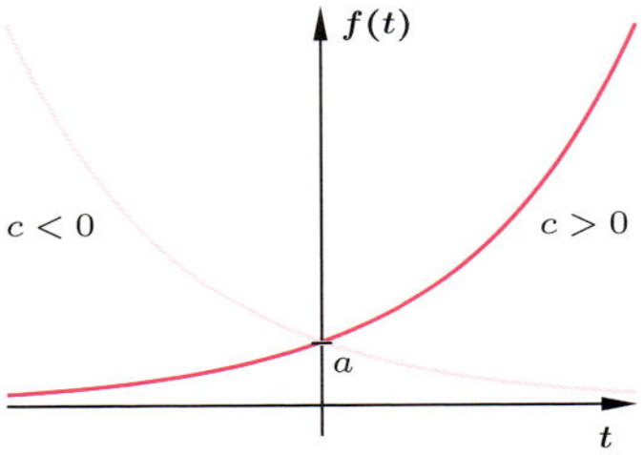

$f'(t) = c \cdot f(t)$
$\Rightarrow f(t) = ae^{ct},\ a > 0$

bounded growth

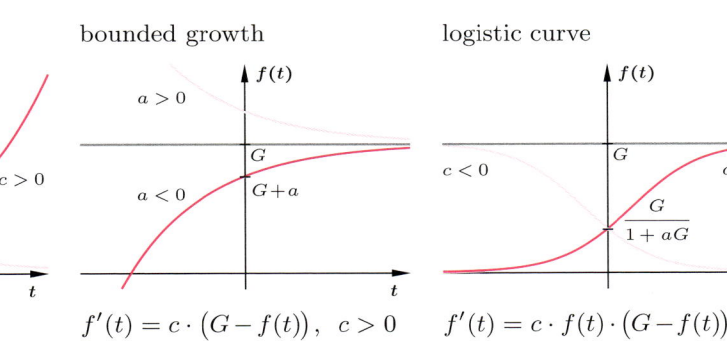

$f'(t) = c \cdot (G - f(t)),\ c > 0$
$\Rightarrow f(t) = G + ae^{-ct}$

logistic curve

$f'(t) = c \cdot f(t) \cdot (G - f(t))$
$\Rightarrow f(t) = \dfrac{G}{1 + aGe^{-cGt}}$

Calculus
MATHEMATICS   PHYSICS   ASTRONOMY   CHEMISTRY

Spirals

spiral of Archimedes

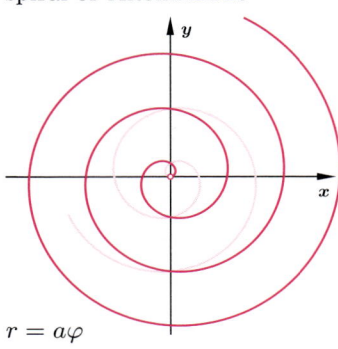

$r = a\varphi$

hyperbolic spiral

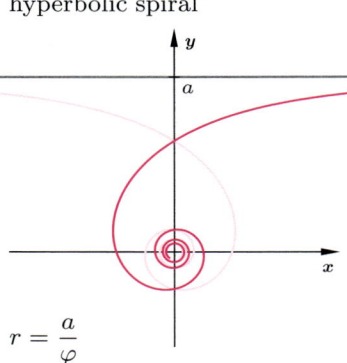

$r = \dfrac{a}{\varphi}$

logarithmic spiral

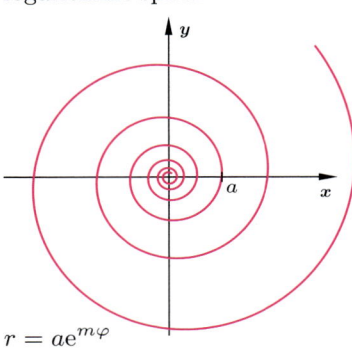

$r = ae^{m\varphi}$

Cycloids and related curves

common cycloid

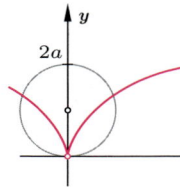

$x = a(t - \sin t)$
$y = a(1 - \cos t)$

$x + \sqrt{y(2a - y)} = a \arccos \dfrac{a - y}{y}$

cardioid

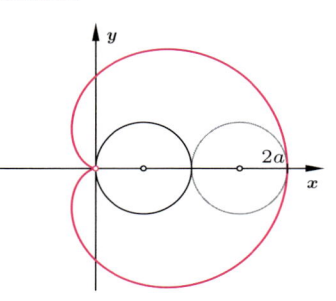

$r = a(1 + \cos \varphi)$
$(x^2 + y^2 - ax)^2 = a^2(x^2 + y^2)$

A common cycloid results from tracing a point at the edge of a circle as it rolls along a straight line. A cardioid results from tracing a point at the edge of a circle as it rolls around another circle of equal radius. ▶

prolate/curtate cycloids (trochoids)

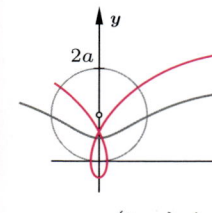

$\lambda = 1.35$
$\lambda = 0.5$

$x = a(t - \lambda \sin t)$
$y = a(1 - \lambda \cos t)$

A prolate or a curtate cycloid results from tracing a point fixed to a circle respectively outside or inside its rolling radius as it rolls along a straight line.

An astroid results from tracing a point at the edge of a circle as it rolls around another circle whose radius is four times as large. ▶

astroid

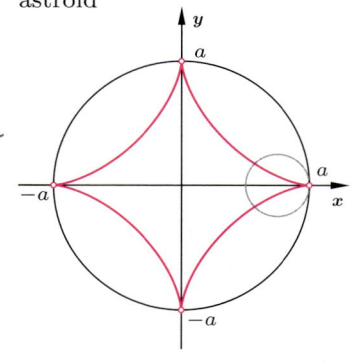

$x = a\cos^3 t, \quad y = a\sin^3 t$

$x^{\frac{2}{3}} + y^{\frac{2}{3}} = a^{\frac{2}{3}}$

Calculus
MATHEMATICS

Miscellaneous selected curves

involute of a circle

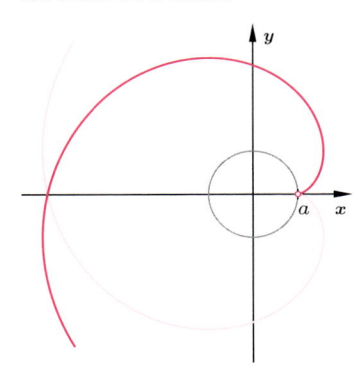

$x = a(\cos t + t \sin t)$
$y = a(\sin t - t \cos t)$

This curve is described by a point fixed at the end of a taut string as it is unwound from a circle.

catenary

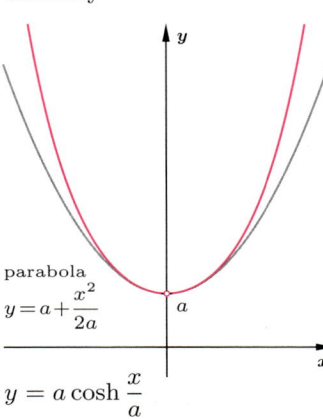

parabola
$y = a + \dfrac{x^2}{2a}$

$y = a \cosh \dfrac{x}{a}$

This is the form assumed by a flexible but non-stretching cable of constant linear density hanging under its own weight between two fixed points.

tractrix

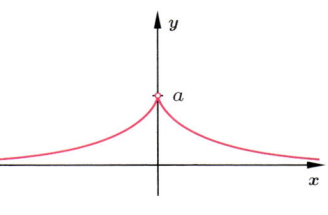

$x = a \cdot \operatorname{arcosh} \dfrac{a}{y} \pm \sqrt{a^2 - y^2} =$
$a \ln \dfrac{a \pm \sqrt{a^2 - y^2}}{y} \pm \sqrt{a^2 - y^2}$

This curve is described by a point mass being towed by a taut cord of length a along a line (here the x-axis) perpendicular to its original offset.

brachistochrone

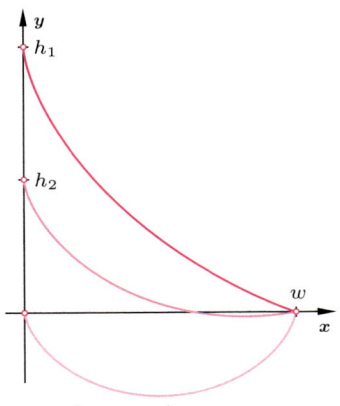

$x = a(t - \sin t)$
$y = a(\cos t - 1) + h$

This curve describes the path which will carry a frictionless point mass under the influence of gravity from one point to another in the shortest possible time. The parameter a is chosen such that a given horizontal distance w is attained. The brachistochrone is a segment of an inverted cycloid.

a heart curve

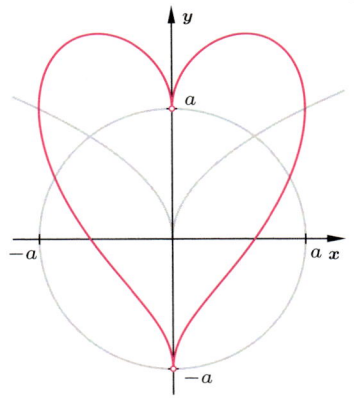

$x = a \cos t$
$y = a(\sin t + \sqrt{|\cos t|})$

$y = a(\sqrt{|x|} \pm \sqrt{1 - x^2})$

folium of DESCARTES

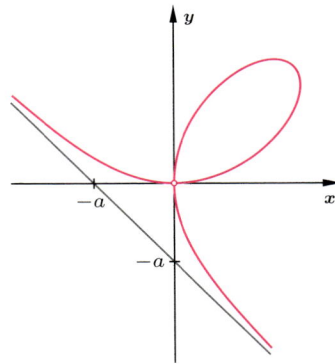

$x = \dfrac{3at}{t^3 + 1}, \quad y = \dfrac{3at^2}{t^3 + 1}$

$x^3 + y^3 - 3axy = 0$

$r = \dfrac{3a \cos \varphi \sin \varphi}{\sin^3 \varphi + \cos^3 \varphi}$

Calculus

MATHEMATICS PHYSICS ASTRONOMY CHEMISTRY

4.5 Integration

Definite integral

Riemann sum
$$S_P(f) = \sum_{k=1}^{n} f(\xi_k)(x_k - x_{k-1}), \quad f \text{ defined on } [a,b]$$
P: partition of $[a,b]$ with points x_i
$a = x_0 < x_1 < \ldots < x_{n-1} < x_n = b$
and arbitrary intermediate points ξ_k
$x_{k-1} \leqslant \xi_k \leqslant x_k, \quad k = 1, \ldots, n$

definite integral
$$\int_a^b f(x)\,dx = \lim S_P(f), \text{ where } P \text{ runs through all partitions of } [a,b] \text{ with } \max(x_k - x_{k-1}) \to 0.$$

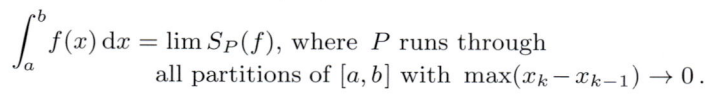

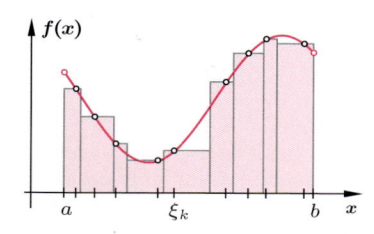

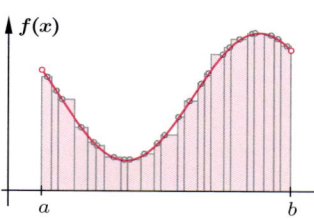

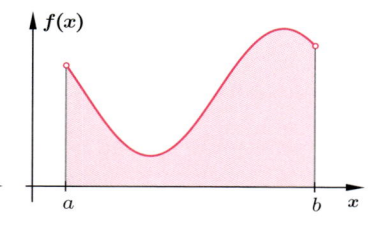

f is integrable

The definite integral $\int_a^b f(x)\,dx$ exists for arbitrary a and b in D.

A function which is continuous on an interval $[a,b]$ is also integrable on $[a,b]$.

- special case: uniform partition

$$x_k - x_{k-1} = \frac{b-a}{n} = \Delta x \text{ for all } k$$

$$\int_a^b f(x)\,dx = \lim_{n \to \infty} \sum_{k=1}^{n} f(\xi_k)\Delta x$$

rules governing limits of integration

For arbitrary r, s, t in $[a,b]$:
$$\int_r^s f(x)\,dx = -\int_s^r f(x)\,dx$$
$$\int_r^t f(x)\,dx = \int_r^s f(x)\,dx + \int_s^t f(x)\,dx$$

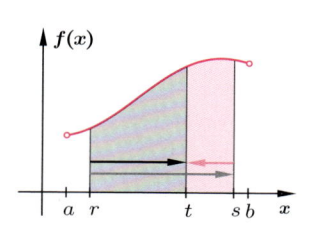

Mean value theorem for integrals

If f is continuous on $[a,b]$, there exists a $\xi \in [a,b]$ such that $\int_a^b f(x)\,dx = (b-a) \cdot f(\xi)$.

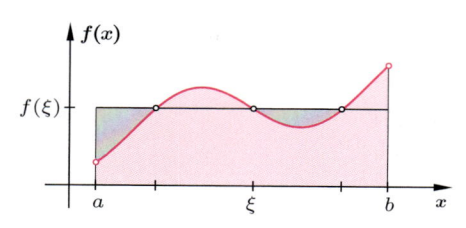

Calculus
MATHEMATICS

Antiderivative, indefinite integral

Let $f\colon [a,b] \to \mathbb{R}$ be a continuous function.

F_a is an integral function of f (with lower integration limit a)	$F_a(x) = \int_a^x f(t)\,\mathrm{d}t, \quad D = [a,b], \quad \int_a^a f(t)\,\mathrm{d}t = 0$
F is an antiderivative of f	$F' = f$
$F, \widetilde{F}$ are antiderivatives of f	$F - \widetilde{F} = \text{const.}$
indefinite integral	the set of all antiderivatives of f
• notations	$\int f(x)\,\mathrm{d}x = F(x) + C \quad \text{or} \quad \int \mathrm{d}F = F + C$
	f is called the integrand, C the constant of integration

Fundamental theorem of calculus

Let f be continuous in the interval $[a,b]$.

1st part: If $F_a(x) = \displaystyle\int_a^x f(t)\,\mathrm{d}t$ is an integral function of f, then $F_a'(x) = f(x)$

2nd part: If F is an arbitrary antiderivative of f, then $\displaystyle\int_a^b f(x)\,\mathrm{d}x = F(b) - F(a)$

• abbreviated notation $\quad F(b) - F(a) = \Big[F(x)\Big]_a^b = F(x)\Big|_a^b$

Rules of integration

The following integration rules apply analogously to indefinite integrals:

sum rule	$\displaystyle\int_a^b \big(f(x) \pm g(x)\big)\,\mathrm{d}x = \int_a^b f(x)\,\mathrm{d}x \pm \int_a^b g(x)\,\mathrm{d}x$
factor rule	$\displaystyle\int_a^b c \cdot f(x)\,\mathrm{d}x = c \cdot \int_a^b f(x)\,\mathrm{d}x$
integration by parts	$\displaystyle\int_a^b f'(x) g(x)\,\mathrm{d}x = \Big[f(x)g(x)\Big]_a^b - \int_a^b f(x) g'(x)\,\mathrm{d}x$
substitution (direct)	$\displaystyle\int_a^b f\big(u(x)\big) u'(x)\,\mathrm{d}x = \int_{u(a)}^{u(b)} f(z)\,\mathrm{d}z, \text{ where } z = u(x)$
(inverse)	$\displaystyle\int_a^b f(x)\,\mathrm{d}x = \int_{u^{-1}(a)}^{u^{-1}(b)} f\big(u(z)\big) u'(z)\,\mathrm{d}z, \text{ where } x = u(z)$
special cases of substitution	$\displaystyle\int_a^b \big(f(x)\big)^s f'(x)\,\mathrm{d}x = \left[\frac{1}{s+1}\big(f(x)\big)^{s+1}\right]_a^b, \quad s \in \mathbb{R},\ s \neq -1$
	$\displaystyle\int_a^b \frac{f'(x)}{f(x)}\,\mathrm{d}x = \Big[\ln|f(x)|\Big]_a^b \qquad\qquad \text{3rd special case} \blacktriangleright \text{p. 72}$

Calculus

	$$\int_a^b f(rx+s)\,dx = \frac{1}{r}\int_{ra+s}^{rb+s} f(z)\,dz$$
monotonicity	$f(x) \leqslant g(x)$ in $[a,b] \Rightarrow \int_a^b f(x)\,dx \leqslant \int_a^b g(x)\,dx$
	in particular: $f(x) \geqslant 0$ in $[a,b] \Rightarrow \int_a^b f(x)\,dx \geqslant 0$
area under the curve	For $f(x) \geqslant 0$ in $[a,b]$, $\int_a^b f(x)\,dx$ is the area bounded by the curve $y = f(x)$, the x-axis, $x = a$ and $x = b$. ▶ p. 75

Improper integrals

integrand undefined at the lower limit of integration	$\int_a^b f(x)\,dx = \lim\limits_{u \to a} \int_u^b f(x)\,dx$
integrand undefined at the upper limit of integration	$\int_a^b f(x)\,dx = \lim\limits_{u \to b} \int_a^u f(x)\,dx$
unbounded limit of integration	$\int_a^\infty f(x)\,dx = \lim\limits_{u \to \infty} \int_a^u f(x)\,dx$
	$\int_{-\infty}^b f(x)\,dx = \lim\limits_{u \to -\infty} \int_u^b f(x)\,dx$

Special indefinite integrals

$$\int 0\,dx = C \qquad\qquad \int a\,dx = ax + C$$

$$\int x^s\,dx = \frac{1}{s+1} x^{s+1} + C,\ s \neq -1 \qquad \int \frac{1}{x}\,dx = \ln|x| + C$$

$$\int (ax+b)^s\,dx = \frac{1}{a(s+1)} (ax+b)^{s+1} + C,\ s \neq -1$$

$$\int \frac{1}{ax+b}\,dx = \frac{1}{a} \ln|ax+b| + C$$

$$\int (ax^p + b)^s x^{p-1}\,dx = \frac{(ax^p+b)^{s+1}}{ap(s+1)} + C,\ s \neq -1,\ a \neq 0,\ p \neq 0$$

$$\int (ax^p + b)^{-1} x^{p-1}\,dx = \frac{1}{ap} \ln|ax^p + b| + C,\ a \neq 0,\ p \neq 0$$

$$\int \frac{ax+b}{cx+d}\,dx = \frac{ax}{c} - \frac{ad-bc}{c^2} \ln|cx+d| + C$$

Calculus
MATHEMATICS

$$\int \frac{ax+b}{x^2+cx+d}\,dx = \frac{a}{2}\ln\left|x^2+cx+d\right| + \frac{b-\frac{ac}{2}}{\sqrt{d-\frac{c^2}{4}}}\arctan\left(\frac{x+\frac{c}{2}}{\sqrt{d-\frac{c^2}{4}}}\right) + C, \quad c^2-4d<0$$

$$\int \frac{1}{x^2+a^2}\,dx = \frac{1}{a}\arctan\frac{x}{a} + C \qquad \int \frac{1}{x^2-a^2}\,dx = \frac{1}{2a}\ln\left|\frac{x-a}{x+a}\right| + C$$

$$\int \sqrt{a^2+x^2}\,dx = \frac{x}{2}\sqrt{a^2+x^2} + \frac{a^2}{2}\ln\left(x+\sqrt{a^2+x^2}\right) + C$$

$$\int \sqrt{a^2-x^2}\,dx = \frac{x}{2}\sqrt{a^2-x^2} + \frac{a^2}{2}\arcsin\frac{x}{|a|} + C$$

$$\int \sqrt{x^2-a^2}\,dx = \frac{x}{2}\sqrt{x^2-a^2} - \frac{a^2}{2}\ln\left|x+\sqrt{x^2-a^2}\right| + C$$

$$\int \frac{1}{\sqrt{x^2+a^2}}\,dx = \ln\left(x+\sqrt{a^2+x^2}\right) + C$$

$$\int \frac{1}{\sqrt{x^2-a^2}}\,dx = \ln\left|x+\sqrt{x^2-a^2}\right| + C \qquad \int \frac{1}{\sqrt{a^2-x^2}}\,dx = \arcsin\frac{x}{|a|} + C$$

$$\int e^{kx}\,dx = \frac{1}{k}e^{kx} + C \qquad \int a^{kx}\,dx = \frac{1}{k\cdot\ln(a)}a^{kx} + C$$

$$\int e^{ax}p(x)\,dx = e^{ax}\left(a^{-1}p(x) - a^{-2}p'(x) + a^{-3}p''(x) - \ldots + (-1)^n a^{-n-1}p^{(n)}(x)\right) + C,$$
$$a \neq 0, \; p: \text{polynomial of degree } n$$

$$\int e^{kx}\sin(ax+b)\,dx = \frac{e^{kx}}{a^2+k^2}\left(k\sin(ax+b) - a\cos(ax+b)\right) + C$$

$$\int e^{kx}\cos(ax+b)\,dx = \frac{e^{kx}}{a^2+k^2}\left(k\cos(ax+b) + a\sin(ax+b)\right) + C$$

$$\int \ln|x|\,dx = x(\ln|x| - 1) + C \qquad \int \log_a|x|\,dx = x\left(\log_a|x| - \log_a(e)\right) + C$$

$$\int x^k \ln(x)\,dx = \frac{x^{k+1}}{k+1}\left(\ln(x) - \frac{1}{k+1}\right) + C, \quad k \neq -1$$

$$\int x^{-1}\ln(x)\,dx = \frac{1}{2}\left(\ln(x)\right)^2 + C$$

$$\int \sin x\,dx = -\cos x + C \qquad \int \sin(ax+b)\,dx = -\frac{1}{a}\cos(ax+b) + C$$

$$\int \cos x\,dx = \sin x + C \qquad \int \cos(ax+b)\,dx = \frac{1}{a}\sin(ax+b) + C$$

$$\int \tan x\,dx = -\ln|\cos x| + C$$

Calculus
MATHEMATICS   PHYSICS   ASTRONOMY   CHEMISTRY

$$\int \sin^2 x \, dx = \frac{1}{2}(x - \sin x \cos x) + C$$

$$\int \frac{1}{\sin x} \, dx = \ln\left|\tan \frac{x}{2}\right| + C$$

$$\int \cos^2 x \, dx = \frac{1}{2}(x + \sin x \cos x) + C$$

$$\int \frac{1}{\cos x} \, dx = \ln\left|\tan\left(\frac{x}{2} + \frac{\pi}{4}\right)\right| + C$$

$$\int \tan^2 x \, dx = \tan x - x + C$$

$$\int \frac{1}{\tan x} \, dx = \ln|\sin x| + C$$

$$\int \sin^n x \, dx = -\frac{1}{n} \sin^{n-1} x \cos x + \frac{n-1}{n} \int \sin^{n-2} x \, dx, \quad n \geqslant 2$$

$$\int \cos^n x \, dx = \frac{1}{n} \sin x \cos^{n-1} x + \frac{n-1}{n} \int \cos^{n-2} x \, dx, \quad n \geqslant 2$$

$$\int \arcsin x \, dx = x \arcsin x + \sqrt{1 - x^2} + C$$

$$\int \arccos x \, dx = x \arccos x - \sqrt{1 - x^2} + C$$

$$\int \arctan x \, dx = x \arctan x - \frac{1}{2} \ln\left(1 + x^2\right) + C$$

$$\int \sinh x \, dx = \cosh x + C$$

$$\int \operatorname{arsinh} x \, dx = x \operatorname{arsinh} x - \sqrt{x^2 + 1} + C$$

$$\int \cosh x \, dx = \sinh x + C$$

$$\int \operatorname{arcosh} x \, dx = x \operatorname{arcosh} x - \sqrt{x^2 - 1} + C$$

$$\int \tanh x \, dx = \ln \cosh x + C$$

$$\int \operatorname{artanh} x \, dx = x \operatorname{artanh} x + \frac{1}{2} \ln\left(1 - x^2\right) + C$$

Special definite integrals

$$\int_0^{2\pi} \sin mx \sin nx \, dx = \int_0^{2\pi} \cos mx \cos nx \, dx = \begin{cases} 0, & \text{if } m \neq n \\ \pi, & \text{if } m = n \neq 0 \end{cases}, \quad m, n \in \mathbb{Z}$$

$$\int_0^{2\pi} \sin mx \cos nx \, dx = 0, \quad m, n \in \mathbb{Z}$$

$$\int_0^\infty \frac{\sin ax}{x} \, dx = \frac{\pi}{2}, \quad a > 0$$

$$\int_0^\infty \sin(x^2) \, dx = \int_0^\infty \cos(x^2) \, dx = \frac{1}{2}\sqrt{\frac{\pi}{2}}$$

$$\int_0^\infty e^{-ax} x^n \, dx = \frac{n!}{a^{n+1}}, \quad a > 0$$

$$\int_0^\infty e^{-ax^2} \, dx = \frac{1}{2}\sqrt{\frac{\pi}{a}}, \quad a > 0$$

$$\int_0^\infty e^{-ax^2} x^{2n} \, dx = \frac{1 \cdot 3 \cdot 5 \cdot \ldots \cdot (2n-1)}{2^{n+1}} \sqrt{\frac{\pi}{a^{2n+1}}}, \quad a > 0, n \in \mathbb{N}$$

Calculus
MATHEMATICS

Area, arc length, volume

A denotes area, s arc length, V_x and V_y the respective volumes of solids of revolution about the x- and y-axes, M the area of a surface of revolution about the x-axis.

Curve defined by $y = f(x)$ (Cartesian coordinates)

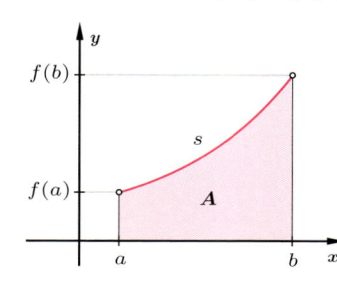

$$A = \int_a^b f(x)\,dx, \quad f(x) \geq 0 \qquad s = \int_a^b \sqrt{1 + (f'(x))^2}\,dx$$

$$V_x = \pi \int_a^b (f(x))^2\,dx$$

$$V_y = \pi \left| \int_a^b x^2 f'(x)\,dx \right| = \pi \left| \int_{f(a)}^{f(b)} x^2\,dy \right|, \quad f \text{ monotonic}$$

$$M = 2\pi \int_a^b f(x) \sqrt{1 + (f'(x))^2}\,dx$$

Curve defined by $\vec{r}(t) = \begin{pmatrix} x(t) \\ y(t) \end{pmatrix}$ (Cartesian coordinates)

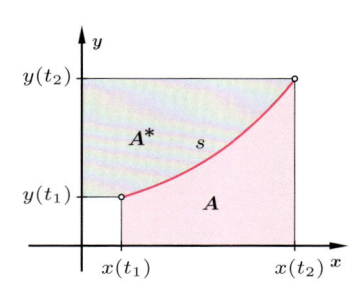

$$s = \int_{t_1}^{t_2} \sqrt{\dot{x}^2 + \dot{y}^2}\,dt$$

x monotonic: $\quad A = \left| \int_{t_1}^{t_2} y\dot{x}\,dt \right|, \, y > 0, \quad V_x = \pi \left| \int_{t_1}^{t_2} y^2 \dot{x}\,dt \right|$

y monotonic: $\quad A^* = \left| \int_{t_1}^{t_2} x\dot{y}\,dt \right|, \, x > 0, \quad V_y = \pi \left| \int_{t_1}^{t_2} x^2 \dot{y}\,dt \right|$

Curve defined by $r = f(\varphi)$ (polar coordinates)

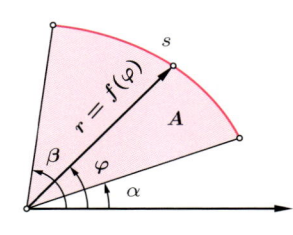

$$A = \frac{1}{2} \int_\alpha^\beta (f(\varphi))^2\,d\varphi \qquad s = \int_\alpha^\beta \sqrt{f^2 + \dot{f}^2}\,d\varphi$$

Solid with cross sectional area $Q(x)$

$$V = \int_a^b Q(x)\,dx$$

JORDAN curve (Cartesian coordinates)

A JORDAN curve is a closed curve in the plane with a continuously differentiable parameter representation $\vec{r}\colon [t_1, t_2] \to \mathbb{R}^2$, $t \mapsto (x(t), y(t))$ which is injective on (t_1, t_2) and satisfies $\vec{r}(t_1) = \vec{r}(t_2)$. In other words, apart from $\vec{r}(t_1)$ where the ends of the curve join, different points on the curve do not intersect.

area $\qquad A = \dfrac{1}{2} \left| \int_{t_1}^{t_2} (x\dot{y} - y\dot{x})\, \mathrm{d}t \right| = \left| \int_{t_1}^{t_2} y\dot{x}\, \mathrm{d}t \right| = \left| \int_{t_1}^{t_2} x\dot{y}\, \mathrm{d}t \right|$

Centre of mass and moment of inertia

Physics ▶ p. 162

Geometry ▶ p. 96

centre of mass $S = (x_S, y_S)$ of the homogeneous planar curve segment $y = f(x)$, $a \leqslant x \leqslant b$

$$x_S = \frac{1}{s} \int_a^b x \sqrt{1 + (f'(x))^2}\, \mathrm{d}x$$

$$y_S = \frac{1}{s} \int_a^b f(x) \sqrt{1 + (f'(x))^2}\, \mathrm{d}x$$

where $\;s = \int_a^b \sqrt{1 + (f'(x))^2}\, \mathrm{d}x$

centre of mass $S = (x_S, y_S)$ of the homogeneous area between $y = 0$ and $y = f(x)$, $f(x) \geqslant 0$ in $[a, b]$

$$x_S = \frac{1}{A} \int_a^b x f(x)\, \mathrm{d}x$$

$$y_S = \frac{1}{2A} \int_a^b (f(x))^2\, \mathrm{d}x$$

where $\;A = \int_a^b f(x)\, \mathrm{d}x$

centre of mass $S = (x_S, y_S, z_S)$ of the homogeneous solid of revolution, generated by rotating the curve $y = f(x)$, $f(x) \geqslant 0$ in $[a, b]$ about the x-axis

$$x_S = \frac{1}{J} \int_a^b x (f(x))^2\, \mathrm{d}x, \quad y_S = z_S = 0$$

where $\;J = \int_a^b (f(x))^2\, \mathrm{d}x$

moment of inertia I of the homogeneous area between $y = 0$ and $y = f(x)$, $f(x) \geqslant 0$ in $[a, b]$ with respect to

- x-axis: $\;I_x = \dfrac{1}{3} \int_a^b (f(x))^3\, \mathrm{d}x$

- y-axis: $\;I_y = \int_a^b x^2 f(x)\, \mathrm{d}x$

Calculus

4.6 Series expansions

Power series

power series in x with coefficients $a_0, a_1, a_2, \ldots$

$$a_0 + a_1 x + a_2 x^2 + a_3 x^3 + \ldots = \sum_{k=0}^{\infty} a_k x^k$$

radius of convergence

There exists an r, $0 \leqslant r \leqslant \infty$, such that the infinite series $\sum_{k=0}^{\infty} a_k x^k$ is absolutely convergent whenever $|x| < r$.
r is called the radius of convergence of the power series.

derivative of a power series

If $f(x) = \sum_{k=0}^{\infty} a_k (x-a)^k$, then $f'(x) = \sum_{k=1}^{\infty} k a_k (x-a)^{k-1}$
and both series have the same radius of convergence.
In particular, f is infinitely differentiable.

Every power series $\sum_{k=0}^{\infty} a_k (x-a)^k$ representing a function f can be expressed in terms of f in the form

$$f(x) = \sum_{k=0}^{\infty} \frac{f^{(k)}(a)}{k!} (x-a)^k.$$

Taylor polynomials and Taylor series

In the definitions below it is assumed that the function $f \colon [a,b] \to \mathbb{R}$ possesses continuous derivatives of sufficiently high order.

Taylor polynomial of degree n of f at the point x_0

$$\sum_{k=0}^{n} \frac{f^{(k)}(x_0)}{k!} (x-x_0)^k$$

Taylor series of f at the point x_0

$$\sum_{k=0}^{\infty} \frac{f^{(k)}(x_0)}{k!} (x-x_0)^k$$

Taylor's theorem concerning the Lagrange remainder term

If $f^{(n+1)}$ exists in (a,b), then for arbitrary points $x, x_0 \in [a,b]$:

$$f(x) = f(x_0) + \frac{f'(x_0)}{1!}(x-x_0) + \frac{f''(x_0)}{2!}(x-x_0)^2 + \ldots + \frac{f^{(n)}(x_0)}{n!}(x-x_0)^n + R_n(x)$$

$$R_n(x) = \frac{f^{(n+1)}(\xi)}{(n+1)!}(x-x_0)^{n+1}, \text{ where } \xi \text{ lies between } x \text{ and } x_0$$

MacLaurin series of f

Taylor series with $x_0 = 0$: $\sum_{k=0}^{\infty} \frac{f^{(k)}(0)}{k!} \cdot x^k$

Calculus
MATHEMATICS PHYSICS ASTRONOMY CHEMISTRY

Taylor polynomials of the function $y = \sin x$ at the point $x_0 = 0$.

The Taylor series converges for every $x \in \mathbb{R}$ to $\sin x$.

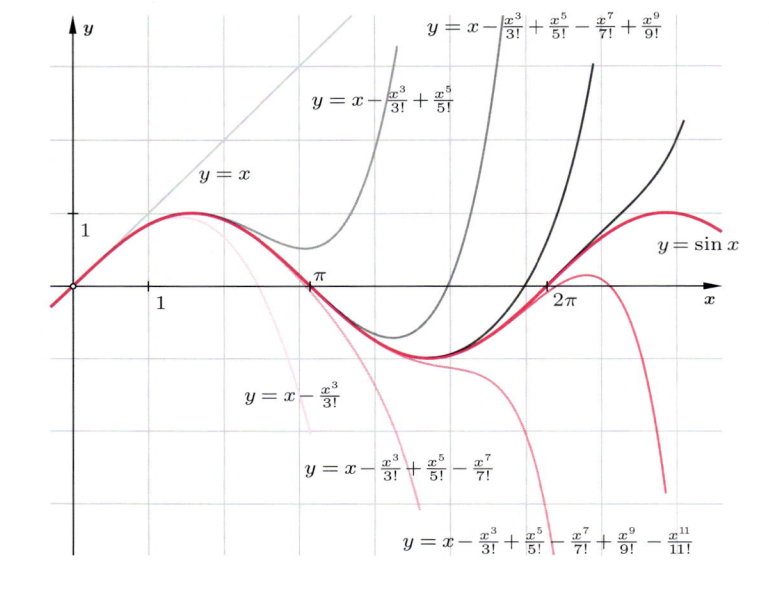

$y = x - \frac{x^3}{3!} + \frac{x^5}{5!} - \frac{x^7}{7!} + \frac{x^9}{9!}$

$y = x - \frac{x^3}{3!} + \frac{x^5}{5!}$

$y = x$

$y = \sin x$

$y = x - \frac{x^3}{3!}$

$y = x - \frac{x^3}{3!} + \frac{x^5}{5!} - \frac{x^7}{7!}$

$y = x - \frac{x^3}{3!} + \frac{x^5}{5!} - \frac{x^7}{7!} + \frac{x^9}{9!} - \frac{x^{11}}{11!}$

Taylor polynomials of the function $y = \frac{1}{1-x}$ at the point $x_0 = 0$.

The Taylor series only converges for $|x| < 1$ to $\frac{1}{1-x}$.

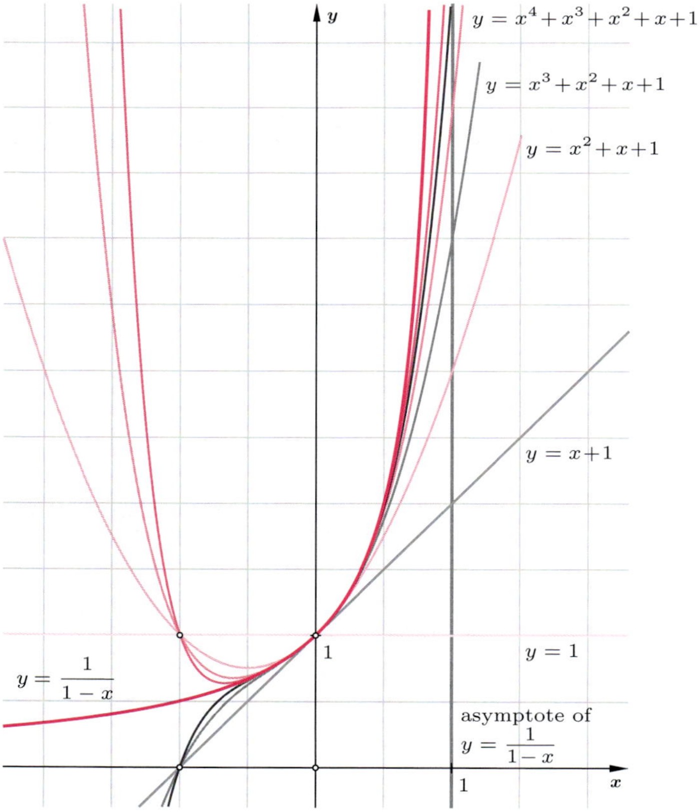

$y = x^4 + x^3 + x^2 + x + 1$

$y = x^3 + x^2 + x + 1$

$y = x^2 + x + 1$

$y = x + 1$

$y = 1$

$y = \frac{1}{1-x}$

asymptote of $y = \frac{1}{1-x}$

Calculus
MATHEMATICS   PHYSICS   ASTRONOMY   CHEMISTRY

Series expansions of special functions

$$(1+x)^\alpha = 1 + \binom{\alpha}{1}x + \binom{\alpha}{2}x^2 + \binom{\alpha}{3}x^3 + \ldots = \sum_{k=0}^{\infty} \binom{\alpha}{k} x^k, \quad |x| < 1, \; \alpha \in \mathbb{R},$$

$$\text{where } \binom{\alpha}{k} = \frac{\alpha(\alpha-1) \cdot \ldots \cdot (\alpha-k+1)}{k!}$$

$$e^{cx} = 1 + \frac{cx}{1!} + \frac{(cx)^2}{2!} + \frac{(cx)^3}{3!} + \ldots = \sum_{k=0}^{\infty} \frac{(cx)^k}{k!}, \quad x \in \mathbb{R}$$

$$(c = \ln(a) \text{ yields the expansion for } a^x.)$$

$$\sin x = x - \frac{x^3}{3!} + \frac{x^5}{5!} - \frac{x^7}{7!} + - \ldots = \sum_{k=0}^{\infty} (-1)^k \frac{x^{2k+1}}{(2k+1)!}, \quad x \in \mathbb{R}$$

$$\cos x = 1 - \frac{x^2}{2!} + \frac{x^4}{4!} - \frac{x^6}{6!} + - \ldots = \sum_{k=0}^{\infty} (-1)^k \frac{x^{2k}}{(2k)!}, \quad x \in \mathbb{R}$$

$$\tan x = x + \frac{1}{3}x^3 + \frac{2}{15}x^5 + \frac{17}{315}x^7 + \frac{62}{2835}x^9 + \frac{1382}{155925}x^{11} + \ldots, \quad |x| < \frac{\pi}{2}$$

$$\arcsin x = x + \frac{1}{2} \cdot \frac{x^3}{3} + \frac{1}{2} \cdot \frac{3}{4} \cdot \frac{x^5}{5} + \frac{1}{2} \cdot \frac{3}{4} \cdot \frac{5}{6} \cdot \frac{x^7}{7} + \ldots = \sum_{k=0}^{\infty} \frac{(2k)!}{2^{2k}(k!)^2(2k+1)} x^{2k+1}, \quad |x| \leqslant 1$$

$$\arccos x = \frac{\pi}{2} - \arcsin x \quad \text{(series expansion of } \arcsin x \text{ as above)}$$

$$\arctan x = x - \frac{x^3}{3} + \frac{x^5}{5} - \frac{x^7}{7} + - \ldots = \sum_{k=0}^{\infty} (-1)^k \frac{x^{2k+1}}{2k+1}, \quad |x| \leqslant 1$$

$$\ln(1+x) = x - \frac{x^2}{2} + \frac{x^3}{3} - \frac{x^4}{4} + - \ldots = \sum_{k=0}^{\infty} \frac{(-1)^k}{k+1} x^{k+1}, \quad -1 < x \leqslant 1$$

$$\ln \frac{x+1}{x-1} = 2\left(\frac{1}{x} + \frac{1}{3x^3} + \frac{1}{5x^5} + \frac{1}{7x^7} + \ldots\right) = 2\sum_{k=0}^{\infty} \frac{1}{(2k+1)x^{2k+1}}, \quad |x| > 1$$

$$\ln \frac{1+x}{1-x} = 2\left(x + \frac{1}{3}x^3 + \frac{1}{5}x^5 + \frac{1}{7}x^7 + \ldots\right) = 2\sum_{k=0}^{\infty} \frac{1}{2k+1} x^{2k+1}, \quad |x| < 1$$

$$\int_0^x e^{-t^2} dt = x - \frac{x^3}{3} + \frac{x^5}{2! \cdot 5} - \frac{x^7}{3! \cdot 7} + \frac{x^9}{4! \cdot 9} - + \ldots = \sum_{k=0}^{\infty} (-1)^k \frac{x^{2k+1}}{k!\,(2k+1)}, \quad x \in \mathbb{R}$$

Calculus

MATHEMATICS PHYSICS ASTRONOMY CHEMISTRY

Fourier series

Given a 2π periodic function $f\colon \mathbb{R}\to\mathbb{R}$, its Fourier series $s_f(x)$ is defined as follows:
$$s_f(x) = a_0 + a_1\cos x + b_1\sin x + a_2\cos 2x + b_2\sin 2x + \ldots = a_0 + \sum_{k=1}^{\infty}\bigl(a_k\cos kx + b_k\sin kx\bigr)$$
where the coefficients are given by
$$a_0 = \frac{1}{2\pi}\int_0^{2\pi} f(x)\,\mathrm{d}x \qquad a_k = \frac{1}{\pi}\int_0^{2\pi} f(x)\cos kx\,\mathrm{d}x \qquad b_k = \frac{1}{\pi}\int_0^{2\pi} f(x)\sin kx\,\mathrm{d}x,\ \ k\in\mathbb{N}$$
In most applications, the Fourier series $s_f(x)$ converges pointwise to $f(x)$.

Examples

The plots illustrate both the function f and the Fourier series approximation with n terms.

- rectangular function

$$f(x) = \begin{cases} \frac{\pi}{2} & \text{for } 0 \leqslant x < \pi \\ -\frac{\pi}{2} & \text{for } \pi \leqslant x < 2\pi \end{cases}$$

(continued with period 2π)

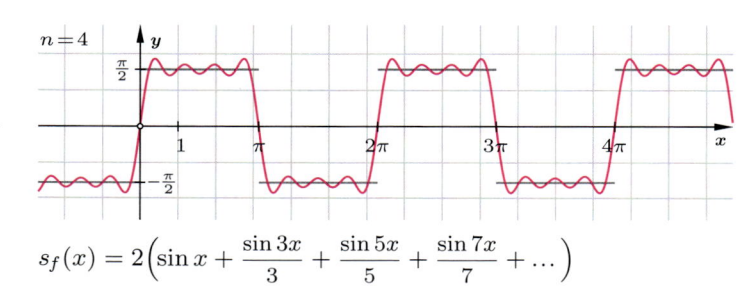

$$s_f(x) = 2\left(\sin x + \frac{\sin 3x}{3} + \frac{\sin 5x}{5} + \frac{\sin 7x}{7} + \ldots\right)$$

- sawtooth function

$f(x) = x$ for $0 \leqslant x < 2\pi$

(continued with period 2π)

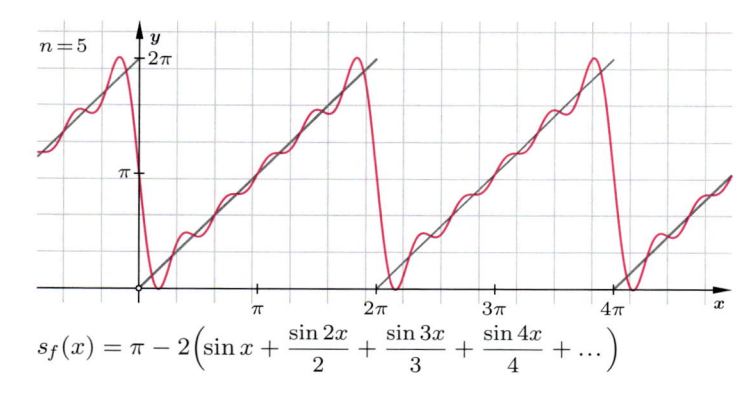

$$s_f(x) = \pi - 2\left(\sin x + \frac{\sin 2x}{2} + \frac{\sin 3x}{3} + \frac{\sin 4x}{4} + \ldots\right)$$

- triangular function

$f(x) = |x|$ for $-\pi \leqslant x < \pi$

(continued with period 2π)

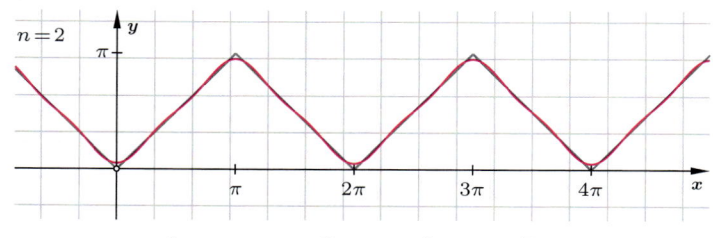

$$s_f(x) = \frac{\pi}{2} - \frac{4}{\pi}\left(\cos x + \frac{\cos 3x}{3^2} + \frac{\cos 5x}{5^2} + \frac{\cos 7x}{7^2} + \ldots\right)$$

Calculus

4.7 Special inequalities and approximations

inequality	domain of validity	criterion for equality
Triangle inequality		
$\lvert x+y \rvert \leq \lvert x \rvert + \lvert y \rvert$	$x, y \in \mathbb{R}$	$x=0$ or $y=0$ or $\operatorname{sgn} x = \operatorname{sgn} y$
$\left\lvert \sum_{k=1}^{n} x_k \right\rvert \leq \sum_{k=1}^{n} \lvert x_k \rvert$	$x_1, x_2, \ldots, x_n \in \mathbb{R}$	All non-vanishing x_i have the same sign.
Inequality of arithmetic and geometric means (AM-GM inequality)		
$\sqrt{xy} \leq \dfrac{x+y}{2}$	$x \geq 0$ and $y \geq 0$	$x = y$ p. 16 ◀
$\sqrt[n]{\prod_{k=1}^{n} x_k} \leq \dfrac{1}{n} \sum_{k=1}^{n} x_k$	$x_i \geq 0,\ i = 1, 2, \ldots, n$	$x_1 = x_2 = x_3 = \ldots = x_n$
Bernoulli's inequality		
$(1+x)^n \geq 1 + nx$	$x > -1,\ n \in \mathbb{N}$	$x = 0$ or $n = 1$
Cauchy-Schwarz inequality		
$\left(\sum_{k=1}^{n} x_k y_k \right)^2 \leq \left(\sum_{k=1}^{n} x_k^2 \right) \left(\sum_{k=1}^{n} y_k^2 \right)$	$x_i, y_i \in \mathbb{R}$ for $i = 1, 2, \ldots, n$	The vectors $\begin{pmatrix} x_1 \\ x_2 \\ \vdots \\ x_n \end{pmatrix}$ and $\begin{pmatrix} y_1 \\ y_2 \\ \vdots \\ y_n \end{pmatrix}$ are linearly dependent.
Stirling's formula		
$n! = \sqrt{2\pi n} \left(\dfrac{n}{e} \right)^n e^s$ where	$\dfrac{1}{12n + \dfrac{2}{5n}} < s < \dfrac{1}{12n},\ n \in \mathbb{N}$	(Stirling's approximation is obtained by setting $s = 0$.) p. 42 ◀

4.8 Differential equations

A differential equation of order n is an equation for an unknown function y relating the nth derivative of y to x, y and the derivatives of y up to order $n-1$:
$$y^{(n)} = f(x, y, y', \ldots, y^{(n-1)})$$
    special case $n = 1$ ▶ p. 142

Separable differential equations

$$\frac{dy}{dx} = g(x) f(y) \qquad\qquad \int \frac{1}{f(y)}\, dy = \int g(x)\, dx + C$$

Special case: logistic differential equation
    p. 67 ◀ graph

$$\frac{dy}{dt} = ay - by^2 = by\left(\frac{a}{b} - y\right) \qquad\qquad y(t) = \frac{a y_0}{b y_0 + (a - b y_0)\, e^{-a(t - t_0)}},\quad y(t_0) = y_0$$

Calculus

MATHEMATICS   PHYSICS   ASTRONOMY   CHEMISTRY

Linear differential equations

equation	general solution	remarks

First order, homogeneous

$y' + u(x)\,y = 0$ $\qquad$ $y(x) = C\mathrm{e}^{-U(x)}$ $\qquad$ $U(x)$ arbitr. antideriv. of $u(x)$

$\dot{y} - \alpha y = 0$, $\alpha = \text{const.}$ $\qquad$ $y(t) = C\mathrm{e}^{\alpha t}$
- $\alpha > 0$: exponential growth
- $\alpha < 0$: exponential decay

p. 67 ◂

First order, inhomogeneous

$y' + u(x)\,y = v(x)$ $\qquad$ $y(x) = \bigl(G(x) + C\bigr)\mathrm{e}^{-U(x)}$ $\qquad$ $U(x)$ arbitr. antideriv. of $u(x)$
$G(x)$ arbit. antideriv. of $v(x)\mathrm{e}^{U(x)}$

Second order, homogeneous with constant coefficients

$ay'' + by' + cy = 0$, $a \neq 0$ $\qquad$ Let the solutions of the corresponding characteristic equation $a\lambda^2 + b\lambda + c = 0$ be $\lambda_{1,2}$.

- $\lambda_{1,2} \in \mathbb{R}$ and $\lambda_1 \neq \lambda_2$ $\qquad$ $y(x) = C_1 \mathrm{e}^{\lambda_1 x} + C_2 \mathrm{e}^{\lambda_2 x}$
- $\lambda_1 = \lambda_2$ $\qquad$ $y(x) = (C_1 + C_2 x)\mathrm{e}^{\lambda_1 x}$
- $\lambda_{1,2} = \alpha \pm i\beta$, $\beta \neq 0$ $\qquad$ $y(x) = (C_1 \sin \beta x + C_2 \cos \beta x)\mathrm{e}^{\alpha x}$

$\ddot{y} + \omega_0^2 y = 0$ $\qquad$ $y(t) = C_1 \cos \omega_0 t + C_2 \sin \omega_0 t$
$\qquad\qquad\qquad\qquad = C \cos(\omega_0 t + \varphi)$ $\qquad$ undamped oscillation

$\ddot{y} + 2\delta \dot{y} + \omega_0^2 y = 0$, $\qquad$ $y(t) = \mathrm{e}^{-\delta t}(C_1 \cos \omega t + C_2 \sin \omega t)$
$\omega_0^2 - \delta^2 = \omega^2 > 0$ $\qquad\qquad = C\mathrm{e}^{-\delta t} \cos(\omega t + \varphi)$ $\qquad$ damped oscillation

Second order, inhomogeneous with constant coefficients (sinusoidal source term)

$\ddot{y} + 2\delta \dot{y} + \omega_0^2 y = A \cos \omega_1 t$
$\omega_1 = \text{const.}$
$\qquad$ $y(t) = \dfrac{A}{\sqrt{(\omega_0^2 - \omega_1^2)^2 + 4\delta^2 \omega_1^2}} \cos(\omega_1 t + \gamma) + h(t)$

h: general solution of $\qquad$ forced oscillation
$\ddot{y} + 2\delta \dot{y} + \omega_0^2 y = 0$ $\qquad$ (with damping)

$\tan \gamma = \dfrac{2\delta \omega_1}{\omega_1^2 - \omega_0^2}$ $\qquad$ $-\pi \leqslant \gamma \leqslant 0$

$\delta = 0$, $\omega_1 = \omega_0$ (resonance) $\qquad$ $y(t) = \dfrac{A}{2\omega_0} t \cdot \sin \omega_0 t + h(t)$ $\qquad$ forced oscillation without damping at resonance frequency

h: general solution of $\ddot{y} + \omega_0^2 y = 0$

Superposition principle

If y_i is any solution of an inhomogeneous linear differential equation of arbitrary order, and y_h is any solution of the corresponding homogeneous differential equation, then $y_i + y_h$ is also a solution of the inhomogeneous differential equation.

5 Geometry

The same notation is used for both geometric objects and their measurements except for lengths between two points (◀ front cover). Angles are specified in degrees.

5.1 Plane geometry

Division ratios and spatial relationships

Division of a line segment AB by a collinear point T in the ratio λ.

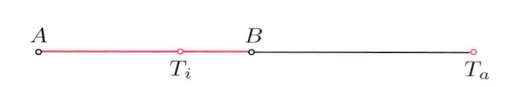

$\lambda = \dfrac{\overline{AT_i}}{\overline{T_iB}}$, where T_i is an interior point

$\lambda = -\dfrac{\overline{AT_a}}{\overline{T_aB}}$, when T_a is an exterior point

These ratios can also be defined with signs reversed.

Harmonic division

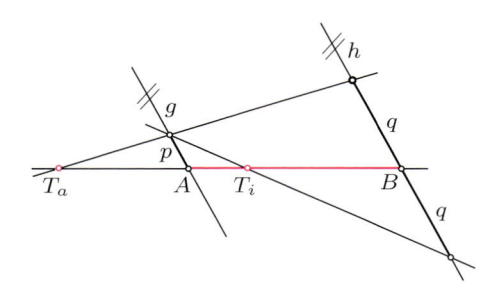

If the line segment AB is divided internally and externally by collinear points such that the ratios are the same except for sign, then they are said to divide the segment harmonically in that ratio. If the ratio is $p:q$, and one of the collinear points is given, then the other point can be constructed using the relation

$\overline{AT_i} : \overline{T_iB} = \overline{AT_a} : \overline{T_aB} = p : q$

as shown in the figure opposite.

Golden ratio

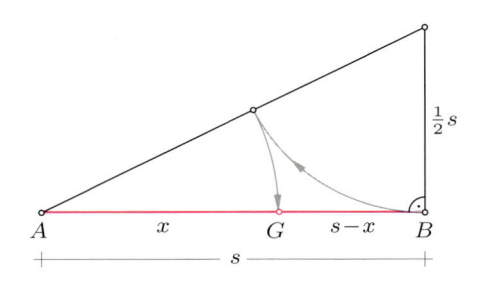

criterion:
$s : x = x : (s - x)$

$\Rightarrow \begin{cases} \dfrac{s}{x} = \dfrac{\sqrt{5}+1}{2} = 1.61803\,39887\ldots = \Phi \\[1em] \dfrac{x}{s} = \dfrac{\sqrt{5}-1}{2} = 0.61803\,39887\ldots = \varphi \end{cases}$

p. 41 ◀ Fibonacci sequence

Geometry

Intercept theorems

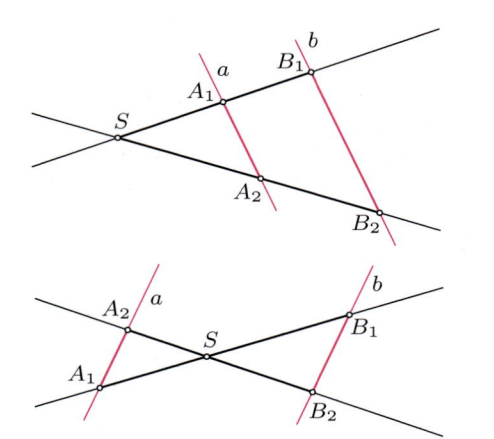

1st statement and its converse

$$a \parallel b \Leftrightarrow \overline{SA_1} : \overline{SB_1} = \overline{SA_2} : \overline{SB_2}$$

2nd statement

$$a \parallel b \Rightarrow \overline{SA_1} : \overline{SB_1} = \overline{A_1A_2} : \overline{B_1B_2}$$

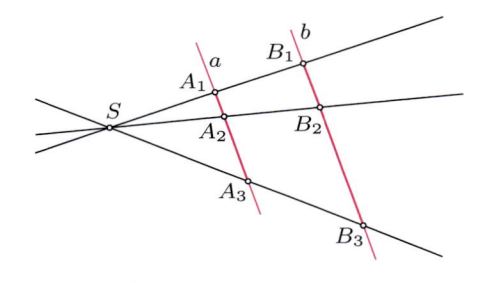

3rd statement and its converse

$$a \parallel b \Leftrightarrow \overline{A_1A_2} : \overline{A_2A_3} = \overline{B_1B_2} : \overline{B_2B_3}$$

Menelaus' theorem

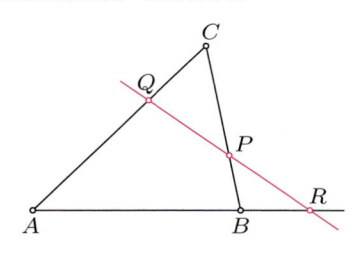

If $\lambda_1, \lambda_2, \lambda_3$ are the ratios by which P, Q, R divide BC, CA, AB respectively, then

P, Q and R are collinear $\Leftrightarrow \lambda_1\lambda_2\lambda_3 = -1$

Ceva's theorem

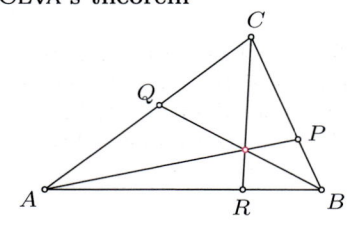

If $\lambda_1, \lambda_2, \lambda_3$ are the ratios by which P, Q, R divide BC, CA, AB respectively, then

AP, BQ and CR intersect at a common point $\Leftrightarrow \lambda_1\lambda_2\lambda_3 = 1$

Geometry

Circle theorems

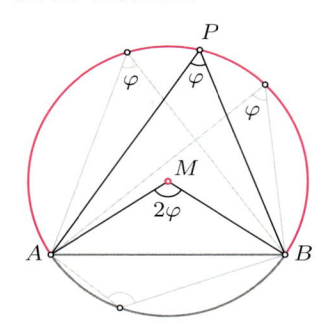

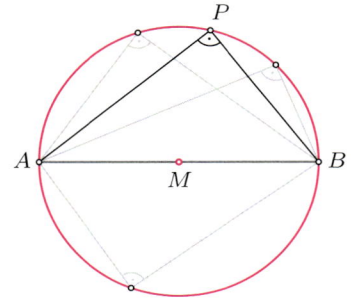

inscribed angle theorem

The central angle AMB in a circle is twice as large as an inscribed angle APB subtending the same arc. In particular, all inscribed angles subtending the same arc AB are equal. Conversely, the locus of all points forming the same angle between two given points A and B is a pair of circles.

THALES' theorem

In a special case of the above theorem, if AB is a diameter of the circle, the inscribed angle is a right angle. Conversely, the locus of all points P forming a right angle between two given points A and B is the circle determined by the diameter AB.

Chords, secants and tangents

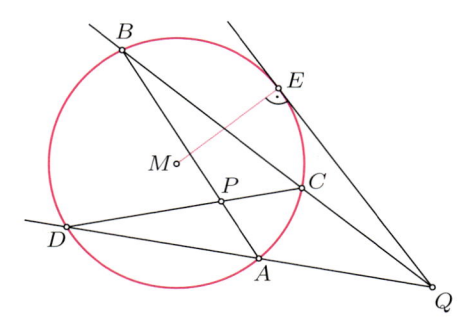

theorem of intersecting chords

$$\overline{PB} \cdot \overline{PA} = \overline{PC} \cdot \overline{PD}$$

tangent-secant theorem

$$\overline{QA} \cdot \overline{QD} = \overline{QC} \cdot \overline{QB} = \overline{QE}^2$$

Circle of APOLLONIUS

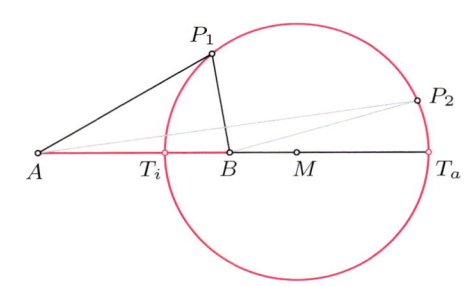

The locus of all points whose distances from two given points A and B have a fixed ratio $a:b$ is a circle with the diameter $T_i T_a$, where T_i and T_a divide the segment AB harmonically in the ratio $a:b$.

Geometry

MATHEMATICS   PHYSICS   ASTRONOMY   CHEMISTRY

Triangles

General triangle

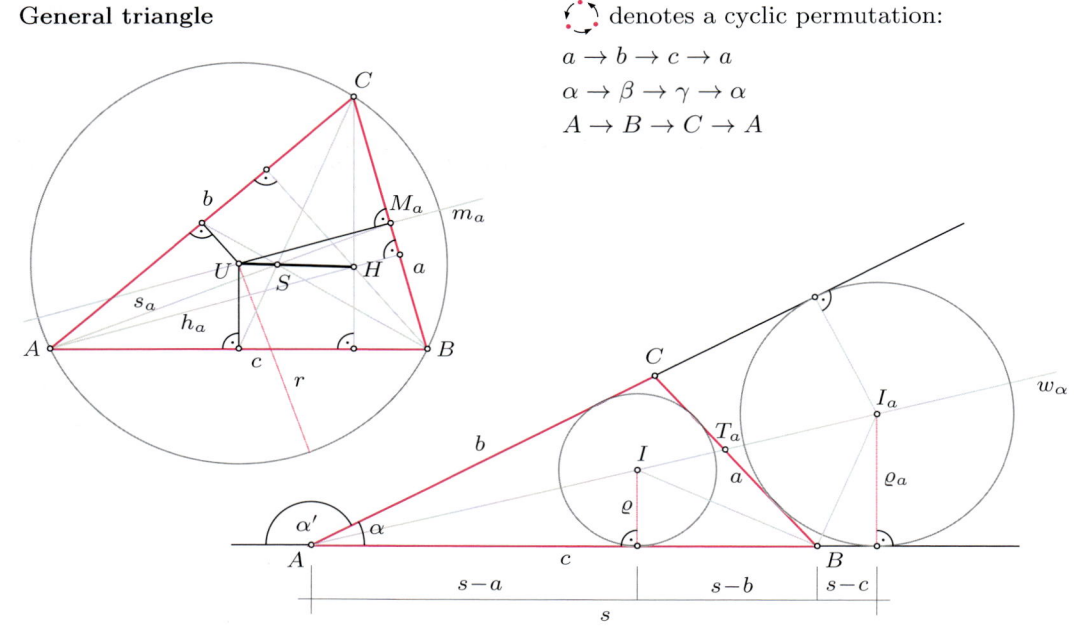

↻ denotes a cyclic permutation:
$a \to b \to c \to a$
$\alpha \to \beta \to \gamma \to \alpha$
$A \to B \to C \to A$

α: interior angle
α': exterior angle
s: semiperimeter $\left(= \dfrac{a+b+c}{2}\right)$

H: orthocentre
U: circumcentre (centre of the circumcircle)
r: circumradius (radius of the circumcircle)
I: incentre (centre of the incircle)
ϱ: inradius (radius of the incircle)

S: centroid (centre of mass)
s_a: median to side a
h_a: altitude to side a
M_a: midpoint of side a
m_a: perpendicular bisector of side a
I_a: excentre (centre of the excircle tangent to side a)
ϱ_a: exradius (radius of the excircle tangent to side a)
w_α: bisector of the angle α
T_a: intersection of the angle bisector w_α with side a

exterior and interior angles	$\alpha + \alpha' = 180°$
sum of interior angles	$\alpha + \beta + \gamma = 180°$
triangle inequality	$a + b > c$ ↻
altitudes	$h_a = c \sin \beta$
	$h_a = \dfrac{2}{a}\sqrt{s(s-a)(s-b)(s-c)}$ ↻
Euler's line	The points H, S and U lie on a common line, and $\overline{HS} : \overline{SU} = 2 : 1$

Geometry
MATHEMATICS   PHYSICS   ASTRONOMY   CHEMISTRY

medians	$\overline{SA} : \overline{SM_a} = 2 : 1$ $s_a = \frac{1}{2}\sqrt{2b^2 + 2c^2 - a^2} = \frac{1}{2}\sqrt{b^2 + c^2 + 2bc\cos\alpha}$	
angle bisectors	$\overline{T_aB} : \overline{T_aC} = \overline{AB} : \overline{AC}$ $w_\alpha = \sqrt{bc\left[1 - \left(\frac{a}{b+c}\right)^2\right]} = \frac{2bc\cos\frac{\alpha}{2}}{b+c}$	
area	$A = \frac{1}{2}ah_a$ $A = \sqrt{s(s-a)(s-b)(s-c)}$ HERON's formula $A = \varrho_a(s-a)$ $A = \varrho s$ $A = \frac{abc}{4r}$ $A = \frac{a^2 \sin\beta \sin\gamma}{2\sin\alpha} = \frac{ab}{2}\sin\gamma = 2r^2 \sin\alpha \sin\beta \sin\gamma$	
inradius and exradii	$\varrho = \frac{A}{s}, \quad \varrho_a = \frac{A}{s-a}$	
circumradius	$r = \frac{abc}{4A} = \frac{a}{2\sin\alpha}$	
sine rule	$\frac{a}{\sin\alpha} = \frac{b}{\sin\beta} = \frac{c}{\sin\gamma} = 2r$	
cosine rule	$a^2 = b^2 + c^2 - 2bc\cos\alpha$	
tangent rule	$\frac{a-b}{a+b} = \frac{\tan\frac{\alpha-\beta}{2}}{\tan\frac{\alpha+\beta}{2}}$	
projection rule	$a = b\cos\gamma + c\cos\beta$	
trigonometric functions of half-angles	$\sin\frac{\alpha}{2} = \sqrt{\frac{(s-b)(s-c)}{bc}}$ $\cos\frac{\alpha}{2} = \sqrt{\frac{s(s-a)}{bc}}$ $\tan\frac{\alpha}{2} = \sqrt{\frac{(s-b)(s-c)}{s(s-a)}}$	

sin, cos, tan ▶ p. 97

Geometry

MATHEMATICS PHYSICS ASTRONOMY CHEMISTRY

congruence theorems for triangles	Two triangles are congruent if any of the following sets are equal: • all three sides • two sides and the included angle • one side and the adjacent angles • two sides and the angle opposite the longer side
similarity theorems for triangles	Two triangles are similar if any of the following conditions hold: • all three pairs of corresponding sides have the same ratio • two pairs of corresponding sides have the same ratio and the included angles are equal • two pairs of corresponding angles are equal • two pairs of corresponding sides have the same ratio and the angles opposite the longer sides are equal

Right-angled triangle

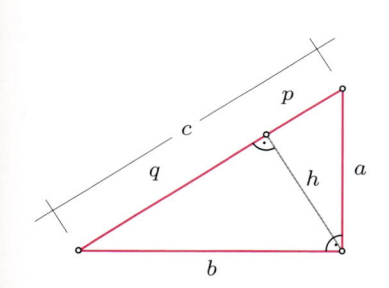

Pythagoras' theorem	$a^2 + b^2 = c^2$
geometric mean theorem	$h^2 = pq$
relations among the sides	$a^2 = pc, \quad b^2 = qc$
altitude	$h = \dfrac{ab}{c}$
circumradius, inradius	$r = \dfrac{c}{2}, \quad \varrho = \dfrac{a+b-c}{2}$

additional formulae ▶ p. 97

Isosceles right-angled triangle

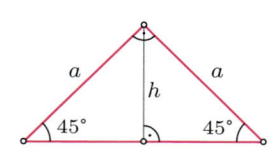

altitude and area	$h = \dfrac{\sqrt{2}}{2}a, \quad A = \dfrac{1}{2}a^2$
circumradius, inradius	$r = \dfrac{\sqrt{2}}{2}a, \quad \varrho = \dfrac{2-\sqrt{2}}{2}a$

Equilateral triangle

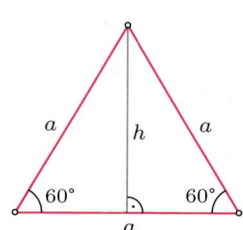

altitude and area	$h = \dfrac{\sqrt{3}}{2}a, \quad A = \dfrac{\sqrt{3}}{4}a^2$
circumradius, inradius	$r = \dfrac{\sqrt{3}}{3}a, \quad \varrho = \dfrac{\sqrt{3}}{6}a$
exradius	$\varrho_a = \dfrac{\sqrt{3}}{2}a$

Geometry

Quadrilaterals

General convex quadrilateral

An object (planar or solid) is called convex if the straight line segment connecting any two points in the object lies entirely within the object.

sum of interior angles $\alpha + \beta + \gamma + \delta = 360°$

diagonals the diagonals are perpendicular to one another if and only if
$$a^2 + c^2 = b^2 + d^2$$

area $A = \dfrac{1}{2} ef \sin \varphi$

$\varphi \neq 90°$: $A = \dfrac{1}{4}\left(b^2 + d^2 - a^2 - c^2\right) \tan \varphi$

$$A = \dfrac{1}{4}\sqrt{4e^2 f^2 - \left(b^2 + d^2 - a^2 - c^2\right)^2}$$

Square

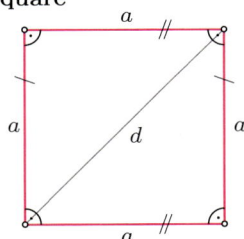

diagonals $d = \sqrt{2}\, a$

area $A = a^2 = \dfrac{d^2}{2}$

circumradius, inradius $r = \dfrac{\sqrt{2}}{2} a = \dfrac{d}{2}, \quad \varrho = \dfrac{a}{2}$

Rectangle

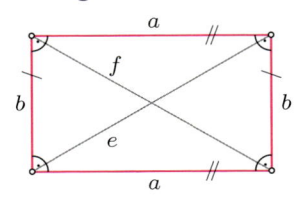

diagonals $e = \sqrt{a^2 + b^2} = f$

area $A = ab$

circumradius $r = \dfrac{e}{2}$

Parallelogram (rhomboid)

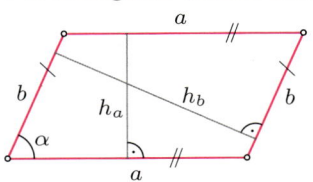

parallelogram identity $e^2 + f^2 = 2\left(a^2 + b^2\right)$
where e and f are the diagonals

area $A = a\, h_a = ab \sin \alpha = b\, h_b$

Geometry

Rhombus

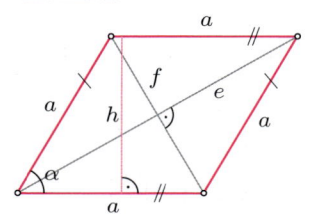

diagonals	$e = 2a \cos \frac{\alpha}{2}$, $\quad f = 2a \sin \frac{\alpha}{2}$
	$e^2 + f^2 = 4a^2$
area	$A = ah = a^2 \sin \alpha = \frac{1}{2} ef$

Trapezoid

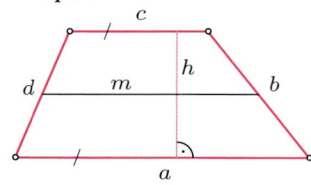

midsegment	$m = \dfrac{a+c}{2}$
area	$A = mh = \dfrac{a+c}{2} h$

Cyclic quadrilateral

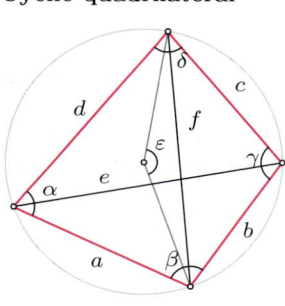

angle criterion	A quadrilateral can be circumscribed if and only if $\alpha + \gamma = \beta + \delta = 180°$
central angle	$\varepsilon = 2\alpha$
PTOLEMY's theorem	$ac + bd = ef$
area (BRAHMAGUPTA's formula)	$A = \sqrt{(s-a)(s-b)(s-c)(s-d)}$ where $s = \dfrac{a+b+c+d}{2}$

Tangential quadrilateral

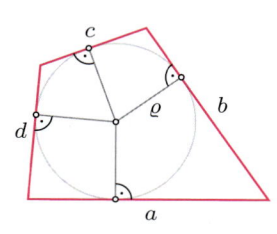

side criterion	A quadrilateral can be inscribed if and only if $a + c = b + d$
area	$A = \dfrac{a+b+c+d}{2} \varrho$

Bicentric quadrilateral

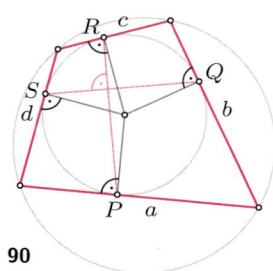

incircle criterion	A tangential quadrilateral is bicentric if and only if $PR \perp SQ$
area	$A = \sqrt{abcd}$

Geometry

Regular pentagon

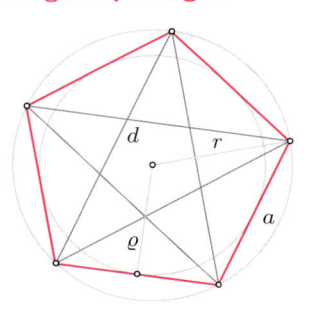

	diagonals	The length ratio between any diagonal and any side is the golden ratio. p. 83 ◀
		$d = \dfrac{\sqrt{5}+1}{2}\, a = \Phi \cdot a$
	area	$A = \dfrac{a^2}{4}\sqrt{25+10\sqrt{5}}$
	circumradius	$r = \dfrac{a}{10}\sqrt{50+10\sqrt{5}}$
	inradius	$\varrho = \dfrac{a}{10}\sqrt{25+10\sqrt{5}}$

Polygon (n-gon)

Simple polygon
(JORDAN polygon)

sum of interior angles	$(n-2)\cdot 180°$
sum of exterior angles	$360°$
number of diagonals	$n_d = \dfrac{n(n-3)}{2}$

Regular convex polygon
(regular n-gon)

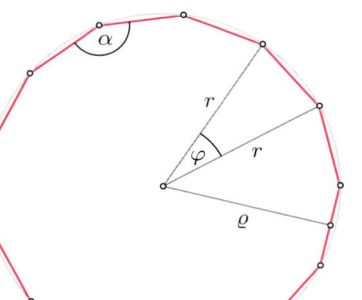

definition	An equilateral and equiangular convex polygon – i.e. a simple polygon in which all sides and all angles are equal.
sum of interior angles	$\alpha = \dfrac{n-2}{n}\cdot 180°$
central angle	$\varphi = \dfrac{360°}{n}$
area	$A = \dfrac{1}{4}\,n\,a^2 \cot\dfrac{\varphi}{2}$
circumradius, inradius	$r = \dfrac{a}{2}\csc\dfrac{\varphi}{2}, \quad \varrho = \dfrac{a}{2}\cot\dfrac{\varphi}{2}$

csc and cot ▶ p. 97

Angles in radian measure

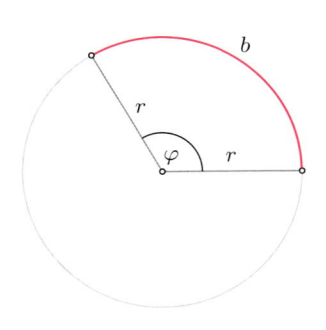

The radian measure $\widehat{\varphi}$ of an angle φ subtended from the centre of a circle by an arc in the circle is the ratio of the arc length to the circumference.

$$\widehat{\varphi} = \frac{b}{r} = \frac{\pi}{180°}\varphi \quad \Leftrightarrow \quad \varphi = \frac{180°}{\pi}\widehat{\varphi}$$

On the unit circle ($r = 1$): $\widehat{\varphi} = b$

The unit of radian measure is the radian (rad). An angle of 1 radian corresponds to a circular arc whose length is equal to the circle's radius.

Geometry

MATHEMATICS   PHYSICS   ASTRONOMY   CHEMISTRY

Circles

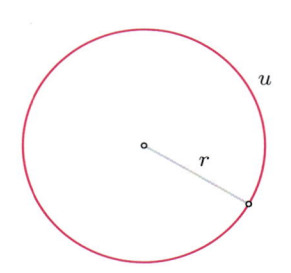

$\pi = 3.14159\,26535\,89793\,23846\,26433\,83279\,50288\,41971\,69399\,37510$ is the ratio of the circumference of a circle to its diameter.

circumference	$u = 2\pi r$
area	$A = \pi r^2$
arc length	$b = \widehat{\beta} r = \dfrac{\pi}{180°} \beta r$

p. 91 ◀ $\widehat{\beta}$ radian measure

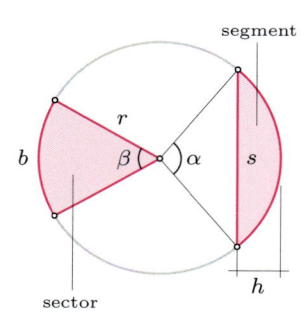

sector area	$A = \dfrac{\widehat{\beta} r^2}{2} = \dfrac{\pi \beta r^2}{360°} = \dfrac{br}{2}$
chord length	$s = 2r \sin \dfrac{\alpha}{2}$
segment height	$h = r \left(1 - \cos \dfrac{\alpha}{2}\right)$
segment area	$A = \dfrac{r^2}{2} (\operatorname{arc} \alpha - \sin \alpha)$

5.2   Solid geometry

Cavalieri's principle

If two solids standing on the same plane have the property that every plane parallel to the base intersects both solids in cross sections of equal area, then the two solids have equal volumes.

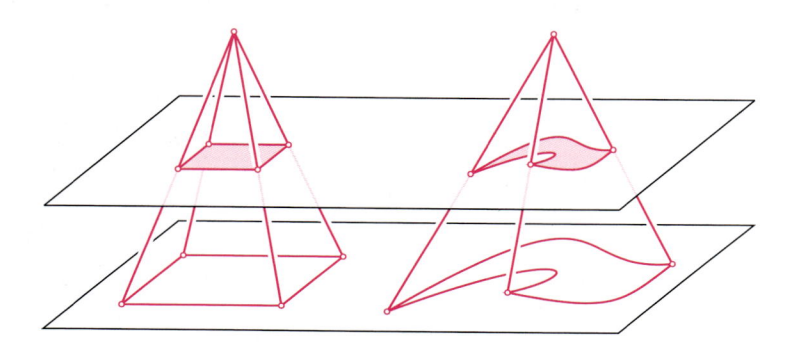

Geometry
MATHEMATICS PHYSICS ASTRONOMY CHEMISTRY

Prisms, pyramids, cylinders and cones

segments, lengths

a, b, c: line segments, lengths
r, r_1, r_2: radii
h: height (altitude)
m: slant height (cone)
d: space diagonal
h': slant height (pyramid)
u: base perimeter

areas

G: area of lower base
D: area of upper base
S: surface area
M: lateral surface area

V: volume of solid

Cube

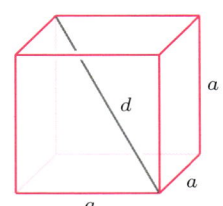

$d = \sqrt{3}\,a$
$S = 6a^2$
$V = a^3$

Cuboid (rectangular prism)

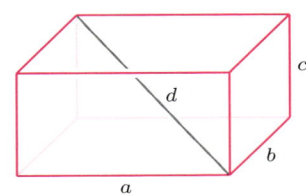

$d = \sqrt{a^2 + b^2 + c^2}$
$S = 2(ab + ac + bc)$
$V = abc$

Parallelepiped

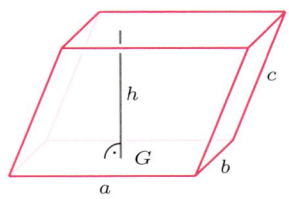

$V = G \cdot h$

triple product ▶ p. 105

Right prism

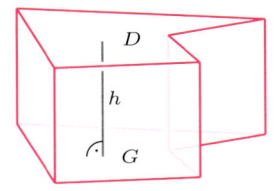

$G = D$
$M = uh$
$V = Gh$

Oblique prism

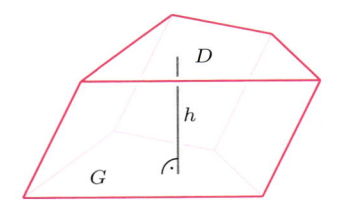

$G = D$
$V = Gh$

Right circular cylinder

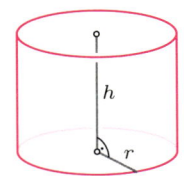

$M = 2\pi rh$
$S = 2\pi r^2 + 2\pi rh = 2\pi r(r+h)$
$V = \pi r^2 h$

Generalized cylinder

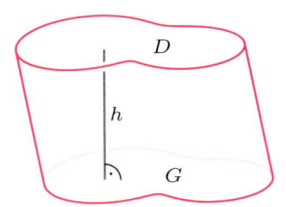

$G = D$
$V = Gh$

Tetrahedron

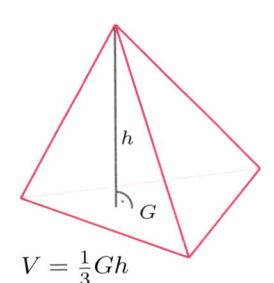

$V = \frac{1}{3}Gh$

Pyramid

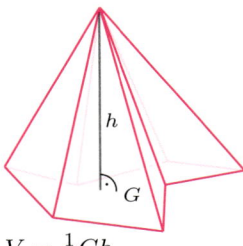

$V = \frac{1}{3}Gh$

Right-regular pyramid

$M = \frac{1}{2}nah'$
$= \frac{1}{2}uh'$

regular n-gon

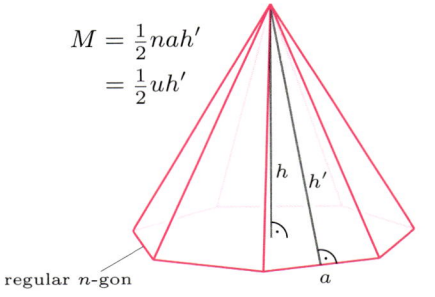

Geometry

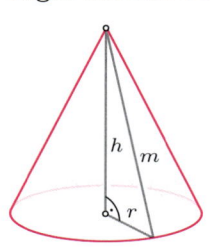

Right circular cone

$M = \pi r m$
$S = \pi r^2 + \pi r m = \pi r(r+m)$
$V = \dfrac{1}{3}\pi r^2 h$

Oblique circular cone

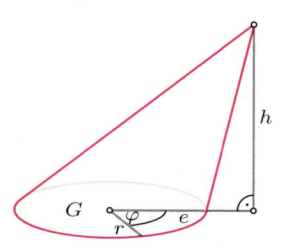

$M = r \displaystyle\int_0^\pi \sqrt{(r - e\cos\varphi)^2 + h^2}\, d\varphi$
$V = \dfrac{1}{3} G h$

Frustra

Pyramidal or conical frustrum

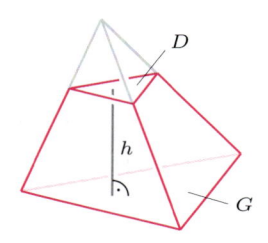

$V = \dfrac{1}{3} h(G + \sqrt{GD} + D)$

Truncated right circular cone

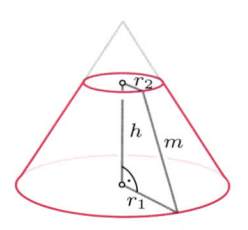

The upper and lower bases are parallel.

$M = \pi(r_1 + r_2) m$
$S = \pi\left(r_1^2 + r_2^2 + m(r_1 + r_2)\right)$
$V = \dfrac{1}{3}\pi(r_1^2 + r_2^2 + r_1 r_2) h$

Prismatoids

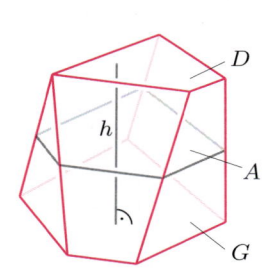

Definition — The upper and lower bases are parallel polygons and the lateral surfaces are triangles or trapezoids. A is the area of the midsection (cross section parallel to the bases at half height).

Volume $\quad V = \dfrac{1}{6} h(G + 4A + D)$

Geometry

MATHEMATICS PHYSICS ASTRONOMY CHEMISTRY

Polyhedra

Euler's polyhedron formula

v: number of vertices
e: number of edges
f: number of faces

For all simple polyhedra (polyhedra which can be transformed by continuous deformations into spheres):

$$v - e + f = 2 \qquad \text{p. 49} \blacktriangleleft \text{Graph theory}$$

Simple polyhedra do not have any holes. The generalization to polyhedra with holes is:

$$v - e + f = 2 - 2g \quad \text{(where } g \text{ is the number of holes)}$$

Regular polyhedra (Platonic solids)

a: edge length ϱ: radius of the insphere r: radius of the circumsphere

	tetrahedron	cube	octahedron	dodecahedron	icosahedron
v	4	8	6	20	12
e	6	12	12	30	30
f	4	6	8	12	20
$\dfrac{S}{a^2}$	$\sqrt{3}$	6	$2\sqrt{3}$	$3\sqrt{5(5+2\sqrt{5})}$	$5\sqrt{3}$
$\dfrac{V}{a^3}$	$\dfrac{\sqrt{2}}{12}$	1	$\dfrac{\sqrt{2}}{3}$	$\dfrac{15+7\sqrt{5}}{4}$	$\dfrac{5(3+\sqrt{5})}{12}$
$\dfrac{\varrho}{a}$	$\dfrac{\sqrt{6}}{12}$	$\dfrac{1}{2}$	$\dfrac{\sqrt{6}}{6}$	$\sqrt{\dfrac{25+11\sqrt{5}}{40}}$	$\dfrac{(3+\sqrt{5})\sqrt{3}}{12}$
$\dfrac{r}{a}$	$\dfrac{\sqrt{6}}{4}$	$\dfrac{\sqrt{3}}{2}$	$\dfrac{\sqrt{2}}{2}$	$\dfrac{(1+\sqrt{5})\sqrt{3}}{4}$	$\dfrac{\sqrt{2(5+\sqrt{5})}}{4}$

Nets of regular polyhedra

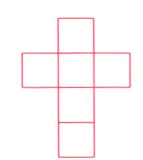

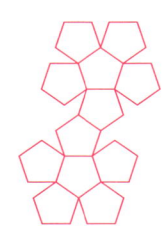

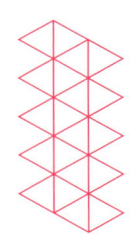

Geometry

Sphere

Volumes

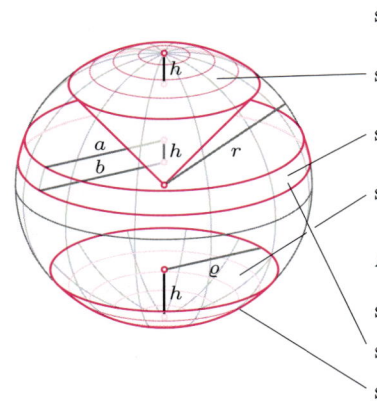

sphere $V = \dfrac{4}{3}\pi r^3$

spherical sector $V = \dfrac{2}{3}\pi r^2 h$

spherical zone $V = \dfrac{1}{6}\pi h(3a^2 + 3b^2 + h^2)$

spherical segment $V = \dfrac{1}{3}\pi h^2(3r - h) = \dfrac{1}{6}\pi h(3\varrho^2 + h^2)$

Areas

surface area $S = 4\pi r^2$

spherical zone $S = 2\pi rh$

spherical cap (dome) $S = 2\pi rh$

Ellipsoid

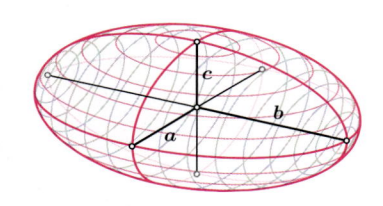

volume $V = \dfrac{4}{3}\pi abc$

Torus

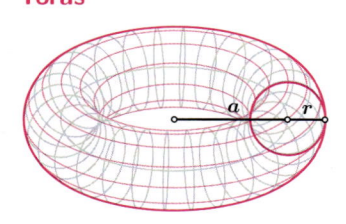

volume $V = 2\pi^2 ar^2$

surface area $S = 4\pi^2 ar$

Solids of revolution

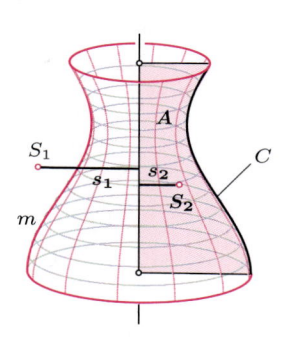

p. 75, 76 ◄ Calculus

C: plane curve generating the solid of revolution
m: length of C
A: area of the plane figure between C and the axis of rotation
S_1: centre of mass of the curve C
s_1: distance of S_1 from the axis of rotation
S_2: centre of mass of the figure between C and the axis of rotation
s_2: distance of S_2 from the axis of rotation

PAPPUS-GULDIN theorem

volume $V = 2\pi s_2 A$

surface area $S = 2\pi s_1 m$

Geometry

5.3 Trigonometry

Definition of the trigonometric functions (circular functions)

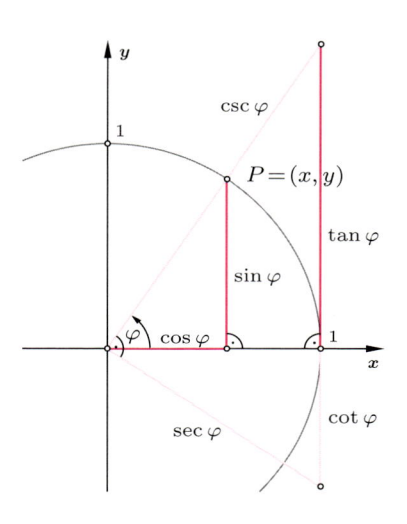

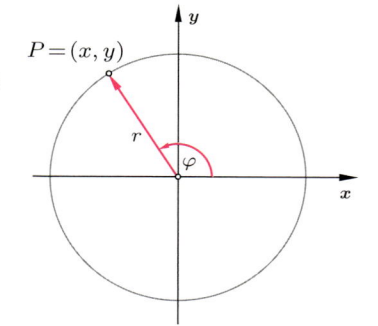

Sine
$$\sin \varphi = \frac{y}{r}$$

Cosine
$$\cos \varphi = \frac{x}{r}$$

Tangent
$$\tan \varphi = \frac{y}{x}, \quad \varphi \neq 90° + k \cdot 180°, \ k \in \mathbb{Z}$$

Secant
$$\sec \varphi = \frac{r}{x} = \frac{1}{\cos \varphi}, \quad \varphi \neq 90° + k \cdot 180°, \ k \in \mathbb{Z}$$

Cosecant
$$\csc \varphi = \frac{r}{y} = \frac{1}{\sin \varphi}, \quad \varphi \neq k \cdot 180°, \ k \in \mathbb{Z}$$

Cotangent
$$\cot \varphi = \frac{x}{y} = \frac{1}{\tan \varphi}, \quad \varphi \neq k \cdot 180°, \ k \in \mathbb{Z}$$

For $0° < \varphi < 90°$ the function values of the trigonometric functions can be represented by the side lengths of triangles constructed on the unit circle.

Definitions in the right-angled triangle

p. 87 ◄ general triangle

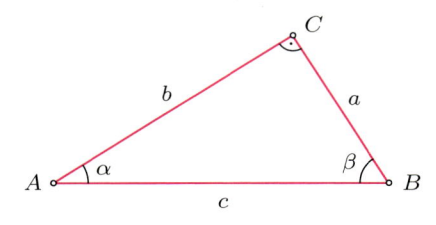

$$\sin \alpha = \frac{a}{c} = \cos \beta$$

$$\cos \alpha = \frac{b}{c} = \sin \beta$$

$$\tan \alpha = \frac{a}{b} = \frac{1}{\tan \beta}$$

Exact function values for selected angles

φ	0°	30°	45°	60°	90°
$\sin \varphi$	0	$\frac{1}{2}$	$\frac{\sqrt{2}}{2}$	$\frac{\sqrt{3}}{2}$	1
$\cos \varphi$	1	$\frac{\sqrt{3}}{2}$	$\frac{\sqrt{2}}{2}$	$\frac{1}{2}$	0
$\tan \varphi$	0	$\frac{\sqrt{3}}{3}$	1	$\sqrt{3}$	—

Basic identities among the trigonometric functions

The following identities hold for all φ for which the functions are defined:

- $\sin^2 \varphi + \cos^2 \varphi = 1$
- $\tan \varphi = \dfrac{\sin \varphi}{\cos \varphi}$
- $1 + \tan^2 \varphi = \dfrac{1}{\cos^2 \varphi}$

Geometry
MATHEMATICS   PHYSICS   ASTRONOMY   CHEMISTRY

Graphs

Sine curve

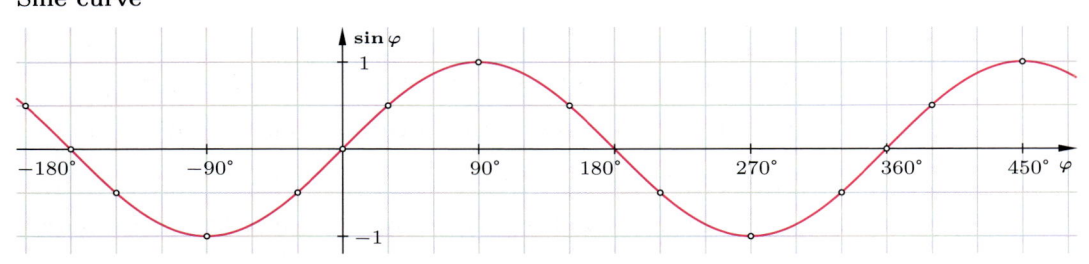

Cosine curve

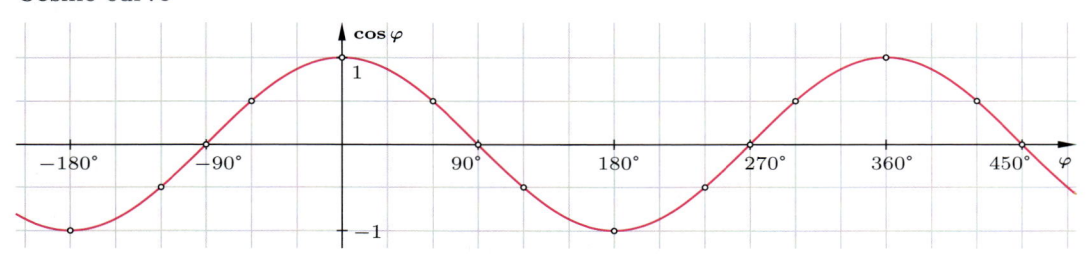

Tangent curve

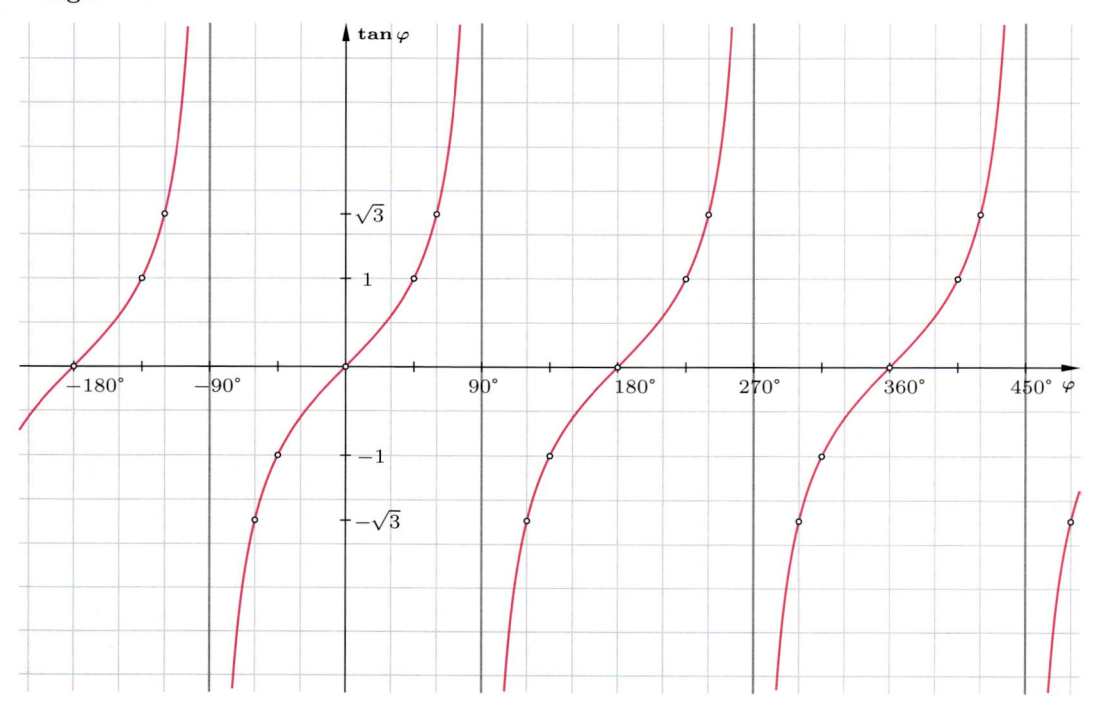

Geometry

MATHEMATICS   PHYSICS   ASTRONOMY   CHEMISTRY

Reduction formulae

(complementary angles, supplementary angles, symmetry and periodicity)

$90° - \alpha$	$\sin(90° - \alpha) = \cos \alpha$	$\cos(90° - \alpha) = \sin \alpha$	$\tan(90° - \alpha) = \dfrac{1}{\tan \alpha}$
$90° + \alpha$	$\sin(90° + \alpha) = \cos \alpha$	$\cos(90° + \alpha) = -\sin \alpha$	$\tan(90° + \alpha) = -\dfrac{1}{\tan \alpha}$
$180° - \alpha$	$\sin(180° - \alpha) = \sin \alpha$	$\cos(180° - \alpha) = -\cos \alpha$	$\tan(180° - \alpha) = -\tan \alpha$
$180° + \alpha$	$\sin(180° + \alpha) = -\sin \alpha$	$\cos(180° + \alpha) = -\cos \alpha$	$\tan(180° + \alpha) = \tan \alpha$
$360° - \alpha$	$\sin(360° - \alpha) = -\sin \alpha$	$\cos(360° - \alpha) = \cos \alpha$	$\tan(360° - \alpha) = -\tan \alpha$
$-\alpha$	$\sin(-\alpha) = -\sin \alpha$	$\cos(-\alpha) = \cos \alpha$	$\tan(-\alpha) = -\tan \alpha$
periodicity $k \in \mathbb{Z}$	$\sin(\alpha + k \cdot 360°) = \sin \alpha$	$\cos(\alpha + k \cdot 360°) = \cos \alpha$	$\tan(\alpha + k \cdot 180°) = \tan \alpha$

Addition formulae ($\alpha \pm \beta$, 2α, 3α, $\frac{\alpha}{2}$)

$$\sin(\alpha \pm \beta) = \sin \alpha \cos \beta \pm \cos \alpha \sin \beta \qquad\qquad \tan(\alpha \pm \beta) = \frac{\tan \alpha \pm \tan \beta}{1 \mp \tan \alpha \tan \beta}$$

$$\cos(\alpha \pm \beta) = \cos \alpha \cos \beta \mp \sin \alpha \sin \beta$$

$$\sin 2\alpha = 2 \sin \alpha \cos \alpha \qquad \begin{aligned}\cos 2\alpha &= \cos^2 \alpha - \sin^2 \alpha \\ &= 2\cos^2 \alpha - 1 \\ &= 1 - 2\sin^2 \alpha\end{aligned} \qquad \tan 2\alpha = \frac{2 \tan \alpha}{1 - \tan^2 \alpha}$$

$$\sin 3\alpha = 3 \sin \alpha - 4 \sin^3 \alpha \qquad \cos 3\alpha = 4 \cos^3 \alpha - 3 \cos \alpha \qquad \tan 3\alpha = \frac{3 \tan \alpha - \tan^3 \alpha}{1 - 3 \tan^2 \alpha}$$

$$\sin^2 \frac{\alpha}{2} = \frac{1 - \cos \alpha}{2} \qquad \cos^2 \frac{\alpha}{2} = \frac{1 + \cos \alpha}{2} \qquad \tan^2 \frac{\alpha}{2} = \frac{1 - \cos \alpha}{1 + \cos \alpha}$$

$$\tan \frac{\alpha}{2} = \frac{1 - \cos \alpha}{\sin \alpha} = \frac{\sin \alpha}{1 + \cos \alpha}$$

Sums and products of trigonometric functions

$$\sin \alpha + \sin \beta = 2 \sin \frac{\alpha + \beta}{2} \cos \frac{\alpha - \beta}{2}$$
$$\sin \alpha - \sin \beta = 2 \cos \frac{\alpha + \beta}{2} \sin \frac{\alpha - \beta}{2}$$
$$\cos \alpha + \cos \beta = 2 \cos \frac{\alpha + \beta}{2} \cos \frac{\alpha - \beta}{2}$$
$$\cos \alpha - \cos \beta = -2 \sin \frac{\alpha + \beta}{2} \sin \frac{\alpha - \beta}{2}$$

$$\sin \alpha \sin \beta = \frac{1}{2} \big[\cos(\alpha - \beta) - \cos(\alpha + \beta)\big]$$
$$\cos \alpha \cos \beta = \frac{1}{2} \big[\cos(\alpha - \beta) + \cos(\alpha + \beta)\big]$$
$$\sin \alpha \cos \beta = \frac{1}{2} \big[\sin(\alpha - \beta) + \sin(\alpha + \beta)\big]$$

Tangent half-angle substitution

For $\tan \dfrac{\alpha}{2} = t$:   • $\sin \alpha = \dfrac{2t}{1 + t^2}$ • $\cos \alpha = \dfrac{1 - t^2}{1 + t^2}$ • $\tan \alpha = \dfrac{2t}{1 - t^2}$

Geometry

5.4 Spherical trigonometry

Spherical triangles

The sides of a spherical triangle are great circles specified by the angles a, b, c (in degrees) which they subtend at the center of the sphere. The angles between the tangents to the great circles at the vertices are α, β, γ. All six angles are less than 180°.

Wherever the ↻ symbol appears, cyclic permutations yield additional, analogous relations.

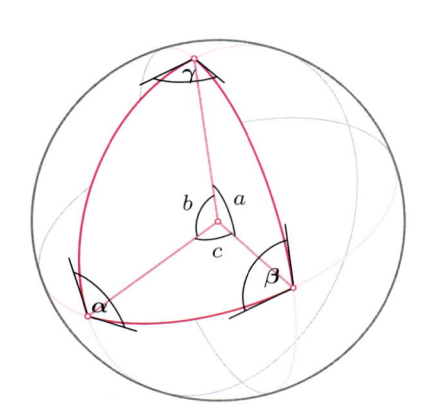

General properties

sum of sides, sum of angles	$0° < a + b + c < 360°$	$180° < \alpha + \beta + \gamma < 540°$
two sides, two angles	$a + b > c$	$\alpha + \beta < \gamma + 180°$ ↻
comparison of sides, angles	$\alpha < \beta \Leftrightarrow a < b$	
sine rule	$\dfrac{\sin \alpha}{\sin a} = \dfrac{\sin \beta}{\sin b} = \dfrac{\sin \gamma}{\sin c}$	
cosine rule for sides	$\cos a = \cos b \cdot \cos c + \sin b \cdot \sin c \cdot \cos \alpha$	↻
cosine rule for angles	$\cos \alpha = -\cos \beta \cdot \cos \gamma + \sin \beta \cdot \sin \gamma \cdot \cos a$	↻
sine-cosine rule	$\sin c \cdot \cos \alpha = \cos a \cdot \sin b - \sin a \cdot \cos b \cdot \cos \gamma$	↻
	$\sin c \cdot \cos \beta = \sin a \cdot \cos b - \cos a \cdot \sin b \cdot \cos \gamma$	↻
polar sine-cosine rule	$\sin \gamma \cdot \cos a = \cos \alpha \cdot \sin \beta + \sin \alpha \cdot \cos \beta \cdot \cos c$	↻
	$\sin \gamma \cdot \cos b = \sin \alpha \cdot \cos \beta + \cos \alpha \cdot \sin \beta \cdot \cos c$	↻

Area of a spherical triangle

spherical excess of a spherical triangle	$\varepsilon = \alpha + \beta + \gamma - 180°$
L'Huilier's theorem for the spherical excess	$\tan \dfrac{\varepsilon}{4} = \sqrt{\tan \dfrac{s}{2} \cdot \tan \dfrac{s-a}{2} \cdot \tan \dfrac{s-b}{2} \cdot \tan \dfrac{s-c}{2}}$, where $s = \dfrac{1}{2}(a + b + c)$
area	$S = \dfrac{\pi}{180°} \varepsilon r^2$, r is the radius of the sphere

Geometry

MATHEMATICS

5.5 Analytical geometry and vectors

In this section a Cartesian coordinate system is assumed.

Analytical geometry in the plane

Points and line segments

points A, B, ...	$A = (x_A, y_A)$, $B = (x_B, y_B)$, ...
distances between two points A and B	$d = \sqrt{(x_B - x_A)^2 + (y_B - y_A)^2}$
midpoint M of a line segment AB	$x_M = \dfrac{x_A + x_B}{2} \qquad y_M = \dfrac{y_A + y_B}{2}$
P divides AB in the ratio $\lambda \neq -1$	$x_P = \dfrac{x_A + \lambda x_B}{1 + \lambda} \qquad y_P = \dfrac{y_A + \lambda y_B}{1 + \lambda}$

p. 83 ◀ division of a line segment

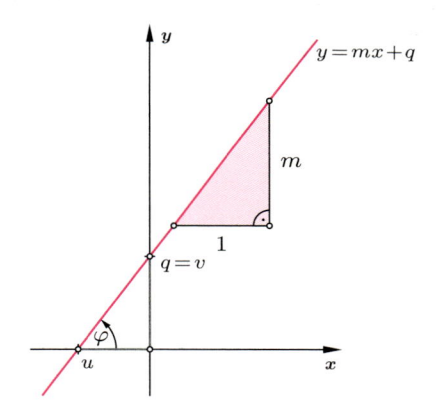

Lines

slope m and inclination φ	$m = \dfrac{y_B - y_A}{x_B - x_A} = \tan \varphi$
equation of the line	$ax + by + c = 0$
line equation in Hesse standard form	$\dfrac{ax + by + c}{\sqrt{a^2 + b^2}} = 0$
line equation in slope-intercept form	$y = mx + q$
line equation in point-slope form	$y - y_P = m(x - x_P)$
line equation in intercept form	$\dfrac{x}{u} + \dfrac{y}{v} = 1$
acute angle of intersection between lines with slopes m_1 and m_2	$\tan \varphi = \left| \dfrac{m_1 - m_2}{1 + m_1 m_2} \right|$

101

Geometry
MATHEMATICS PHYSICS ASTRONOMY CHEMISTRY

two lines with slopes m_1 and m_2 are perpendicular or parallel to one another	$m_1 m_2 = -1 \quad \text{or} \quad m_1 = m_2$
distance of a point P from the line $ax + by + c = 0$	$d = \left\| \dfrac{ax_P + by_P + c}{\sqrt{a^2 + b^2}} \right\|$

Circles

equation of a circle with centre M, radius r	$(x - x_M)^2 + (y - y_M)^2 = r^2$
general equation of a circle	$x^2 + y^2 + ax + by + c = 0$
tangent to the circle at the point P	$(x_P - x_M)(x - x_M) + (y_P - y_M)(y - y_M) = r^2$

Vectors in the plane and in three-dimensional space

vector	A vector is understood to be the set of all arrows which have the same length (magnitude), same direction and same orientation.
arrow (graphical representation of a vector)	An ordered pair of points in the plane or in space
position vector	A graphical representation in which the initial point is the origin of the coordinate system.

Graphical representation of position vectors in the plane

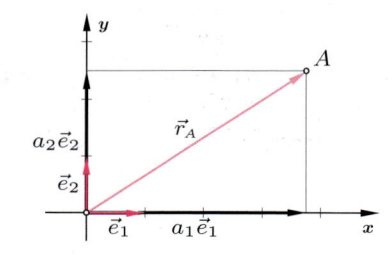

$$\vec{r}_A = a_1 \vec{e}_1 + a_2 \vec{e}_2 = \begin{pmatrix} a_1 \\ a_2 \end{pmatrix}$$

basis vectors

$$\vec{e}_1 = \begin{pmatrix} 1 \\ 0 \end{pmatrix}, \quad \vec{e}_2 = \begin{pmatrix} 0 \\ 1 \end{pmatrix}$$

Graphical representation of position vectors in three-dimensional space

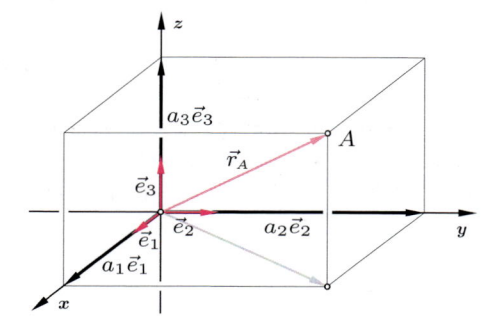

$$\vec{r}_A = a_1 \vec{e}_1 + a_2 \vec{e}_2 + a_3 \vec{e}_3 = \begin{pmatrix} a_1 \\ a_2 \\ a_3 \end{pmatrix}$$

basis vectors

$$\vec{e}_1 = \begin{pmatrix} 1 \\ 0 \\ 0 \end{pmatrix}, \quad \vec{e}_2 = \begin{pmatrix} 0 \\ 1 \\ 0 \end{pmatrix}, \quad \vec{e}_3 = \begin{pmatrix} 0 \\ 0 \\ 1 \end{pmatrix}$$

Geometry
MATHEMATICS   PHYSICS   ASTRONOMY   CHEMISTRY

With the exception of the vector product and triple products, all of the operations below are defined analogously for vectors in the plane.

Sum and difference

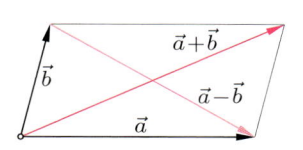

$$\vec{a} \pm \vec{b} = \begin{pmatrix} a_1 \\ a_2 \\ a_3 \end{pmatrix} \pm \begin{pmatrix} b_1 \\ b_2 \\ b_3 \end{pmatrix} = \begin{pmatrix} a_1 \pm b_1 \\ a_2 \pm b_2 \\ a_3 \pm b_3 \end{pmatrix}$$

$$\vec{a} - \vec{a} = \begin{pmatrix} 0 \\ 0 \\ 0 \end{pmatrix} = \vec{0} \quad \text{(null vector)}$$

Scalar multiple

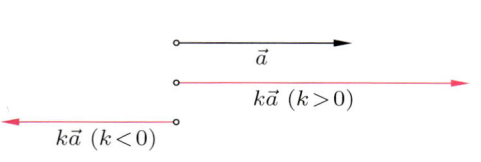

$$k\vec{a} = k\begin{pmatrix} a_1 \\ a_2 \\ a_3 \end{pmatrix} = \begin{pmatrix} ka_1 \\ ka_2 \\ ka_3 \end{pmatrix}, \quad k \in \mathbb{R}$$

$$0\vec{a} = \vec{0}, \quad (-1)\vec{a} = -\vec{a} \quad \text{(opposite vector)}$$

Vector relationships

collinear vectors — Two vectors $\vec{a}$ and $\vec{b}$ are said to be collinear (linearly dependent) if they are both parallel to a common line.

coplanar vectors — Three vectors $\vec{a}, \vec{b}$ and $\vec{c}$ are said to be coplanar (linearly dependent) if they are all parallel to a common plane.

decomposition with respect to two non-collinear vectors — If $\vec{a}$ and $\vec{b}$ are two non-collinear vectors, every vector $\vec{c}$ which is coplanar with $\vec{a}$ and $\vec{b}$ can be expressed uniquely as the sum of two vectors parallel to $\vec{a}$ and $\vec{b}$ respectively, i.e. as the linear combination:
$\vec{c} = x\vec{a} + y\vec{b}$

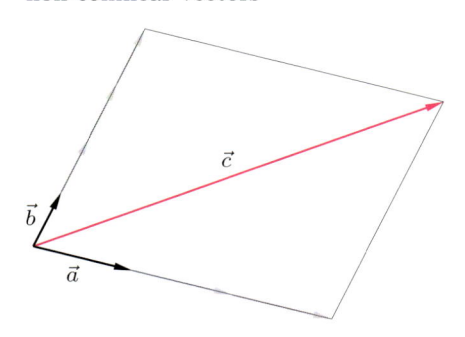

The two vectors $x\vec{a}$ and $y\vec{b}$ are called the vector components of $\vec{c}$; the two numbers x and y are called the scalar components of $\vec{c}$.

decomposition with respect to three non-coplanar vectors — If $\vec{a}, \vec{b}$ and $\vec{c}$ are three non-coplanar vectors, an arbitrary vector can be expressed uniquely as the sum of three vectors parallel to $\vec{a}, \vec{b}$ and $\vec{c}$,
i.e. as the linear combination:
$\vec{d} = x\vec{a} + y\vec{b} + z\vec{c}$

Geometry

Magnitude (norm)

length of $\vec{a}$

$$|\vec{a}| = a = \left|\begin{pmatrix} a_1 \\ a_2 \\ a_3 \end{pmatrix}\right| = \sqrt{a_1^2 + a_2^2 + a_3^2}$$

$$|k\vec{a}| = |k||\vec{a}|, \quad k \in \mathbb{R}$$

triangle inequality

$$|\vec{a} + \vec{b}| \leqslant |\vec{a}| + |\vec{b}|$$

Scalar product (dot product, inner product)

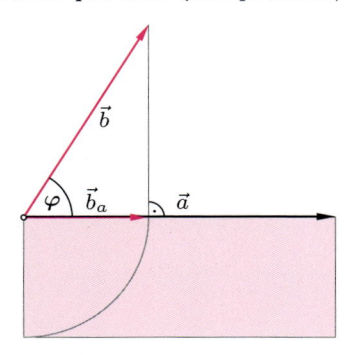

$$\vec{a} \cdot \vec{b} = |\vec{a}||\vec{b}| \cos \varphi$$

$$\vec{a} \cdot \vec{b} = \begin{pmatrix} a_1 \\ a_2 \\ a_3 \end{pmatrix} \cdot \begin{pmatrix} b_1 \\ b_2 \\ b_3 \end{pmatrix} = a_1 b_1 + a_2 b_2 + a_3 b_3$$

$$\vec{a} \cdot \vec{b} = 0 \iff \varphi = 90°, \text{ if } |\vec{a}| \neq 0, |\vec{b}| \neq 0$$

sign of the scalar product:

$$\vec{a} \cdot \vec{b} = \begin{cases} |\vec{a}||\vec{b}_a|, & \text{if } \varphi \text{ acute} \\ -|\vec{a}||\vec{b}_a|, & \text{if } \varphi \text{ obtuse} \\ 0, & \text{if } \varphi = 90° \end{cases}$$

algebraic properties

$$\vec{a} \cdot \vec{b} = \vec{b} \cdot \vec{a}$$

$$\vec{a} \cdot (\vec{b} + \vec{c}) = \vec{a} \cdot \vec{b} + \vec{a} \cdot \vec{c}$$

$$(k\vec{a}) \cdot \vec{b} = k(\vec{a} \cdot \vec{b}), \quad k \in \mathbb{R}$$

CAUCHY-SCHWARZ inequality

$$(\vec{a} \cdot \vec{b})^2 \leqslant \vec{a}^2 \vec{b}^2$$

vector projection of $\vec{b}$ on $\vec{a}$

$$\vec{b}_a = \frac{\vec{a} \cdot \vec{b}}{\vec{a} \cdot \vec{a}} \vec{a} = \frac{\vec{a} \cdot \vec{b}}{a^2} \vec{a}$$

Vector product (cross product)

$$\vec{a} \times \vec{b} = \begin{pmatrix} a_1 \\ a_2 \\ a_3 \end{pmatrix} \times \begin{pmatrix} b_1 \\ b_2 \\ b_3 \end{pmatrix} = \begin{pmatrix} \left|\begin{matrix} a_2 & b_2 \\ a_3 & b_3 \end{matrix}\right| \\ -\left|\begin{matrix} a_1 & b_1 \\ a_3 & b_3 \end{matrix}\right| \\ \left|\begin{matrix} a_1 & b_1 \\ a_2 & b_2 \end{matrix}\right| \end{pmatrix} = \begin{pmatrix} a_2 b_3 - a_3 b_2 \\ a_3 b_1 - a_1 b_3 \\ a_1 b_2 - a_2 b_1 \end{pmatrix}$$

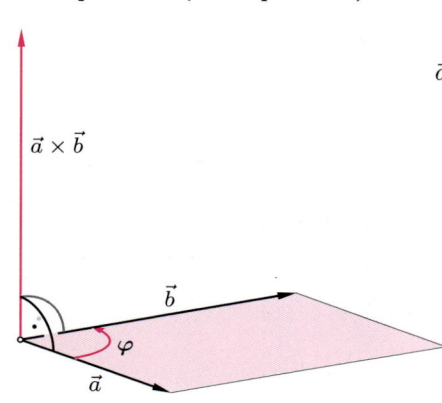

$\vec{a} \times \vec{b}$ is defined uniquely by the following criteria:

- $\vec{a} \times \vec{b}$ is perpendicular to both $\vec{a}$ and $\vec{b}$.
- $|\vec{a} \times \vec{b}|$ is equal to the area of the parallelogram spanned by $\vec{a}$ and $\vec{b}$:
  $|\vec{a} \times \vec{b}| = |\vec{a}||\vec{b}| \sin \varphi, \quad 0° \leqslant \varphi \leqslant 180°$
- $\vec{a}, \vec{b}$ and $\vec{a} \times \vec{b}$ form a right-handed system.

Geometry

MATHEMATICS

right-handed system

The non-coplanar vectors $\vec{a}$, $\vec{b}$ and $\vec{c}$ with a common initial point form a right-handed system in the specified order if, as viewed from the end point of $\vec{c}$, $\vec{a}$ can be rotated into the direction of $\vec{b}$ by less than 180° anticlockwise.

geometric and algebraic properties

$\vec{a} \times \vec{b} = \vec{0} \iff \vec{a}, \vec{b}$ are collinear

$\vec{a} \times \vec{b} = -(\vec{b} \times \vec{a})$

$\vec{a} \times (\vec{b} + \vec{c}) = (\vec{a} \times \vec{b}) + (\vec{a} \times \vec{c})$

$(k\vec{a}) \times \vec{b} = k(\vec{a} \times \vec{b}) = \vec{a} \times (k\vec{b}), \ k \in \mathbb{R}$

vector triple product

$\vec{a} \times (\vec{b} \times \vec{c}) = (\vec{a} \cdot \vec{c})\vec{b} - (\vec{a} \cdot \vec{b})\vec{c}$

BINET-CAUCHY identity

$(\vec{a} \times \vec{b}) \cdot (\vec{c} \times \vec{d}) = (\vec{a} \cdot \vec{c})(\vec{b} \cdot \vec{d}) - (\vec{b} \cdot \vec{c})(\vec{a} \cdot \vec{d})$

special case: LAGRANGE's identity

$(\vec{a} \times \vec{b})^2 = \vec{a}^2 \vec{b}^2 - (\vec{a} \cdot \vec{b})^2$

Scalar triple product

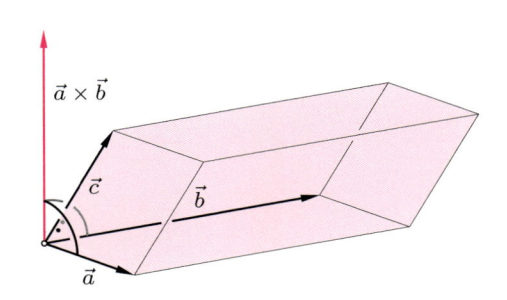

p. 31 ◀ evaluating determinants

$[\vec{a}, \vec{b}, \vec{c}] = (\vec{a} \times \vec{b}) \cdot \vec{c} = \begin{vmatrix} a_1 & b_1 & c_1 \\ a_2 & b_2 & c_2 \\ a_3 & b_3 & c_3 \end{vmatrix}$

geometric interpretation

$|[\vec{a}, \vec{b}, \vec{c}]|$: volume of the parallelepiped spanned by $\vec{a}, \vec{b}, \vec{c}$

$[\vec{a}, \vec{b}, \vec{c}] > 0 \iff \vec{a}, \vec{b}, \vec{c}$ form a right-handed system

$[\vec{a}, \vec{b}, \vec{c}] = 0 \iff \vec{a}, \vec{b}, \vec{c}$ are coplanar

$[\vec{a}, \vec{b}, \vec{c}] < 0 \iff \vec{a}, \vec{b}, \vec{c}$ form a left-handed system

algebraic properties

$[\vec{a}, \vec{b}, \vec{c}] = [\vec{b}, \vec{c}, \vec{a}] = [\vec{c}, \vec{a}, \vec{b}]$

$[\vec{a}, \vec{b}, \vec{c}] = -[\vec{a}, \vec{c}, \vec{b}] = -[\vec{b}, \vec{a}, \vec{c}] = -[\vec{c}, \vec{b}, \vec{a}]$

$[(\vec{a}+\vec{b}), \vec{c}, \vec{d}] = [\vec{a}, \vec{c}, \vec{d}] + [\vec{b}, \vec{c}, \vec{d}]$

$[(k\vec{a}), \vec{b}, \vec{c}] = k[\vec{a}, \vec{b}, \vec{c}], \ k \in \mathbb{R}$

$[\vec{a}, \vec{b}, \vec{c}] = [\vec{a}, \vec{b}, \vec{c} + k\vec{a}], \ k \in \mathbb{R}$

Geometry

MATHEMATICS PHYSICS ASTRONOMY CHEMISTRY

Analytical geometry in three-dimensional space

Special vectors and points

position vector at point $A = (x_A, y_A, z_A)$	$\vec{r}_A = \begin{pmatrix} x_A \\ y_A \\ z_A \end{pmatrix}$
displacement vector from A to B	$\overrightarrow{AB} = \vec{r}_B - \vec{r}_A$
unit vector in the direction of $\vec{a}$	$\vec{e}_a = \dfrac{1}{|\vec{a}|}\vec{a} = \dfrac{\vec{a}}{a} = \dfrac{1}{\sqrt{a_1^2 + a_2^2 + a_3^2}}\begin{pmatrix} a_1 \\ a_2 \\ a_3 \end{pmatrix}$
midpoint M of the line segment AB	$\vec{r}_M = \dfrac{1}{2}(\vec{r}_A + \vec{r}_B)$
centre of mass S of the triangle ABC	$\vec{r}_S = \dfrac{1}{3}(\vec{r}_A + \vec{r}_B + \vec{r}_C)$
centre of mass S of the tetrahedron $ABCD$	$\vec{r}_S = \dfrac{1}{4}(\vec{r}_A + \vec{r}_B + \vec{r}_C + \vec{r}_D)$

Areas and volumes

area A of the parallelogram or triangle spanned by $\vec{a}$ and $\vec{b}$	$A = |\vec{a} \times \vec{b}|$ or $A = \dfrac{1}{2}|\vec{a} \times \vec{b}|$
volume V of the parallelepiped or tetrahedron spanned by $\vec{a}$, $\vec{b}$ and $\vec{c}$	$V = |[\vec{a}, \vec{b}, \vec{c}]|$ or $V = \dfrac{1}{6}|[\vec{a}, \vec{b}, \vec{c}]|$

Lines and planes

parameter representation of the line through A with direction vector $\vec{v}$	$\vec{r}(t) = \vec{r}_A + t\vec{v}, \ t \in \mathbb{R}$
parameter representation of the line through two points A and B	$\vec{r}(t) = \vec{r}_A + t(\vec{r}_B - \vec{r}_A), \ t \in \mathbb{R}$
parameter representation of the plane through A with direction vectors $\vec{u}$ and $\vec{v}$	$\vec{r}(t, s) = \vec{r}_A + s\vec{u} + t\vec{v}, \ s, t \in \mathbb{R}$
plane through A perpendicular to $\vec{n}$ (normal vector)	$\vec{n} \cdot (\vec{r} - \vec{r}_A) = 0$
coordinate equation of the plane	$ax + by + cz + d = 0$
Hesse normal form of the equation of the plane	$\dfrac{ax + by + cz + d}{\sqrt{a^2 + b^2 + c^2}} = 0$
intercept form of the equation of the plane with intercepts $X = (u, 0, 0),\ Y = (0, v, 0),\ Z = (0, 0, w)$	$\dfrac{x}{u} + \dfrac{y}{v} + \dfrac{z}{w} = 1$

Geometry

MATHEMATICS   PHYSICS   ASTRONOMY   CHEMISTRY

Circles and spheres

equation of the circle or sphere with centre M and radius ϱ	$(\vec{r} - \vec{r}_M)^2 = \varrho^2$
tangent at the point Q on the circle or tangent plane at the point Q on the sphere	$(\vec{r}_Q - \vec{r}_M) \cdot (\vec{r} - \vec{r}_M) = \varrho^2$
polar line or polar plane of a pole Q ($Q \neq M$)	$(\vec{r}_Q - \vec{r}_M) \cdot (\vec{r} - \vec{r}_M) = \varrho^2$
power q of the point Q	$q = (\vec{r}_Q - \vec{r}_M)^2 - \varrho^2$

Angles

two vectors $\vec{a} \neq \vec{0}$ and $\vec{b} \neq \vec{0}$ are perpendicular (orthogonal) or parallel to one another	$\vec{a} \cdot \vec{b} = 0 \quad \text{or} \quad \vec{a} = k\vec{b}, \ k \in \mathbb{R} \setminus \{0\}$
angle φ between vectors $\vec{a}$ and $\vec{b}$	$\cos\varphi = \dfrac{\vec{a} \cdot \vec{b}}{a\,b}$ or $\cos\varphi = \vec{e}_a \cdot \vec{e}_b = \dfrac{\vec{a} \cdot \vec{b}}{|\vec{a}||\vec{b}|}$ p. 106 ◀ $\vec{e}_a$
acute angle of intersection between planes with normal vectors $\vec{n}_1$ and $\vec{n}_2$	$\cos\varphi = \dfrac{|\vec{n}_1 \cdot \vec{n}_2|}{n_1 n_2}$
acute angle of intersection between a line and a plane	$\sin\varphi = \dfrac{|\vec{n} \cdot \vec{v}|}{n\,v}$, $\vec{v}$ and $\vec{n}$ are the direction vector and normal vector respectively

Projections

vector component of $\vec{a}$ in the direction of $\vec{b}$ or orthogonal projection of $\vec{a}$ onto $\vec{b}$	$\vec{a}_b = \dfrac{\vec{a} \cdot \vec{b}}{b^2} \vec{b} = (\vec{a} \cdot \vec{e}_b)\vec{e}_b$
scalar component of $\vec{a}$ in the direction of $\vec{b}$	$\dfrac{\vec{a} \cdot \vec{b}}{b} = \vec{a} \cdot \vec{e}_b, \ |\vec{a} \cdot \vec{e}_b| = |\vec{a}_b|$
component of $\vec{a}$ perpendicular to $\vec{b}$	$\vec{a}_b^{\perp} = \dfrac{(\vec{b} \times \vec{a}) \times \vec{b}}{b^2} = (\vec{e}_b \times \vec{a}) \times \vec{e}_b$
orthogonal decomposition of $\vec{a}$ with respect to the direction of $\vec{b}$	$\vec{a} = \vec{a}_b + \vec{a}_b^{\perp}$

Distances

distance between two points A and B	$d(A,B) = |\overrightarrow{AB}| = |\vec{r}_B - \vec{r}_A|$
distance between the point P and the line g: $\vec{r}(t) = \vec{r}_A + t \cdot \vec{v}$	$d(P,g) = \dfrac{|\overrightarrow{AP} \times \vec{v}|}{v} = |\overrightarrow{AP} \times \vec{e}_v|$

Geometry

MATHEMATICS   PHYSICS   ASTRONOMY   CHEMISTRY

distance between two parallel lines
$g_1\colon \vec{r}(t) = \vec{r}_A + t\vec{v}$ and $g_2\colon \vec{r}(s) = \vec{r}_B + s\vec{v}$

$$d(g_1, g_2) = \frac{|\overrightarrow{AB} \times \vec{v}|}{v} = |\overrightarrow{AB} \times \vec{e}_v|$$

distance between the point P and the plane
$\varepsilon\colon \vec{n} \cdot (\vec{r} - \vec{r}_A) = 0$

$$d(P, \varepsilon) = \frac{|\overrightarrow{AP} \cdot \vec{n}|}{n} = |\overrightarrow{AP} \cdot \vec{e}_n|$$

distance between two parallel planes
$\varepsilon_1\colon \vec{n} \cdot (\vec{r} - \vec{r}_A) = 0$ and $\varepsilon_2\colon \vec{n} \cdot (\vec{r} - \vec{r}_B) = 0$

$$d(\varepsilon_1, \varepsilon_2) = \frac{|\overrightarrow{AB} \cdot \vec{n}|}{n} = |\overrightarrow{AB} \cdot \vec{e}_n|$$

distance between two skew lines
$g_1\colon \vec{r}(t) = \vec{r}_A + t\vec{u}$ and $g_2\colon \vec{r}(s) = \vec{r}_B + s\vec{v}$

$$d(g_1, g_2) = \frac{|\overrightarrow{AB} \cdot \vec{n}|}{n} = |\overrightarrow{AB} \cdot \vec{e}_n|$$
where $\vec{n} = \vec{u} \times \vec{v}$

GRAM-SCHMIDT orthogonalization procedure

Given any set of three linearly independent vectors $\vec{b}_1, \vec{b}_2, \vec{b}_3$, using the procedure opposite, three vectors $\vec{d}_1, \vec{d}_2, \vec{d}_3$ can be defined such that they are pairwise perpendicular to one another.

$$\vec{d}_1 = \vec{b}_1$$

$$\vec{d}_2 = \vec{b}_2 - \frac{\vec{b}_2 \cdot \vec{d}_1}{\vec{d}_1 \cdot \vec{d}_1} \cdot \vec{d}_1$$

$$\vec{d}_3 = \vec{b}_3 - \frac{\vec{b}_3 \cdot \vec{d}_1}{\vec{d}_1 \cdot \vec{d}_1} \cdot \vec{d}_1 - \frac{\vec{b}_3 \cdot \vec{d}_2}{\vec{d}_2 \cdot \vec{d}_2} \cdot \vec{d}_2$$

Conic sections

Definition as second-order curves

Any curve in $\mathbb{R}^2$ described by a quadratic equation in x and y of the form

$$ax^2 + 2bxy + cy^2 + 2dx + 2ey + f = 0, \quad (a, b, c) \neq (0, 0, 0)$$

is defined as a conic section. They can be classified as follows:

criterion	case	possible curve
$ac - b^2 > 0$	elliptic	ellipse (circle), point, empty set
$ac - b^2 = 0$	parabolic	parabola, pair of parallel lines, line
$ac - b^2 < 0$	hyperbolic	hyperbola, pair of intersecting lines

The equation of a conic section can be simplified if one chooses the coordinate system such that the coordinate axes correspond to the symmetry axes of the curve.

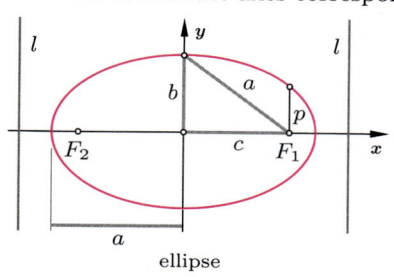

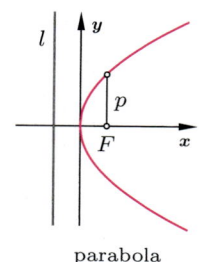

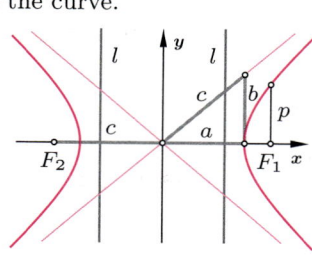

ellipse   parabola   hyperbola

Geometry

MATHEMATICS   PHYSICS   ASTRONOMY   CHEMISTRY

Analytical properties

	ellipse	parabola	hyperbola
linear eccentricity c	$c^2 = a^2 - b^2$		$c^2 = a^2 + b^2$
eccentricity ε	$\varepsilon = \dfrac{c}{a} < 1$	$\varepsilon = 1$	$\varepsilon = \dfrac{c}{a} > 1$
focal parameter p	$p = \dfrac{b^2}{a}$	p	$p = \dfrac{b^2}{a}$
area	$A = \pi a b$		
equation	$\dfrac{x^2}{a^2} + \dfrac{y^2}{b^2} = 1$	$y^2 = 2px$	$\dfrac{x^2}{a^2} - \dfrac{y^2}{b^2} = 1$
tangent at point P on the curve	$\dfrac{x_P x}{a^2} + \dfrac{y_P y}{b^2} = 1$	$y_P y = p(x + x_P)$	$\dfrac{x_P x}{a^2} - \dfrac{y_P y}{b^2} = 1$
asymptotes			$y = \pm \dfrac{b}{a} x$
foci	$F_1 = (c, 0)$ $F_2 = (-c, 0)$	$F = \left(\dfrac{p}{2}, 0\right)$	$F_1 = (c, 0)$ $F_2 = (-c, 0)$
directrices	$x = \pm \dfrac{a^2}{c}$	$x = -\dfrac{p}{2}$	$x = \pm \dfrac{a^2}{c}$
parametric representation	$x(t) = a \cos t$ $y(t) = b \sin t$		$x(t) = \pm a \cosh t$ $y(t) = b \sinh t$
vertex equations	$y^2 = 2px - \dfrac{p}{a} x^2$	$y^2 = 2px$	$y^2 = 2px + \dfrac{p}{a} x^2$

vertex equation (all three cases)	$y^2 = 2px - (1 - \varepsilon^2) x^2$
equation in polar coordinates with the origin at one focus and the polar axis through the nearer vertex	$r = \dfrac{p}{1 + \varepsilon \cos \varphi}$

Definition in terms of directrices

Let a point F (focus) and a line l (directrix) be given. A conic section is the locus of all points the ratio of whose respective distances from F and l is ε.

The resulting curve is

- an ellipse, if $\varepsilon < 1$
- a parabola, if $\varepsilon = 1$
- a hyperbola, if $\varepsilon > 1$

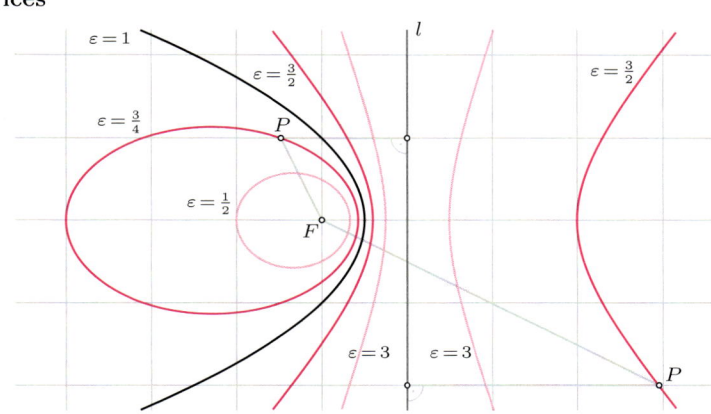

Geometry

Definition in terms of foci

Let either two foci F_1 and F_2 or a focus F and a directrix l be given. A conic section is the locus of all points satisfying the distance relations indicated below:

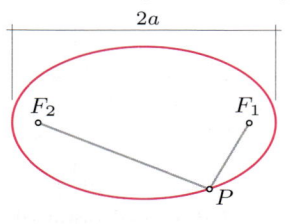

$\overline{PF_1} + \overline{PF_2} = 2a$
ellipse

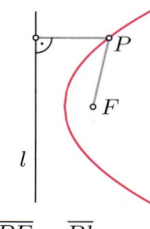

$\overline{PF} = \overline{Pl}$
parabola

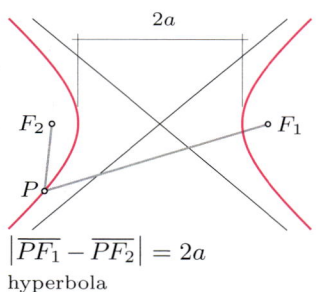

$|\overline{PF_1} - \overline{PF_2}| = 2a$
hyperbola

Definition as conic sections

Let a double right circular cone K with aperture 2α and a plane E intersecting the axis of K away from its vertex at an angle β be given. The angle between the axis and a generatrix of K is α. The curve resulting from the intersection of K and E is

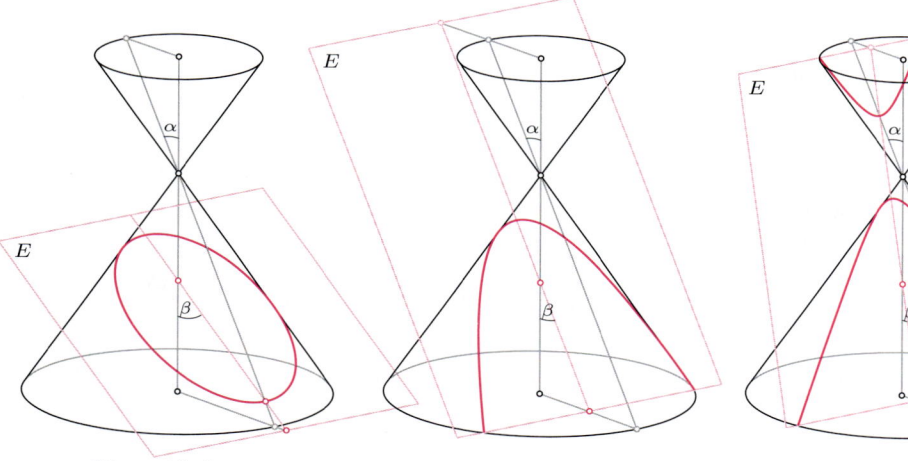

- an ellipse, if $\beta > \alpha$
- a parabola, if $\beta = \alpha$
- a hyperbola, if $\beta < \alpha$

The eccentricity is given by

$$\varepsilon = \frac{\cos \beta}{\cos \alpha}$$

A DANDELIN sphere is tangent to both the plane E and the interior of the cone K. Each sphere touches K in a circle and E at a focus F of the conic section, and the intersection of the tangent circle with E is the directrix l associated with that focus.

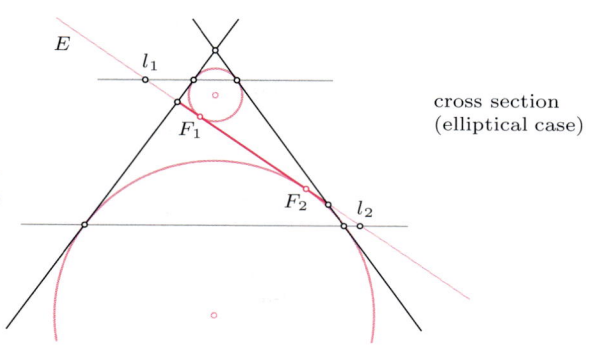

cross section
(elliptical case)

5.6 Affine maps

Affine transformations in the plane

An affinity or affine transformation is an invertible transformation of the plane which preserves straight lines – i.e. the image of a line is itself a line. It can be specified in terms of two arbitrary triangles, in which the second is the image of the first. The special cases in which the two triangles are similar or congruent correspond to a similarity transformation or isometry respectively. The set of each of the three types of transformation forms a group. Quantities and geometric objects which remain unchanged by a transformation are called invariants. A point P which remains unchanged by a transformation is called a fixed point of the transformation.

Invariants

affine transformation	similarity transformation	isometry
lines, line segments		
ellipses, hyperbolas, parabolas	*in addition:*	*in addition:*
parallelism		
division ratios of points on line segments	circles	line segment lengths
length ratios of parallel line segments	angles	areas
area ratio of two figures		

Matrix representation p. 27 ◀ Linear algebra

The points in the plane are specified below by their position vectors $\vec{x}$.
Every affine transformation is of the form

$$\vec{x} \mapsto \vec{x}' = A\vec{x} + \vec{v} \quad \text{or} \quad \begin{pmatrix}x\\y\end{pmatrix} \mapsto \begin{pmatrix}x'\\y'\end{pmatrix} = \begin{pmatrix}a_1 & b_1\\a_2 & b_2\end{pmatrix}\begin{pmatrix}x\\y\end{pmatrix} + \begin{pmatrix}v_1\\v_2\end{pmatrix}$$

where $\det A \neq 0$. In the case of isometries, for an appropriate value of φ the matrix takes the form

$$A = \begin{pmatrix}\cos\varphi & -\sin\varphi\\ \sin\varphi & \cos\varphi\end{pmatrix} \quad \text{or} \quad A = \begin{pmatrix}\cos\varphi & \sin\varphi\\ \sin\varphi & -\cos\varphi\end{pmatrix}$$

The former describes a rotation by an angle φ about the origin, the latter the same rotation preceded by reflection about the x-axis. In general $\det A = \pm 1$. In the case of similarity transformations, A is a scalar multiple of the matrix for an isometry.

Special affine transformations

affinity with all points on the x-axis fixed
$$\begin{pmatrix}x'\\y'\end{pmatrix} = \begin{pmatrix}1 & b_1\\0 & b_2\end{pmatrix}\begin{pmatrix}x\\y\end{pmatrix}$$

affinity perpendicular to the x-axis
$$\begin{pmatrix}x'\\y'\end{pmatrix} = \begin{pmatrix}1 & 0\\0 & b_2\end{pmatrix}\begin{pmatrix}x\\y\end{pmatrix}$$

affinity parallel to the (fixed) x-axis
(shear parallel to the x-axis)
$$\begin{pmatrix}x'\\y'\end{pmatrix} = \begin{pmatrix}1 & b_1\\0 & 1\end{pmatrix}\begin{pmatrix}x\\y\end{pmatrix}$$

Geometry

MATHEMATICS   PHYSICS   ASTRONOMY   CHEMISTRY

Special similarity transformations

homogeneous dilation with centre $\begin{pmatrix} 0 \\ 0 \end{pmatrix}$ and factor k
$$\begin{pmatrix} x' \\ y' \end{pmatrix} = \begin{pmatrix} k & 0 \\ 0 & k \end{pmatrix} \begin{pmatrix} x \\ y \end{pmatrix}$$

homogeneous dilation with centre $\begin{pmatrix} z_1 \\ z_2 \end{pmatrix}$ and factor k
$$\begin{pmatrix} x' \\ y' \end{pmatrix} = \begin{pmatrix} k & 0 \\ 0 & k \end{pmatrix} \begin{pmatrix} x \\ y \end{pmatrix} + (1-k) \begin{pmatrix} z_1 \\ z_2 \end{pmatrix}$$

Special isometries

translation by the vector $\begin{pmatrix} v_1 \\ v_2 \end{pmatrix}$
$$\begin{pmatrix} x' \\ y' \end{pmatrix} = \begin{pmatrix} x \\ y \end{pmatrix} + \begin{pmatrix} v_1 \\ v_2 \end{pmatrix}$$

reflection about the line $y = x \cdot \tan \varphi$
$$\begin{pmatrix} x' \\ y' \end{pmatrix} = \begin{pmatrix} \cos 2\varphi & \sin 2\varphi \\ \sin 2\varphi & -\cos 2\varphi \end{pmatrix} \begin{pmatrix} x \\ y \end{pmatrix}$$

rotation about $(0,0)$ by the angle θ
$$\begin{pmatrix} x' \\ y' \end{pmatrix} = \begin{pmatrix} \cos \theta & -\sin \theta \\ \sin \theta & \cos \theta \end{pmatrix} \begin{pmatrix} x \\ y \end{pmatrix}$$

Affine transformations in space

Consider a rotation about the origin in space. A positive rotation angle corresponds to an anticlockwise rotation as viewed towards the origin from the end point of the vector defining the rotation axis.

rotation about $\vec{e}_1$ (x-axis) by the angle θ
$$\begin{pmatrix} x' \\ y' \\ z' \end{pmatrix} = \begin{pmatrix} 1 & 0 & 0 \\ 0 & \cos \theta & -\sin \theta \\ 0 & \sin \theta & \cos \theta \end{pmatrix} \begin{pmatrix} x \\ y \\ z \end{pmatrix}$$

rotation about $\vec{e}_2$ (y-axis) by the angle θ
$$\begin{pmatrix} x' \\ y' \\ z' \end{pmatrix} = \begin{pmatrix} \cos \theta & 0 & \sin \theta \\ 0 & 1 & 0 \\ -\sin \theta & 0 & \cos \theta \end{pmatrix} \begin{pmatrix} x \\ y \\ z \end{pmatrix}$$

rotation about $\vec{e}_3$ (z-axis) by the angle θ
$$\begin{pmatrix} x' \\ y' \\ z' \end{pmatrix} = \begin{pmatrix} \cos \theta & -\sin \theta & 0 \\ \sin \theta & \cos \theta & 0 \\ 0 & 0 & 1 \end{pmatrix} \begin{pmatrix} x \\ y \\ z \end{pmatrix}$$

rotation matrix for a rotation about the axis through the origin with unit vector $\vec{v}$ by the angle θ

$$\begin{pmatrix} \cos \theta + v_1^2(1-\cos \theta) & v_1 v_2 (1-\cos \theta) - v_3 \sin \theta & v_1 v_3 (1-\cos \theta) + v_2 \sin \theta \\ v_1 v_2 (1-\cos \theta) + v_3 \sin \theta & \cos \theta + v_2^2(1-\cos \theta) & v_2 v_3 (1-\cos \theta) - v_1 \sin \theta \\ v_1 v_3 (1-\cos \theta) - v_2 \sin \theta & v_2 v_3 (1-\cos \theta) + v_1 \sin \theta & \cos \theta + v_3^2(1-\cos \theta) \end{pmatrix}$$

In vector notation, $\vec{r}_P$ is transformed to the vector
$$\vec{r}_P{}' = (\vec{v} \cdot \vec{r}_P)(1-\cos \theta) \vec{v} + (\cos \theta) \vec{r}_P + (\sin \theta)(\vec{v} \times \vec{r}_P)$$

orthogonal projection onto the yz-plane
$$\begin{pmatrix} x' \\ y' \\ z' \end{pmatrix} = \begin{pmatrix} 0 & 0 & 0 \\ 0 & 1 & 0 \\ 0 & 0 & 1 \end{pmatrix} \begin{pmatrix} x \\ y \\ z \end{pmatrix}$$

Geometry
MATHEMATICS

orthogonal projection onto the xz-plane
$$\begin{pmatrix} x' \\ y' \\ z' \end{pmatrix} = \begin{pmatrix} 1 & 0 & 0 \\ 0 & 0 & 0 \\ 0 & 0 & 1 \end{pmatrix} \begin{pmatrix} x \\ y \\ z \end{pmatrix}$$

orthogonal projection onto the xy-plane
$$\begin{pmatrix} x' \\ y' \\ z' \end{pmatrix} = \begin{pmatrix} 1 & 0 & 0 \\ 0 & 1 & 0 \\ 0 & 0 & 0 \end{pmatrix} \begin{pmatrix} x \\ y \\ z \end{pmatrix}$$

p. 29 ◀ composition of transformations

5.7 Coordinate transformations

Transformations in the plane

Cartesian coordinates $(x, y) \leftrightarrow$ Cartesian coordinates (x', y')

Given two Cartesian coordinate systems in the plane, it is often necessary to transform the coordinates (x, y) of P with respect to one coordinate system into the corresponding coordinates (x', y') with respect to the other, and vice versa. This type of transformation is called a coordinate transformation.

In the plane it is sufficient to consider two types: the new coordinate may result from

- translation of the original coordinate system by $\vec{a} = \begin{pmatrix} a_1 \\ a_2 \end{pmatrix}$

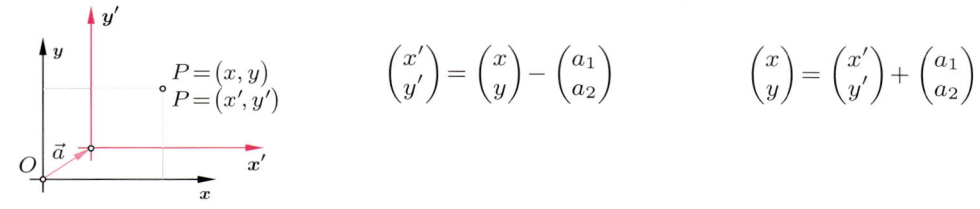

$$\begin{pmatrix} x' \\ y' \end{pmatrix} = \begin{pmatrix} x \\ y \end{pmatrix} - \begin{pmatrix} a_1 \\ a_2 \end{pmatrix} \qquad \begin{pmatrix} x \\ y \end{pmatrix} = \begin{pmatrix} x' \\ y' \end{pmatrix} + \begin{pmatrix} a_1 \\ a_2 \end{pmatrix}$$

- rotation of the original coordinate system about the origin by the angle θ

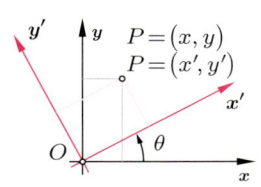

$$\begin{pmatrix} x' \\ y' \end{pmatrix} = \begin{pmatrix} \cos\theta & \sin\theta \\ -\sin\theta & \cos\theta \end{pmatrix} \begin{pmatrix} x \\ y \end{pmatrix} \qquad \begin{pmatrix} x \\ y \end{pmatrix} = \begin{pmatrix} \cos\theta & -\sin\theta \\ \sin\theta & \cos\theta \end{pmatrix} \begin{pmatrix} x' \\ y' \end{pmatrix}$$

Cartesian coordinates $(x, y) \leftrightarrow$ polar coordinates (r, φ)

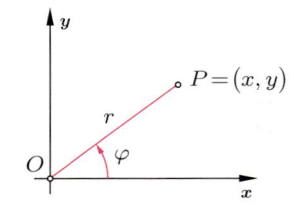

$$x = r\cos\varphi$$
$$y = r\sin\varphi$$

$$r = \sqrt{x^2 + y^2}$$
$$\cos\varphi = \frac{x}{r}, \quad \sin\varphi = \frac{y}{r}$$

Geometry

MATHEMATICS PHYSICS ASTRONOMY CHEMISTRY

Transformations in space

Cartesian coordinates $(x, y, z) \leftrightarrow$ Cartesian coordinates (x', y', z')

Let two Cartesian coordinate systems in space be given, and let the point P have coordinates (x, y, z) with respect to one coordinate system and (x', y', z') with respect to the other. As in the plane, there are two types of coordinate transformations in space:

- translation by $\vec{a}$. The transformation equations are analogous to those in the plane.
- rotation (assuming both coordinate systems have the same origin)

$\vec{e}_1, \vec{e}_2, \vec{e}_3$ and $\vec{e}_1\,', \vec{e}_2\,', \vec{e}_3\,'$	unit basis vectors of two coordinate systems with a common origin
$a_{ij} = \vec{e}_i \cdot \vec{e}_j\,' = \cos(\vec{e}_i, \vec{e}_j\,')$	direction cosines of $\vec{e}_i$ and $\vec{e}_j\,'$

Then the transformation is given by the equations:

$$\begin{pmatrix} x \\ y \\ z \end{pmatrix} = \begin{pmatrix} a_{11} & a_{12} & a_{13} \\ a_{21} & a_{22} & a_{23} \\ a_{31} & a_{32} & a_{33} \end{pmatrix} \begin{pmatrix} x' \\ y' \\ z' \end{pmatrix} \qquad \begin{pmatrix} x' \\ y' \\ z' \end{pmatrix} = \begin{pmatrix} a_{11} & a_{21} & a_{31} \\ a_{12} & a_{22} & a_{32} \\ a_{13} & a_{23} & a_{33} \end{pmatrix} \begin{pmatrix} x \\ y \\ z \end{pmatrix}$$

The matrices are transposes of one another. p. 28 ◀ matrix operations

Cartesian coordinates $(x, y, z) \leftrightarrow$ cylindrical polar coordinates (r, φ, z)

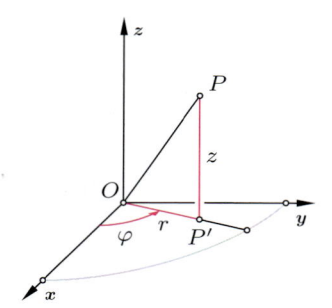

$$x = r \cos \varphi \qquad r = \sqrt{x^2 + y^2}$$
$$y = r \sin \varphi \qquad \cos \varphi = \frac{x}{r}, \quad \sin \varphi = \frac{y}{r}$$
$$z = z \qquad z = z$$

Cartesian coordinates $(x, y, z) \leftrightarrow$ spherical polar coordinates (r, ϑ, φ)

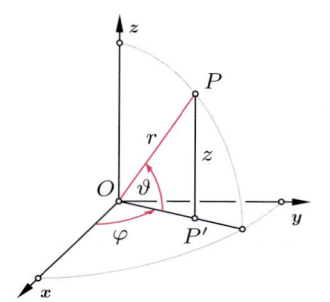

$$x = r \cos \vartheta \cos \varphi \qquad r = \sqrt{x^2 + y^2 + z^2}$$
$$y = r \cos \vartheta \sin \varphi \qquad \sin \vartheta = \frac{z}{r}, \quad -90° \leqslant \vartheta \leqslant 90°$$
$$z = r \sin \vartheta \qquad \cos \varphi = \frac{x}{r \cos \vartheta}, \quad \sin \varphi = \frac{y}{r \cos \vartheta}$$

6 Probability and Statistics

6.1 Descriptive Statistics

Univariate Data

Ungrouped data (individual values)

Let a sample of size n with individual values $x_1, x_2, \ldots, x_n$ be given.

Measures of location and dispersion (summary statistics)

arithmetic mean	$\overline{x} = \dfrac{1}{n} \sum_{i=1}^{n} x_i$
variance (empirical)	$s^2 = \dfrac{1}{n-1} \sum_{i=1}^{n} (x_i - \overline{x})^2$
standard deviation (empirical)	$s = \sqrt{\dfrac{1}{n-1} \sum_{i=1}^{n} (x_i - \overline{x})^2}$
coefficient of variation	$v = \dfrac{s}{\overline{x}} \cdot 100\%$, assuming all $x_i > 0$
median	assuming $x_1, \ldots, x_n$ are in ascending order: • the middle value, if n is odd • the average of the two middle values, if n is even
1st quartile	the median of the values below the median
3rd quartile	the median of the values above the median
interquartile range	3rd quartile $-\ 1^{\text{st}}$ quartile

A box plot is a graphical representation of the location, dispersion and skewness of a set of data. It shows the range of normal data, which are those values which deviate from the nearest quartile by at most 1.5 times the interquartile range.
All other observations are considered extreme (also termed outliers) and are plotted individually.
Box plots allow quick qualitative comparisons among different sets of data.

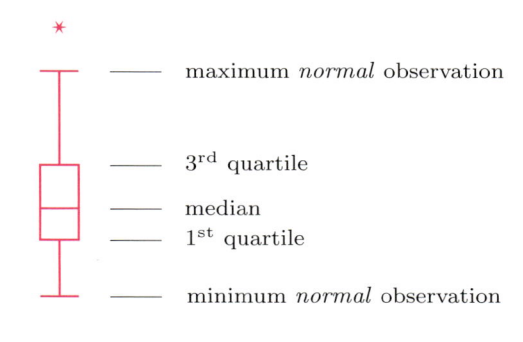

— maximum *normal* observation

— 3rd quartile
— median
— 1st quartile

— minimum *normal* observation

— outlier
(*extreme* observation)

Probability and Statistics
MATHEMATICS PHYSICS ASTRONOMY CHEMISTRY

Grouped data (classified data)

Data may be grouped (or classified) by subdividing the n individual values into k class intervals with class midpoints z_j. The absolute frequency of class j is n_j; the relative frequency is n_j/n. It follows that

$$\sum_{j=1}^{k} n_j = n$$

A histogram is a graphical representation of grouped values by adjacent rectangles above the class intervals such that the area of each rectangle is proportional to the corresponding class frequency.

If the individual values are unknown, the arithmetic mean and sample standard deviation are calculated with the following formulae:

$$\overline{x} = \frac{1}{n}\sum_{j=1}^{k} n_j z_j, \quad s^2 = \frac{1}{n-1}\sum_{j=1}^{k} n_j (z_j - \overline{x})^2$$

Bivariate Data

Let a sample of size n with pairs of values (x_1, y_1), (x_2, y_2), ..., (x_n, y_n) be given. A scatter diagram is a plot in which the values of the pairs are represented as points in the plane.

In addition to the univariate measures of location and dispersion, such as $\overline{x}$, s_x, $\overline{y}$ and s_y, a measure of the statistical dependence between the x and y data is required. A standard summary statistic for this dependence is the empirical correlation coefficient

$$r_{xy} = \frac{\sum_{i=1}^{n}(x_i - \overline{x})(y_i - \overline{y})}{\sqrt{\sum_{i=1}^{n}(x_i - \overline{x})^2 \cdot \sum_{i=1}^{n}(y_i - \overline{y})^2}} = \frac{s_{xy}}{s_x s_y}$$

where s_{xy} denotes the empirical covariance

$$s_{xy} = \frac{1}{n-1}\sum_{i=1}^{n}(x_i - \overline{x})(y_i - \overline{y})$$

The correlation coefficient r_{xy} measures the degree and direction of linear correlation between the two variables. The larger $|r_{x,y}|$ is, the closer the points (x_i, y_i) lie to a straight line whose slope has the same sign as r_{xy}. The maximum value of $|r_{x,y}|$ is one, which is attained if and only if the points (x_i, y_i) lie exactly on a straight line. Since the dependence between the x and y data may be nonlinear, and because r_{xy} can be strongly affected by outliers, the scatter plot can often be more informative than the correlation coefficient.

The correlation coefficient r_{xy} also appears in the determination of the linear regression line of y on x. The formula is given by

$$y - \overline{y} = a(x - \overline{x}), \quad \text{where} \quad a = \frac{s_{xy}}{s_x^2} = r_{xy} \cdot \frac{s_y}{s_x}$$

computational details ▶ p. 136
regression line in statistical inference ▶ p. 132

6.2 Probability

Events and probabilities

A random experiment is a procedure whose outcome cannot be predicted with certainty. Its sample space Ω is the set of all possible outcomes ω of the random experiment.
Events $A, B, C, \ldots$ correspond to subsets of Ω, and an event A is deemed to occur whenever the actual outcome ω is an element of A. An event consisting of a single outcome is called an elementary event (or simple event).

Basic notation and operations involving events:

Ω	the certain event
$\emptyset$	the impossible event
$\bar{A} = \Omega \setminus A$	the event that A *does not occur*
$A \cup B$	the event A *or* B, i.e. the event that *at least one of A and B occurs*
$A \cap B$	the event A *and* B, i.e. the event that *both A and B occur*
$A \subset B$	B follows from A, i.e. *if A occurs, B must also occur*
$A \cap B = \emptyset$	A and B are mutually exclusive (or disjoint)

In the discrete case – i.e. if Ω is finite, $\Omega = \{\omega_1, \omega_2, \ldots, \omega_m\}$, or countable, $\Omega = \{\omega_1, \omega_2, \ldots\}$ – every subset of Ω defines an event. The collection $\mathbb{E}$ of all possible events is simply the set of all subsets of Ω, namely the power set of Ω. Given the probabilities $p(\omega_i)$ of all elementary events $\{\omega_i\}$, the probability of an arbitrary event A is determined by

$$P(A) = \sum_{i,\, \omega_i \in A} p(\omega_i)$$

The probabilities $p(\omega_i) \geqslant 0$ can be arbitrary apart from the constraint that their sum must be one:

$$\sum_{i,\, \omega_i \in \Omega} p(\omega_i) = 1$$

Probabilities defined in this way satisfy the KOLMOGOROV axioms:

- $P(A) \geqslant 0$ for all $A \in \mathbb{E}$
- $P(\Omega) = 1$
- For all sets of mutually exclusive events $A_1, A_2, \ldots \in \mathbb{E}$ (i.e. $A_i \cap A_j = \emptyset$ for $i \neq j$): $P(A_1 \cup A_2 \cup \ldots) = P(A_1) + P(A_2) + \ldots$.

If Ω is uncountable – e.g. $\Omega = [0, 1]$ – then only *reasonable* subsets of Ω can be interpreted as events (for instance subintervals of $\Omega = [0, 1]$). The collection $\mathbb{E}$ of all events must constitute a sigma algebra (σ-algebra) closed with respect to complements and countable unions:

- $A \in \mathbb{E} \Rightarrow \bar{A} \in \mathbb{E}$
- $\Omega \in \mathbb{E}$
- $A_1, A_2, \ldots \in \mathbb{E} \Rightarrow A_1 \cup A_2 \cup \ldots \in \mathbb{E}$

A probability function $P\colon \mathbb{E} \to [0,1]$ must, just as in the discrete case, satisfy the Kolmogorov axioms. The triple $(\Omega, \mathbb{E}, P)$ is called a probability space. In contrast with the discrete case, the construction of $\mathbb{E}$ and the definition of P satisfying the Kolmogorov axioms require special additional consideration.

Consequences arising from the KOLMOGOROV axioms

- $0 \leqslant P(A) \leqslant 1$
- $P(\bar{A}) = 1 - P(A)$
- $P(\emptyset) = 0$
- $A \subset B \Rightarrow P(A) \leqslant P(B)$
- $A, B \subset \Omega,\ A \cap B = \emptyset \ \Rightarrow\ P(A \cup B) = P(A) + P(B)$
- $P(A \cup B) = P(A) + P(B) - P(A \cap B)$ (addition law)

Determination of probabilities

The actual determination of the probability function P – or the probabilities $p(\omega_i)$ in the discrete case – is beyond the scope of the Kolmogorov axioms. Indeed, it frequently requires modelling considerations in the context of applications outside mathematics. Nevertheless, there are three general approaches:

- Assumption of equally likely events: In random experiments with a finite number of distinct but otherwise equivalent outcomes one postulates that all of the probabilities $p(\omega_i)$ are equal because of the underlying symmetry. It follows that

$$P(A) = \frac{\text{number of elements of } A}{\text{number of elements of } \Omega} = \frac{\text{number of "favourable outcomes"}}{\text{number of "possible outcomes"}}$$

For $\Omega = [a, b]$, the analogous postulate requires the probabilities of equally long subintervals to be equal. Consequently

$$P([c, d]) = \frac{d-c}{b-a}, \quad a \leqslant c \leqslant d \leqslant b$$

If the sample space Ω is a bounded subset of $\mathbb{R}^2$ or $\mathbb{R}^3$, the equal likelihood assumption results in probabilities based on analogous area or volume ratios respectively.

- Empirical determination of probabilities: Whenever random experiments are repeated many times, the relative frequencies observed for a given event A appear to converge to a stable value as the number of repetitions N is increased. Consequently $P(A)$ can be regarded as an idealized relative frequency of A – i.e. the limit of the relative frequencies of A as $N \to \infty$. It can be approximated by relative frequencies recorded for large numbers of repetitions.

- A subjective approach: One can regard $P(A)$ as a subjective degree of belief (or credence) that A will occur. In order to determine $P(A)$ in percent, one can consider what stake would be fair in a wager in which one wins 100 francs if A occurs, and nothing otherwise.

Probability and Statistics

Conditional probability

Definition of conditional probability

The conditional probability that A occurs, given that B has occurred, is

$$P(A|B) = P_B(A) = \frac{P(A \cap B)}{P(B)}, \quad P(B) \neq 0$$

Product rule

If a conditional probability of A given B and the probability of the condition B are known, the corresponding joint probability of A and B can be calculated.

$$P(A \cap B) = P(A) \cdot P(B|A) = P(B) \cdot P(A|B)$$

Independent events

A and B are defined to be independent if and only if $P(A \cap B) = P(A) \cdot P(B)$.

Law of total probability

If $\{A_1, A_2, \ldots, A_n\}$ is a partition of Ω with $P(A_i) > 0$ for all i, i.e. $A_1 \cup A_2 \cup \ldots \cup A_n = \Omega$ and the A_i are mutually exclusive – then for an arbitrary event $B \subset \Omega$:

$$P(B) = P(A_1) \cdot P(B|A_1) + P(A_2) \cdot P(B|A_2) + \ldots + P(A_n) \cdot P(B|A_n)$$

Bayes' theorem

If $\{A_1, A_2, \ldots, A_n\}$ is a partition of Ω with $P(A_i) > 0$ for all i, then for an arbitrary event B with $P(B) \neq 0$:

$$P(A_i|B) = \frac{P(A_i) \cdot P(B|A_i)}{\sum_{j=1}^{n} P(A_j) \cdot P(B|A_j)}$$

Random variables

Random variables $X, Y, \ldots$ are mappings (functions) $\Omega \to \mathbb{R}$. Each possible outcome ω of the random experiment is assigned a real number $x = X(\omega)$. The value x is called a realization of the random variable. Of interest are the probabilities associated with sets of possible values of X:

$$P(X \in A) = P(\{\omega;\ X(\omega) \in A\})$$

for sets $A \subset \mathbb{R}$. The set of all these probabilities is called the distribution of the random variable X.

Discrete random variables

X is called discrete if the set of possible values it can assume is finite $\{x_1, x_2, \ldots, x_n\}$ or countable $\{x_1, x_2, \ldots\}$. The distribution of a discrete random variable X is determined by the probabilities $p(x_i)$ of the possible values x_i:

$$p(x_i) = P(X\!=\!x_i) = \sum_{j,\, X(\omega_j)=x_i} p(\omega_j)$$

For an arbitrary set $A \subset \mathbb{R}$:
$$P(X \in A) = \sum_{i,\, x_i \in A} p(x_i)$$

Two discrete random variables X and Y defined on the same sample set Ω are defined to be independent, if for all possible possible values x_i of X and y_j of Y:

$$P(X\!=\!x_i \text{ and } Y\!=\!y_j) = P(X\!=\!x_i) \cdot P(Y\!=\!y_j)$$

Continuous random variables

A random variable is called continuous if the set of possible values it can assume forms a finite or infinite interval. Here only those random variables whose distributions are defined by probability densities will be considered.

f is called a probability density function if $f(x) \geqslant 0$ for all x and $\int_{-\infty}^{+\infty} f(x)\,\mathrm{d}x = 1$.

The random variable X has the probability density function f if, for all $a < b$,

$$P(a \leqslant X \leqslant b) = \int_a^b f(x)\,\mathrm{d}x$$

However, for any given value x, it follows that $P(X\!=\!x) = 0$. Consequently one makes use of an integral function of f

$$F(x) = P(X \leqslant x) = \int_{-\infty}^{x} f(z)\,\mathrm{d}z$$

called the cumulative distribution function (or distribution function) of X.
It follows that $P(a \leqslant X \leqslant b) = F(b) - F(a)$.

Expected value (or expectation) of the random variable X

notations: $E(X)$ or μ_X or μ

definition:
$$E(X) = \sum_{\omega_j \in \Omega} X(\omega_j) p(\omega_j) = \sum_i x_i p(x_i) \qquad (X \text{ discrete})$$

$$E(X) = \int_{-\infty}^{\infty} x f(x)\,\mathrm{d}x \qquad (X \text{ continuous})$$

properties:
$$E(a + bX) = a + bE(X) \qquad (a, b \in \mathbb{R})$$
$$E(X + Y) = E(X) + E(Y)$$
$$E(g(X)) = \sum_i g(x_i) p(x_i) \quad \text{or} \quad \int_{-\infty}^{\infty} g(x) f(x)\,\mathrm{d}x, \quad g \colon \mathbb{R} \to \mathbb{R}$$

If X and Y are independent, $E(X \cdot Y) = E(X) \cdot E(Y)$ holds.

Probability and Statistics

Variance and standard deviation of the random variable X

notations: $\text{Var}(X)$ or σ_X^2 or σ^2 for the variance
$\sqrt{\text{Var}(X)}$ or σ_X or σ for the standard deviation

definition:
$$\text{Var}(X) = E\big((X-\mu_X)^2\big) = \sum_i (x_i-\mu)^2 \, p(x_i) \qquad (X \text{ discrete})$$
$$= \int_{-\infty}^{+\infty} (x-\mu)^2 f(x)\,dx \qquad (X \text{ continuous})$$

properties:
$$\text{Var}(a+bX) = b^2 \cdot \text{Var}(X) \qquad (a, b \in \mathbb{R})$$
$$\text{Var}(X) = E(X^2) - \big(E(X)\big)^2$$

If X and Y are independent, $\text{Var}(X+Y) = \text{Var}(X) + \text{Var}(Y)$ holds.

Chebyshev's inequality

$$P\big(|X-\mu| \geq k\sigma\big) \leq \frac{1}{k^2}$$

The probability that the values of a random variable deviate from its expected value by at least k times its standard deviation cannot exceed $1/k^2$.

Distributions

Binomial distribution

Definition: A random variable X with possible values $x = 0, 1, \ldots, n$ is binomially distributed if
$$P(X=x) = P_{n,p}(x) = \binom{n}{x} p^x (1-p)^{n-x}, \quad 0 < p < 1 \qquad \text{p. 42} \blacktriangleleft \text{binomial coefficients}$$

Usage: the distribution of the frequency of occurrence X of an event A in n independent trials of a particular random experiment. The probability that A occurs in any particular trial is assumed constant and is denoted by p.

Special case: Suppose balls are drawn at random from an urn containing r red and $m-r$ white balls and replaced after each draw. The number of red balls in a selection of n balls drawn in this manner is binomially distributed with $p = r/m$.

Recursive formula:
$$P_{n,p}(0) = (1-p)^n, \quad P_{n,p}(x) = \frac{n-x+1}{x} \cdot \frac{p}{1-p} P_{n,p}(x-1), \quad x = 1, 2, \ldots, n$$

If X is binomially distributed, then $E(X) = np$ and $\text{Var}(X) = np(1-p)$.

Approximations:
- If $np^2 \leqslant 0.025$, using the POISSON distribution
$$P_{n,p}(x) \approx e^{-np}\frac{(np)^x}{x!}, \quad x = 0, 1, \ldots$$
- If $npq > 9$, using the normal distribution
$$P_{n,p}(x) \approx \frac{1}{\sqrt{2\pi np(1-p)}} e^{-\frac{(x-np)^2}{2np(1-p)}}, \quad x \approx np$$

$$\sum_{x=a}^{b} P_{n,p}(x) \approx \Phi\left(\frac{b - np + \frac{1}{2}}{\sqrt{np(1-p)}}\right) - \Phi\left(\frac{a - np - \frac{1}{2}}{\sqrt{np(1-p)}}\right)$$

tables of Φ-values ▶ p. 149

Hypergeometric distribution

Definition: A random variable X whose possible values x are integers ranging between $\max(0, n-m+r)$ and $\min(n, r)$ is hypergeometrically distributed if

$$P(X = x) = P_{n,m,r}(x) = \frac{\binom{r}{x}\binom{m-r}{n-x}}{\binom{m}{n}}, \quad n < m, \ r < m$$

Usage: Suppose n balls are drawn at random without replacement from an urn containing r red and $m - r$ white balls. The number of red balls in the selection is hypergeometrically distributed.

Recursive formula:

$$P_{n,m,r}(x) = \frac{n - x + 1}{x} \cdot \frac{r - x + 1}{m - r - n + x} \cdot P_{n,m,r}(x-1)$$

If X is hypergeometrically distributed, then

$$E(X) = n \cdot \frac{r}{m} \quad \text{and} \quad \text{Var}(X) = n \cdot \frac{r}{m} \cdot \left(1 - \frac{r}{m}\right) \cdot \frac{m-n}{m-1}$$

If $\dfrac{n}{m} < 0.1$ and $m \geqslant 60$, the hypergeometric distribution can be approximated by the binomial distribution with $p = \dfrac{r}{m}$.

POISSON distribution

Definition: A random variable X with possible values $x = 0, 1, \ldots$ is Poisson-distributed if
$$P(X = x) = P_\lambda(x) = e^{-\lambda}\frac{\lambda^x}{x!}, \quad \lambda > 0$$

Usage: Distribution of the number of events occurring in a given time interval or region of space, assuming the events occur independently and with the same average rate – e.g. radioactive decay. It is the limiting case of the binomial distribution for $n \to \infty$, $p \to 0$, $np \to \lambda$.

Recursive formula:
$$P_\lambda(0) = e^{-\lambda}, \quad P_\lambda(x) = \frac{\lambda}{x} \cdot P_\lambda(x-1), \quad x = 1, 2, \ldots$$

If X is Poisson-distributed, then $E(X) = \mathrm{Var}(X) = \lambda$

If $\lambda > 9$, the Poisson distribution can be approximated by a normal distribution:
$$\sum_{x=a}^{b} P_\lambda(x) \approx \Phi\left(\frac{b - \lambda + 0.5}{\sqrt{\lambda}}\right) - \Phi\left(\frac{a - \lambda - 0.5}{\sqrt{\lambda}}\right)$$

Normal distribution

Definition: A continuous random variable X is normally distributed with mean μ and standard deviation σ if its probability density is given by the GAUSSIAN function
$$\varphi_{\mu,\sigma}(x) = \frac{1}{\sqrt{2\pi}\,\sigma} e^{-\frac{(x-\mu)^2}{2\sigma^2}}$$

Usage: description of errors of measurement resulting from the accumulation of many small effects.

If X is normally distributed as above, its expected value and variance are indeed $E(X) = \mu$ and $\mathrm{Var}(X) = \sigma^2$. The random variable given by $U = \frac{X-\mu}{\sigma}$ is also normally distributed, with mean 0 and standard deviation 1. Its distribution is called the standard normal distribution.

Computation: The cumulative distribution function Φ of U
$$P(U \leqslant u) = \Phi(u) = \frac{1}{\sqrt{2\pi}} \int_{-\infty}^{u} e^{-\frac{z^2}{2}} \, dz \qquad \blacktriangleright \text{p. 149}$$

cannot be expressed in terms of elementary functions. Consequently one makes use of tables (p. 149) or numerical approximations. If X is normally distributed with mean μ and standard deviation σ, it can be written in terms of U above as $X = \mu + \sigma U$. Hence the probability that it assumes a value x between a and b is given in terms of the standard function Φ by
$$P(a \leqslant X \leqslant b) = \Phi(u_2) - \Phi(u_1) \quad \text{where} \quad u_1 = \frac{a-\mu}{\sigma} \quad \text{and} \quad u_2 = \frac{b-\mu}{\sigma}$$

Distributions used in statistical tests

The chi-squared distribution and STUDENT's t-distribution are derived from the standard normal distribution. They incorporate an additional parameter ν, a positive integer specifying the number of degrees of freedom.

- If $X_1, X_2, \ldots, X_\nu$ are independent and standard normally distributed, then the random variable $Y = X_1^2 + X_2^2 + \ldots + X_\nu^2$ is chi-squared distributed with ν degrees of freedom.
- If X is standard normally distributed and Y chi-squared distributed with ν degrees of freedom, then the random variable $T = \frac{X}{\sqrt{Y/\nu}}$ is t-distributed with ν degrees of freedom.

These distributions play an important role in statistical inference. In statistical tests the number of degrees of freedom is closely related to the number of observations.

6.3 Statistical inference

Sample and statistical population

Statistical inference is the process of drawing conclusions about a statistical population based on information from a sample of that population. To avoid possibly distorting the conclusions it is important that the choice of the sample be random.

Finite statistical populations

Here the statistical population is a specific set of N elements (persons, objects, etc.) for which a given attribute ξ is of interest. Suppose the values of the attribute in the population are listed $\xi_1, \xi_2, \ldots, \xi_N$. If elements $j_1, j_2, \ldots, j_n$ are chosen from the population, the sample data consists of $x_1 = \xi_{j_1}, x_2 = \xi_{j_2}, \ldots, x_n = \xi_{j_n}$. Random samples are chosen by drawing lots or by the use of random numbers.

Infinite statistical populations

The statistical population can also be an abstract set of measurements or observations which could be carried out in principle. This population can be described as a discrete or continuous random variable. The sample consists of the measurements or observations that are actually carried out – i.e. the values $x_1, x_2, \ldots, x_n$. The sample may be considered random if all the measurements are carried out under the same conditions and no measurement result is affected by the other measurements (independence).

Parameter estimation

A parameter is a quantity which is characteristic of the statistical population. An estimate is an approximation of the parameter value making use of only the sample values $x_1, x_2, \ldots, x_n$.

Important special cases:

- Finite population $\xi_1, \xi_2, \ldots, \xi_N$. The parameter of interest is the arithmetic mean of the population

$$\mu = \frac{1}{N} \sum_{i=1}^{N} \xi_i$$

The estimate is the arithmetic mean of the sample

$$\widehat{\mu} = \overline{x} = \frac{1}{n} \sum_{i=1}^{n} x_i = \frac{1}{n} \sum_{i=1}^{n} \xi_{j_i}$$

- Infinite population consisting of all possible measurements of a quantity ξ. The parameter of interest is the expected value $\mu = E(\xi)$ in the population. It corresponds to the value that one would obtain if measurement errors could be eliminated. The estimate is the arithmetic mean of the sample

$$\widehat{\mu} = \overline{x} = \frac{1}{n} \sum_{i=1}^{n} x_i$$

Probability and Statistics
MATHEMATICS   PHYSICS   ASTRONOMY   CHEMISTRY

- Infinite population consisting of all possible repetitions of a random experiment. The parameter of interest is the probability $p = P(A)$ of a particular event A. Suppose that in a sample of n repetitions of the experiment, A occurred k times. The estimate is the relative frequency of A

$$\widehat{p} = \frac{k}{n}$$

Estimates fluctuate at random, depending on the particular sample. Consequently they themselves are random variables.

Statistical hypothesis testing

Hypothesis tests can be carried out whenever there is a reasonable conjecture (hypothesis) regarding the distribution of the random variable of interest. Since one cannot verify the conjecture directly, one attempts to verify it indirectly, in that

- a contrary hypothesis, usually the so-called null hypothesis H_0 is posed, and
- one attempts to use the statistical data to disprove (reject) the null hypothesis.

One rejects H_0, if the data in the statistical sample are incompatible with the assumptions of H_0. To this end a test quantity T is chosen for which large values of T would confirm the original conjecture. The rejection region takes the form $[t_c, \infty)$, where the critical value t_c is determined such that if H_0 were indeed true, the event $T \geqslant t_c$ would occur with at most a low prescribed probability α. This probability α is called the level of significance. As a rule, α is chosen to be 5% or 1%.

Usually H_0 asserts that a population parameter assumes a particular value or lies in a given range of values. One rejects H_0 if the statistical estimate is too far away from this value or the range. Furthermore, one takes the accuracy of the estimate into account – i.e. which deviations are typical and which not. Consequently, the test quantity T often takes the form

$$\frac{|\text{parameter estimate} - \text{value of the parameter in the null hypothesis}|}{\text{estimated standard deviation of the parameter estimate}}.$$

If the test quantity does not fall within the rejection region, then one retains H_0: the result from the sample is compatible with H_0 – i.e. there is insufficient reason to reject H_0. The test does not indicate to what degree H_0 might be considered correct if it is not rejected. That also depends on what alternative explanations for the observed data are considered.

Probability and Statistics
MATHEMATICS PHYSICS ASTRONOMY CHEMISTRY

Possible errors: In each statistical test it is possible to make one of the following errors:

- H_0 is rejected even though it is true. This is called a type I error. The test is designed to ensure that the probability of a type I error is at most α.

- H_0 is not rejected even though it is false. This is called a type II error. The probability of a type II error depends on the alternative hypothesis chosen and the size of the sample.

Confidence intervals

A confidence interval is an interval $[g_1, g_2]$, calculated from the sample values, which contains the parameter being estimated with a specified probability K. The end points g_1 and g_2 are called confidence limits. The probability K is called the confidence level and is normally chosen close to 1.

Confidence intervals can be derived from hypothesis tests concerning a parameter θ. For a fixed significance level α one considers null hypotheses $\theta = \theta_0$ ranging over all possible values of θ_0. Those values of θ_0 for which the null hypothesis would not be rejected form an interval with confidence level $K = 1 - \alpha$. Thus the confidence interval consists of all parameter values which are compatible with the sample data.

Many confidence intervals are expressed in terms of an estimate of the parameter plus/minus a multiple of the sample standard deviation. The value of this multiple depends on the confidence level K.

6.4 Important statistical tests and confidence intervals

Six statistical tests are described below together with their associated confidence intervals. They deal with simple statistical questions and data types and serve as key examples. The flow chart opposite indicates which statistical tests are applied in which situations. In the literature for statistics on can find many other tests for more complex statistical questions.

Test and confidence interval for a probability (binomial test)

Situation
In n repetitions of a random experiment a particular event A has occurred k times.

Question addressed by the confidence interval
What values of $p = P(A)$ are compatible with these statistical data?

Question addressed by the hypothesis test
Does the probability $P(A)$ differ from a specified value p_0? Corresponding null hypothesis H_0: $P(A) = p_0$.

Probability and Statistics
MATHEMATICS   PHYSICS   ASTRONOMY   CHEMISTRY

```
                    question concerning
              probabilities │ expectations of
                            │ measured quantities
```

Flowchart nodes:

- **question concerning probabilities**
  - **one event** → **binomial test, confidence level**
    - *conservative* → critical values given by 1st formula
    - *approximate* → critical values given by 2nd formula
  - **of m events A_i** $(A_i \cap A_j = \emptyset, \bigcup A_i = \Omega)$ → **chi-square test**

- **question concerning expectations of measured quantities**
  - **populations**
    - **one** → reduction to 1 population by computing differences → **assumption of normal distribution**
      - *yes* → **t-test**
      - *no* → **reduction to ranks / signs**
        - *ranks* → **Wilcoxon test on 1 sample**
        - *signs* → **sign-test**
    - **two** → **measurements**
      - *paired* → (reduction to 1 population by computing differences)
      - *unpaired* → **assumption of normal distribution**
        - *yes* → **t-test on 2 samples**
        - *no* → **Wilcoxon test on 2 samples**
  - **regression model** → **regression analysis (t-test)**

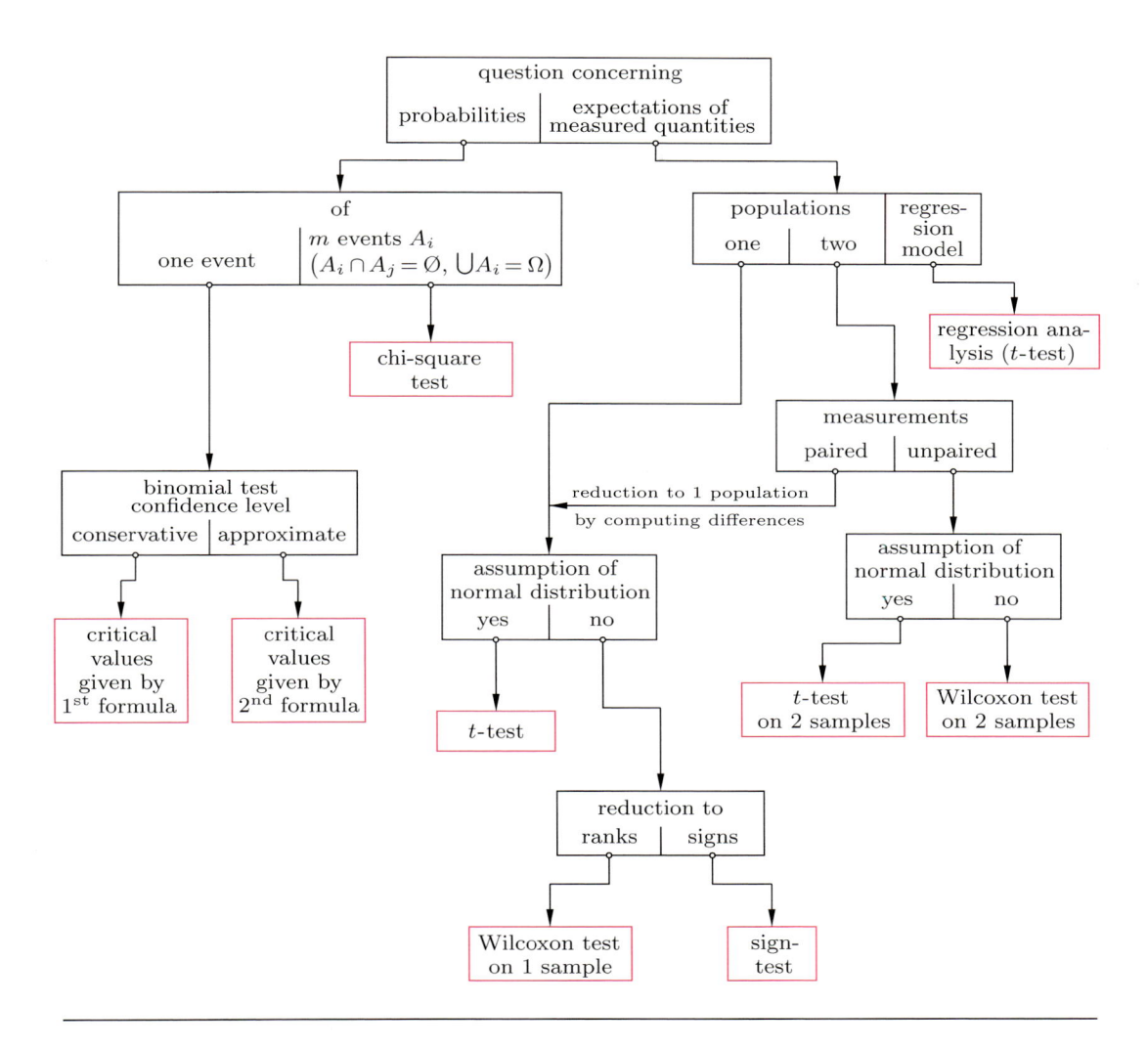

Assumptions
Repetitions of the experiment are independent; the probability of A is constant.

Rejection region
H_0 is rejected if $k \leqslant k_1$ or $k \geqslant k_2$, where k_1 and k_2 are given by

$$k_1 = \max\left\{k,\ \sum_{j=0}^{k} \binom{n}{j} p_0^j (1-p_0)^{n-j} \leqslant \frac{\alpha}{2}\right\}$$

$$k_2 = \min\left\{k,\ \sum_{j=k}^{n} \binom{n}{j} p_0^j (1-p_0)^{n-j} \leqslant \frac{\alpha}{2}\right\}$$

Probability and Statistics
MATHEMATICS   PHYSICS   ASTRONOMY   CHEMISTRY

Approximate determination of k_1 and k_2: graphically by means of the point of intersection of the horizontal line $p = p_0$ with the curve plots on p. 150 for the appropriate value of n, computationally by

$$k_1 \approx np_0 - 0.5 - u_{1-\frac{\alpha}{2}}\sqrt{np_0(1-p_0)}, \quad k_2 \approx np_0 + 0.5 + u_{1-\frac{\alpha}{2}}\sqrt{np_0(1-p_0)}$$

where the critical value $u_{1-\frac{\alpha}{2}}$ is obtained from the standard normal distribution.
▶ p. 149

Confidence interval

(p_1, p_2) where $p_1 = p_1(k)$ and $p_2 = p_2(k)$ are the respective solutions of the equations

$$\sum_{j=k}^{n} \binom{n}{j} p^j (1-p)^{n-j} = \frac{\alpha}{2} \quad (k > 0), \quad \sum_{j=0}^{k} \binom{n}{j} p^j (1-p)^{n-j} = \frac{\alpha}{2} \quad (k < n)$$

with respect to p in the interval $(0, 1)$. By convention, $p_1(0) = 0$ and $p_2(n) = 1$.

Approximate determination of p_1 and p_2: graphically by means of the point of intersection of the vertical line $\widehat{p} = \frac{k}{n}$ with the curve plots on p. 150 for the appropriate value of n, computationally by

$$p_1 \approx \frac{k-0.5}{n} - \frac{1}{\sqrt{n}}\sqrt{\frac{k}{n}\left(1-\frac{k}{n}\right)}\, u_{1-\frac{\alpha}{2}}, \quad p_2 \approx \frac{k+0.5}{n} + \frac{1}{\sqrt{n}}\sqrt{\frac{k}{n}\left(1-\frac{k}{n}\right)}\, u_{1-\frac{\alpha}{2}}$$

Test and confidence interval for the expected value of a normally distributed random variable (Student's t-test)

Situation
A sample of n measured values $(x_1, \ldots, x_n)$ has been obtained.

Question addressed by the confidence interval
What values of the expectation μ are compatible with the sample data?

Question addressed by the hypothesis test
Does the expected value μ of the population differ from a specified value μ_0?
Corresponding null hypothesis H_0: $\mu = \mu_0$.

Assumptions
The individual measurements are independent and normally distributed with mean μ and standard deviation σ.

Rejection region

$$\frac{|\overline{x} - \mu_0|}{s/\sqrt{n}} > t_{1-\frac{\alpha}{2}}(n-1)$$

where $\overline{x}$ is the sample mean, s is the empirical standard deviation of the sample, and $t_{1-\frac{\alpha}{2}}(n-1)$ denotes the critical value of Student's t-distribution with $n-1$ degrees of freedom. Correspondingly, the test is called Student's t-test, or simply the t-test.
▶ p. 151

Probability and Statistics

Confidence interval

$$\left(\bar{x} - \frac{s}{\sqrt{n}} t_{1-\frac{\alpha}{2}}(n-1),\ \bar{x} + \frac{s}{\sqrt{n}} t_{1-\frac{\alpha}{2}}(n-1)\right)$$

Alternative tests in the same situation

Even if the overall population is not normally distributed, the level of significance is still approximately α. The larger n is, the better the approximation. Alternatively, there are two tests in which the level of significance can be calculated exactly while making significantly fewer assumptions about the distribution of X. However, they differ formally from the t-test in testing a location parameter which differs from the mean whenever the distribution is not symmetric about $x = E(X)$. The sign test tests the null hypothesis that the population median is m_0. The parameter tested by the WILCOXON signed-rank test is usually close to the median. In the symmetric case, all these location parameters coincide. In both tests, the level of significance is exactly the same as the chosen value of α for arbitrary continuous distributions. In the Wilcoxon test involving non-normal distributions in the population, the probability of type II errors is usually smaller than in the t-test or sign test.

Rejection region for the sign test

One determines the number k of values x_i in the sample for which $x_i > m_0$. This number is binomially distributed with $p = P(X_i > m_0)$. Consequently, one can apply the binomial test with $p_0 = 0.5$.

Rejection region for the WILCOXON signed-rank test

One arranges the absolute values of the differences $|x_i - m_0|$ in ascending order and assigns each x_i a rank $1, 2, \ldots, n$ according to the position of $|x_i - m_0|$ in the list. Then one calculates r_+, the sum of the ranks of the values x_i for which $x_i > m_0$. H_0 is rejected if

$$r_+ \leqslant r_{\frac{\alpha}{2}}(n) \quad \text{or} \quad r_+ \geqslant \frac{n(n+1)}{2} - r_{\frac{\alpha}{2}}(n)$$

$r_{\frac{\alpha}{2}}(n)$ ▶ p. 151

Chi-squared test for a set of probabilities

Situation

Let a set of mutually exclusive events A_i be given such that $A_1 \cup A_2 \cup \ldots \cup A_m = \Omega$, and suppose that in n repetitions of the corresponding random experiment each event A_i occurs $b(i)$ times $(i = 1, 2, \ldots, m)$.

Question addressed by the hypothesis test

Are the probabilities $(P(A_1), \ldots, P(A_m))$ different from the prescribed values $(P_0(A_1), \ldots, P_0(A_m))$?
Corresponding null hypothesis H_0: $P(A_i) = P_0(A_i)$ for $i = 1, 2, \ldots, m$

Assumptions

Repetitions of the experiment are independent, the probabilities $P_0(A_i)$ are constant, $n P_0(A_i) \geqslant 1$ for all i and $n P_0(A_i) \geqslant 5$ for at least 80% of the events A_i.

Rejection region

$$\sum_{i=1}^{m} \frac{(b(i) - nP_0(A_i))^2}{nP_0(A_i)} > \chi^2_{1-\alpha}(m-1),$$

where $\chi^2_{1-\alpha}(\nu)$ denotes the critical value of the chi-squared distribution with ν degrees of freedom.

▶ p. 151

Tests and confidence intervals for the difference between expected values in paired samples (matched pairs t-test)

Situation

A sample of n pairs of measured values (x_1, y_1), (x_2, y_2), ..., (x_n, y_n) has been obtained. Each data pair is obtained from the same element in the population. Thus the values x_i and y_i with the same index are associated with one another and are in general dependent.

Question addressed by the confidence interval

If μ_1 and μ_2 denote the respective expected values of X and Y in the population, what values of the difference $\mu_1 - \mu_2$ are compatible with the data in the sample?

Question addressed by the hypothesis test

Are the expected values μ_1 and μ_2 different? Corresponding null hypothesis H_0: $\mu_1 = \mu_2$.

Implementation

If one considers the differences $d_i = x_i - y_i$, then their expected value in the population is $\mu_1 - \mu_2$. Consequently one can implement Student's t-test for the expectation of a normally distributed random variable (with $\mu_0 = 0$) and calculate the corresponding confidence limits.

Assumptions

The differences d_i are independent and normally distributed with mean μ and standard deviation σ.

Tests and confidence intervals for the difference between expected values in separate samples (t-test on two independent samples)

Situation

Two independent samples of measured values have been obtained from two different populations. The first consists of n_1 values $x_1, x_2, \ldots, x_{n_1}$ and the second of n_2 values $y_1, y_2, \ldots, y_{n_2}$. The standard deviation in both populations is assumed to be the same, but no assumptions are made concerning the respective expected values μ_1 and μ_2.

Question addressed by the confidence interval

What values of the difference of the expected values μ_1 and μ_2 are compatible with the data in both samples?

Question addressed by the hypothesis test

Are the expected values μ_1 and μ_2 different? Corresponding null hypothesis H_0: $\mu_1 = \mu_2$.

Assumptions

All values are independent, the x and y values in their respective populations are normally distributed with means μ_1 and μ_2, respectively, and standard deviation σ.

Rejection region

$$\frac{|\bar{x} - \bar{y}|}{s_{\text{comb}}\sqrt{\frac{1}{n_1} + \frac{1}{n_2}}} > t_{1-\frac{\alpha}{2}}(n_1 + n_2 - 2)$$

where $t_{1-\frac{\alpha}{2}}(\nu)$ denotes the critical value of the t-distribution with ν degrees of freedom and s_{comb} the combined sample standard deviation of a single measurement:

$$s_{\text{comb}}^2 = \frac{\sum_{i=1}^{n_1}(x_i - \bar{x})^2 + \sum_{i=1}^{n_2}(y_i - \bar{y})^2}{n_1 + n_2 - 2} = s_x^2 \frac{n_1 - 1}{n_1 + n_2 - 2} + s_y^2 \frac{n_2 - 1}{n_1 + n_2 - 2}$$

Confidence interval

The confidence limits are given by

$$\bar{x} - \bar{y} \pm s_{\text{comb}}\sqrt{\frac{1}{n_1} + \frac{1}{n_2}}\; t_{1-\frac{\alpha}{2}}(n_1 + n_2 - 2)$$

Variants

There is a variant in which the standard deviations of the two populations cannot be assumed equal. In this case the significance level of the t-test and the confidence level are only approximate. However, except in extreme situations, this variant leads to similar conclusions.

If the x and y values are not normally distributed, the significance level of the t-test and the confidence level are only approximate, although the larger the sample sizes are, the better the approximation. The WILCOXON-MANN-WHITNEY test makes no assumptions concerning the distributions in the respective populations. It yields the correct level of significance with respect to the more general null hypothesis that the distributions in both populations are the same. Furthermore, in this test non-normal distributions in the population usually result in a reduction of the probability of type II errors.

Rejection region for the WILCOXON-MANN-WHITNEY test

One arranges the $n_1 + n_2$ values in both samples in ascending order and assigns each value a rank $1, 2, \ldots, n_1 + n_2$ according to its position in the list. The sum r_x of the ranks of all the values in the first sample is the test quantity. H_0 is rejected if

$$r_x \leqslant \frac{n_1(n_1+1)}{2} + w_{\frac{\alpha}{2}}(n_1, n_2) \quad \text{or} \quad r_x \geqslant n_1 n_2 + \frac{n_1(n_1+1)}{2} - w_{\frac{\alpha}{2}}(n_1, n_2)$$

critical value $w_{\frac{\alpha}{2}}(n_1, n_2)$ ▶ p. 152

Test and confidence interval for the slope of a regression line (t-test in regression analysis)

Situation

We consider a population in which the expected value of a variable Y depends linearly on an explanatory variable X – i.e. for a given input value x, $E(Y) = \alpha x + \beta$. A sample consisting of n pairs of measured values (x_i, y_i) has been obtained. The values x_i need not be random; they could be chosen by the experimenter.

Question addressed by the confidence interval

What values of the slope α of the regression line are compatible with the data in the sample?

Question addressed by the hypothesis test

Does the explanatory variable affect the value of the response variable?
Corresponding null hypothesis H_0: $\alpha = 0$.

Assumptions

All values are independent. In the overall population the response variable Y for a given x is normally distributed with mean $\alpha x + \beta$ and standard deviation σ.

Least squares estimate

$$\widehat{\alpha} = \frac{\sum (x_i - \overline{x})(y_i - \overline{y})}{\sum (x_i - \overline{x})^2}$$

Rejection region

$$\frac{|\widehat{\alpha}|}{s/\sqrt{\sum (x_i - \overline{x})^2}} > t_{1-\frac{\alpha}{2}}(n-2)$$

where $t_{1-\frac{\alpha}{2}}(\nu)$ denotes the critical value of the t-distribution with ν degrees of freedom and s the estimate of the standard deviation σ in the model

$$s^2 = \frac{1}{n-2} \sum r_i^2$$

where r_i denotes the i-th residual (vertical deviation from the regression line):

$$r_i = y_i - \overline{y} - \widehat{\alpha}(x_i - \overline{x})$$

Confidence interval

The confidence limits are given by

$$\widehat{\alpha} \pm \frac{s}{\sqrt{\sum (x_i - \overline{x})^2}} \, t_{1-\frac{\alpha}{2}}(n-2)$$

Checking the assumptions

Departures from either of the assumptions that the model is linear and that the standard deviation σ is independent of x become evident if one plots the residuals r_i against the values x_i (so-called TUKEY-ANSCOMBE plot).

7 Numerical Analysis

Explanation of notation

$s := A$ denotes an assignment. The value or expression A on the right is first determined and then assigned to the variable with the symbol s. If the symbol s also appears in A, then in general it is understood to have different values to the left and right of the $:=$ sign.

7.1 Polynomials

$$p\colon x \mapsto a_n x^n + a_{n-1} x^{n-1} + \ldots + a_2 x^2 + a_1 x + a_0$$

Statement of problems

(P1) determine $p(x_0)$
(P2) divide $p(x)$ by $x - x_0$
(P3) simultaneously determine p and its derivatives $p', \ldots, p^{(m)}$ at the point x_0
(P4) expand $p(x)$ in powers of $x - x_0$

HORNER's method

	a_{n-1}	a_{n-2}	a_{n-3}			a_2	a_1	a_0
a_n	v_{n-1}	v_{n-2}				v_2	v_1	v_0
a_n							w_1	
a_n						w_2		
a_n								
a_n								
a_n								
a_n		w_{n-2}						
a_n	w_{n-1}							
a_n								

computational scheme:

		b
	a	c

$c := a x_0 + b$

For problems (P1) and (P2) only the first two rows need be calculated. For problem (P3) the first $m+2$ rows are needed, and for problem (P4) all $n+2$ rows are required.

Algorithm

1. The values of $a_{n-1}, \ldots, a_0$ are entered in the first row, and a_n is entered repeatedly in the first column.
2. In each row, starting from the left, the entries are calculated by multiplying the entry to the left by x_0 and adding the entry above (see computational scheme above).

Then, if $w_n := v_n := a_n$ and $w_0 := v_0$, the solutions to the above problems are given by:

(S1) $p(x_0) = v_0$
(S2) $p(x) = (x - x_0)(v_n x^{n-1} + \ldots + v_1) + v_0$
(S3) $p^{(i)}(x_0) = w_i \cdot i!$ $\quad (i = 0, \ldots, m)$
(S4) $p(x) = w_n (x - x_0)^n + w_{n-1}(x - x_0)^{n-1} + \ldots + w_1 (x - x_0) + w_0$

Numerical Analysis

7.2 Interpolation

Suppose a function f is given whose values are specified at a finite set of points. An interpolating function is sought whose values coincide with those of f at the specified points and which provides an approximation of f elsewhere.

Polynomial interpolation

Let $n+1$ ordered pairs of numbers (x_i, y_i), $i = 0, \ldots, n$, be given such that their x values x_i are distinct. Then there exists a unique polynomial function p of degree at most n which satisfies

$$p(x_i) = y_i \quad (i = 0, \ldots, n)$$

LAGRANGE polynomials

The polynomial function p above can be constructed from a basis of Lagrange polynomials of degree n defined by

$$l_i \colon x \mapsto (x - x_0) \cdot \ldots \cdot (x - x_{i-1}) \cdot (x - x_{i+1}) \cdot \ldots \cdot (x - x_n) \quad (i = 0, \ldots, n)$$

These polynomials satisfy $l_i(x_k) = 0$ for $k \neq i$. Consequently,

$$p \colon x \mapsto \sum_{i=0}^{n} y_i \lambda_i l_i(x), \qquad \lambda_i := \frac{1}{l_i(x_i)} \quad (i = 0, \ldots, n)$$

Evaluation of p at the point x

A computationally efficient means of evaluating $p(x)$ uses the barycentric formula:

$$p(x) = \begin{cases} y_i & \text{if } x = x_i \quad (i = 0, \ldots, n) \\ \dfrac{\sum_{i=0}^{n} w_i y_i}{\sum_{i=0}^{n} w_i} & \text{otherwise, where} \quad w_i := \dfrac{\lambda_i}{x - x_i} \quad (i = 0, \ldots, n) \end{cases}$$

Interpolation with cubic splines

Problem statement

Let $n \geqslant 2$ points (x_i, y_i), $i = 1, \ldots, n$ be given such that $x_1 < x_2 < \ldots < x_n$. A piecewise smooth polynomial $p(x)$ is sought which satisfies the following conditions:

1. $p(x_i) = y_i \quad (i = 1, \ldots, n)$
2. p is twice continuously differentiable on $[x_1, x_n]$
3. In each interval (x_i, x_{i+1}), p is defined by a cubic polynomial $p_i(x) \quad (i = 1, \ldots, n-1)$
4. $p''(x_1) = p''(x_n) = 0$

Algorithm

One introduces the slopes y'_i, $i=1,\ldots,n$, at the interpolation points x_i as unknowns. With respect to these slopes, p is determined by

$$p_i(x) = y_i\, P_0(s) + y_{i+1}\, P_1(s) + h_i\left(y'_i\, Q_0(s) + y'_{i+1}\, Q_1(s)\right) \qquad (x_i \leqslant x \leqslant x_{i+1})$$

where $h_i := x_{i+1} - x_i$, $s := \dfrac{x - x_i}{h_i} \in [0,1]$ and $P_l(s), Q_l(s)$ are the cubic basis polynomials:

$$P_0(s) = (1+2s)\,(s-1)^2, \quad P_1(s) = P_0(1-s), \quad Q_0(s) = s\,(s-1)^2, \quad Q_1(s) = -Q_0(1-s)$$

The unknowns y'_i are determined by the conditions $p''_1(x_1) = p''_{n-1}(x_n) = 0$ and $p''_{i-1}(x_i) = p''_i(x_i)$, $i = 2, 3, \ldots, n-1$. Using the auxiliary variables

$$r_i = \frac{1}{h_i}, \quad c_i = r_i^2\,(y_{i+1} - y_i), \quad i = 1, \ldots, n-1$$

one obtains the following system of n linear equations for $y'_1, \ldots, y'_n$:

$$\begin{vmatrix} 2r_1 y'_1 \;+\;\; r_1 y'_2 & = & 3c_1 \\ \vdots & & \\ r_{i-1} y'_{i-1} + 2(r_{i-1}+r_i)y'_i + r_i y'_{i+1} & = & 3(c_{i-1}+c_i) \\ \vdots & & \\ r_{n-1} y'_{n-1} \;+\;\; 2r_{n-1} y'_n & = & 3c_{n-1} \end{vmatrix} \qquad (i = 2, 3, \ldots, n-1)$$

7.3 Systems of linear equations

Problem

Given the linear coefficients a_{ij} and the constant terms b_i, determine the solution set of the system of equations:

$$\begin{vmatrix} a_{11}x_1 + a_{12}x_2 + \ldots + a_{1n}x_n & = & b_1 \\ a_{21}x_1 + a_{22}x_2 + \ldots + a_{2n}x_n & = & b_2 \\ & \vdots & \\ a_{n1}x_1 + a_{n2}x_2 + \ldots + a_{nn}x_n & = & b_n \end{vmatrix}$$

The Gaussian elimination algorithm

The solution set remains unaltered under the following two operations:
- interchanging two equations
- subtracting a multiple of an equation from another equation

By repeated application of these operations a new system of equations can be derived which has the same solution set L as the original system of equations and in which each equation contains fewer unknowns than the previous.

At the start of the algorithm set $i := 1$, $j := 1$. The goal of the j-th elimination step is to eliminate the unknown x_j from equations $i+1, i+2, \ldots, n$. If $a_{ij} = a_{i+1,j} = \ldots = a_{n,j} = 0$, no action is required: i is left unchanged and j is incremented by 1 (i.e. the value of j is increased by 1). Otherwise, by interchanging two rows if necessary, one can ensure that $a_{ij} \neq 0$. Then, for $k = i+1, i+2, \ldots, n$, one subtracts a_{kj}/a_{ij} times the i-th equation from the k-th equation. At the completion of this sequence of steps, i and j are each incremented by 1.

In the so-called regular case the algorithm terminates with $i = n$. The resulting system is in upper triangular form:

$$\begin{vmatrix} a_{11}x_1 + a_{12}x_2 + \ldots + a_{1n}x_n &= b_1 \\ a_{22}x_2 + \ldots + a_{2n}x_n &= b_2 \\ & \vdots \\ a_{nn}x_n &= b_n \end{vmatrix}$$

where $a_{11} \neq 0, a_{22} \neq 0, \ldots, a_{nn} \neq 0$. In this case the solution is unique and can be determined by solving the last equation and, using back substitution, successively solving the preceding equations.

In the so-called singular case, at least one of the equations contains at least two fewer unknowns than the previous. For instance, for $n = 4$ the final system of equations might have the following form:

$$\begin{vmatrix} a_{11}x_1 + a_{12}x_2 + a_{13}x_3 + a_{14}x_4 &= b_1 \\ a_{23}x_3 + a_{24}x_4 &= b_2 \\ a_{34}x_4 &= b_3 \\ 0 &= b_4 \end{vmatrix}$$

where $a_{11} \neq 0$, $a_{23} \neq 0$, $a_{34} \neq 0$. If $b_4 \neq 0$, then the last equation is unsolvable, and consequently the whole system of equations is unsolvable: $L = \emptyset$. If $b_4 = 0$, then the last equation, and hence the system of equations has infinitely many solutions: x_3 and x_4 are determined from the two middle equations, x_2 is arbitrary and x_1 is determined in terms of x_2 by solving the first equation.

7.4 Least squares approximations

Linear least squares (GAUSS)

Consider an overdetermined system of linear equations with p unknowns $z_1, \ldots, z_p$ and $n > p$ equations:

$$\sum_{j=1}^{p} M_{ij} z_j = y_i \qquad (i = 1, \ldots, n)$$

In general, an overdetermined system does not have any exact solutions. The least squares fit determines an approximate solution for which the residuals

$$r_i := \sum_{j=1}^{n} M_{ij} z_j - y_i$$

are made as small as possible in the sense that the sum of their squares $\sum_{i=1}^{n} r_i^2$ is minimal.

Numerical Analysis
MATHEMATICS PHYSICS ASTRONOMY CHEMISTRY

The solution of the above linear least squares problem is given by the solution of the following system of linear equations:

$$\sum_{l=1}^{p} C_{kl} z_l = b_k, \qquad (k=1,\ldots,p)$$

where

$$C_{kl} := \sum_{i=1}^{n} M_{ik} M_{il} \quad (k,l=1,\ldots,p)$$

$$b_k := \sum_{i=1}^{n} M_{ik} y_i \quad (k=1,\ldots,p)$$

If the columns of the matrix (M_{ij}) are linearly independent, then this system of equations has a unique solution.

Special case: polynomial regression

Consider n ordered pairs of numbers

$$(x_i, y_i) \qquad (i=1,2,\ldots,n)$$

Given m, where $m < n-1$, a polynomial function

$$p\colon x \mapsto a_m x^m + \ldots + a_0$$

is sought which approximates the given values y_i at the points x_i. This means that the coefficients $a_0, \ldots, a_m$ should be chosen as an approximate solution of the system of equations

$$\sum_{j=0}^{m} x_i^j a_j = y_i \qquad (i=1,2,\ldots,n)$$

The algorithm given above can be used, if one sets $p = m+1$, $z_j = a_{j-1}$ and $M_{ij} = x_i^{j-1}$ ($1 \leqslant i \leqslant n$, $1 \leqslant j \leqslant p$).

Special case: linear regression ($m=1$)

$p\colon x \mapsto a_1 x + a_0$

Letting $\bar{x} = \frac{1}{n}\sum x_i$ and $\bar{y} = \frac{1}{n}\sum y_i$ one obtains

$$a_1 = \frac{\sum(x_i - \bar{x})(y_i - \bar{y})}{\sum(x_i - \bar{x})^2}, \qquad a_0 = \bar{y} - a_1 \bar{x},$$

where the range of summation is understood to be $i=1,\ldots,n$.

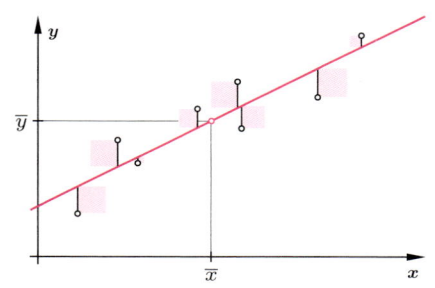

The regression line is chosen such that the sum of the squared residuals is minimal.

The equation of the line resulting from this linear least squares fit is $y = a_1 x + a_0$. It is identical with the regression line used in statistics.

p. 116/132 ◀ linear regression of y with respect to x

Numerical Analysis
MATHEMATICS PHYSICS ASTRONOMY CHEMISTRY

7.5 Numerical solution of equations in one unknown

Problem statement
Let f be a continuous function defined on a closed interval I and suppose f changes sign within I. Determine a root of f in I as accurately as possible – i.e. a point s in I for which $f(s)=0$.

Bisection method

Algorithm
Choose $a_0, b_0 \in I$ such that $f(a_0)<0$ and $f(b_0)>0$.
Then, for $i=0,1,\ldots$, iterate:

- $x_i := \dfrac{a_i + b_i}{2}$
- If $f(x_i) < 0$, set $a_{i+1} := x_i$, $b_{i+1} := b_i$
- If $f(x_i) > 0$, set $a_{i+1} := a_i$, $b_{i+1} := x_i$

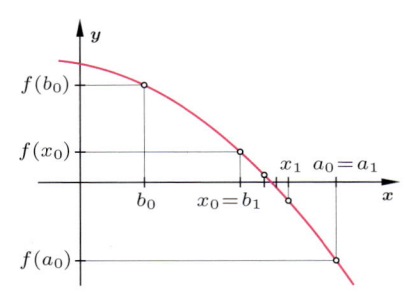

Continue the iteration until either $f(x_i)=0$ (i.e. $s=x_i$) or $|a_i - b_i|$ becomes sufficiently small.

Iteration termination error $\quad |x_i - s| < |b_i - a_i|$

Secant method

Here it is assumed that the function is continuously differentiable with a non-vanishing derivative on I (i.e. the function is monotone on I).

Algorithm
Choose two distinct starting points x_0 and x_1 in I and, for $i=1,2,\ldots$, iterate:

- $x_{i+1} := x_i - f(x_i) \dfrac{x_i - x_{i-1}}{f(x_i) - f(x_{i-1})}$

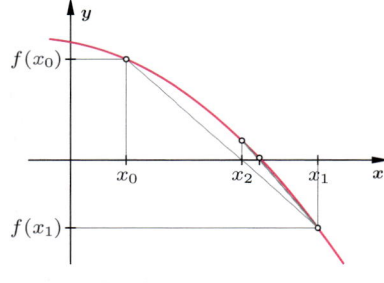

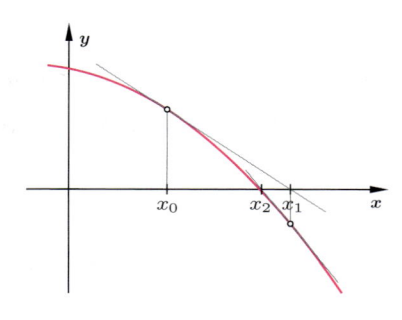

Continue the iteration until $|x_{i+1} - x_i|$ becomes sufficiently small.

Properties
Normally the secant method converges faster than the bisection method. However, in the secant method, the root may lie outside the interval $[x_i, x_{i+1}]$. Consequently, the method does not provide arbitrarily close upper and lower bounds for the root.

Newton-Raphson method

Here it is also assumed that the function is continuously differentiable on I.

Algorithm
Choose a starting value $x_0 \in I$ such that $f(x_0) \neq 0$ and $f'(x_0) \neq 0$, and, for $i=0,1,\ldots$, iterate:

- $x_{i+1} := x_i - \dfrac{f(x_i)}{f'(x_i)}$

Numerical Analysis

Continue the iteration until $|x_{i+1} - x_i|$ becomes sufficiently small.

Properties

If x_0 is chosen sufficiently close to s and f is twice continuously differentiable, then there exists a constant $C \approx \left| \dfrac{f''(s)}{2f'(s)} \right|$ such that

$$|x_{i+1} - s| \leq C |x_i - x_{i-1}|^2 \quad (i = 1, 2, \ldots)$$

Fixed-point iteration

Algorithm

Choose a function $g : I \to I$ such that the roots of f coincide with solutions of the equation $g(x) = x$ (so-called fixed points of g). Choose an arbitrary starting value $x_0 \in I$, and, for $i = 0, 1, \ldots$, iterate:

- $x_{i+1} := g(x_i)$

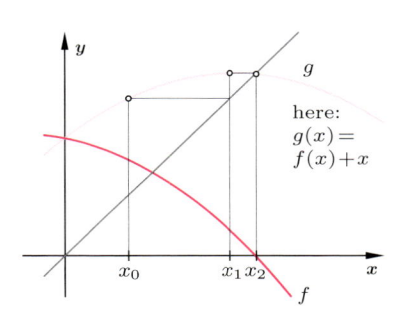

here: $g(x) = f(x) + x$

Continue the iteration until $|x_{i+1} - x_i|$ becomes sufficiently small.

Properties

If there exists a constant L ($0 < L < 1$) such that for all $x_1, x_2 \in I$, $|g(x_2) - g(x_1)| \leq L |x_2 - x_1|$, then $\lim\limits_{i \to \infty} x_i = s$ and s is the only root of f (the only fixed point of g) in I.

Iteration termination error (BANACH fixed-point theorem)

$$\left. \begin{aligned} |x_i - s| &\leq \frac{L}{1 - L} |x_i - x_{i-1}| \quad \text{(a posteriori)} \\ |x_i - s| &\leq \frac{L^i}{1 - L} |x_1 - x_0| \quad \text{(a priori)} \end{aligned} \right\} \quad (i = 1, 2, \ldots)$$

7.6 Numerical integration

Problem statement

Given an interval $[a, b]$ ($-\infty < a < b < \infty$) and a function f that is sufficiently many times continuously differentiable on $[a, b]$, approximate the integral $I := \int_a^b f(x) \, dx$ by an expression of the form

$$\sum_{i=1}^n w_i f(x_i)$$

where $x_i \in [a, b]$ are the integration points and w_i the corresponding weights.

Numerical Analysis

Trapezoidal rule

Let $[a, b]$ be uniformly partitioned into n subintervals by $n+1$ equidistant integration points defined by $x_i = a + ih$ $(i = 0, 1, \ldots, n)$ with increment $h := \dfrac{b-a}{n}$.

- trapezoidal rule approximation:
$$T_n = h \left[\frac{f(x_0) + f(x_n)}{2} + \sum_{k=1}^{n-1} f(x_k) \right]$$

- systematic doubling of the number of subintervals: $T_{2n} = \dfrac{1}{2}(T_n + M_n)$

where $M_n = h \sum_{k=1}^{n} f\!\left(a + (k - \tfrac{1}{2})h\right)$ denotes the midpoint rule approximation, which uses the n subinterval midpoints as integration points.

Error estimate

$$R_n := T_n - I = \frac{(b-a)^3}{12n^2} f''(\xi)$$

where $\xi \in (a, b)$ depends on n. A useful estimate of R_{2n}, based on the difference between successive trapezoidal rule approximation, is given by $\dfrac{1}{3}(T_n - T_{2n}) = \dfrac{1}{6}(T_n - M_n)$.

Modification of the trapezoidal rule: SIMPSON's rule

Subtracting the above estimate of R_{2n} from T_{2n}, one obtains the improved approximation

$$I \approx \frac{1}{3}(4T_{2n} - T_n) = \frac{1}{3}(T_n + 2M_n)$$

The last expression is the SIMPSON's rule spproximation S_n corresponding to T_n. Its integration points include both the end points and the midpoints of the n subintervals. As a rule, whenever R_{2n} is small, this approximation is more exact than T_{2n}.

Special case

For $n = 1$ SIMPSON's rule reduces to the three-point NEWTON-COTES formula (known in German as the "KEPLER'sche Fassregel").

$$I \approx \frac{b-a}{6}\left(f(a) + f(b) + 4f\!\left(\frac{a+b}{2}\right)\right)$$

Gaussian quadrature

Here the n integration points x_i and the weights w_i are chosen such that the approximation is exact for all polynomials of degree less than $2n$. In this case non-equidistant integration points are required. The n integration points do not allow an exact approximation for all polynomials of degree $2n$, as may be verified with the example $f(x) = (x - x_1)^2 \cdot \ldots \cdot (x - x_n)^2$.

The calculation to determine the integration points x_i and the weights w_i is complicated. Consequently such points are usually listed in tables or stored electronically. The tables list integration points for a standard integration interval $[a, b] = [-1, 1]$. A further difficulty is that no integration points are common to different values of of n, except possibly for the midpoint of $[a, b]$. As in the case of the trapezoidal rule, one needs approximations for various values of n in order to estimate the approximation error.

Numerical Analysis
MATHEMATICS   PHYSICS   ASTRONOMY   CHEMISTRY

The GAUSS-KRONROD quadrature formula makes use of $n+1$ additional integration points, such that the resulting approximation is exact for all polynomials of degree less than or equal to $3n+1$ (n even) or $3n+2$ (n odd). However, all $2n+1$ weights must be calculated afresh.

Example

Gauss $n=3$ exact for degree $\leqslant 5$		Kronrod $n=7$ exact for polynomials of degree $\leqslant 11$	
x_i	w_i	x_i	w_i
0	$\dfrac{8}{9}$	0	$\dfrac{22016}{48825}$
		$\pm\dfrac{1}{3}\sqrt{5-2\sqrt{\dfrac{30}{11}}}$	$\dfrac{8019}{350\left(138-49\sqrt{\dfrac{30}{11}}\right)}$
$\pm\sqrt{\dfrac{3}{5}}$	$\dfrac{5}{9}$	$\pm\sqrt{\dfrac{3}{5}}$	$\dfrac{12500}{46557}$
		$\pm\dfrac{1}{3}\sqrt{5+2\sqrt{\dfrac{30}{11}}}$	$\dfrac{8019}{350\left(138+49\sqrt{\dfrac{30}{11}}\right)}$

The integration points $x=0$ and $x=\pm\sqrt{\dfrac{3}{5}}$ are common to both formulae.
Consequently, the corresponding function values need only be computed once. An estimate of the approximation error is provided by a comparison of the two results:

$$\int_a^b f(x)\,dx \approx \frac{b-a}{2}\sum_{k=1}^n w_k\, f\left(\frac{b+a}{2}+\frac{b-a}{2}x_k\right)$$

The GAUSS-KRONROD approximation is more precise.

7.7 Numerical differentiation

Problem statement

Given a function f which is at least three times continuously differentiable and whose values $f_j = f(x_j)$, $j=0,1,2$, are specified at the equidistant data points x_0, $x_1=x_0+h$, $x_2=x_0+2h$ ($h\neq 0$), approximate the values of its first and second derivatives.

Two- and three-point formulae

$$f'(x_1) \approx \frac{1}{2h}(f_2 - f_0)$$
$$f'(x_0) \approx \frac{1}{2h}(-f_2 + 4f_1 - 3f_0)$$
$$f'(x_2) \approx \frac{1}{2h}(3f_2 - 4f_1 + f_0)$$
$$f''(x_1) \approx \frac{1}{h^2}(f_2 - 2f_1 + f_0)$$

In general, numerical differentiation results in a loss of numerical precision. If the the function values f_j are known to within an error $\varepsilon > 0$, the optimal increment for the x values is $h \approx \varepsilon^{1/3}$ for first derivatives and $h \approx \varepsilon^{1/4}$ for second derivatives. The resulting approximation errors of the above two- and three-point formulae will be about h^2.

Numerical Analysis

7.8 Numerical solution of differential equations

Initial value problem

Let $G \subset \mathbb{R}^2$ and let a function $f \colon G \to \mathbb{R}$ which is continuous on G be given. A function $x \mapsto y$ is sought which, together with its derivative $x \mapsto y'$, satisfies both the differential equation

$$y' = f(x, y)$$

and the initial condition

$$x_0 \mapsto y_0, \quad A = (x_0, y_0) \in G.$$

$$\text{e. g. } y' = x - y + 1, \ A = (0, 1)$$

The explicit first-order differential equation $y' = f(x, y)$ defines a direction field, in which a slope given by $f(x, y)$ is assigned to every point $(x, y) \in G$. Any solution curve passing through this point must have this given slope.

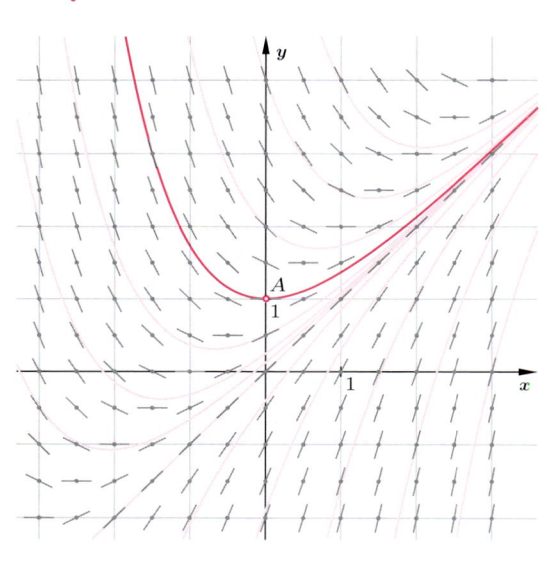

A sufficient condition for the existence and uniqueness of a solution is the existence of a constant L such that

$$\left| f(x, y_2) - f(x, y_1) \right| \leqslant L \left| y_2 - y_1 \right| \quad (x, y_i) \in G \quad (i = 1, 2)$$

$$\text{or} \quad \left| f_y(x, y) \right| \leqslant L \quad (x, y) \in G$$

where f_y denotes the partial derivative of f with respect to its second variable – i.e. $f_y(x, y)$ is the value of the derivative of $u \mapsto f(x, u)$ w.r.t. u at the point $u = y$.   p. 63 ◂

Euler method

A sequence of ordered pairs of values (x_i, y_i) is generated such that the y_i approximate the function values of the solution y at the data points x_i.

One begins with the point (x_0, y_0) corresponding to the initial condition, chooses a step size h and sets $i := 0$. Then the sequence is generated by the recurrence relation

$$x_{i+1} := x_i + h, \quad y_{i+1} := y_i + h f(x_i) \quad (i = 0, 1, \ldots)$$

Limitations of the Euler method are slow convergence of the y_i to the exact y values as $h \to 0$ and the possibility of numerical instability.

Runge-Kutta method

In contrast to the EULER method, the computation of y_{i+1} in the RUNGE-KUTTA method also makes use of the derivative at intermediate points of the interval $[x_i, x_i + h]$. As before, one starts with the point (x_0, y_0) and sets $i := 0$. In the i-th step $(i = 0, 1, \ldots)$

one calculates
$$k_1 := hf(x_i, y_i)$$
$$k_2 := hf(x_i+\tfrac{h}{2},\ y_i+\tfrac{k_1}{2})$$
$$k_3 := hf(x_i+\tfrac{h}{2},\ y_i+\tfrac{k_2}{2})$$
$$k_4 := hf(x_i+h,\ y_i+k_3)$$
$$x_{i+1} := x_i + h$$
$$y_{i+1} := y_i + \frac{k_1 + 2k_2 + 2k_3 + k_4}{6}$$

Controlling the step size

The step size h can be varied in the course of the algorithm.
Initially, a step size should be chosen such that
$$|h| < \frac{1}{5|f_y(x_0, y_0)|}.$$
If, during the course of the algorithm, the condition
$$\left|\frac{k_2 - k_3}{k_1 - k_2}\right| > \frac{1}{10}$$
occurs, then the calculations should be continued with a reduced step size.

Error estimate

It is advisable to continually check the accuracy of the computed results by generating two parallel sequences $(x_i^{(1)}, y_i^{(1)})$ and $(x_i^{(2)}, y_i^{(2)})$ in which the step size of the former is half the step size of the latter. Then $x_{2i}^{(1)} = x_i^{(2)}$ and
$$\frac{y_{2i}^{(1)} - y_i^{(2)}}{15}$$
yields an estimate of the error of $y_{2i}^{(1)}$. Furthermore, the expression
$$\frac{16 y_{2i}^{(1)} - y_i^{(2)}}{15}$$
is a better estimate of the solution at the point $x_i^{(2)}$ than $y_{2i}^{(1)}$, in general. Consequently, it can be used to continue the computation.

7.9 Discrete Fourier transform (DFT)

If one approximates the Fourier coefficients of a 2π-periodic function using the trapezoidal rule, taking $f(0) = f(2\pi)$ into account, one obtains
$$\int_0^{2\pi} f(x) \cos kx \, dx \approx \frac{2\pi}{n} \sum_{j=0}^{n-1} f\left(\frac{2\pi j}{n}\right) \cos \frac{2\pi k j}{n}$$
for the coefficients of the cosine terms and an analogous expression for the coefficients of the sine terms.

The discrete Fourier transform of n real or complex numbers $(h_0, h_1, \ldots, h_{n-1})$ is defined as

$$H_k = \sum_{j=0}^{n-1} h_j e^{-2\pi i k j/n} \qquad (k = 0, 1, \ldots, n-1)$$

where
$$e^{-2\pi i j k/n} = \cos(2\pi j k/n) - i \sin(2\pi j k/n).$$
p. 18 ◀ EULER's formula

Thus the Fourier cosine and sine coefficients of f are approximately $\frac{2\pi}{n}$ times the real and imaginary parts, respectively, of the discrete Fourier transform of $(f(0), f(\frac{2\pi}{n}), \ldots, f((n-1)\frac{2\pi}{n}))$.

The inverse discrete Fourier transform is given by a similar formula:

$$h_j = \frac{1}{n} \sum_{k=0}^{n-1} H_k e^{2\pi i j k/n} \qquad (j = 0, 1, \ldots, n-1)$$

The computation of the discrete Fourier transform as defined above requires $\frac{1}{2}n^2$ computations of cosine and sine values as well as n^2 multiplications. A recursive algorithm, called the fast Fourier transform (FFT), requires significantly fewer operations for the calculation. If $n = 2^m$ the fast Fourier transform is particularly efficient, requiring just $2nm = 2n \log_2(n)$ operations. Whenever n is even, one can separate the terms with odd and even indices in the discrete Fourier transform:

$$\begin{aligned} H_k &= \sum_{j=0}^{n/2-1} h_{2j} e^{-2\pi i k(2j)/n} + \sum_{j=0}^{n/2-1} h_{2j+1} e^{-2\pi i k(2j+1)/n} \\ &= \sum_{j=0}^{n/2-1} h_{2j} e^{-2\pi i k j/(n/2)} + e^{-2\pi i k/n} \cdot \sum_{j=0}^{n/2-1} h_{2j+1} e^{-2\pi i k j/(n/2)} \end{aligned}$$

Instead of a discrete Fourier transform with n terms one has two discrete Fourier transforms with $\frac{n}{2}$ terms plus an additional n evaluations of complex exponential functions and n multiplications. If n is a power of two, one can recursively apply this expansion to the reduced discrete Fourier transforms until one is left with discrete Fourier transforms of length 2, which only involve sums and differences.

7.10 Random number generation

In many applications it is desirable to have a deterministic algorithm which can generate a sequence of real numbers $u_1, u_2, \ldots$ in the interval $[0, 1)$ such they share the properties of random numbers which are independent and uniformly distributed in the interval. Such an algorithm is called a pseudorandom number generator (PRNG).

The best known such algorithm is the linear congruential generator:

$$x_n := \mathrm{mod}(a x_{n-1} + c, m), \quad u_n := \frac{x_n}{m} \quad (n = 1, 2, \ldots)$$

where the modulus $m > 0$, the multiplier a $(1 \leqslant a < m)$ and the increment c $(0 \leqslant c < m)$ are integer parameters of the algorithm. The initial value x_0, called the seed, is also an integer and can be chosen by the user. With the possible exception of some initial terms, the sequence is necessarily periodic.

Numerical Analysis

The modulus m should be chosen as large as possible, usually a power of two in binary computers. The multiplier a and the increment c should be chosen such that the period length, which cannot exceed m, is as large as possible. The period length will be m for every x_0 if and only if the following three conditions are met:
- c and m are relatively prime.
- Every prime factor of m is a factor of $a-1$.
- If 4 is a factor of m, then 4 is a factor of $a-1$.

For $c=0$ the maximum period length is $m-1$. A necessary and sufficient condition that the period length is indeed $m-1$ is that m is prime and $\mod(a^{(m-1)/p}, m) \neq 1$ for all prime factors p of $m-1$. For $c=0$ and $m=2^k \geq 16$, the maximum period length is $\frac{m}{4}$. In this case, a necessary and sufficient condition is that $\mod(a,8) \in \{3,5\}$ and x_0 is odd.

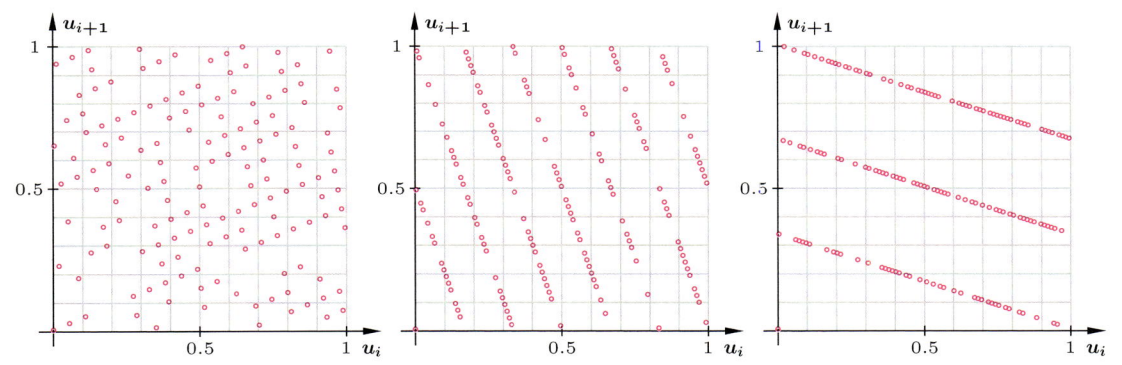

However, a long period length is not the only criterion for a good generator. In addition, coordinate pairs (u_n, u_{n+1}) constructed from pairs of successive terms in the original sequence should cover the unit square as uniformly as possible. Similarly, coordinate triples (u_n, u_{n+1}, u_{n+2}) constructed from triples of successive terms should fill the unit cube as uniformly as possible, etc. Here the choice of c is of no consequence, so that one usually takes $c=0$ or $c=1$. The choice of the multiplier a is crucial, as illustrated by the examples in the diagrams below. Out of the m^2 possible points of the form $\left(\frac{k}{m}, \frac{j}{m}\right)$ only m occur, and for an unsuitable choice of a, they can be strongly separated from one another in certain directions. There are no simple sufficient criteria for the choice of a multiplier. Consequently, it is necessary to undertake comprehensive tests before a random generator can be put into use.

150 pairs (u_n, u_{n+1}) of the linear congruential generator with $m=256$, $c=1$, and $a=165$ (left), $a=125$ (centre) and $a=85$ (right). The figure at the left displays the best behaviour. The behaviour displayed by the centre figure is unsatisfactory, and the behaviour in the right figure is totally unacceptable for a random number generator.

Since the generator is periodic, no more than $\frac{m}{1000}$ values should be used. There are more complex algorithms which have much longer periods and for which the requirement of uniform distribution of d-tuples is better satisfied. A relatively simple algorithm is the WICHMANN-HILL random number generator, which combines three linear congruential generators:

$$x_n := \mod(171 x_{n-1}, 30269), \quad y_n := \mod(172 y_{n-1}, 30307), \quad z_n := \mod(170 z_{n-1}, 30323)$$

$$u_n := \mod\left(\frac{x_n}{30269} + \frac{y_n}{30307} + \frac{z_n}{30323}, 1\right)$$

Its period length is equal to $\frac{1}{4} \cdot 30268 \cdot 30306 \cdot 30322$.

8 Mathematical Tables

Prime numbers and selected prime factorizations (up to 4049)

Examples in the use of the table:
$1247 = 1230 + 17 = 29 \cdot 43$ $1249 = 1230 + 19$ prime $1251 = 1230 + 21$ divisible by 3

n	$n+1$	$n+7$	$n+11$	$n+13$	$n+17$	$n+19$	$n+23$	$n+29$
0	—	2 3 5 7	11	13	17	19	23	29
30	31	37	41	43	47	7 · 7	53	59
60	61	67	71	73	7 · 11	79	83	89
90	7 · 13	97	101	103	107	109	113	7 · 17
120	11 · 11	127	131	7 · 19	137	139	11 · 13	149
150	151	157	7 · 23	163	167	13 · 13	173	179
180	181	11 · 17	191	193	197	199	7 · 29	11 · 19
210	211	7 · 31	13 · 17	223	227	229	233	239
240	241	13 · 19	251	11 · 23	257	7 · 37	263	269
270	271	277	281	283	7 · 41	17 · 17	293	13 · 23
300	7 · 43	307	311	313	317	11 · 29	17 · 19	7 · 47
330	331	337	11 · 31	7 · 7 · 7	347	349	353	359
360	19 · 19	367	7 · 53	373	13 · 29	379	383	389
390	17 · 23	397	401	13 · 31	11 · 37	409	7 · 59	419
420	421	7 · 61	431	433	19 · 23	439	443	449
450	11 · 41	457	461	463	467	7 · 67	11 · 43	479
480	13 · 37	487	491	17 · 29	7 · 71	499	503	509
510	7 · 73	11 · 47	521	523	17 · 31	23 · 23	13 · 41	7 · 7 · 11
540	541	547	19 · 29	7 · 79	557	13 · 43	563	569
570	571	577	7 · 83	11 · 53	587	19 · 31	593	599
600	601	607	13 · 47	613	617	619	7 · 89	17 · 37
630	631	7 · 7 · 13	641	643	647	11 · 59	653	659
660	661	23 · 29	11 · 61	673	677	7 · 97	683	13 · 53
690	691	17 · 41	701	19 · 37	7 · 101	709	23 · 31	719
720	7 · 103	727	17 · 43	733	11 · 67	739	743	7 · 107
750	751	757	761	7 · 109	13 · 59	769	773	19 · 41
780	11 · 71	787	7 · 113	13 · 61	797	17 · 47	11 · 73	809
810	811	19 · 43	821	823	827	829	7 · 7 · 17	839
840	29 · 29	7 · 11 · 11	23 · 37	853	857	859	863	11 · 79
870	13 · 67	877	881	883	887	7 · 127	19 · 47	29 · 31
900	17 · 53	907	911	11 · 83	7 · 131	919	13 · 71	929
930	7 · 7 · 19	937	941	23 · 41	947	13 · 73	953	7 · 137
960	31 · 31	967	971	7 · 139	977	11 · 89	983	23 · 43
990	991	997	7 · 11 · 13	17 · 59	19 · 53	1009	1013	1019
1020	1021	13 · 79	1031	1033	17 · 61	1039	7 · 149	1049
1050	1051	7 · 151	1061	1063	11 · 97	1069	29 · 37	13 · 83
1080	23 · 47	1087	1091	1093	1097	7 · 157	1103	1109
1110	11 · 101	1117	19 · 59	1123	7 · 7 · 23	1129	11 · 103	17 · 67
1140	7 · 163	31 · 37	1151	1153	13 · 89	19 · 61	1163	7 · 167
1170	1171	11 · 107	1181	7 · 13 · 13	1187	29 · 41	1193	11 · 109
1200	1201	17 · 71	7 · 173	1213	1217	23 · 53	1223	1229
1230	1231	1237	17 · 73	11 · 113	29 · 43	1249	7 · 179	1259
1260	13 · 97	7 · 181	31 · 41	19 · 67	1277	1279	1283	1289
1290	1291	1297	1301	1303	1307	7 · 11 · 17	13 · 101	1319
1320	1321	1327	11 · 11 · 11	31 · 43	7 · 191	13 · 103	17 · 79	19 · 71
1350	7 · 193	23 · 59	1361	29 · 47	1367	37 · 37	1373	7 · 197
1380	1381	19 · 73	13 · 107	7 · 199	11 · 127	1399	23 · 61	1409
1410	17 · 83	13 · 109	7 · 7 · 29	1423	1427	1429	1433	1439
1440	11 · 131	1447	1451	1453	31 · 47	1459	7 · 11 · 19	13 · 113
1470	1471	7 · 211	1481	1483	1487	1489	1493	1499

Mathematical Tables
MATHEMATICS   PHYSICS   ASTRONOMY   CHEMISTRY

n	$n+1$	$n+7$	$n+11$	$n+13$	$n+17$	$n+19$	$n+23$	$n+29$
1500	19·79	11·137	1511	17·89	37·41	7·7·31	1523	11·139
1530	1531	29·53	23·67	1543	7·13·17	1549	1553	1559
1560	7·223	1567	1571	11·11·13	19·83	1579	1583	7·227
1590	37·43	1597	1601	7·229	1607	1609	1613	1619
1620	1621	1627	7·233	23·71	1637	11·149	31·53	17·97
1650	13·127	1657	11·151	1663	1667	1669	7·239	23·73
1680	41·41	7·241	19·89	1693	1697	1699	13·131	1709
1710	29·59	17·101	1721	1723	11·157	7·13·19	1733	37·47
1740	1741	1747	17·103	1753	7·251	1759	41·43	29·61
1770	7·11·23	1777	13·137	1783	1787	1789	11·163	7·257
1800	1801	13·139	1811	7·7·37	23·79	17·107	1823	31·59
1830	1831	11·167	7·263	19·97	1847	43·43	17·109	11·13·13
1860	1861	1867	1871	1873	1877	1879	7·269	1889
1890	31·61	7·271	1901	11·173	1907	23·83	1913	19·101
1920	17·113	41·47	1931	1933	13·149	7·277	29·67	1949
1950	1951	19·103	37·53	13·151	7·281	11·179	1973	1979
1980	7·283	1987	11·181	1993	1997	1999	2003	7·7·41
2010	2011	2017	43·47	7·17·17	2027	2029	19·107	2039
2040	13·157	23·89	7·293	2053	11·11·17	29·71	2063	2069
2070	19·109	31·67	2081	2083	2087	2089	7·13·23	2099
2100	11·191	7·7·43	2111	2113	29·73	13·163	11·193	2129
2130	2131	2137	2141	2143	19·113	7·307	2153	17·127
2160	2161	11·197	13·167	41·53	7·311	2179	37·59	11·199
2190	7·313	13·13·13	31·71	2203	2207	47·47	2213	7·317
2220	2221	17·131	23·97	7·11·29	2237	2239	2243	13·173
2250	2251	37·61	7·17·19	31·73	2267	2269	2273	43·53
2280	2281	2287	29·79	2293	2297	11·11·19	7·7·47	2309
2310	2311	7·331	11·211	23·101	13·179	17·137	2333	2339
2340	2341	2347	2351	13·181	2357	7·337	17·139	23·103
2370	2371	2377	2381	2383	7·11·31	2389	2393	2399
2400	7·7·7·7	29·83	2411	19·127	2417	41·59	2423	7·347
2430	11·13·17	2437	2441	7·349	2447	31·79	11·223	2459
2460	23·107	2467	7·353	2473	2477	37·67	13·191	19·131
2490	47·53	11·227	41·61	2503	23·109	13·193	7·359	11·229
2520	2521	7·19·19	2531	17·149	43·59	2539	2543	2549
2550	2551	2557	13·197	11·233	17·151	7·367	31·83	2579
2580	29·89	13·199	2591	2593	7·7·53	23·113	19·137	2609
2610	7·373	2617	2621	43·61	37·71	11·239	2633	7·13·29
2640	19·139	2647	11·241	7·379	2657	2659	2663	17·157
2670	2671	2677	7·383	2683	2687	2689	2693	2699
2700	37·73	2707	2711	2713	11·13·19	2719	7·389	2729
2730	2731	7·17·23	2741	13·211	41·67	2749	2753	31·89
2760	11·251	2767	17·163	47·59	2777	7·397	11·11·23	2789
2790	2791	2797	2801	2803	7·401	53·53	29·97	2819
2820	7·13·31	11·257	19·149	2833	2837	17·167	2843	7·11·37
2850	2851	2857	2861	7·409	47·61	19·151	13·13·17	2879
2880	43·67	2887	7·7·59	11·263	2897	13·223	2903	2909
2910	41·71	2917	23·127	37·79	2927	29·101	7·419	2939
2940	17·173	7·421	13·227	2953	2957	11·269	2963	2969
2970	2971	13·229	11·271	19·157	29·103	7·7·61	41·73	2999
3000	3001	31·97	3011	23·131	7·431	3019	3023	13·233
3030	7·433	3037	3041	17·179	11·277	3049	43·71	7·19·23
3060	3061	3067	37·83	7·439	17·181	3079	3083	3089
3090	11·281	19·163	7·443	29·107	13·239	3109	11·283	3119
3120	3121	53·59	31·101	13·241	3137	43·73	7·449	47·67
3150	23·137	7·11·41	29·109	3163	3167	3169	19·167	11·17·17
3180	3181	3187	3191	31·103	23·139	7·457	3203	3209
3210	13·13·19	3217	3221	11·293	7·461	3229	53·61	41·79
3240	7·463	17·191	3251	3253	3257	3259	13·251	7·467
3270	3271	29·113	17·193	7·7·67	19·173	11·13·23	37·89	3299

147

Mathematical Tables
MATHEMATICS   PHYSICS   ASTRONOMY   CHEMISTRY

n	$n+1$	$n+7$	$n+11$	$n+13$	$n+17$	$n+19$	$n+23$	$n+29$
3300	3301	3307	7·11·43	3313	31·107	3319	3323	3329
3330	3331	47·71	13·257	3343	3347	17·197	7·479	3359
3360	3361	7·13·37	3371	3373	11·307	31·109	17·199	3389
3390	3391	43·79	19·179	41·83	3407	7·487	3413	13·263
3420	11·311	23·149	47·73	3433	7·491	19·181	11·313	3449
3450	7·17·29	3457	3461	3463	3467	3469	23·151	7·7·71
3480	59·59	11·317	3491	7·499	13·269	3499	31·113	11·11·29
3510	3511	3517	7·503	13·271	3527	3529	3533	3539
3540	3541	3547	53·67	11·17·19	3557	3559	7·509	43·83
3570	3571	7·7·73	3581	3583	17·211	37·97	3593	59·61
3600	13·277	3607	23·157	3613	3617	7·11·47	3623	19·191
3630	3631	3637	11·331	3643	7·521	41·89	13·281	3659
3660	7·523	19·193	3671	3673	3677	13·283	29·127	7·17·31
3690	3691	3697	3701	7·23·23	11·337	3709	47·79	3719
3720	61·61	3727	7·13·41	3733	37·101	3739	19·197	23·163
3750	11·11·31	13·17·17	3761	53·71	3767	3769	7·7·7·11	3779
3780	19·199	7·541	17·223	3793	3797	29·131	3803	13·293
3810	37·103	11·347	3821	3823	43·89	7·547	3833	11·349
3840	23·167	3847	3851	3853	7·19·29	17·227	3863	53·73
3870	7·7·79	3877	3881	11·353	13·13·23	3889	17·229	7·557
3900	47·83	3907	3911	7·13·43	3917	3919	3923	3929
3930	3931	31·127	7·563	3943	3947	11·359	59·67	37·107
3960	17·233	3967	11·19·19	29·137	41·97	23·173	7·569	3989
3990	13·307	7·571	4001	4003	4007	19·211	4013	4019
4020	4021	4027	29·139	37·109	11·367	7·577	13·311	4049

Pythagorean triples and quadruples

$a^2 + b^2 = c^2$

a, b relatively prime
$a, b \leqslant 200$

a	b	c
3	4	5
5	12	13
7	24	25
8	15	17
9	40	41
11	60	61
12	35	37
13	84	85
15	112	113
16	63	65
17	144	145
19	180	181
20	21	29
20	99	101
24	143	145
28	45	53

a	b	c
28	195	197
33	56	65
36	77	85
39	80	89
44	117	125
48	55	73
51	140	149
52	165	173
57	176	185
60	91	109
65	72	97
84	187	205
85	132	157
88	105	137
95	168	193
104	153	185
119	120	169
133	156	205
140	171	221

$d^2 + e^2 + f^2 = g^2$

d, e, f relatively prime
$d, e, f \leqslant 25$

d	e	f	g
1	2	2	3
1	4	8	9
1	6	18	19
1	12	12	17
2	3	6	7
2	5	14	15
2	6	9	11
2	10	11	15
2	10	25	27
2	14	23	27
3	4	12	13
3	6	22	23
3	14	18	23
3	16	24	29
4	4	7	9
4	5	20	21

d	e	f	g
4	8	19	21
4	13	16	21
6	6	7	11
6	6	17	19
6	10	15	19
6	13	18	23
6	21	22	31
7	14	22	27
8	9	12	17
8	11	16	21
8	20	25	33
9	12	20	25
10	10	23	27
11	12	24	29
12	15	16	25
12	16	21	29
14	18	21	31
17	20	20	33
23	24	24	41

There are infinitely many Pythagorean triples (x, y, z). Using the following formulae, they can easily be constructed from two (relatively prime) natural numbers n, m ($n > m$):

$$x = n^2 - m^2, \quad y = 2mn, \quad z = n^2 + m^2$$

Mathematical Tables
MATHEMATICS   PHYSICS   ASTRONOMY   CHEMISTRY

Cumulative normal distribution

Cumulative distribution function of the standard normal distribution ($\mu = 0$, $\sigma = 1$):

$$\Phi(u) = \frac{1}{\sqrt{2\pi}} \int_{-\infty}^{u} e^{-\frac{z^2}{2}} \, dz$$

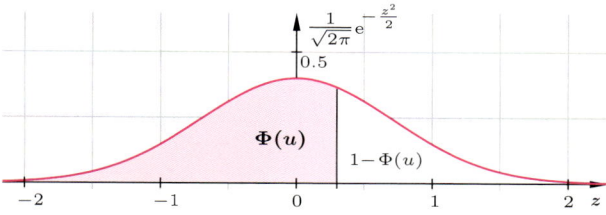

u	+0.00	+0.01	+0.02	+0.03	+0.04	+0.05	+0.06	+0.07	+0.08	+0.09
0.0	0.5000	0.5040	0.5080	0.5120	0.5160	0.5199	0.5239	0.5279	0.5319	0.5359
0.1	0.5398	0.5438	0.5478	0.5517	0.5557	0.5596	0.5636	0.5675	0.5714	0.5753
0.2	0.5793	0.5832	0.5871	0.5910	0.5948	0.5987	0.6026	0.6064	0.6103	0.6141
0.3	0.6179	0.6217	0.6255	0.6293	0.6331	0.6368	0.6406	0.6443	0.6480	0.6517
0.4	0.6554	0.6591	0.6628	0.6664	0.6700	0.6736	0.6772	0.6808	0.6844	0.6879
0.5	0.6915	0.6950	0.6985	0.7019	0.7054	0.7088	0.7123	0.7157	0.7190	0.7224
0.6	0.7257	0.7291	0.7324	0.7357	0.7389	0.7422	0.7454	0.7486	0.7517	0.7549
0.7	0.7580	0.7611	0.7642	0.7673	0.7704	0.7734	0.7764	0.7794	0.7823	0.7852
0.8	0.7881	0.7910	0.7939	0.7967	0.7995	0.8023	0.8051	0.8078	0.8106	0.8133
0.9	0.8159	0.8186	0.8212	0.8238	0.8264	0.8289	0.8315	0.8340	0.8365	0.8389
1.0	0.8413	0.8438	0.8461	0.8485	0.8508	0.8531	0.8554	0.8577	0.8599	0.8621
1.1	0.8643	0.8665	0.8686	0.8708	0.8729	0.8749	0.8770	0.8790	0.8810	0.8830
1.2	0.8849	0.8869	0.8888	0.8907	0.8925	0.8944	0.8962	0.8980	0.8997	0.9015
1.3	0.9032	0.9049	0.9066	0.9082	0.9099	0.9115	0.9131	0.9147	0.9162	0.9177
1.4	0.9192	0.9207	0.9222	0.9236	0.9251	0.9265	0.9279	0.9292	0.9306	0.9319
1.5	0.9332	0.9345	0.9357	0.9370	0.9382	0.9394	0.9406	0.9418	0.9429	0.9441
1.6	0.9452	0.9463	0.9474	0.9484	0.9495	0.9505	0.9515	0.9525	0.9535	0.9545
1.7	0.9554	0.9564	0.9573	0.9582	0.9591	0.9599	0.9608	0.9616	0.9625	0.9633
1.8	0.9641	0.9649	0.9656	0.9664	0.9671	0.9678	0.9686	0.9693	0.9699	0.9706
1.9	0.9713	0.9719	0.9726	0.9732	0.9738	0.9744	0.9750	0.9756	0.9761	0.9767
2.0	0.97725	0.97778	0.97831	0.97882	0.97932	0.97982	0.98030	0.98077	0.98124	0.98169
2.1	0.98214	0.98257	0.98300	0.98341	0.98382	0.98422	0.98461	0.98500	0.98537	0.98574
2.2	0.98610	0.98645	0.98679	0.98713	0.98745	0.98778	0.98809	0.98840	0.98870	0.98899
2.3	0.98928	0.98956	0.98983	0.99010	0.99036	0.99061	0.99086	0.99111	0.99134	0.99158
2.4	0.99180	0.99202	0.99224	0.99245	0.99266	0.99286	0.99305	0.99324	0.99343	0.99361
2.5	0.99379	0.99396	0.99413	0.99430	0.99446	0.99461	0.99477	0.99492	0.99506	0.99520
2.6	0.99534	0.99547	0.99560	0.99573	0.99585	0.99598	0.99609	0.99621	0.99632	0.99643
2.7	0.99653	0.99664	0.99674	0.99683	0.99693	0.99702	0.99711	0.99720	0.99728	0.99736
2.8	0.99744	0.99752	0.99760	0.99767	0.99774	0.99781	0.99788	0.99795	0.99801	0.99807
2.9	0.99813	0.99819	0.99825	0.99831	0.99836	0.99841	0.99846	0.99851	0.99856	0.99861
3.0	0.998650		0.998736		0.998817		0.998893		0.998965	
3.1	0.999032		0.999096		0.999155		0.999211		0.999264	
3.2	0.999313		0.999359		0.999402		0.999443		0.999481	
3.3	0.999517		0.999550		0.999581		0.999610		0.999638	
3.4	0.999663		0.999687		0.999709		0.999730		0.999749	
3.5	0.999767		0.999784		0.999800		0.999815		0.999828	
3.6	0.999841		0.999853		0.999864		0.999874		0.999883	
3.7	0.9998922		0.9999004		0.9999080		0.9999150		0.9999216	
3.8	0.9999276		0.9999333		0.9999385		0.9999433		0.9999478	
3.9	0.9999519		0.9999557		0.9999592		0.9999625		0.9999655	

Values with negative arguments can be derived from $\Phi(-u) = 1 - \Phi(u)$.

Critical values $u_{1-\alpha}$ for statistical tests are obtained by solving the equation

$$\Phi(u_{1-\alpha}) = 1 - \alpha$$

In particular: $u_{0.95} = 1.645$, $u_{0.975} = 1.960$, $u_{0.99} = 2.326$, $u_{0.995} = 2.576$

Mathematical Tables
MATHEMATICS   PHYSICS   ASTRONOMY   CHEMISTRY

Rejection regions and confidence intervals for binomial distributions
(for 5% significance level or 95% confidence)

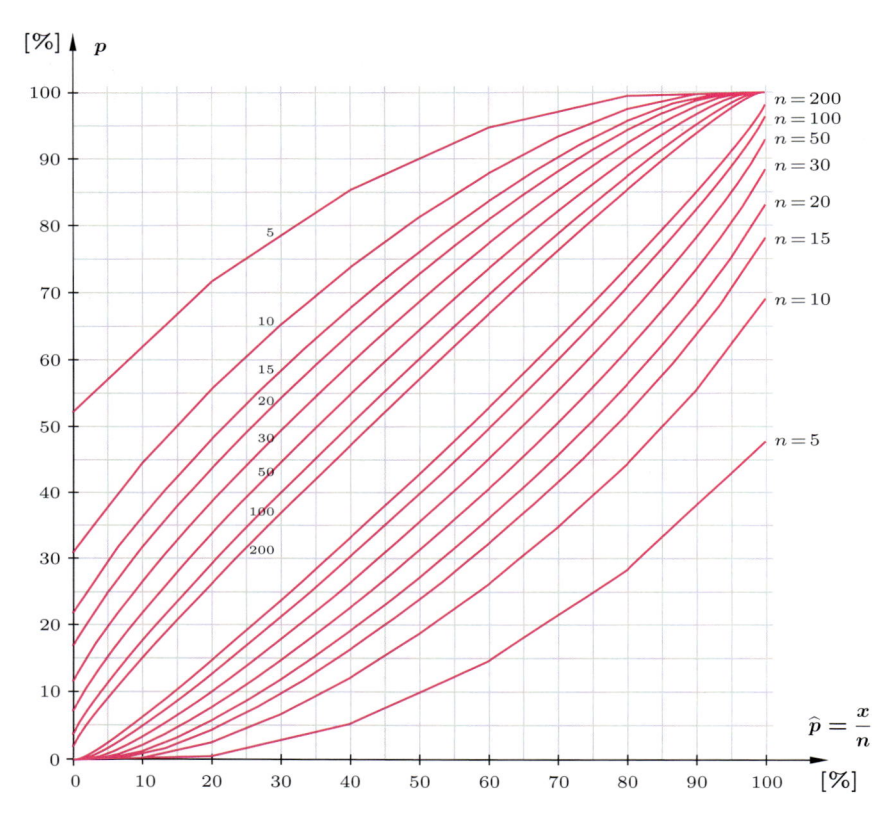

Curves for the approximate determination of rejection regions and confidence intervals for binomial distributions

Examples in the use of the graphs

Suppose a coin is tossed $n = 30$ times. What results would lead to rejection of the hypothesis that $p = 0.5$ with a significance level of 5%? The horizontal line $p = 50\%$ intersects the two curves for $n = 30$ at the points ($\frac{x}{n} = 0.305, p = 50\%$) and ($\frac{x}{n} = 0.695, p = 50\%$). Consequently, a test at a 5% significance level would reject the null hypothesis if either $x \leqslant 30 \cdot 0.305 \Leftrightarrow x \leqslant 9$ or $x \geqslant 30 \cdot 0.695 \Leftrightarrow x \geqslant 21$.

Suppose that in $n = 20$ independent repetitions of a random experiment an event occurs $x = 5$ times. Find a 95% confidence interval for the unknown probability of the event. The vertical line $\frac{x}{n} = 0.25$ intersects the two curves for $n = 20$ at the points ($\frac{x}{n} = 0.25, p = 8\%$) and ($\frac{x}{n} = 0.25, p = 49\%$). Consequently, the 95% confidence interval is $(0.08, 0.49)$.

For sample sizes not shown, one can use linear interpolation between the pair of illustrated curves most closely corresponding to the sample size.

Critical values of the chi-squared distribution

Critical values $\chi^2_{1-\alpha}(\nu)$ of the chi-squared distribution with ν degrees of freedom:

ν	1	2	3	4	5	6	7	8	9	10
$\alpha = 0.05$	3.84	5.99	7.81	9.49	11.07	12.59	14.07	15.51	16.92	18.31
$\alpha = 0.01$	6.63	9.21	11.34	13.28	15.09	16.81	18.48	20.09	21.67	23.21
ν	11	12	13	14	15	16	17	18	19	20
$\alpha = 0.05$	19.68	21.03	22.36	23.68	25.00	26.30	27.59	28.87	30.14	31.41
$\alpha = 0.01$	24.72	26.22	27.69	29.14	30.58	32	33.41	34.81	36.19	37.57
ν	25	30	35	40	50	60	70	80	90	100
$\alpha = 0.05$	37.65	43.77	49.80	55.76	67.5	79.08	90.53	101.88	113.15	124.34
$\alpha = 0.01$	44.31	50.89	57.34	63.69	76.15	88.38	100.43	112.33	124.12	135.81

For $\nu \to \infty$ the critical values asymptotically approach $\nu + 1.65 \cdot \sqrt{2\nu}$ and $\nu + 2.33 \cdot \sqrt{2\nu}$, respectively.

Critical values of Student's t-distribution

Critical values $t_{1-\frac{\alpha}{2}}(\nu)$ of Student's t-distribution with ν degrees of freedom:

ν	1	2	3	4	5	6	7	8	9	10	11	12
$\alpha = 0.05$	12.71	4.30	3.18	2.78	2.57	2.45	2.36	2.31	2.26	2.23	2.20	2.18
$\alpha = 0.01$	63.66	9.92	5.84	4.60	4.03	3.71	3.50	3.36	3.25	3.17	3.11	3.05
ν	13	14	15	16	18	20	25	30	40	60	100	200
$\alpha = 0.05$	2.16	2.14	2.13	2.12	2.10	2.09	2.06	2.04	2.02	2.00	1.98	1.97
$\alpha = 0.01$	3.01	2.98	2.95	2.92	2.88	2.85	2.79	2.75	2.70	2.66	2.63	2.60

For $\nu \to \infty$ the critical values converge to the corresponding values 1.96 and 2.58 of the normal distribution.

Critical values for the Wilcoxon signed-rank test

Critical value $r_{0.025}(n)$ for carrying out the Wilcoxon signed-rank test at a significance level of 5%: The null hypothesis is rejected if

$$r_+ \leqslant r_{0.025}(n) \quad \text{or} \quad r_+ \geqslant \frac{n(n+1)}{2} - r_{0.025}(n)$$

For $n < 6$ the critical values are undefined; the null hypothesis is never rejected at a 5% significance level.

n	6	7	8	9	10	11	12	13	14	15	16	17	18	19	20	21	22	23
$r_{0.025}$	0	2	3	5	8	10	13	17	21	25	29	34	40	46	52	58	65	73

For larger values of n, the asymptotic approximation

$$r_{0.025}(n) \approx \frac{n(n+1)}{4} - 1.96\sqrt{\frac{n(n+1)(2n+1)}{24}}$$

can be used.

Critical values for the Wilcoxon-Mann-Whitney test

Critical value $w_{0.025}(n_1, n_2)$ for carrying out the WILCOXON-MANN-WHITNEY test at a significance level of 5%: The null hypothesis is rejected if

$$r_x \leqslant \frac{n_1(n_1+1)}{2} + w_{0.025}(n_1, n_2) \quad \text{or} \quad r_x \geqslant n_1 n_2 + \frac{n_1(n_1+1)}{2} - w_{0.025}(n_1, n_2)$$

n_1	$n_2 = 3$	4	5	6	7	8	9	10	11	12	13	14	15	16	17	18
3	–	–	0	1	1	2	2	3	3	4	4	5	5	6	6	7
4		0	1	2	3	4	4	5	6	7	8	9	10	11	11	12
5	0	1	2	3	5	6	7	8	9	11	12	13	14	15	17	18
6	1	2	3	5	6	8	10	11	13	14	16	17	19	21	22	24
7	1	3	5	6	8	10	12	14	16	18	20	22	24	26	28	30
8	2	4	6	8	10	13	15	17	19	22	24	26	29	31	34	36
9	2	4	7	10	12	15	17	20	23	26	28	31	34	37	39	42
10	3	5	8	11	14	17	20	23	26	29	33	36	39	42	45	48
11	3	6	9	13	16	19	23	26	30	33	37	40	44	47	51	55
12	4	7	11	14	18	22	26	29	33	37	41	45	49	53	57	61
13	4	8	12	16	20	24	28	33	37	41	45	50	54	59	63	67
14	5	9	13	17	22	26	31	36	40	45	50	55	59	64	69	74
15	5	10	14	19	24	29	34	39	44	49	54	59	64	70	75	80
16	6	11	15	21	26	31	37	42	47	53	59	64	70	75	81	86
17	6	11	17	22	28	34	39	45	51	57	63	69	75	81	87	93
18	7	12	18	24	30	36	42	48	55	61	67	74	80	86	93	99

A dash entry means that the null hypothesis is never rejected at a 5% significance level.

For larger values of n_1 and n_2 the asymptotic approximation

$$w_{0.025}(n_1, n_2) \approx \frac{n_1 n_2}{2} - 1.96 \sqrt{\frac{n_1 n_2 (n_1 + n_2 + 1)}{12}}$$

can be used.

Actuarial life tables

On the use of the table on the opposite page

$l_x(k)$ denotes the probability that a newborn male lives to his k-th birthday, multiplied by the factor 100 000. This can be used to calculate the conditional probability that a man who has passed his k-th birthday lives to his $(k+n)$-th birthday.

$$P_x(k+n) = \frac{l_x(k+n)}{l_x(k)}$$

$e_x(k)$ denotes the expected remaining lifetime of a man still living on his k-th birthday.

$$e_x(k) = \sum_{n=1}^{\omega_x+1-k} \left(n - \frac{1}{2}\right) \frac{l_x(k+n-1) - l_x(k+n)}{l_x(k)} = \sum_{n=1}^{\omega_x-k} \frac{l_x(k+n)}{l_x(k)} + \frac{1}{2},$$

where ω_x is the highest age listed in the table.

The quantities $l_y(k)$ and $e_y(k)$ are correspondingly defined for women.

Mathematical Tables
MATHEMATICS PHYSICS ASTRONOMY CHEMISTRY

exact age k	men $l_x(k)$	$e_x(k)$	women $l_y(k)$	$e_y(k)$	exact age k	men $l_x(k)$	$e_x(k)$	women $l_y(k)$	$e_y(k)$
0	100 000	77.22	100 000	82.82	55	92 831	25.28	95 978	29.72
1	99 466	76.63	99 583	82.16	56	92 305	24.42	95 670	28.81
2	99 426	75.66	99 548	81.19	57	91 731	23.57	95 336	27.91
3	99 395	74.69	99 528	80.21	58	91 105	22.73	94 977	27.01
4	99 372	73.70	99 512	79.22	59	90 421	21.89	94 589	26.12
5	99 354	72.72	99 498	78.23	60	89 674	21.07	94 171	25.24
6	99 340	71.73	99 487	77.24	61	88 861	20.26	93 721	24.35
7	99 326	70.74	99 477	76.25	62	87 975	19.46	93 237	23.48
8	99 314	69.75	99 468	75.25	63	87 010	18.67	92 715	22.61
9	99 302	68.75	99 460	74.26	64	85 961	17.89	92 153	21.74
10	99 290	67.76	99 453	73.27	65	84 821	17.12	91 545	20.88
11	99 278	66.77	99 445	72.27	66	83 584	16.37	90 887	20.03
12	99 263	65.78	99 436	71.28	67	82 240	15.63	90 173	19.19
13	99 247	64.79	99 427	70.28	68	80 784	14.90	89 397	18.35
14	99 228	63.80	99 415	69.29	69	79 207	14.19	88 552	17.52
15	99 205	62.82	99 401	68.30	70	77 500	13.49	87 627	16.70
16	99 176	61.84	99 383	67.31	71	75 654	12.81	86 614	15.89
17	99 137	60.86	99 362	66.33	72	73 660	12.14	85 499	15.09
18	99 084	59.89	99 337	65.35	73	71 509	11.49	84 270	14.30
19	99 016	58.93	99 309	64.36	74	69 192	10.86	82 910	13.53
20	98 933	57.98	99 278	63.38	75	66 700	10.25	81 401	12.77
21	98 839	57.04	99 247	62.40	76	64 026	9.65	79 721	12.03
22	98 740	56.09	99 215	61.42	77	61 167	9.08	77 850	11.30
23	98 642	55.15	99 184	60.44	78	58 124	8.53	75 766	10.60
24	98 545	54.20	99 153	59.46	79	54 899	8.00	73 444	9.92
25	98 451	53.25	99 122	58.48	80	51 504	7.50	70 863	9.26
26	98 359	52.30	99 090	57.50	81	47 955	7.02	68 004	8.63
27	98 269	51.35	99 058	56.52	82	44 277	6.56	64 850	8.03
28	98 180	50.40	99 025	55.54	83	40 501	6.12	61 393	7.45
29	98 091	49.44	98 990	54.55	84	36 667	5.71	57 631	6.91
30	98 003	48.49	98 954	53.57	85	32 821	5.32	53 577	6.39
31	97 914	47.53	98 915	52.59	86	29 013	4.95	49 256	5.91
32	97 824	46.57	98 875	51.62	87	25 298	4.61	44 713	5.46
33	97 733	45.62	98 831	50.64	88	21 729	4.28	40 012	5.04
34	97 639	44.66	98 784	49.66	89	18 356	3.97	35 235	4.65
35	97 541	43.70	98 734	48.69	90	15 229	3.69	30 481	4.30
36	97 439	42.75	98 681	47.71	91	12 385	3.42	25 856	3.98
37	97 332	41.80	98 623	46.74	92	9 854	3.17	21 473	3.69
38	97 218	40.84	98 560	45.77	93	7 654	2.94	17 434	3.43
39	97 097	39.89	98 493	44.80	94	5 790	2.72	13 822	3.20
40	96 967	38.95	98 420	43.83	95	4 255	2.52	10 694	2.99
41	96 826	38.00	98 340	42.87	96	3 030	2.34	8 070	2.80
42	96 674	37.06	98 254	41.91	97	2 084	2.18	5 936	2.63
43	96 510	36.12	98 159	40.95	98	1 382	2.03	4 254	2.47
44	96 330	35.19	98 056	39.99	99	882	1.90	2 968	2.32
45	96 135	34.26	97 943	39.04	100	540	1.78	2 014	2.18
46	95 922	33.34	97 818	38.08	101	318	1.68	1 328	2.04
47	95 689	32.42	97 682	37.14	102	179	1.59	849	1.92
48	95 435	31.50	97 531	36.19	103	97	1.51	525	1.79
49	95 156	30.59	97 366	35.25	104	51	1.43	312	1.67
50	94 851	29.69	97 184	34.32	105	26	1.34	178	1.54
51	94 517	28.79	96 984	33.39	106	13	1.20	97	1.41
52	94 151	27.90	96 764	32.46	107	6	0.93	50	1.27
53	93 750	27.02	96 525	31.54	108	3	0.50	24	1.11
54	93 311	26.14	96 263	30.63	109			11	0.89
					110			4	0.50

© SFSO, Swiss life tables 1998/2003 (BFS, Sterbetafeln für die Schweiz 1998/2003)

Mathematical Tables
MATHEMATICS · PHYSICS · ASTRONOMY · CHEMISTRY

Random numbers and the first 2000 digits of the decimal expansion of π

$\pi \approx 3.$	0	1	2	3	4	5	6	7	8	9
0	14159	26535	89793	23846	26433	83279	50288	41971	69399	37510
1	58209	74944	59230	78164	06286	20899	86280	34825	34211	70679
2	82148	08651	32823	06647	09384	46095	50582	23172	53594	08128
3	48111	74502	84102	70193	85211	05559	64462	29489	54930	38196
4	44288	10975	66593	34461	28475	64823	37867	83165	27120	19091
5	45648	56692	34603	48610	45432	66482	13393	60726	02491	41273
6	72458	70066	06315	58817	48815	20920	96282	92540	91715	36436
7	78925	90360	01133	05305	48820	46652	13841	46951	94151	16094
8	33057	27036	57595	91953	09218	61173	81932	61179	31051	18548
9	07446	23799	62749	56735	18857	52724	89122	79381	83011	94912
10	98336	73362	44065	66430	86021	39494	63952	24737	19070	21798
11	60943	70277	05392	17176	29317	67523	84674	81846	76694	05132
12	00056	81271	45263	56082	77857	71342	75778	96091	73637	17872
13	14684	40901	22495	34301	46549	58537	10507	92279	68925	89235
14	42019	95611	21290	21960	86403	44181	59813	62977	47713	09960
15	51870	72113	49999	99837	29780	49951	05973	17328	16096	31859
16	50244	59455	34690	83026	42522	30825	33446	85035	26193	11881
17	71010	00313	78387	52886	58753	32083	81420	61717	76691	47303
18	59825	34904	28755	46873	11595	62863	88235	37875	93751	95778
19	18577	80532	17122	68066	13001	92787	66111	95909	21642	01989
20	38095	25720	10654	85863	27886	59361	53381	82796	82303	01952
21	03530	18529	68995	77362	25994	13891	24972	17752	83479	13151
22	55748	57242	45415	06959	50829	53311	68617	27855	88907	50983
23	81754	63746	49393	19255	06040	09277	01671	13900	98488	24012
24	85836	16035	63707	66010	47101	81942	95559	61989	46767	83744
25	94482	55379	77472	68471	04047	53464	62080	46684	25906	94912
26	93313	67702	89891	52104	75216	20569	66024	05803	81501	93511
27	25338	24300	35587	64024	74964	73263	91419	92726	04269	92279
28	67823	54781	63600	93417	21641	21992	45863	15030	28618	29745
29	55706	74983	85054	94588	58692	69956	90927	21079	75093	02955
30	32116	53449	87202	75596	02364	80665	49911	98818	34797	75356
31	63698	07426	54252	78625	51818	41757	46728	90977	77279	38000
32	81647	06001	61452	49192	17321	72147	72350	14144	19735	68548
33	16136	11573	52552	13347	57418	49468	43852	33239	07394	14333
34	45477	62416	86251	89835	69485	56209	92192	22184	27255	02542
35	56887	67179	04946	01653	46680	49886	27232	79178	60857	84383
36	82796	79766	81454	10095	38837	86360	95068	00642	25125	20511
37	73929	84896	08412	84886	26945	60424	19652	85022	21066	11863
38	06744	27862	20391	94945	04712	37137	86960	95636	43719	17287
39	46776	46575	73962	41389	08658	32645	99581	33904	78027	59009

The sequence of digits in the decimal expansion of the irrational number π can be used to generate random numbers. The groups of five digits can be regarded as random integers uniformly distributed over the set $\{0, 1, \ldots, 99999\}$. The fractions resulting from division by 10^5 are uniformly distributed in $[0, 1)$.

Example: Choose 12 objects out of 366 (numbered from 000 to 365) by drawing at random with replacement.

- Arbitrarily choose a row number and a column number $\rightarrow$ initial number.
- Specify a step rule (e.g. move two blocks to the left and five down).
- Procedure: For each number chosen use only the first three digits. Disregard any number whose first 3 digits exceed 365.

In the case of random draws without replacement, disregard any numbers which have already been used.

PHYSICS

1 Classical Mechanics

1.1 Kinematics

Linear motion

displacement s or position coordinates x, y, z		$[s] = \text{m}$
average velocity	$\bar{v} = \dfrac{\Delta s}{\Delta t}$	$[v] = \text{m/s}$
instantaneous velocity	$v = \lim\limits_{\Delta t \to 0} \dfrac{\Delta s}{\Delta t} = \dfrac{\mathrm{d}s}{\mathrm{d}t} = \dot{s}$	
average acceleration	$\bar{a} = \dfrac{\Delta v}{\Delta t}$	$[a] = \text{m/s}^2$
instantaneous acceleration	$a = \lim\limits_{\Delta t \to 0} \dfrac{\Delta v}{\Delta t} = \dfrac{\mathrm{d}v}{\mathrm{d}t} = \dot{v} = \ddot{s}$	Note: v or a a can also be negative!
uniform linear motion	$s = s_0 + vt$	s_0: initial displacement, $v = \text{const.}$
uniformly accelerated motion	$v = v_0 + at$	v_0: initial velocity
	$s = s_0 + v_0 t + \tfrac{1}{2} a t^2$	$a = \text{const.}$
	$v^2 = v_0^2 + 2a(s - s_0)$	
	$\bar{v} = \dfrac{v_1 + v_2}{2}$	
linear motion	$\Delta s = \bar{v} \Delta t$	

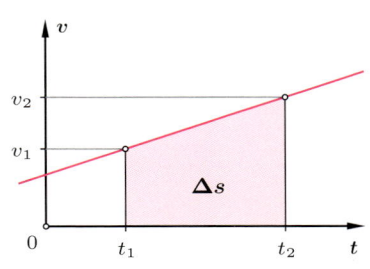

Uniform circular motion ($\omega = \text{const.}$)

period	T	$[T] = \text{s}$
frequency	$f = \dfrac{1}{T}$	$[f] = \text{s}^{-1} = \text{Hz (Hertz)}$
angle	$\varphi = \dfrac{b}{r}$	$[\varphi] = \text{rad} = \text{m/m}$
angular velocity	$\omega = \dfrac{\Delta \varphi}{\Delta t} = \dfrac{2\pi}{T} = 2\pi f$	$[\omega] = \text{rad/s} = \text{s}^{-1}$

Classical Mechanics

speed	$v = r\omega$
centripetal acceleration	$a_z = \dfrac{v^2}{r} = r\omega^2$

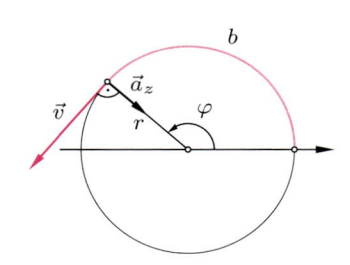

Motion in three dimensions

position vector	$\vec{r} = \begin{pmatrix} x \\ y \\ z \end{pmatrix}$
velocity	$\vec{v} = \dfrac{\mathrm{d}\vec{r}}{\mathrm{d}t} = \dot{\vec{r}}$
speed	$v = |\vec{v}|$
acceleration	$\vec{a} = \dfrac{\mathrm{d}\vec{v}}{\mathrm{d}t} = \dot{\vec{v}} = \ddot{\vec{r}}$

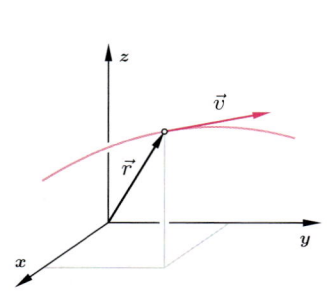

uniformly accelerated motion	$\vec{v} = \vec{v}_0 + \vec{a}t$	$\vec{v}_0$: initial velocity
	$\vec{r} = \vec{r}_0 + \vec{v}_0\, t + \tfrac{1}{2}\vec{a}t^2$	$\vec{r}_0$: initial position
	$\vec{a} = \dot{\vec{v}} = \ddot{\vec{r}} = \text{const.}$	straight-line or parabolic motion

ballistic trajectory	$\vec{a} = \begin{pmatrix} 0 \\ -g \end{pmatrix}$	g: acceleration of free fall
		▶ p. 204
	$y = x \tan \alpha_0 - \dfrac{g}{2v_0^2 \cos^2 \alpha_0} x^2$	
	$y_{\max} = \dfrac{v_0^2 \sin^2 \alpha_0}{2g}$	
	$x_w = \dfrac{v_0^2 \sin 2\alpha_0}{g}$	
		α_0: angle of elevation

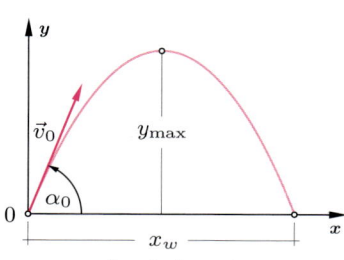

general trajectory	$\vec{a} = \vec{a}_t + \vec{a}_n$	
	$a_t = \dfrac{\mathrm{d}v}{\mathrm{d}t} = \dot{v}$	
	$a_n = \dfrac{v^2}{\varrho}$	

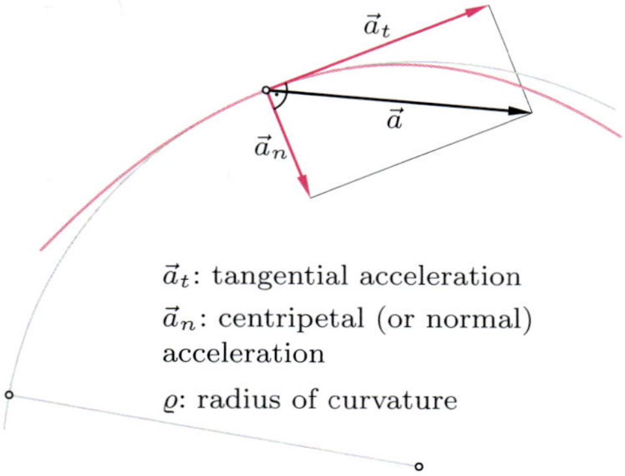

$\vec{a}_t$: tangential acceleration
$\vec{a}_n$: centripetal (or normal) acceleration
ϱ: radius of curvature

Classical Mechanics

1.2 Dynamics of a point mass

mass	m	$[m] = \text{kg}$	
density	$\varrho = \dfrac{m}{V}$	$[\varrho] = \text{kg/m}^3$	▶ p. 187
momentum	$\vec{p} = m\vec{v}$	$[p] = \text{kg·m/s} = \text{N·s}$	

theory of special relativity ▶ p. 181

Force

NEWTON's second law of motion

$$\vec{F}_{\text{res}} = \lim_{\Delta t \to 0} \frac{\Delta \vec{p}}{\Delta t} = \frac{d\vec{p}}{dt} = \dot{\vec{p}}$$

general equation of motion
$\vec{F}_{\text{res}}$: resultant force
$[F] = \text{kg·m/s}^2 = \text{N}$ (Newton)

$$\vec{F}_{\text{res}} = m\vec{a}$$

$m = \text{const.}$

NEWTON's third law of motion (actio = reactio)

$$\vec{F}_{12} = -\vec{F}_{21}$$

- gravitational force, weight $F_G = mg$ g: acceleration of free fall ▶ p. 204

- kinetic friction $F_f = \mu_k F_n$ μ_k: coefficient of kinetic friction ▶ p. 189
  F_n: normal force

- static friction $F_f \leqslant \mu_s F_n$ μ_s: coefficient of static friction ▶ p. 189

- rolling resistance $F_r = C_{\text{rr}} F_n$ C_{rr}: coefficient of rolling resistance ▶ p. 189

- elastic force (HOOKE's law) $F = ky$ $y = |l - l_0|$
  l_0: length of unstretched spring
  l: length of stretched spring
  k: spring constant $[D] = \text{N/m}$

impulse $\vec{F}\Delta t = \Delta \vec{p}$ if $\vec{F}$ const.

$$\int_{t_1}^{t_2} \vec{F}\,dt = \vec{p}_2 - \vec{p}_1$$

if $\vec{F}$ variable

conservation of momentum $\vec{p}_{\text{tot}} = \sum_i \vec{p}_i = \text{const.}$

$\vec{p}_{\text{tot}}$: total momentum in closed system
$\vec{p}_i$: individual momenta
Punktsysteme ▶ p. 161

elastic and inelastic collisions

head-on collisions ▶ p. 159

Classical Mechanics

Work and energy

Work W $[W] = \text{N·m} = \text{W·s} = \text{J}$ (Joule)

- **constant force**
$$W = F_s s$$
$$= Fs \cos\alpha = \vec{F} \cdot \vec{s}$$
$$(\vec{F} = \text{const.}, \alpha = \text{const.})$$

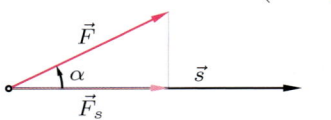

- **general case**
$$W_{AB} = \int_{s_A}^{s_B} F_s \, ds$$
$$= \int_{s_A}^{s_B} \vec{F} \cdot d\vec{s}$$

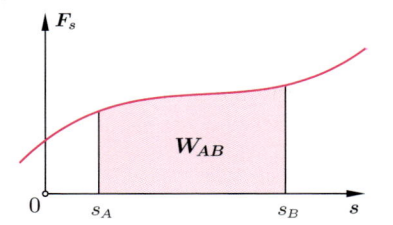

Energy E $[E] = \text{J} = \text{W·s}$

relationship between work and energy
$$\Delta E = W_{AB}$$

ΔE: energy change in an open system

W_{AB}: work done on this system by an external force

- **kinetic energy**
$$E_k = \tfrac{1}{2} m v^2$$

- **potential energy in a uniform gravitational field**
$$E_p = mgh$$

g: acceleration of free fall
h: height above a freely chosen reference level
   non-unif. grav. field ▶ p. 161

- **potential energy of a stretched spring**
$$E_p = \tfrac{1}{2} k y^2$$

k: spring constant
y: displacement from equilibrium   p. 157 ◀ Hooke's law

conservation of energy
$$E_{\text{tot}} = \sum_i E_i = \text{const.}$$

E_{tot}: total energy in a closed system
E_i: component energies

Power P $[P] = \text{J/s} = \text{W}$ (Watt)

- **average power**
$$\overline{P} = \frac{W_{AB}}{\Delta t} = \frac{\Delta E}{\Delta t}$$

- **instantaneous power**
$$P = \frac{dW}{dt} = \vec{F} \cdot \vec{v}$$

efficiency
$$\eta = \frac{W_2}{W_1} = \frac{P_2}{P_1}$$

W_1, P_1: work, power supplied
W_2, P_2: useful work, power extracted

Classical Mechanics

Head-on collision

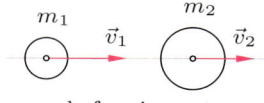

before impact — after impact

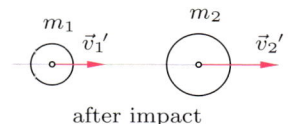

- elastic collision

$$\vec{v}_1' = \frac{(m_1 - m_2)\vec{v}_1 + 2m_2\vec{v}_2}{m_1 + m_2}$$

$$\vec{v}_2' = \frac{(m_2 - m_1)\vec{v}_2 + 2m_1\vec{v}_1}{m_1 + m_2}$$

$E_{k_{tot}} = E'_{k_{tot}}$
$E_{def} = 0$

- perfectly inelastic collision

$$\vec{v}_1' = \vec{v}_2' = \vec{v}'$$

$$\vec{v}' = \frac{m_1\vec{v}_1 + m_2\vec{v}_2}{m_1 + m_2}$$

$$E_{def} = \frac{m_1 m_2 (\vec{v}_1 - \vec{v}_2)^2}{2(m_1 + m_2)}$$

$E_{def} = E_{k_{tot}} - E'_{k_{tot}}$

E_{def}: energy of deformation

Uniform circular motion

centripetal force

$$F_Z = ma_z = \frac{mv^2}{r} = mr\omega^2$$

F_Z: radial component of F_{res}

p. 156 ◀ centripetal acceleraton

Fictitious forces in uniformly rotating systems

coriolis force

$$\vec{F}_C = -2m(\vec{\Omega} \times \vec{v})$$
$$F_C = 2m\Omega v \sin\alpha$$

$\vec{v}$: velocity in rotating reference system;
$\alpha = \angle(\vec{\Omega}, \vec{v})$

centrifugal force

$$\vec{F}_{ZF} = -m \cdot \vec{\Omega} \times (\vec{\Omega} \times \vec{r})$$
$$F_{ZF} = m\Omega^2 r \sin\alpha$$

$\vec{\Omega}$: angular velocity of the reference system;
$\alpha = \angle(\vec{\Omega}, \vec{r})$

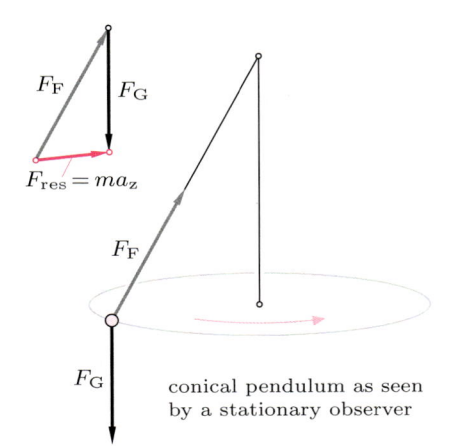

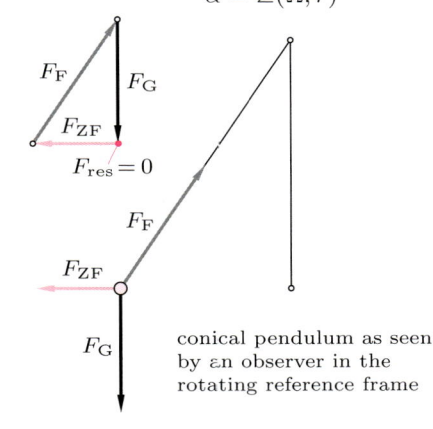

conical pendulum as seen by a stationary observer

conical pendulum as seen by an observer in the rotating reference frame

Classical Mechanics

Harmonic oscillator

circular frequency	$\omega = \dfrac{2\pi}{T} = 2\pi f$	T: period f: frequency
time-dependent displacement	$y = \hat{y}\sin(\omega t + \varphi_0)$	$\hat{y}$: amplitude $\omega t + \varphi_0$: time-dependent phase (phase angle) φ_0: initial phase
velocity	$v = \dot{y} = \omega \hat{y}\cos(\omega t + \varphi_0)$	$\hat{v} = \omega \hat{y}$
acceleration	$a = \dot{v} = \ddot{y} = -\omega^2 y$ $a = -\omega^2 \hat{y}\sin(\omega t + \varphi_0)$	$\hat{a} = \omega^2 \hat{y}$
force law	$\vec{F} = -k\vec{y}$	$[k] = \mathrm{N/m}$ k: force constant spring: $k =$ spring constant
period	$T = 2\pi\sqrt{\dfrac{m}{k}}$	
simple pendulum	$T \approx 2\pi\sqrt{\dfrac{l}{g}}$	for small amplitudes $\hat{y}$
compound pendulum (physical pendulum)		rigid bodies ▶ p. 162

Kepler's laws

I orbit: ellipse with m_z at one of its two foci
           p. 108 ◀ ellipse

II area law: $\dfrac{\Delta A}{\Delta t} = \mathrm{const.}$

$\dfrac{\Delta A}{\Delta t} = \dfrac{1}{2}(a-c)v_P = \dfrac{1}{2}(a+c)v_A = \dfrac{\pi a b}{T}$

III $\dfrac{a^3}{T^2} = \dfrac{Gm_z}{4\pi^2} = \mathrm{const.}$

aphelion A: farthest point from the sun
perihelion P: nearest point to the sun

$\varepsilon = \dfrac{c}{a}$: eccentricity

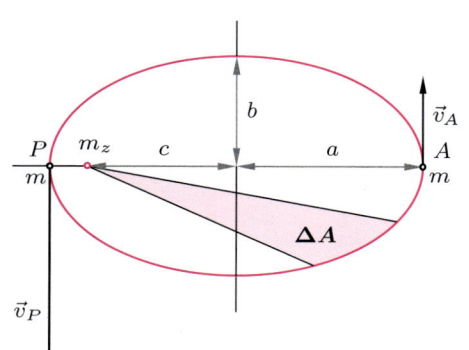

central mass $m_Z \gg m$
a, b: semi-major, semi-minor axes
c: linear eccentricity
T: orbital period
G: gravitational constant
▶ inside back cover

Classical Mechanics

Gravitation

gravitational force between two point masses	$F_G = G\dfrac{m_1 m_2}{r^2}$	G: gravitational constant ▶ inside back cover
	$\vec{F}_G = -G\dfrac{m_1 m_2}{r^2} \cdot \dfrac{\vec{r}}{r}$	
potential energy	$E_p = -G\dfrac{m_1 m_2}{r}$	$E_p = 0$ for $r \to \infty$
gravitational potential	$\Phi = -G\dfrac{m}{r}$	reference point at infinity
standard gravitational parameter	$\mu = Gm$	m: mass of the central body

Systems of point masses

centre of mass	$\vec{r}_{cm} = \dfrac{\sum_i m_i \vec{r}_i}{m_{tot}}$	$m_{tot} = \sum_i m_i$
velocity of the centre of mass	$\vec{v}_{cm} = \dfrac{\sum_i m_i \vec{v}_i}{m_{tot}} = \dfrac{\sum_i \vec{p}_i}{m_{tot}}$	$\vec{v}_{cm}$ = const. in a closed system
internal forces	$\sum_{i,j} \vec{F}_{i,j} = 0$	
external forces	$\sum_k \vec{F}_k = m_{tot} \vec{a}_{cm}$	$\vec{a}_{cm}$: acceleration of the centre of mass
angular momentum of a point mass	$\vec{L} = \vec{r} \times \vec{p}$	$[L]$ = N·m·s $\vec{r}$: position vector; $\vec{p} = m\vec{v}$
angular momentum of a system	$\vec{L}_{tot} = \sum_i \vec{L}_i$	
moment of force (torque)	$\vec{M} = \vec{r} \times \vec{F}$ $M = rF \sin\varphi$	$[M]$ = N·m $\varphi = \angle(\vec{r}, \vec{F})$
total moment of force	$\vec{M}_{tot} = \sum_i \vec{M}_i$	
angular impulse	$\int_{t_1}^{t_2} \vec{M}\,dt = \vec{L}_2 - \vec{L}_1$	
	$\vec{M}\Delta t = \Delta\vec{L}$	if $\vec{M}$ = const.
	$\vec{M} = \dfrac{d\vec{L}}{dt} = \dot{\vec{L}}$	
conservation of angular momentum	$\vec{L}_{tot} = \sum_i \vec{L}_i =$ const.	$\vec{L}_{tot}$: total angular momentum in a closed system

Classical Mechanics

1.3 Rigid bodies (rotation about a fixed axis)

equilibrium criteria	$\vec{F}_{\text{res}} = \sum_i \vec{F}_i = \vec{0}$	
	$\vec{M}_{\text{tot}} = \sum_i \vec{M}_i = \vec{0}$	reference point arbitrary
angular displacement	φ	
angular velocity	$\omega = \dfrac{\mathrm{d}\varphi}{\mathrm{d}t} = \dot{\varphi}$	
angular acceleration	$\alpha = \dfrac{\mathrm{d}\omega}{\mathrm{d}t} = \dot{\omega} = \ddot{\varphi}$	
linear velocity and acceleration of a point	$\vec{v}_i = \vec{\omega} \times \vec{r}_i$ $a_i = r_i \alpha$	
rotational motion with constant angular acceleration	$\omega = \omega_0 + \alpha t$ $\varphi = \varphi_0 + \omega_0 t + \tfrac{1}{2}\alpha t^2$	ω_0, φ_0: initial values
moment of inertia	$I \approx \sum_i r_i^2 \Delta m_i$	Δm_i: mass element at a distance of r_i from the rotation axis
	$I = \displaystyle\int_K r^2 \, dm$	$[I] = \text{kg}\cdot\text{m}^2$

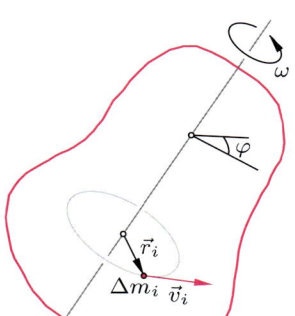

Moments of inertia of selected bodies (axis through the centre of mass)

• thin rod (l)	$I_{\text{cm}} \approx \dfrac{1}{12} m l^2$	axis $\perp$ rod
• rectangular solid (a, b, c)	$I_{\text{cm}} = \dfrac{1}{12} m (a^2 + b^2)$	axis $\parallel c$
• solid cylinder (r, h)	$I_{\text{cm}} = \dfrac{1}{2} m r^2$	axis $\parallel h$
	$I_{\text{cm}} = m \left(\dfrac{r^2}{4} + \dfrac{h^2}{12} \right)$	axis $\perp h$
• hollow cylinder (r_1, r_2, h)	$I_{\text{cm}} = \dfrac{1}{2} m (r_1^2 + r_2^2)$	axis $\parallel h$
• solid sphere	$I_{\text{cm}} = \dfrac{2}{5} m r^2$	
• hollow sphere	$I_{\text{cm}} \approx \dfrac{2}{3} m r^2$	shell thickness $d \ll r$

Classical Mechanics

parallel axis theorem (HUYGENS-STEINER theorem)	$I_{\text{cm}} + ms^2$	I_{cm}: moment of inertia about centre of mass
		I: moment of inertia about parallel axis at distance s
fundamental equation of rotation	$M = I\alpha$	$I = $ const.
	M: total moment of force w. r. t. rotation axis	
	$M = \sum_i r_i F_i$	
		$\vec{r}_i \perp \vec{F}_i$
angular momentum	$L = I\omega$	for symmetric bodies w. r. t. symmetry axis
	$M = \dfrac{\mathrm{d}L}{\mathrm{d}t} = \dot{L}$	
rotational energy	$E_{\text{rot}} = \dfrac{1}{2} I \omega^2$	
work	$W = M\varphi$	$M = $ const.
power	$P = M\omega$	
angular harmonic oscillator	$M = -k\varphi = I\ddot{\varphi}$	φ: angular displacement
		k: torsion coefficient
	$\varphi = \hat{\varphi} \sin(\omega t + \delta_0)$	$[k] = $ N·m/rad
	$T = \dfrac{2\pi}{\omega} = 2\pi \sqrt{\dfrac{I}{k}}$	$\hat{\varphi}$: angular amplitude
		δ_0: initial phase
physical pendulum	$T \approx 2\pi \sqrt{\dfrac{I_s + ms^2}{mgs}}$	
	for small amplitudes $\hat{\varphi}$	

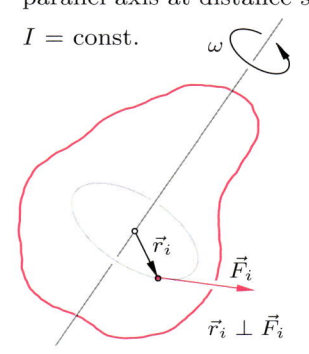

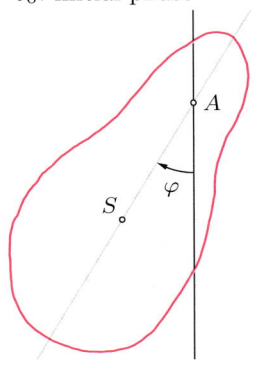

rotation axis through A perpendicular to plane of paper; $\overline{AS} = s$

I_s: moment of inertia about parallel axis through S

m: total mass

Classical Mechanics

1.4 Continuous media

Elasticity of solids (homogeneous and isotropic)

normal stress	$\sigma = \dfrac{\Delta F_\mathrm{N}}{\Delta A}$	$[\sigma] = \mathrm{N/m^2}$ ΔA: surface element ΔF_n: force $\perp \Delta A$
HOOKE's law	$\sigma = E \cdot \varepsilon$	$\varepsilon = \Delta l / l$: strain E: elastic modulus (YOUNG's modulus) $[E] = \mathrm{N/m^2}$ ▶ p. 188
energy density	$w = \dfrac{\sigma^2}{2E}$	$[w] = \mathrm{J/m^3}$

Liquids and gases

pressure	$p = \dfrac{F_\mathrm{n}}{A}$	if $p = \mathrm{const.}$ over A F_n: force $\perp$ surface A
	$p = \dfrac{\Delta F_\mathrm{n}}{\Delta A}$	$[p] = \mathrm{N/m^2} = \mathrm{Pa}$ (Pascal)
hydrostatic pressure	$\Delta p = \varrho g h$	ϱ: constant density h: height difference in fluid
barometric formula	$p = p_0 \cdot \mathrm{e}^{-\frac{\varrho_0 g}{p_0} \cdot h}$	ideal gas; T constant g: const. acceleration of free fall p_0, ϱ_0: values at $h = 0$
ISA model for standard pressure vs. height (polytropic atmosphere)	$p = p_0 \left(1 - \dfrac{\alpha \cdot h}{T_0}\right)^\beta$	for troposphere ($h \leqslant 11\,\mathrm{km}$): $p_0 = 101\,325\,\mathrm{Pa}$ $T_0 = 288.15\,\mathrm{K}$ $\alpha = 0.006\,500\,\mathrm{K/m}$ $\beta = 5.255\,877$
buoyancy	$F_B = \varrho_\mathrm{F} g V_K$	V_K: displacement volume of body ϱ_F: density of fluid
compression	$\Delta V = -\chi V \Delta p$	χ: compressibility; $[\chi] = \mathrm{Pa}^{-1}$ ▶ p. 188
surface tension	$\gamma = \dfrac{\Delta W}{\Delta A} = \dfrac{F}{l}$	$[\gamma] = \mathrm{J/m^2} = \mathrm{N/m}$ ▶ p. 188 ΔA: surface element l: length of boundary

Classical Mechanics

work of compression	$\Delta W = -p\Delta V$	p: constant pressure
	$W = -\int p\,dV$	
volume flow	$Q = \dfrac{\Delta V}{\Delta t}$	$[Q] = \mathrm{m}^3/\mathrm{s}$
continuity equation	$Q = v_1 A_1 = v_2 A_2 = \text{const.}$	for an imaginary tube in an incompressible fluid

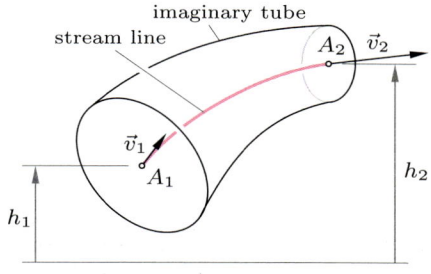

BERNOULLI's principle	$p + \tfrac{1}{2}\varrho v^2 + \varrho g h = \text{const.}$	along a streamline; stationary flow of an inviscid and incompressible fluid
shear strain	$\tau = \dfrac{\Delta F_t}{\Delta A}$	$[\tau] = \mathrm{N/m}^2$ ΔA: surface element ΔF_t: force $\parallel \Delta A$
	$\tau = \eta \dfrac{\Delta v}{\Delta z}$	η: dynamic viscosity; $[\eta] = \mathrm{N{\cdot}s/m}^2$ ▶ p. 189
STOKES flow	$F_D = 6\pi\eta r v$	laminar flow around a sphere of radius r F_D: drag v: velocity of the undisturbed flow
HAGEN-POISEUILLE law	$\bar{v} = \left(\dfrac{\Delta p}{\Delta l}\right) \cdot \dfrac{r^2}{8\eta}$	laminar flow in cylindrical pipe $\bar{v}$: mean flow velocity $\Delta p/\Delta l$: pressure gradient along pipe axis
drag in turbulent flow	$F_D = c_D \cdot \dfrac{\varrho v^2}{2} \cdot A$	c_D: drag coefficient ▶ p. 189 A: cross-sectional area $\perp \vec{v}$
dynamic lift in turbulent flow	$F_L = c_L \cdot \dfrac{\varrho v^2}{2} \cdot A$	c_L: lift coefficient A: planform (wing) area

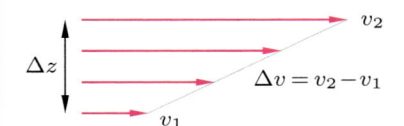

2 Waves, Optics and Acoustics

sine wave (harmonic wave)	$u(x,t) = \hat{u}\sin(kx - \omega t)$	stationary waves ▶ p. 169
circular frequency	$\omega = 2\pi f = \dfrac{2\pi}{T}$	$[\omega] = \text{s}^{-1}$, f: frequency T: period
wave number	$k = \dfrac{2\pi}{\lambda}$	$[k] = \text{m}^{-1}$, λ: wavelength
wavelength	$\lambda = \dfrac{c}{f}$	$[\lambda] = \text{m}$, c: propagation velocity
energy flux density	$J = \dfrac{\mathrm{d}P}{\mathrm{d}A}$	$[J] = \text{W/m}^2$

Electromagnetic waves

• propagation velocity	$c = \sqrt{\dfrac{1}{\varepsilon\mu}} = \dfrac{c_{\text{vac}}}{\sqrt{\varepsilon_r\mu_r}} = \dfrac{c_{\text{vac}}}{n}$	$\varepsilon = \varepsilon_0\varepsilon_r$, $\mu = \mu_0\mu_r$ $n = \sqrt{\varepsilon_r\mu_r}$ index of refraction ▶ p. 193 ε_r, μ_r ▶ p. 195 c_{vac} ▶ inside back cover
• energy flux density in vacuum	$J = \dfrac{1}{2}\varepsilon_0 c E^2$	E: electric field amplitude

Pressure and sound waves

• in gases	$c = \sqrt{\varkappa\dfrac{RT}{M}}$	R: universal gas constant ▶ inside back cover T: abs. temperature, $[T] = \text{K}$ M: molar mass, $[M] = \text{kg/mol}$ $\varkappa = \dfrac{C_p}{C_v}$ ▶ p. 191
	$J = \dfrac{p^2}{2c\varrho}$	p: sound pressure amplitude ϱ: density
• in liquids	$c = \dfrac{1}{\sqrt{\varrho\chi}}$	χ: compressibility ▶ p. 188
• in a rod	$c = \sqrt{\dfrac{E}{\varrho}}$	E: elastic modulus ▶ p. 188
• on a string	$c = \sqrt{\dfrac{\sigma}{\varrho}} = \sqrt{\dfrac{F}{\mu}}$	σ: normal stress F: string tension $\mu = \Delta m/\Delta l$, $[\mu] = \text{kg/m}$

Waves, Optics and Acoustics

Geometrical optics

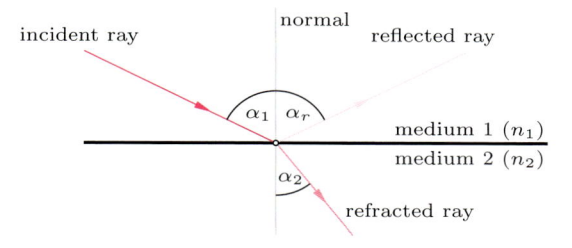

incident ray — normal — reflected ray
α_1, α_r
medium 1 (n_1)
medium 2 (n_2)
α_2
refracted ray

law of reflection	$\alpha_r = \alpha_1$	
refractive index	$n = \dfrac{c_{\text{vacuum}}}{c_{\text{medium}}} \approx \dfrac{c_{\text{air}}}{c_{\text{medium}}}$	▶ p. 193
SNELL's law	$\dfrac{\sin \alpha_1}{\sin \alpha_2} = \dfrac{c_1}{c_2} = \dfrac{n_2}{n_1} = n_{21}$	n_{21}: relative refractive index

Spherical mirrors and thin lenses

radii of curvature r

r_1, r_2

$r > 0$: mirror surface concave
$r_i > 0$: lens surface convex

Focal length

• of a spherical mirror	$f \approx \dfrac{r}{2}$	$[f] = \text{m}$
• of a parabolic mirror	$f = \dfrac{1}{4a}$	parabolic section $y = ax^2$
• of a thin lens	$\dfrac{1}{f} \approx (n-1)\left(\dfrac{1}{r_1} + \dfrac{1}{r_2}\right)$	
optical power	$D = \dfrac{1}{f}$	$[D] = \text{m}^{-1} = \text{dpt (dioptre)}$
lens system	$D_{\text{res}} = D_1 + D_2$	
thin lens formula, mirror equation	$\dfrac{1}{a} + \dfrac{1}{b} \approx \dfrac{1}{f}$	a: object distance b: image distance
linear magnification	$\dfrac{B}{A} = \dfrac{b}{a}$	A: lateral size of object B: lateral size of image

Wave optics

Diffraction

- diffraction grating

$$\sin \alpha_m = m \frac{\lambda}{d}$$

$$m = 0, \pm 1, \pm 2, \ldots$$

intensity maxima at α_m
d: grating constant
m: diffraction order

- single-slit diffraction

$$\sin \alpha_k = k \frac{\lambda}{s}$$

$$k = \pm 1, \pm 2, \pm 3, \ldots$$

intensity minima at α_k
s: width of slit

- circular aperture

$$\sin \alpha_k = z_k \cdot \frac{\lambda}{d}$$

d: diameter of aperture
$z_1 \approx 1.2197$ (1st minimum)
$z_2 \approx 2.2331$ (2nd minimum)
$z_3 \approx 3.2383$ (3rd minimum)

Photometry

luminous intensity I

$[I] = \text{cd}$ (Candela)

luminance $L = \dfrac{dI}{dA \cos \alpha}$

$[L] = \text{cd/m}^2$
α: angle between beam direction and normal to emission surface

solid angle $\Omega = \dfrac{A}{r^2}$

A: area on a sphere of radius r
$[\Omega] = \dfrac{\text{m}^2}{\text{m}^2} = \text{sr}$ (steradian)

luminous flux $\Phi = I\Omega$

$[\Phi] = \text{lm}$ (lumen)
Ω: solid angle ($[\Omega] = \text{sr}$)

illuminance $E = \dfrac{d\Phi}{dA}$

$[E] = \text{lx} = \text{lm/m}^2$ (lux)

law of illumination
(inverse square law
and cosine law)

$$E = \frac{I}{r^2} \cos \beta$$

β: angle between beam direction and normal to illuminated surface

Waves, Optics and Acoustics

Acoustics

sound intensity	$I = \dfrac{\mathrm{d}P}{\mathrm{d}A}$	$[I] = \mathrm{W/m^2}$; p. 166 ◀ energy flux density
sound intensity level	$L = 10 \log_{10}\left(\dfrac{I}{I_0}\right)$	I_0: hearing threshold at 1 kHz $I_0 = 10^{-12}\,\mathrm{W/m^2}$ L: specified in dB (decibel)
musical interval = frequency ratio	$\dfrac{f_2}{f_1}$	f_1: frequency of lower pitch f_2: frequency of higher pitch ▶ p. 188
standing wave	$u(x,t) = \hat{u} \cdot \sin(kx) \cdot \cos(\omega t)$	$\hat{u}$: amplitude
overtones • in string / open pipe	$f_n = n \cdot f_1$	$f_1 = \dfrac{c}{2l}$: fundamental frequency l: string or pipe length, $n = 1, 2, 3\ldots$
• gedackt pipe	$f_n = (2n-1) \cdot f_1$	$f_1 = \dfrac{c}{4l}$

Doppler effekt (longitudinal)

acoustic DOPPLER effect	$f_R = f_S \dfrac{c \pm v_R}{c \mp v_S}$	$f_{S,R}$: frequency of source, receiver $v_{S,R}$: speed of source, receiver (relative to medium) The upper signs apply to the situation illustrated.
MACH number	$M = \dfrac{v}{c}$	v: object velocity relative to medium c: speed of sound in medium
optical DOPPLER effect	$\dfrac{\Delta\lambda}{\lambda} \approx \dfrac{v_r}{c} \approx -\dfrac{\Delta f}{f}$	$v_r \ll c$: relative radial velocity λ, f: source wavelength, frequency $\Delta\lambda, \Delta f$: wavelength, frequency shift c: speed of light theory of relativity ▶ p. 181

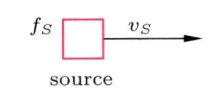

3 Thermodynamics

thermodynamic temperature (absolute temperature)	T	$[T] = $ K (Kelvin)
Celsius temperature (centigrade temperature)	$\vartheta \mathrel{\hat{=}} T - T_0$	$[\vartheta] = $ °C (degree Celsius) T_0: standard temperautre ▶ inside back cover
temperature increment	$\Delta T = \Delta \vartheta$	K or °C
linear expansion	$\Delta l \approx \alpha l \Delta T$	α: coefficient of linear expansion ▶ p. 190
volume expansion	$\Delta V \approx \gamma V \Delta T$	γ: coeffcient of volume expansion ▶ p. 191 isotropic solid: $\gamma \approx 3\alpha$
quantity of heat	Q	$[Q] = $ J
internal energy	U	$[U] = $ J
specific heat c (specific heat capacity)	$\Delta Q = cm\Delta T$	$[c] = $ J/(kg·K) ▶ p. 190/191 c_p: at const. pressure c_v: at const. pressure
molar heat capacity C	$\Delta Q = nC\Delta T$	$[C] = $ J/(mol·K) ▶ p. 191
amount of substance	$n = \dfrac{m}{M}$	$[n] = $ mol (mole) M: molar mass; $[M] = $ kg/mol
latent heat of fusion L_f	$Q = L_f m$	$[L_f] = $ J/kg ▶ p. 190/191
latent heat of vaporization or heat of condensation L_v	$Q = L_v m$	$[L_v] = $ J/kg ▶ p. 191
heating value H	$Q = Hm$	$[H] = $ J/kg ▶ p. 193

First law of thermodynamics	$\Delta U = Q + W$	ΔU: change in internal energy $Q > 0$: heat supplied to system $W > 0$: work done on system
	$dU = TdS - pdV + \mu dn + \ldots$	S: entropy, μ: chemical potential, n: amount of substance

Thermodynamics

ideal gas law	$pV = NkT = nRT$	N: no. of particles; n: amount of substance k: BOLTZMANN's constant ▶ inside back cover R: univ. gas constant ▶ p. 191 $R = N_A k \qquad N = n N_A$ N_A: AVOGADRO's constant ▶ inside back cover
molar heat capacity of an ideal gas	$C_p - C_v = R$	• ideal gases: $C_v = \frac{1}{2} f R$ (f: no. of degrees of freedom) • solids: $C_p = 3R$ (DULONG-PETIT law)
adiabatic change of state of an ideal gas	$pV^\varkappa = $ const. $TV^{\varkappa-1} = $ const. $p^{1-\varkappa} T^\varkappa = $ const.	$\varkappa = \dfrac{c_p}{c_v} = \dfrac{C_p}{C_v}$ ▶ p. 191
equation of state of a VAN DER WAALS gas	$\left(p + a\left(\dfrac{n}{V}\right)^2\right)(V - bn) = nRT$	a, b: VAN DER WAALS- constants ▶ p. 191
pressure of an ideal gas (kinetic theory)	$p = \dfrac{1}{3}\dfrac{N}{V} m\overline{v^2} = \dfrac{2}{3}\dfrac{N}{V} \overline{E}_k$	m: particle mass
mean translational kinetic energy of a particle	$\overline{E}_k = \dfrac{1}{2} m \overline{v^2} = \dfrac{3}{2} kT$	k: BOLTZMANN's constant ▶ inside back cover
MAXWELL-BOLTZMANN distribution of particle speeds in an ideal gas	$\dfrac{\mathrm{d}N}{N} = 4\pi v^2 \left(\dfrac{m}{2\pi kT}\right)^{\frac{3}{2}} \cdot \mathrm{e}^{-\frac{mv^2}{2kT}} \mathrm{d}v$	fraction of particles with speeds between v and $v + \mathrm{d}v$
mean speed	$\bar{v} = \overline{|\vec{v}|} = \sqrt{\dfrac{8kT}{\pi m}}$	
rms speed	$v_\mathrm{rms} = \sqrt{\overline{v^2}} = \sqrt{\dfrac{3kT}{m}}$	rms: root mean square
most probable speed	$v_w = \sqrt{\dfrac{2kT}{m}}$	
Entropy	S	$[S] = \mathrm{J/K}$
• thermodynamic	$\Delta S = \dfrac{\Delta Q_\mathrm{rev}}{T}$ $\mathrm{d}S = \dfrac{\delta Q_\mathrm{rev}}{T}$	for reversible processes
• statistical	$S = k \ln(\Omega)$	Ω: number of states for given total energy and no. of particles

Thermodynamics

Second law of thermodynamics $\Delta S \geqslant 0$ equivalent to $\eta \leqslant \eta_{\mathrm{C}}$

in a closed system; for reversible processes $\Delta S = 0$

CARNOT efficiency $\eta_{\mathrm{C}} = \dfrac{T_H - T_C}{T_H}$

maximum efficiency of a cyclic heat engine

T_H: temp. of hot reservoir
T_C: temp. of cold reservoir

maximum coefficient of performance of a heat pump $COP_{\mathrm{heat}} = \dfrac{T_H}{T_H - T_C}$

maximum coefficient of performance of a refrigerator $COP_{\mathrm{cool}} = \dfrac{T_C}{T_H - T_C}$

thermal conduction

- general

$$\dfrac{\Delta Q}{\Delta t} = -\lambda A \dfrac{\Delta T}{\Delta x}$$

A: cross-sectional area
$\dfrac{\Delta T}{\Delta x}$: temperature gradient
λ: thermal conductivity
$[\lambda] = \mathrm{W/(m \cdot K)}$ ▶ p. 190/191

- in building structures

$$\dfrac{\Delta Q}{\Delta t} = UA\Delta T$$

ΔT: interior–exterior air temperature difference
U: thermal transmittance
$[U] = \mathrm{W/(m^2 \cdot K)}$ ▶ p. 190

thermal radiation $P = \dfrac{\Delta Q}{\Delta t} = \varepsilon \sigma T^4 \cdot A$

ε: emissivity ▶ p. 190
σ: STEFAN-BOLTZMANN constant ▶ inside back cover
T: absolute temp. of emitting surface
A: surface area

Atomic Physics ▶ p. 182

4 Electricity and Magnetism

4.1 Electrostatics

Charge	Q, q	$[Q] = [q] = \text{A·s} = \text{C}$ (coulomb)
conservation of charge	$Q_{\text{tot}} = \sum_i Q_i = \text{const.}$	Q_{tot}: total charge in a closed system
COULOMB's law for point charges	$F = \dfrac{1}{4\pi\varepsilon} \cdot \dfrac{Q_1 Q_2}{r^2}$ $\vec{F} = \dfrac{1}{4\pi\varepsilon} \cdot \dfrac{Q_1 Q_2}{r^2} \cdot \dfrac{\vec{r}}{r}$	$\varepsilon = \varepsilon_0 \varepsilon_r$ ε_0: vacuum permittivity ▶ inside back cover ε_r: relative permittivity (dielectric constant) ▶ p. 195
electric field	$\vec{E} = \dfrac{\vec{F}}{q}$	$[E] = \text{V/m} = \text{N/C}$ q: test charge
electric displacement field	$\vec{D} = \varepsilon \vec{E}$	$[D] = \text{C/m}^2$
electric field of a point charge (or outside a uniformly charged or conducting sphere)	$E = \dfrac{1}{4\pi\varepsilon} \cdot \dfrac{Q}{r^2}$ $\vec{E} = \dfrac{1}{4\pi\varepsilon} \cdot \dfrac{Q}{r^2} \cdot \dfrac{\vec{r}}{r}$	r: distance from the charge (or from the sphere's centre)
electric flux	$\Phi_e = \sum E_n \cdot \Delta A$ $\Phi_e = \displaystyle\int_A \vec{E} \cdot \mathrm{d}\vec{A}$	$[\Phi_e] = \text{V·m}$ E_n: normal component
electric displacement flux	$\Psi = \sum D_n \cdot \Delta A$ $\Psi = \displaystyle\int_A \vec{D} \cdot \mathrm{d}\vec{A}$	$[\Psi] = \text{C}$
GAUSS' law	$\Phi_e = \dfrac{1}{\varepsilon} \displaystyle\sum_A Q_e$ $\Psi = \displaystyle\sum_A Q_e$	A: closed surface Q_e: enclosed charge
electric dipole moment	$\vec{p}_e = |Q|\vec{d}$	$[p_e] = \text{C·m}$ $\ominus \xrightarrow{p_e} \oplus$ $-Q \quad\quad +Q$

Electricity and Magnetism

torque acting on electric dipole	$\vec{M} = \vec{p}_e \times \vec{E}$ $M = p_e E \sin \varphi$	

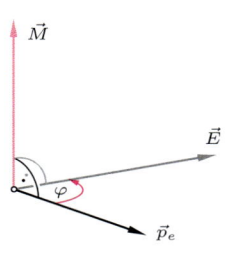

voltage (potential difference)	$V_{AB} = \dfrac{W_{AB}}{q}$	$[V] = \text{J/C} = \text{V}$ (volt)
	$V_{AB} = \vec{E} \cdot \vec{s}$	in a homogeneous field $\vec{s} = \overrightarrow{AB}$
	$V_{AB} = \displaystyle\int_A^B \vec{E} \cdot \mathrm{d}\vec{s}$	
electric potential	$\varphi_A = V_{AZ} = -\displaystyle\int_Z^A \vec{E} \cdot \mathrm{d}\vec{s}$	$[\varphi_A] = \text{V}$ Z: reference point ($\varphi_Z = 0$)
	$\varphi_A - \varphi_B = V_{AB}$	applies only to electrostatic fields
electric potential due to a point charge	$\varphi = \dfrac{1}{4\pi\varepsilon} \cdot \dfrac{Q}{r}$	zero potential at infinity
potential energy of a charged particle	$E_p = q\varphi$	

Capacitance

Capacitance	$C = \dfrac{Q}{U}$	$[C] = \text{C/V} = \text{F}$ (farad)
• capacitance of a parallel-plate capacitor	$C = \varepsilon \dfrac{A}{d}$	d: distance between plates A: area of one plate; $d \ll \sqrt{A}$
• capacitance of a conducting sphere in free space	$C = 4\pi\varepsilon r$	
• capacitance of a cylindrical capacitor (or coaxial cable)	$C = \dfrac{2\pi\varepsilon l}{\ln \dfrac{r_2}{r_1}}$	r_1, r_2: inner, outer radii l: cylinder length; $l \gg r_2$
• capacitance of a spherical capacitor (concentric spheres)	$C = 4\pi\varepsilon \cdot \left(\dfrac{1}{r_1} - \dfrac{1}{r_2}\right)^{-1}$	r_1, r_2: inner, outer radii

Combinations of capacitors

• capacitors in series	$\dfrac{1}{C} = \displaystyle\sum_i \dfrac{1}{C_i}$	
• capacitors in parallel	$C = \displaystyle\sum_i C_i$	

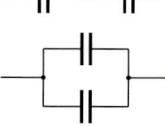

Electricity and Magnetism

electric field in a parallel-plate capacitor	$E = \dfrac{Q}{\varepsilon A} = \dfrac{V}{d}$	$d \ll \sqrt{A}$
electric field in a cylindrical capacitor	$E = \dfrac{1}{2\pi\varepsilon} \cdot \dfrac{Q/l}{r}$	$r \ll l,\ r_1 < r < r_2$
electric field in a spherical capacitor	$E = \dfrac{1}{4\pi\varepsilon} \cdot \dfrac{Q}{r^2}$	$r_1 < r < r_2$
capacitor discharge	$V = V_0\, e^{-\tfrac{t}{RC}}$	V_0: initial value of the voltage R: resistance of discharge circuit
energy stored in a charged capacitor	$E_p = \dfrac{QV}{2} = \dfrac{CV^2}{2} = \dfrac{Q^2}{2C}$	
energy density of an electric field	$w_e = \dfrac{1}{2}\varepsilon E^2 = \dfrac{ED}{2}$	$[w_e] = \mathrm{J/m^3}$

4.2 Direct current

electric current	$I = \dfrac{\Delta Q}{\Delta t}$	$[I] = \mathrm{A}$ (ampere)
	$I = \displaystyle\lim_{\Delta t \to 0} \dfrac{\Delta Q}{\Delta t} = \dfrac{\mathrm{d}Q}{\mathrm{d}t} = \dot{Q}$	conventional current: flow direction of positive charge-carriers
	$I = nqvA$	n: charge-carrier density ▶ p. 195 q: particle charge v: drift velocity A: cross-sectional area of conductor
current density	$J = \dfrac{\Delta I}{\Delta A}$	$[J] = \mathrm{A/m^2}$ $\Delta A \perp$ current direction
electrical resistance (static resistance)	$R = \dfrac{V}{I}$	$[R] = \mathrm{V/A} = \Omega$ (ohm)
differential resistance	$R = \dfrac{\Delta V}{\Delta I} = \dfrac{\mathrm{d}V}{\mathrm{d}I}$	$[R] = \mathrm{V/A} = \Omega$ (ohm)
Ohm's law	$R = \mathrm{const.},\ V \propto I$	
electrical resistivity ϱ_{el}	$R = \varrho_{\mathrm{el}} \dfrac{l}{A}$	$[\varrho_{\mathrm{el}}] = \Omega\cdot\mathrm{m}$ ▶ p. 194

Electricity and Magnetism

temperature dependence of resistance	$R(T) = R_0 + \alpha R_0 \cdot (T - T_0)$	$[\alpha] = \text{K}^{-1}$ α: temperature coefficient of resistivity at T_0 ▶ p. 194 T_0: reference temperature R_0: resistance at T_0
electrical conductance	$G = \dfrac{1}{R} = \dfrac{I}{V}$	$[G] = \text{A}/\text{V} = \Omega^{-1} = \text{S}$ (siemens)
electrical conductivity	$\sigma_{\text{el}} = \dfrac{1}{\varrho_{\text{el}}}$ $\vec{J} = \sigma \vec{E}$	$[\sigma_{\text{el}}] = (\Omega \cdot \text{m})^{-1} = \text{S}/\text{m}$

Combinations of resistors

• resistors in series	$R = \sum_i R_i$	
• resistors in parallel	$\dfrac{1}{R} = \sum_i \dfrac{1}{R_i}$	

Kirchhoff's laws

• Kirchhoff's current law (Kirchhoff's 1st law)	$\sum_k I_k = 0$	at a junction (node); signs of currents I_k into and out of node different!
• Kirchhoff's voltage law (Kirchhoff's 2nd law)	$\sum_k (IR)_k = \sum_i V_i$	for every closed loop; signs of voltage drops and gains w.r.t. loop direction V_i: voltage sources (emf's)
electric power	$P = VI$	$[P] = \text{W}$ (watt)
Joule heating (resistive heating)	$W = R I^2 \Delta t = \dfrac{V^2}{R} \Delta t$	
terminal voltage of an electrical power source	$V_\text{T} = V_0 - IR_i$	V_0: open-circuit voltage (zero load) R_i: internal resistance
Faraday's laws of electrolysis	$m = \dfrac{MQ}{zF}$	m: mass liberated/deposited at electrodes; Q: total charge M: molar mass; z: ionic valency; $F = N_A e$: Faraday constant ▶ inside back cover

4.3 Magnetism

Magnetic field — Depending on the context, the term magnetic field may refer to the magnetic flux density B or the magnetic field strength H.

magnetic flux density — B — $[B] = \text{V·s/m}^2 = \text{T}$ (tesla)

LORENTZ-force (magnetic term) — $\vec{F} = q(\vec{v} \times \vec{B})$; $F = qvB\sin\varphi$

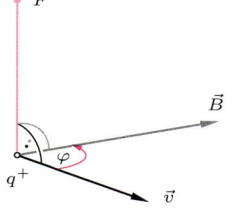

magnetic flux density in material medium — $\vec{B} = \mu_r \vec{B}_0$ — B_0: magnetic flux density in vacuum; μ_r: relative permeability ▶ p. 195

magnetic field strength — $\vec{H} = \dfrac{\vec{B}}{\mu}$ — $[H] = \text{A/m}$; $\mu = \mu_0 \mu_r$; μ_0: vacuum permeability (magnetic constant) ▶ inside back cover

force on a current-carrying wire element in a magnetic field — $\vec{F} = I(\vec{l} \times \vec{B})$; $F = IlB\sin\varphi$ — $\vec{l}$: direction of conductor = conventional-current direction; φ: angle between field and current directions

force on a current-carrying wire element — $d\vec{F} = I(d\vec{l} \times \vec{B})$

torque on a planar current loop — $\vec{M} = I(\vec{A} \times \vec{B})$ — $\vec{A}$: loop area, vector $\perp$ loop plane (right hand grip rule)

magnetic dipole moment $\vec{p}_m$ — $\vec{M} = \vec{p}_m \times \vec{B}$ — $[p_m] = \text{A·m}^2$; S ⟶ N

magnetic field generated by a current element (BIOT-SAVART law) — $d\vec{B} = \dfrac{\mu_0 I}{4\pi} \cdot \dfrac{d\vec{l} \times \vec{r}}{r^3}$ — $d\vec{l}$: current element; $\vec{r}$: displacement vector from current element to field point

magnetic field generated by an infinitely long straight current-carrying wire — $B = \dfrac{\mu I}{2\pi r}$ — $\mu = \mu_0 \mu_r$; r: distance from wire

Electricity and Magnetism

magnetic field on the axis of a circular current loop	$B = \dfrac{\mu I R^2}{2(z^2 + r^2)^{3/2}}$	z: axial distance from the centre of the loop
magnetic field at the centre of a circular current loop	$B = \dfrac{\mu I}{2r}$	r: circle radius
magnetic field inside a current-carrying cylindrical solenoid (exact at centre, approx. elsewhere)	$B = \dfrac{\mu N I}{\sqrt{l^2 + d^2}}$	N: number of turns $\\$ l: length of solenoid $\\$ d: diameter of solenoid
	$B \approx \dfrac{\mu N I}{l}$	for $l \gg d$
magnetic field at centre of a current-carrying HELMHOLTZ coil pair	$B = \left(\dfrac{4}{5}\right)^{\tfrac{3}{2}} \cdot \dfrac{\mu N I}{r}$ $\\$ $\approx 0.716 \cdot \dfrac{\mu N I}{r}$	N: no. of turns in one coil $\\$ r: radius and separation distance of the coils
MAXWELL-AMPÈRE equation	$\oint_C \vec{B} \cdot d\vec{s} =$ $\\$ $\mu_0 \sum I_A + \mu_0 \varepsilon_0 \dfrac{d\Phi_e}{dt}$	Φ_e: electric flux $\\$ I_A: current through an arbitrary area enclosed by C
Magnetic flux	Φ_m	$[\Phi_m] = \text{V·s} = \text{Wb}$ (weber)
• homogeneous field	$\Phi_m = B_n A$	B_n: normal component $\\$ A: planar area
• general case	$\Phi_m = \displaystyle\int_S \vec{B} \cdot d\vec{A}$	S: arbitrary surface
GAUSS' law for magnetism	$\Phi_m = 0$	for closed surfaces
Law of induction	$V_{\text{ind}} = -\dfrac{\Delta \Phi_m}{\Delta t}$	FARADAY's induction law
MAXWELL-FARADAY equation	$V_{\text{ind}} = \displaystyle\oint_c \vec{E} \cdot d\vec{s}$ $\\$ $= -\dfrac{d\Phi_m}{dt}$ $\\$ $= -\dot{\Phi}_m$	c: closed curve; orientation w. r. t. area normal by right hand grip rule $\\$ Φ_m: magnetic flux through an arbritrary surface enclosed by c
inductance L (self induction)	$\Phi_m = LI$	$[L] = \text{V·s/A} = \text{H}$ (henry)
induced electromotive force (emf) in a coil	$V_{\text{ind}} = -\dfrac{d\Phi_m}{dt} = -L\dfrac{dI}{dt}$	

Electricity and Magnetism

inductance of a long, thin solenoid	$L = \dfrac{\mu N^2 A}{l}$	$\mu = \mu_r \mu_0$ A: cross-sectional area l: solenoid length; $l \gg \sqrt{A}$
switch-on transient current through inductor	$I(t) = I_\infty \left(1 - e^{-\frac{Rt}{L}}\right)$	I_∞: steady-state DC current
energy E_m stored in a current-carrying coil	$E_m = \dfrac{1}{2} L I^2$	
energy density of a magnetic field	$w_m = \dfrac{B^2}{2\mu} = \dfrac{BH}{2}$	

4.4 Alternating current

sinusoidal alternating voltage	$v = \hat{v} \cos(\omega t + \varphi_1)$ $\tilde{v} = \hat{v} e^{j(\omega t + \varphi_1)}$ $V = \dfrac{\hat{v}}{\sqrt{2}}$	v, i: instantaneous values $\hat{v}, \hat{\imath}$: amplitudes, peak values $\tilde{v}, \tilde{\imath}$: complex notation j: imaginary unit $(j^2 = -1)$ V, I: effective values
sinusoidal alternating current	$i = \hat{\imath} \cos(\omega t + \varphi_2)$ $\tilde{\imath} = \hat{\imath} e^{j(\omega t + \varphi_2)}$ $I = \dfrac{\hat{\imath}}{\sqrt{2}}$	φ_1, φ_2: initial phases
impedance	$Z = \dfrac{\hat{v}}{\hat{\imath}} = \dfrac{V}{I}$ $\tilde{Z} = \dfrac{\tilde{v}}{\tilde{\imath}}$	$[Z] = \Omega$ $\lvert \tilde{Z} \rvert = Z$ und $\arg \tilde{Z} = \varphi_1 - \varphi_2$
real power (active power)	$P = VI \cos(\varphi_1 - \varphi_2)$	$[P] = \text{W}$ (watt)
apparent power	$S = VI$	$[S] = \text{VA}$ (volt-ampere)
reactive power	$Q = VI \sin(\varphi_1 - \varphi_2)$	$[Q] = \text{var}$ (volt-ampere reactive)
power factor	$\lambda = \dfrac{P}{S} = \cos(\varphi_1 - \varphi_2)$	

Electricity and Magnetism

Impedance and phase shift

- resistance $\quad Z = R, \quad \varphi_1 - \varphi_2 = 0 \quad\quad \tilde{Z} = R$

- ideal inductor $\quad Z = \omega L, \quad \varphi_1 - \varphi_2 = +\dfrac{\pi}{2} \quad\quad \tilde{Z} = \mathrm{j}\omega L$

- ideal capacitor $\quad Z = \dfrac{1}{\omega C}, \quad \varphi_1 - \varphi_2 = -\dfrac{\pi}{2} \quad\quad \tilde{Z} = \dfrac{1}{\mathrm{j}\omega C}$

- R, C, L in series
$$Z = \sqrt{R^2 + \left(\omega L - \dfrac{1}{\omega C}\right)^2} \quad\quad \tilde{Z} = \sum_i \tilde{Z}_i$$

$$\tan(\varphi_1 - \varphi_2) = \dfrac{\omega L - \dfrac{1}{\omega C}}{R}$$

- R, C, L in parallel
$$\dfrac{1}{Z} = \sqrt{\dfrac{1}{R^2} + \left(\dfrac{1}{\omega L} - \omega C\right)^2} \quad\quad \dfrac{1}{\tilde{Z}} = \sum_i \dfrac{1}{\tilde{Z}_i}$$

$$\tan(\varphi_1 - \varphi_2) = R\left(\dfrac{1}{\omega L} - \omega C\right)$$

resonance frequency of an undamped oscillating circuit $\quad f_{\text{res}} = \dfrac{1}{2\pi\sqrt{LC}}$

resonance frequency of a dipole antenna $\quad f_{\text{res}} = \dfrac{c}{\lambda_{\text{res}}} = \dfrac{c}{2l} \quad\quad l$: antenna length
$\quad c$: speed of light

Levels

- for voltages $\quad L_V = 20\log_{10}\left(\dfrac{V}{V_0}\right) \quad\quad$ specified in dB (decibel)

- for currents $\quad L_I = 20\log_{10}\left(\dfrac{I}{I_0}\right)$

- for power $\quad L_P = 10\log_{10}\left(\dfrac{P}{P_0}\right)$

Transformers

- no load $\quad \dfrac{V_2}{V_1} = \dfrac{N_2}{N_1} \quad\quad$ 1, 2: primary, secondary coil

- ideal transformer, full load $\quad \dfrac{I_2}{I_1} = \dfrac{N_1}{N_2}$

5 Special Relativity

LORENTZ factor
$$\gamma = \frac{1}{\sqrt{1 - \frac{v^2}{c^2}}}$$

v: velocity of the coordinate system $0'x'y'z'$ with respect to the system $0\,x\,y\,z$

c: speed of light in vacuum

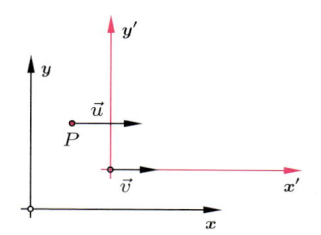

LORENTZ transformation
$$x' = \gamma(x - vt)$$
$$y' = y$$
$$z' = z$$
$$t' = \gamma\left(t - \frac{v}{c^2}x\right)$$

v in x direction

Transformation of related quantities

- velocity addition
$$u' = \frac{u - v}{1 - \frac{uv}{c^2}}$$

- length contraction
$$l = \frac{l_0}{\gamma}$$

- time dilation
$$\Delta t = \gamma \Delta t_0$$

$l, \Delta t$: values measured in a system in which the object moves with velocity v.

$l_0, \Delta t_0$: values measured in a system in which the object is at rest.

- frequency
$$f = f_0 \sqrt{\frac{c - v}{c + v}}$$
$$= f_0 \cdot \gamma \cdot \left(1 - \frac{v}{c}\right)$$

f_0: source frequency
f: observed frequency
v: relative velocity between source and observer moving apart

Relativistic dynamics

- invariant mass $\quad m \quad$ also: rest mass

- momentum $\quad \vec{p} = \gamma m \vec{v}$

- relativistic mass $\quad m_{\text{rel}} = \gamma m = \frac{p}{v} \quad$ (no longer used)

- force $\quad \vec{F} = \dfrac{\mathrm{d}\vec{p}}{\mathrm{d}t} = \dot{\vec{p}}$

- rest energy $\quad E_0 = mc^2$

- total energy $\quad E = \gamma E_0 = \sqrt{(mc^2)^2 + (pc)^2}$

- kinetic energy $\quad E_k = E - E_0 = (\gamma - 1)mc^2$

6 Atomic Physics

DE BROGLIE relation	$p = \dfrac{h}{\lambda}$	h: PLANCK constant ▶ inside back cover
photon energy	$E = hf = \hbar\omega$	$\hbar = h/(2\pi)$
photoelectric emission	$hf = W_A + \tfrac{1}{2}mv^2$	W_A: work function of the material ▶ p. 195
time-independent SCHRÖDINGER equation	$\dfrac{\hbar^2}{2m} \cdot \dfrac{\mathrm{d}^2\Psi}{\mathrm{d}x^2} = (E_p - E)\Psi$	$\|\Psi\|^2$: probability density E: total energy E_p: potential energy
HEISENBERG uncertainty principle	$\Delta x \cdot \Delta p_x \geqslant \tfrac{1}{2}\hbar$ $\Delta E \cdot \Delta t \geqslant \tfrac{1}{2}\hbar$	$\Delta x, \Delta p_x$: uncertainties in simultaneous measurements of x and p_x (similarly for ΔE and Δt)

BOHR model of the hydrogen atom

- orbital radii

$$r_n = \dfrac{\varepsilon_0 h^2}{\pi e^2 m_e} \cdot n^2 = r_1 n^2$$

m_e: electron mass, $n = 1, 2, 3, \ldots$: principal quantum number, $r_1 \approx 0.0529\,\mathrm{nm}$

- electron energy in the n-th level

$$E_n = \dfrac{-1}{8\varepsilon_0^2} \cdot \dfrac{m_e \cdot e^4}{h^2 \cdot n^2}$$
$$= -hcR_\infty \cdot \dfrac{1}{n^2} = E_1 \cdot \dfrac{1}{n^2}$$

R_∞: RYDBERG constant ▶ inside back cover
$E_1 \approx -13.6\,\mathrm{eV}$: energy of the ground state

- BOHR frequency condition (transition $m \to n$)

$$hf = |E_n - E_m|$$

$E_n < E_m$: emission
$E_n > E_m$: absorption

- orbital angular momentum of an electron

$$|\vec{L}| = \hbar\sqrt{l(l+1)}$$
$$L_z = m\hbar$$

$l = 0, 1, \ldots, n-1$: azimuthal (or orbital) quantum number
$m = 0, \pm 1, \pm 2, \ldots, \pm l$: magnetic quantum number

Black body radiation laws

- PLANCK's law

$$\dfrac{\mathrm{d}I}{\mathrm{d}f} = \dfrac{2\pi h f^3}{c^2} \cdot \dfrac{1}{\mathrm{e}^{\frac{hf}{kT}} - 1}$$

I: radiant intensity at temperature T;
$[I] = \mathrm{W/m^2}$

- STEFAN-BOLTZMANN law

$$I = \sigma T^4$$

I: radiant intensity
σ: STEFAN-BOLTZMANN constant ▶ inside back cover

- WIEN's displacement law

$$\lambda_{\max} T = b$$

$\lambda_{\max}$: peak wavelength
b: WIEN's displacement constant ▶ inside back cover

7 Nuclear Physics

mass number (or nucleon number)	$A = Z + N$	A: mass number, Z: atomic number (no. of protons) N: neutron number
mass defect	$\Delta m \approx Z(m_p + m_e) + N m_n - m_a$	the mass defect corresponds to the (nuclear) binding energy, m_a: atomic mass ▶ p. 196
nuclear radius	$r \approx r_0 \sqrt[3]{A}$	$r_0 \approx 1.2 \cdot 10^{-15}$ m

Radioactivity

• exponential decay law	$N = N_0 e^{-\lambda t}$	N: number of nuclei, λ: decay constant
• half life	$T_{1/2} = \dfrac{\ln(2)}{\lambda}$	▶ p. 199
• mean lifetime	$\tau = \dfrac{1}{\lambda} = \dfrac{T_{1/2}}{\ln(2)}$	
• activity	$A = -\dfrac{dN}{dt} = \lambda N$	$[A] = \text{Bq} = \text{s}^{-1}$ (becquerel) Ci (Curie) ▶ p. 186
absorption of gamma rays	$I = I_0 e^{-\mu x}$	I: intensity x: thickness of layer μ: absorption coefficient
half-value layer (HVL)	$x_{1/2} = \dfrac{\ln(2)}{\mu}$	▶ p. 201

Radiological units, dosimetry

activity		see above
exposure	$X = \dfrac{\Delta Q}{\Delta m}$	$[X] = \text{C/kg}$ total ion charge of one sign caused by ionizing radiation in dry air per unit mass
absorbed dose	$D = \dfrac{\Delta W}{\Delta m}$	$[D] = \text{J/kg} = \text{Gy}$ (gray)
dose equivalent	$H = w_R D$	$[H] = \text{J/kg} = \text{Sv}$ (sievert) w_R: radiation weighting factor ▶ p. 203 $[w_R] = \text{Sv/Gy}$
effective dose	$E = \sum w_T H$	$[E] = \text{Sv}$ w_T: tissue weighting factor ▶ p. 203

8 Measurement Errors

Error bounds (maximum errors)

maximum absolute measurement error of the quantity a	$\Delta a \geqslant 0$	a lies between $a - \Delta a$ and $a + \Delta a$
maximum relative measurement error of the quantity a	$r_a = \dfrac{\Delta a}{a}$	or $= \dfrac{\Delta a}{a} \cdot 100\%$
expressing the precision of measured quantities	$(a \pm \Delta a)$ or $(1 \pm r_a) \cdot a$	e.g. $(1.58 \pm 0.25) \cdot 10^3$ m or $(1 \pm 0.16) \cdot 1.58$ km

Propagation of measurement-error bounds

addition, subtraction	$\Delta(a \pm b) = \Delta a + \Delta b$	maximum absolute error
multiplication, division	$r_{a \cdot b} = r_{a/b} \approx r_a + r_b$	maximum relative error
powers	$r_{a^p} \approx \|p\| \cdot r_a$	maximum relative error
e.g. roots	e.g. $r(\sqrt{a}) \approx \dfrac{1}{2} \cdot r_a$	
in general	$\Delta f(a, b, \ldots) \approx$ $\left\|\dfrac{\partial f}{\partial a}\right\| \Delta a + \left\|\dfrac{\partial f}{\partial b}\right\| \Delta b + \ldots$	maximum absolute error

Random errors

Let δa be the estimate of random measurement errors of a obtained from the empirical standard deviation of repeated measurements.   p. 115 ◀ descriptive statistics

If a is normally distributed, then it may be expected that:
- 68% of the measurements lie in the range $a \pm \delta a$
- 95.4% of the measurements lie in the range $a \pm 2\delta a$
- 99.7% of the measurements lie in the range $a \pm 3\delta a$

Propagation of random errors   (approximations for small errors)

addition, subtraction	$\sqrt{(\delta a)^2 + (\delta b)^2}$	standard deviation of absolute errors
multiplication, division	$\sqrt{\left(\dfrac{\delta a}{a}\right)^2 + \left(\dfrac{\delta b}{b}\right)^2}$	standard deviation of relative errors
powers	$\sqrt{p^2 \cdot \left(\dfrac{\delta a}{a}\right)^2}$	standard deviation of relative errors
in general	$\sqrt{\left(\dfrac{\partial f}{\partial a} \delta a\right)^2 + \left(\dfrac{\partial f}{\partial b} \delta b\right)^2 + \ldots}$	standard deviation of absolute errors

9 Physical Data

9.1 Units

fundamental physical constants ▶ inside back cover

Base units of the International System of Units (SI)

(The definitions below are quoted from the English versions published by the International Committee of Weights and Measures (CIPM); the official definitions are recorded in French.)

The metre is the distance travelled by light in vacuum during a time interval of $\frac{1}{299792458}$ of a second. (1983)   1 m

The kilogram is the unit of mass; it is equal to the mass of the international prototype of the kilogram. (1889)   1 kg

The second is the duration of 9 192 631 770 periods of the radiation corresponding to the transition between the two hyperfine levels of the ground state of the caesium 133 atom. (1967)   1 s

The ampere is that constant current which, if maintained in two straight parallel conductors of infinite length, of negligible circular cross-section, and placed 1 metre apart in vacuum, would produce between these conductors a force equal to $2 \cdot 10^{-7}$ newton per metre of length. (1948)   1 A

The kelvin, unit of thermodynamic temperature, is the fraction $\frac{1}{273.16}$ of the thermodynamic temperature of the triple point of water. (1967)   1 K

The candela is the luminous intensity, in a given direction, of a source that emits monochromatic radiation of frequency $540 \cdot 10^{12}$ hertz and that has a radiant intensity in that direction of $\frac{1}{683}$ watt per steradian. (1979)   1 cd

The mole is the amount of substance of a system which contains as many elementary entities as there are atoms in 0.012 kilogram of carbon 12.   1 mol

When the mole is used, the elementary entities must be specified and may be atoms, molecules, ions, electrons, other particles, or specified groups of such particles. (1967) In this definition, it is understood that unbound atoms of carbon 12, at rest and in their ground state, are referred to. (1980)

Conversion table for non-SI units

(equals signs in this table denote definitions)

Length	1 Å (Ångström)	$= 10^{-10}$ m	
	1 in (inch)	$= 2.540 \cdot 10^{-2}$ m	
	1 ft (foot)	$= 12$ in	$= 0.3048$ m
	1 yd (yard)	$= 3$ ft	$= 0.9144$ m
	1 mi (mile)	$= 5280$ ft	$= 1609.344$ m
	1 nmi (international nautical mile)		$= 1852$ m
Volume	1 gal (US gallon)	$= 3.785\,411\,784 \cdot 10^{-3}$ m^3	
	1 pt (UK pint)	$= 0.568\,261\,25 \cdot 10^{-3}$ m^3	
Speed	1 kn (knot)	$= 1.852$ km/h	≈ 0.5144 m/s

Physical Data

MATHEMATICS **PHYSICS** ASTRONOMY CHEMISTRY

Mass	1 lb (pound)	$= 0.45359237$ kg	
	1 ct (metric carat)	$= 0.2 \cdot 10^{-3}$ kg	
Force	1 dyn (dyne)	$= 10^{-5}$ N	
	1 kp (kilopond)	$= 9.80665$ N	
	1 lbf (pound-force)	$= 4.4482216152605$ N	
Energy	1 erg	$= 10^{-7}$ J	
	1 kpm (kilopond-metre)	$= 9.80665$ J	
	1 cal$_{IT}$ (international Steam Table calorie)	$= 4.1868$ J	
	1 kWh (kilowatt-hour)	$= 3.6 \cdot 10^6$ J	
	1 kgce (kilogram SCE)	$\approx 7.000 \cdot 10^3$ kcal$_{IT}$	$\approx 2.93076 \cdot 10^7$ J
	1 latm (litre-atmosphere)		$= 1.01325 \cdot 10^2$ J
	1 eV (electron volt)	$\approx 1.602176487 \cdot 10^{-19}$ J	
	1 eV/particle	≈ 96.485 kJ/mol	≈ 23.045 kcal/mol
Power	1 PS (metric horsepower)	$= 75$ kp·m/s	$= 735.49875$ W
Pressure	1 bar	$= 10^5$ N/m^2	$= 10^5$ Pa
	1 kp/m^2	$= 9.80665$ Pa	
	1 at (technical atmosphere)	$= 1$ kp/cm^{-2}	$= 98066.5$ Pa
	1 atm (standard atmosphere)	$= 101325$ Pa	$= 1.01325$ bar
	1 Torr	$= \frac{1}{760}$ atm ≈ 1.333 mbar ≈ 1 mm Hg	
Temperature	K → °C	$\vartheta_{\text{Celsius}} = (T_K - 273.15\,\text{K}) \cdot \frac{°C}{K}$	
	°F → °C	$\vartheta_{\text{Celsius}} = (T_F - 32\,°F) \cdot \frac{5\,°C}{9\,°F}$	
	°C → °F	$T_F = \vartheta_{\text{Celsius}} \cdot \frac{9\,°F}{5\,°C} + 32\,°F$	
Luminance	1 stilb	$= 1$ cd/cm^2	
Magnetic field	1 G (gauss)	$= 10^{-4}$ T	
	1 Oe (oersted)	$= \frac{250}{\pi}$ A/m	
Magnetic flux	1 Mx (maxwell)	$= 10^{-8}$ V·s	
Dosimetry	1 Ci (curie)	$= 3.7 \cdot 10^{10}$ Bq	
	1 R (roentgen)	$= 2.85 \cdot 10^{-4}$ C/kg	
	1 rad (radiation absorbed dose)	$= 0.01$ Gy	
	1 rem (roentgen equivalent in man)	$= 0.01$ Sv	
Angle measurement	6400 (angular mil)	$= 360°$	$= 2\pi$ rad
	100 gon (gradian)	$= 90°$	$= \frac{\pi}{2}$ rad

Equivalence of mass and energy units

based on the equations $E = mc^2$ and $E = kT$ — more precise values ▶ inside back cover

	u*	kg	MeV	K	J
1 u $\cong$	1	$1.6605 \cdot 10^{-27}$	$9.3149 \cdot 10^2$	$1.0809 \cdot 10^{13}$	$1.4924 \cdot 10^{-10}$
1 kg $\cong$	$6.0221 \cdot 10^{26}$	1	$5.6096 \cdot 10^{29}$	$6.5096 \cdot 10^{39}$	$8.9876 \cdot 10^{16}$
1 MeV $\cong$	$1.0735 \cdot 10^{-3}$	$1.7827 \cdot 10^{-30}$	1	$1.1605 \cdot 10^{10}$	$1.6022 \cdot 10^{-13}$
1 K $\cong$	$9.2511 \cdot 10^{-14}$	$1.5362 \cdot 10^{-40}$	$8.6173 \cdot 10^{-11}$	1	$1.3807 \cdot 10^{-23}$
1 J $\cong$	$6.7005 \cdot 10^9$	$1.1127 \cdot 10^{-17}$	$6.2415 \cdot 10^{12}$	$7.2430 \cdot 10^{22}$	1

Physical Data

9.2 Mechanics

Density ϱ

Common solids at 20 °C

	in 10^3 kg/m^3
aluminium	2.70
beech wood (dry)*	0.7
brass (65% Cu, 35% Zn)	8.47
brick*	1.6
carbon steel (1% C)	7.83
cast iron (grey)*	7.2
concrete*	2.2
copper	8.92
cork*	0.3
corundum (99.9% Al_2O_3*)	4.0
diamond	3.51
fir wood (dry)*	0.5
fused quartz	2.2
germanium	5.35
glass-ceramic*	2.53
gold	19.29
graphite	2.24
ice (at 0 °C)	0.917
invar (64% Fe, 36% Ni)	8.00
iron	7.86
lead	11.34
limestone*	2.7
marble*	2.7
mercury (at −39 °C)	14.19
natural rubber	0.945
nickel	8.90
oak wood (dry)*	0.7
paraffin*	0.9
platinum	21.45
Plexiglas	1.18
porcelain*	2.4
rigid polyvinyl chloride (uPVC)	1.40
silicon	2.42
silver	10.5
sodium	0.97
stainless steel (V2A: 74% Fe, 18% Cr, 8% Ni)	7.9
styrofoam*	0.02
tin (white)	7.29
tungsten	19.3
uranium	18.7
window glass*	2.5
zinc	7.14

densities of elements ▶ p. 228

Common liquids at 20 °C

		in 10^3 kg/m^3
acetone	$(CH_3)_2CO$	0.791
ammonia (at −40 °C)	NH_3	0.690
benzene	C_6H_6	0.879
carbon tetrachloride	CCl_4	1.594
diethyl ether	$(C_2H_5)_2O$	0.714
ethanol	C_2H_5OH	0.789
glycerol	$C_3H_5(OH)_3$	1.261
heating oil EL*		0.86
mercury (▶ p. 192)	Hg	13.546
methanol	CH_3OH	0.792
olive oil (typ.)*		0.92
petrol (gasoline)*		0.75
petroleum*		0.85
sulphuric acid (conc.)	H_2SO_4	1.84
toluene	C_7H_8	0.867
water (▶ S. 192)	H_2O	0.998
heavy water	D_2O	1.105

Common gases at 0 °C and standard pressure

		in kg/m^3
air (by mass: 23% O_2, 76% N_2, 1% Ar)		1.293
ammonia	NH_3	0.771
argon	Ar	1.784
butane	C_4H_{10}	2.732
carbon dioxide	CO_2	1.977
carbon monoxide	CO	1.250
Freon 12	CF_2Cl_2	5.510
helium	He	0.1785
hydrogen	H_2	0.0899
methane	CH_4	0.717
natural gas*		0.83
neon	Ne	0.900
nitrogen	N_2	1.250
oxygen	O_2	1.429
propane	C_3H_8	2.010
sulphur dioxide	SO_2	2.926
xenon	Xe	5.897

*typical values

Physical Data

Elastic modulus E and tensile strength σ_B

(typical values)

	E in 10^{10} N/m²	σ_B in 10^7 N/m²
aluminium (99.99%)		
soft	7.1	5
work hardened	7.1	13
brass (65% Cu, 35% Zn)		
soft	11	29
work hardened	11	54
carbon steel ($\approx 1\%$ C)	21	70
cast iron ($\approx 3\%$ Graphit)	11	22
copper soft	13	22
corundum (99% Al_2O_3)	44	40
diamond (monocrystalline)	114	
fused quartz	7.31	11
iron (99.8%)	21.9	20
Kevlar	10	270
nickel	20	44
nylon 6,6	0.33	8.2
piano wire	21	196
platinum	17	14
Plexiglas	0.3	7
rubber (vulcanized, high quality)	–	0.015
silver	8	17
stainless steel (V2A: 74% Fe, 18% Cr, 8% Ni)	19.1	64

Compressibility χ

of common liquids at 20°C and a pressure of a few bars

	χ in 10^{-10} Pa^{-1}
acetone	12
ethanol	11
mercury	0.38
oil	6
water	4.45

Surface tension γ

of common liquids at 20°C

	γ in N/m
acetone	0.02330
ethanol	0.0223
ethyl ether	0.017
mercury	0.475
olive oil (typ.)	0.033
soap solution	0.030
water	0.07275
water (100°C)	0.0589

Propagation velocity c

for sound waves
(at 20°C and standard pressure)

	c in m/s
Gases	
air	344
carbon dioxide	268
helium	1005
hydrogen	1310
methane	445
nitrogen	349
oxygen	326
Liquids	
acetone	1190
benzene	1326
ethanol	1180
glycerol	1923
water (dist.)	1483
Solids	
longitudinal waves in rods, thickness $d \ll \lambda$	
aluminium	5240
brass	3420
fused quartz	5970
lead	1250
steel	5050

Musical intervals

	$f_2 : f_1$
octave	2 : 1
seventh	15 : 8
major sixth	5 : 3
fifth	3 : 2
fourth	4 : 3
major third	5 : 4
minor third	6 : 5
major second (greater)	9 : 8
major second (lesser)	10 : 9
minor second	16 : 15
semitone (equal-tempered)	$\sqrt[12]{2} \approx 1.0595$

Standard concert pitch (ISO)

	f
A_4	440 Hz

Physical Data

Coefficients of friction μ

Coefficients of rolling resistance
(typical values)

	C_{rr}
bicycle tyre on asphalt	0.007
car tyres on asphalt	0.008 ± 0.002
car tyres on loose sand	0.3 ± 0.1
car tyres on gravel	0.02 ± 0.01
railway wheel on rail	0.0015 ± 0.0005

Dynamic viscosity η

	η in Ns/m^2
air at 20 °C and standard pressure	$1.82 \cdot 10^{-5}$
ethanol 20 °C	$1.20 \cdot 10^{-3}$
glycerol 20 °C	1.48
honey (typical)	5000
mercury 20 °C	$1.55 \cdot 10^{-3}$
water 0 °C	$1.79 \cdot 10^{-3}$
water 20 °C	$1.00 \cdot 10^{-3}$
water 40 °C	$0.65 \cdot 10^{-3}$
water 60 °C	$0.47 \cdot 10^{-3}$

Drag coefficients c_D (turbulent flow)

person (erect)		0.78
passenger car (closed)		0.2–0.4
lorry (truck)		0.6–1.5
sphere	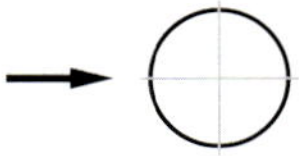	0.47
hemisphere	hollow	0.34
	solid	0.40
hemisphere	hollow	1.33
	solid	1.17
hollow cone	$\alpha = 30°$	0.34
	$\alpha = 60°$	0.51
narrow solid cone	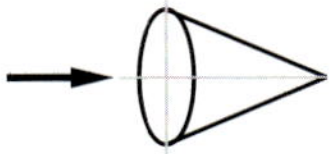	0.58

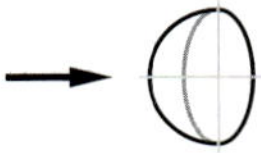

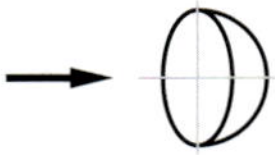

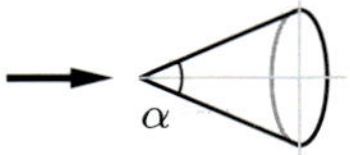

Coefficients of kinetic and static friction
(typical values for smooth, dry surfaces)

	kinetic μ_k	static μ_s
tyre on dry asphalt	0.65 ± 0.15	0.85 ± 0.15
brake pads on disc brakes	0.35 ± 0.15	
glass on glass	0.40	0.94
joint (e.g. shoulder)	0.003	0.01
leather on metal	0.3	0.4
NaCl on NaCl	1.2	1.5
ski on snow	0.12 ± 0.08	0.2 ± 0.1
steel on ice	0.014	0.027
steel on steel (hard)	0.42	0.78
steel on teflon	0.04	0.04
wood on wood	0.3 ± 0.1	0.4 ± 0.2
wood on stone	0.3	0.7

flow $\parallel$ or $\perp$ to symmetry axes of figures shown

circular disc	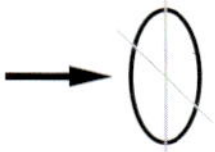	1.11

circular cylinder	l/d	
	1	0.91
	2	0.85
	4	0.87
	7	0.99

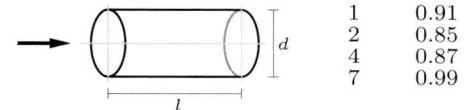

circular cylinder	l/d	
	1	0.63
	2	0.68
	5	0.74
	10	0.82
	40	0.98
	∞	1.20

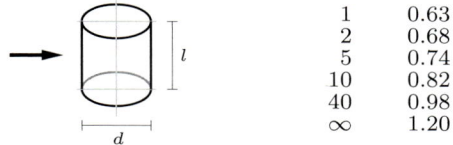

aerofoil	l/d	
	2	0.2
	3	0.1
	5	0.06
	10	0.083

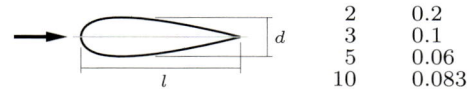

rectangular plate	a/b	
	1	1.10
	2	1.15
	4	1.19
	10	1.29
	18	1.40
	∞	2.01

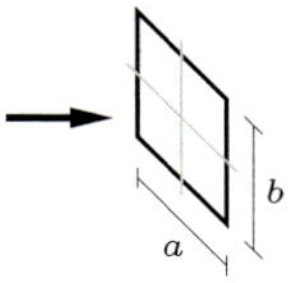

streamlined body		0.05

9.3 Thermodynamics

Thermodynamic properties of common solids

α coefficient of linear expansion (in the range 0°C to 100°C)
c specific heat at 20°C
ϑ_f melting point
L_f latent heat of fusion
λ thermal conductivity at 20°C

	α 10^{-6} K^{-1}	c J/(kg·K)	ϑ_f °C	L_f 10^5 J/kg	λ W/(m·K)
aluminium	23.8	896	660.1	3.97	239
brass	18	380	905	1.6	79
carbon steel ($\approx$ 1% C)	11	452	1450		45
cast iron	10	540	1200	1.3	50
copper	16.8	383	1083	2.05	390
corundum (99% Al$_2$O$_3$)	6.5	754	2053	10.93	41.9
diamond	1.18	510	3820	1.05	2000
fused quartz	0.55	710	1610	(cryst. quartz)	1.36
glass-ceramic (typical)	0 ± 0.1	800			1.46
gold	14.3	129	1063.0	0.64	312
ice (at 0°C)	37	2100	0	3.338	2.2
invar (64% Fe, 36% Ni)	0.2 − 1.6	460	1436		11
iron (pure)	12	450	1535	2.77	80
lead	31.3	129	327.4	0.23	34.8
nickel	12.8	448	1453	3.03	81
platinum	9.0	133	1769.3	1.11	70.1
silver	19.7	235	960.8	1.045	428
tin	27	227	231.9	0.596	64
tungsten	4.3	134	3380	1.92	177
window glass (typical)	8.5	800			0.8
zinc	26.3	385	419.5	1.11	112

Emissivity ε

at 20°C surface temperature

aluminium, anodized	0.92
aluminium, oxidized	0.3
aluminium, polished	0.04
aluminium, rough	0.06
black body	1.0
glass	0.9
human skin	0.95–0.98
ice	0.97
paint	0.95
silver, polished	0.02
textile	0.75–0.95
water	0.98

Thermal conductivity λ

of construction materials in $\dfrac{W}{mK}$

brick	0.47
concrete, lightweight	0.22
concrete, reinforced	1.85
fir panels	0.15
insulation material	0.04
still air	0.025
window glass	0.8

Thermal transmittance U

of structural components

	thickness in cm	U in $\dfrac{W}{m^2 K}$
brick wall plastered both sides	30	1.15
window		
single pane		5.9
double pane		2.5
insulated glazing		1.1
lightw. concrete wall	25	
with ext. insulation	15	0.2
solid wood wall	20	0.5
Plexiglas pane	0.5	5.3
cavity wall	15+15	
with insulation	10	0.30

Physical Data

Thermodynamic properties of common liquids

- γ coefficient of volume expansion (at 20 °C)
- c_p specific heat (at 20 °C)
- L_f latent heat of fusion
- L_v latent heat of vaporization
- ϑ_f freezing point
- ϑ_v boiling point (at standard pressure)
- p_s vapour pressure (at 20 °C)
- λ thermal conductivity (at 20 °C)

	γ $10^{-3}\,\frac{1}{K}$	c_p $10^3\,\frac{J}{kg\,K}$	L_f $10^5\,\frac{J}{kg}$	L_v $10^6\,\frac{J}{kg}$	ϑ_f °C	ϑ_v °C	p_s $10^3\,Pa$	λ $\frac{W}{m\,K}$
acetone	1.49	2.16	0.98	0.525	−94.86	56.25	24	0.162
benzene	1.23	1.725	1.28	0.394	5.53	80.10	10	0.148
diethyl ether	1.62	2.310	1.00	0.384	−116.3	34.5	58.4	0.13
ethanol	1.10	2.43	1.08	0.840	−114.5	78.33	5.87	0.165
glycerol	0.50	2.39	2.01	0.854	18.4	290.5		0.285
mercury	0.182	0.139	0.118	0.285	−38.87	356.58	0.000163	8.2
methanol	1.20	2.495	0.92	1.10	−97.7	64.6	12.9	0.198
olive oil (typ.)	2.16	2.0			−6	300		0.17
sodium (400 °C)	0.27	1.28	1.13	0.390	97.8	890	0.060	
water	0.207	4.182	3.338	2.257	0	100.0	2.34	0.598

Thermodynamic properties of common gases

- $c_{p,v}$ specific heat at constant pressure, volume (at 20 °C)
- $C_{p,v}$ molar heat capacity at constant pressure, volume (at 20 °C)
- κ adiabatic constant
- ϑ_s condensation point (at standard pressure)
- ϑ_f freezing point
- ϑ_c critical temperature
- p_c critical pressure
- ϱ_c critical density
- a, b VAN DER WAALS constants

	c_p $10^3\,\frac{J}{kg\,K}$	C_p $\frac{J}{mol\,K}$	$\kappa=\frac{C_p}{C_v}$	ϑ_s °C	ϑ_f °C	ϑ_c °C	p_c $10^6\,Pa$	ϱ_c $\frac{kg}{m^3}$	a $\frac{N\,m^4}{mol^2}$	b $\frac{m^3}{10^5\,mol}$
air	1.005	29.1	1.402			−140.73	3.78	328	0.135	3.65
ammonia	2.160	36.8	1.305	−33.4	−77.7	+132.4	11.30	235	0.423	3.71
argon	0.523	20.9	1.648	−185.88	−189.38	−122.29	4.90	536	0.136	3.20
butane	1.67	97.2	1.091	−0.5	−138.4	152	3.80	228	1.466	12.26
carbon dioxide	0.837	36.8	1.293	−78.45	(subl.)	+31.0	7.38	468	0.366	4.29
Freon 12	0.502	60.7	1.14	−29.8	−158.2	+112.0	4.12	558	0.837	7.75
helium	5.23	20.9	1.63	−268.94		−267.95	0.229	69.4	0.0035	2.38
hydrogen	14.32	28.9	1.41	−252.77	−259.20	−239.91	1.297	30.1	0.0245	2.65
methane	2.219	35.6	1.308	−161.5	−182.52	−82.3	4.64	162	0.230	4.31
neon	1.031	20.8	1.64	−246.06	−248.61	−228.75	2.65	484	0.0208	1.67
nitrogen	1.038	29.1	1.401	−195.82	−210.00	−146.9	3.39	311	0.137	3.87
oxygen	0.917	29.3	1.398	−182.97	−218.79	−118.38	5.08	430	0.138	3.19
propane	1.64	72.4	1.136	−42.09	−187.6	96.7	4.25	224	0.8779	8.445
water vapour	1.863	33.6	1.33	+100	0.00	+374.0	22.06	322	0.554	3.05

Physical Data

Saturated vapour pressures p_s and densities ϱ_s of water

over water

ϑ in °C	p_s in kPa	ϱ_s in kg/m³
−10	0.285	0.00236
−5	0.421	0.00332
0	0.611	0.00485
2	0.705	0.00557
4	0.813	0.00637
6	0.935	0.00727
8	1.072	0.00828
10	1.227	0.00941
12	1.401	0.01067
14	1.597	0.01208
16	1.817	0.01365
18	2.062	0.01539
20	2.337	0.01732
22	2.642	0.01944
24	2.984	0.02181
26	3.361	0.02440
28	3.780	0.02726
30	4.242	0.03039
35	5.624	0.03963
40	7.378	0.05017
45	9.586	0.06545
50	12.34	0.0830
60	19.92	0.130
70	31.16	0.198
80	47.34	0.293
85	57.81	0.353
90	70.10	0.424
95	84.51	0.5045
96	87.68	0.5222
97	90.94	0.5403
98	94.30	0.5589
99	97.76	0.5781
100	101.32	0.5977
105	120.80	0.7045
110	143.26	0.8265
120	198.53	1.122
130	270.13	1.496
140	361.4	1.967
150	476.0	2.548
160	618.1	3.260
170	792.1	4.122
180	1002.6	5.157
190	1255.0	6.392
200	1554.4	7.857
250	3975.4	19.98
300	8590.3	46.24
350	16532	113.6
374.2	22060	328

over ice

ϑ in °C	p_s in kPa	ϱ_s in kg/m³
−30	0.037	0.00035
−25	0.063	0.00057
−20	0.103	0.00091
−15	0.165	0.00139
−10	0.260	0.00215
−5	0.401	0.00325

Saturated vapour pressures p_s of refrigerants

ϑ in °C	ammonia NH$_3$; R 717 p_s in bar	propane C$_3$H$_8$; R 290 p_s in bar	Freon 22 CHClF$_2$; R 22 p_s in bar	carbon dioxide CO$_2$; R 744 p_s in bar
−100		0.033	0.0201	0.139*
−90		0.062	0.0479	0.372*
−80		0.133	0.104	0.896*
−70	0.1092	0.276	0.205	1.981*
−60	0.2190	0.451	0.375	4.099*
−50	0.4087	0.705	0.647	6.84
−40	0.7176	1.09	1.056	10.05
−30	1.1954	1.640	1.65	14.27
−20	1.9024	2.455	2.46	19.67
−10	2.9087	3.550	3.56	26.47
0	4.294	4.980	4.99	34.85
10	6.150	6.803	6.85	45.06
20	8.572	9.081	9.17	57.33
30	11.66	11.880	12.03	71.92
40	15.54	15.269	15.48	
50	20.33	19.327	19.61	
60	26.13	24.146		

* over solid CO$_2$

Densities ϱ of water and mercury

(at standard pressure)

temperature in °C	water in kg/m³	mercury in kg/m³
−10	998.109 (liq.)	13620
−5	999.255 (liq.)	13607.4
0	999.840	13595.1
3	999.964	13587.7
4	999.972	13585.2
5	999.964	13582.8
10	999.700	13570.5
15	999.101	13558.2
20	998.206	13545.9
25	997.047	13533.6
30	995.650	13521.4
40	992.22	13497.0
50	988.04	13472.6
60	983.20	13448.3
70	977.76	13424.0
80	971.79	13399.8
90	965.30	13375.7
100	958.35	13351.6
150	916.8*	13233
200	864.7*	13115
250	799.2*	12997
300	712.2*	12880
350	574.3*	12764

* at boiling pressure

Physical Data

Latent heats of vaporization of water

temperature in °C	L_v in 10^6 J/kg
0	2.5009
25	2.4419
40	2.4064
60	2.3582
80	2.3084
100	2.2569
200	1.9407
300	1.4044
374.2	0

Heating values H_L of common fuels

lower heating values (LHV), i. e. end products vaporized (at 25 °C, standard pressure)

	H_L in 10^6 J/kg
anthracite	32
butane	45.7
coke	29
ethanol	26.7
fir wood	15
heating oil	42.7
hydrogen	120.0
methane	50.1
methanol	22.7
natural gas	38
paraffin	45
petrol (gasoline)	43.5
propane	46.4

Triple points of selected substances

	T_{tp} in K	p_{tp} in Pa
carbon dioxide CO_2	216.6	$5.18 \cdot 10^5$
iodine I_2	383	$1.1 \cdot 10^4$
mercury Hg	234.2	$1.7 \cdot 10^{-4}$
hydrogen*	13.96	$6.8 \cdot 10^3$
nitrogen N_2	63.1	$1.2 \cdot 10^4$
oxygen O_2	54.3	$1.6 \cdot 10^2$
water H_2O	273.16	$6.11 \cdot 10^2$

* 75% ortho-, 25% para-H_2

9.4 Optics

Indices of refraction   selected materials at 20 °C

The indices of refraction n and wavelengths λ are specified with respect to air at 20 °C and standard pressure (partial pressure of water vapour 1.3% of standard pressure).

Fraunhofer line element wavelength in nm colour	G'(H_γ) H 434.048 blue-violet	F(H_β) H 486.135 azure	D Na 589.30 yellow	C(H_α) H 656.282 red	A' K 768.20 red	He-Ne laser 632.8 red-orange	Ga-As laser 840 infrared
Jena glass FK3	1.47333	1.46939	1.46444	1.46232	1.45968	1.4629	
K3	1.52932	1.52433	1.51814	1.51554	1.51250	1.5163	
SF4	1.79201	1.77471	1.75496	1.74728	1.73886	1.7497	
fused quartz SiO_2	1.4669	1.4631	1.4584	1.4563	1.4539	1.4571	
crystalline quartz SiO_2							
$\perp$ opt. axis: ord. ray	1.55394	1.54966	1.54422	1.54187	1.53903	1.5426	1.5353
extr. ray	1.56337	1.55896	1.55332	1.55089	1.54794	1.5517	
carbon disulphide CS_2	1.6750	1.65225	1.62774	1.61820	1.6080	1.6211	
water H_2O	1.34034	1.33712	1.33300	1.33115	1.32889	1.3317	1.3277

Indices of refraction n_{20}^D   selected materials w. r. t air (20 °C, standard pressure)

		n_{20}^D			n_{20}^D
diamond	C	2.4173	air (w. r. t. vacuum)		1.000272
ethanol	C_2H_5OH	1.3617	Plexiglas M222 (acrylic)		1.491
glycerol (free of water)	$C_3H_8O_3$	1.455	polystyrene		1.588
Jena glass BK7		1.5163	common salt	NaCl	1.5443
Jena glass SFS1		1.9225	cinnamaldehyde	C_9H_8O	1.6195
methanol	CH_3OH	1.3290	ethyl cinnamate (trans)	$C_{11}H_{12}O_2$	1.5598

Physical Data

Wavelengths

selected spectral lines in air (20°C, standard pressure) in nm

H	He	Hg	Na	selected laser lines
H_δ 410.17 violet	447.15 blue	404.66 violet	466.86 blue	337.1 N_2
H_γ 434.05 blue-violet	471.31 blue	407.78 violet	498.29 azure	488.0 Ar
H_β 486.13 azure	492.19 azure	435.84 blue-violet	514.91 green	514.5 Ar
H_α 656.27 red	501.57 green	491.61 azure	515.37 green	632.8 HeNe
	587.56 yellow	546.07 green	589.00 yellow	694.3 ruby
	667.82 red	576.96 yellow	589.59 yellow	1064 Nd:YAG
	706.52 red	579.07 yellow	615.43 orange	10600 CO_2
		623.44 red	616.08 orange	

9.5 Electricity and Magnetism

Electrical resistivities ϱ_{el} and temperature coefficients α

(conductors and semiconductors at 20°C)

	ϱ_{20} in $\Omega \cdot$m	α_{20} in K^{-1}
aluminium	$2.65 \cdot 10^{-8}$	$+3.9 \cdot 10^{-3}$
brass (65% Cu, 35% Zn)	$8.0 \cdot 10^{-8}$	$+1.0 \cdot 10^{-3}$
constantan (55% Cu, 44% Ni, 1% Mn)	$49 \cdot 10^{-8}$	$\pm 0.04 \cdot 10^{-3}$
copper (pure) cold-drawn (wire)	$1.75 \cdot 10^{-8}$	$+3.9 \cdot 10^{-3}$
soft	$1.68 \cdot 10^{-8}$	$+3.9 \cdot 10^{-3}$
fat tissue	33	
germanium (pure)	0.46	$-48 \cdot 10^{-3}$
gold	$2.21 \cdot 10^{-8}$	$+3.9 \cdot 10^{-3}$
graphite (arc lamp)	$300 \cdot 10^{-8}$	$-0.2 \cdot 10^{-3}$
iron (pure*)	$9.61 \cdot 10^{-8}$	$+5.6 \cdot 10^{-3}$
lead	$20.8 \cdot 10^{-8}$	$+4.2 \cdot 10^{-3}$
manganin (84% Cu, 12% Mn, 4% Ni)	$43 \cdot 10^{-8}$	$+1 \cdot 10^{-5}$
mercury	$95.76 \cdot 10^{-8}$	$+0.9 \cdot 10^{-3}$
muscle tissue	2	
nichrome (80% Ni, 20% Cr)	$103 \cdot 10^{-8}$	$+0.17 \cdot 10^{-3}$
nickel (pure)	$6.93 \cdot 10^{-8}$	$+6.7 \cdot 10^{-3}$
platinum	$10.5 \cdot 10^{-8}$	$+3.8 \cdot 10^{-3}$
silicon (pure*)	640	$-75 \cdot 10^{-3}$
silver	$1.59 \cdot 10^{-8}$	$+3.8 \cdot 10^{-3}$
steel (1% C)	$20.0 \cdot 10^{-8}$	$+2.9 \cdot 10^{-3}$
sulphuric acid 30%	$1.31 \cdot 10^{-2}$	$-16 \cdot 10^{-3}$
tin	$10.9 \cdot 10^{-8}$	$+4.5 \cdot 10^{-3}$
tungsten	$5.5 \cdot 10^{-8}$	$+4.6 \cdot 10^{-3}$
at 727°C	$24.3 \cdot 10^{-8}$	
at 1727°C	$55.7 \cdot 10^{-8}$	
at 2727°C	$90.4 \cdot 10^{-8}$	
at 3227°C	$108.5 \cdot 10^{-8}$	
zinc	$5.90 \cdot 10^{-8}$	$+3.7 \cdot 10^{-3}$

* impurity concentration $< 10^{18}/$m^3

Physical Data

Electrical resistivities ϱ_{el} and dielectric constants ε_r

(typical values for insulators at 20 °C)

	ϱ in $\Omega\cdot$m	ε_r
air (standard pressure)	10^{13}	1.000536
amber	10^{18}	2.9
ebonite	10^{15}	2.8
fused quartz	10^{12}	3.8
mica	$5\cdot 10^{14}$	7.0
paper (dry)	10^{10}	2.0
paraffin	$3\cdot 10^{16}$	2.2
Plexiglas	10^{13}	3.4
polystyrene (styrofoam)	10^{17}	1.03
polyvinyl chloride (PVC)	$5\cdot 10^{12}$	3.4
porcelain	10^{11}	6
pyrex glass	10^{11}	4.7
sulphur	10^{15}	1.7
teflon	10^{15}	2.0
water (distilled)	bis 10^5	80.4

Permeabilities μ_r

ferromagnetic materials	at 2 mT	max.
cobalt	70	250
iron	200	5000
nickel	100	1000
permalloy (78.5% nickel, 21.5% iron)	8000	100000

paramagnetic materials	$\mu_r - 1$
air	$0.4\cdot 10^{-6}$
aluminium	$22\cdot 10^{-6}$
iron oxide	$7200\cdot 10^{-6}$
platinum	$260\cdot 10^{-6}$

diamagnetic materials	$\mu_r - 1$
bismuth	$-166\cdot 10^{-6}$
copper	$-6.4\cdot 10^{-6}$
gold	$-29\cdot 10^{-6}$
lead	$-18\cdot 10^{-6}$
mercury	$-29\cdot 10^{-6}$
superconductor (ideal diamagnet)	-1
water	$-9.1\cdot 10^{-6}$

9.6 Atomic and nuclear Physics

Concentrations n_e of free electrons in selected substances

at 20 °C

		n_e in m^{-3}
copper	Cu	$11.6\cdot 10^{28}$
germanium*	Ge	$1.1\cdot 10^{19}$
silicon*	Si	$1.0\cdot 10^{16}$
silver	Ag	$6.9\cdot 10^{28}$

* intrinsic carrier concentration

Work functions W_A and cutoff wavelengths λ_0 of selected substances

(photoelectric effect)

	W_A in eV	λ_0 in nm
barium	2.56	492
caesium	1.94	639
copper	4.84	256
germanium	5.02	247
silicon	3.59	345
tungsten	4.57	271
zinc	4.34	286

Elementary particles

	quarks			leptons		
name	up	charm	top	electron	muon	tau
symbol	u	c	t	neutrino ν_e	neutrino ν_μ	neutrino ν_τ
el. charge in e	2/3	2/3	2/3	0	0	0
mass in MeV	1.5…3	1250 ± 90	$\approx 173\,000$	$< 2\cdot 10^{-6}$	< 0.19	< 18
name	down	strange	bottom	electron	muon	tau
symbol	d	s	b	e	μ	τ
el. charge in e	$-1/3$	$-1/3$	$-1/3$	-1	-1	-1
mass in MeV	3…7	95 ± 25	≈ 4200	0.510999	105.66	1776.9

For each of these particles there is a corresponding antiparticle with the same mass but with opposite charge. Quarks q and antiquarks $\bar{q}$ can only appear in combinations whose total electrical charge is an integer multiple of e (*hadrons*):

mesons $= q\bar{q}$ or *baryons* $= qqq$ or *antibaryons* $= \bar{q}\bar{q}\bar{q}$ (proton $= uud$; neutron $= udd$)

Physical Data

PHYSICS

Force carriers of the fundamental interactions (bosons)

interaction	gravitation	elektromagnetic	weak	strong
particle	graviton	photon	W and Z boson	gluon
symbol	not yet discovered	γ	W^+, W^-, Z^0	**g**
electr. charge in e	0	0	$+1, -1, 0$	0
mass in MeV	0	0	$W^\pm$: 80410, Z: 91187	0
acts on	mass, energy	electr. charge	leptons, quarks	quarks, hadrons
rel. strength on				
• quarks	10^{-41}	1	$10^{-4} - 1$	25–60
• protons in nucleus	10^{-36}	1	10^{-7}	20

Unstable particles

		mass in MeV	$T_{1/2}$ in s	typical decay	interaction
muon	μ^-	105.658367	$1.522856 \cdot 10^{-6}$	$\mu^- \to e^- + \bar{\nu}_e + \nu_\mu$	weak
π meson (pion)	π^0	134.9766	$5.8 \cdot 10^{-17}$	$\pi^0 \to \gamma + \gamma \,(98.8\%)$	electromagnetic
				$\pi^0 \to \gamma + e^+ + e^- \,(1.2\%)$	electromagnetic
	$\pi^\pm$	139.5702	$1.8045 \cdot 10^{-8}$	$\pi^\pm \to \mu^\pm + \nu_\mu$	weak
neutron	n	939.56536	$6.139 \cdot 10^2$	$n \to p + e^- + \bar{\nu}_e$	weak
K meson (kaon)	$K^\pm$	493.68	$8.581 \cdot 10^{-9}$	$K^+ \to \pi^+ + \pi^+ + \pi^-$	weak
Λ baryon	Λ^0	1115.683	$1.82 \cdot 10^{-10}$	$\Lambda^0 \to p + \pi^-$	weak

Table of stable nuclides   (lifetime $\gtrsim 10^9$ years)

(all stable isotopes according to G. Audi, et al. in *Nuclear Physics A 729*, 3-128 (2003))

- Z atomic number
- sym chemical symbol
- A mass number
- NA natural abundance of the isotope as fraction of the isotopic mixture on the earth (% of atoms)
- m_a atomic mass in u   ▶ inside back cover
- M molar mass in 10^{-3} kg/mol

Z element	sym	A	m_a, M	NA	Z element	sym	A	m_a, M	NA
1 hydrogen	H	1	1.007 825 0	99.985			15	15.000 109	0.368
		2	2.014 101 8	0.015	8 oxygen	O	16	15.994 915	99.757
2 helium	He	3	3.016 029 3	0.000137			17	16.999 132	0.038
		4	4.002 603 3	99.999863			18	17.999 160	0.205
3 lithium	Li	6	6.015 122	7.5	9 fluorine	F	19	18.998 403	100
		7	7.016 004	92.5	10 neon	Ne	20	19.992 440	90.48
4 beryllium	Be	9	9.012 182	100			21	20.993 847	0.27
5 boron	B	10	10.012 937	19.9			22	21.991 385	9.25
		11	11.009 305	80.1	11 sodium	Na	23	22.989 770	100
6 carbon	C	12	12 (exakt)	98.93	12 magnesium	Mg	24	23.985 042	78.99
		13	13.003 355	1.07			25	24.985 837	10.00
7 nitrogen	N	14	14.003 074	99.632			26	25.982 593	11.01

Physical Data

Z element	sym	A	m_a, M	NA	Z element	sym	A	m_a, M	NA
13 aluminium	Al	27	26.981 538	100			66	65.926 037	27.90
14 silicon	Si	28	27.976 927	92.230			67	66.927 131	4.10
		29	28.976 495	4.683			68	67.924 848	18.75
		30	29.973 770	3.087			70	69.925 325	0.62
15 phosphorous	P	31	30.973 762	100	31 gallium	Ga	69	68.925 581	60.108
16 sulphur	S	32	31.972 071	94.93			71	70.924 705	39.892
(sulfur)		33	32.971 458	0.76	32 germanium	Ge	70	69.924 250	20.84
		34	33.967 867	4.29			72	71.922 076	27.54
		36	35.967 081	0.02			73	72.923 459	7.73
17 chlorine	Cl	35	34.968 853	75.78			74	73.921 178	36.28
		37	36.965 903	24.22			76	75.921 403	7.61
18 argon	Ar	36	35.967 546	0.337	33 arsenic	As	75	74.921 596	100
		38	37.962 732	0.063	34 selenium	Se	74	73.922 477	0.89
		40	39.962 383	99.600			76	75.919 214	9.37
19 potassium	K	39	38.963 707	93.258			77	76.919 915	7.63
		40	39.963 999	0.012			78	77.917 310	23.77
		41	40.961 826	6.730			80	79.916 522	49.61
20 calcium	Ca	40	39.962 591	96.941			82	81.916 700	8.73
		42	41.958 618	0.647	35 bromine	Br	79	78.918 338	50.69
		43	42.958 767	0.135			81	80.916 291	49.31
		44	43.955 481	2.086	36 krypton	Kr	78	77.920 386	0.35
		46	45.953 693	0.004			80	79.916 378	2.28
		48	47.952 534	0.187			82	81.913 485	11.58
21 scandium	Sc	45	44.955 910	100			83	82.914 136	11.49
22 titanium	Ti	46	45.952 629	8.25			84	83.911 507	57.00
		47	46.951 764	7.44			86	85.910 610	17.30
		48	47.947 947	73.72	37 rubidium	Rb	85	84.911 789	72.17
		49	48.947 871	5.41			87	86.909 183	27.83
		50	49.944 792	5.18	38 strontium	Sr	84	83.913 425	0.56
23 vanadium	V	50	49.947 163	0.250			86	85.909 262	9.86
		51	50.943 964	99.750			87	86.908 879	7.00
24 chromium	Cr	50	49.946 050	4.345			88	87.905 614	82.58
		52	51.940 512	83.789	39 yttrium	Y	89	89.905 848	100
		53	52.940 654	9.501	40 zirconium	Zr	90	89.904 702	51.45
		54	53.938 885	2.365			91	90.905 644	11.22
25 manganese	Mn	55	54.938 050	100			92	91.905 040	17.15
26 iron	Fe	54	53.939 615	5.845			94	93.906 316	17.38
		56	55.934 942	91.754			96	95.908 276	2.80
		57	56.935 399	2.119	41 niobium	Nb	93	92.906 378	100
		58	57.933 280	0.282	42 molybdenum	Mo	92	91.906 810	14.84
27 cobalt	Co	59	58.933 200	100			94	93.905 088	9.25
28 nickel	Ni	58	57.935 348	68.077			95	94.905 841	15.92
		60	59.930 791	26.223			96	95.904 679	16.68
		61	60.931 060	1.140			97	96.906 021	9.55
		62	61.928 349	3.635			98	97.905 408	24.13
		64	63.927 970	0.926			100	99.907 477	9.63
29 copper	Cu	63	62.929 601	69.17	44 ruthenium	Ru	96	95.907 598	5.54
		65	64.927 794	30.83			98	97.905 287	1.87
30 zinc	Zn	64	63.929 147	48.63			99	98.905 939	12.76

Physical Data
PHYSICS

Z element	sym	A	m_a, M	NA	Z element	sym	A	m_a, M	NA
		100	99.904 220	12.60			131	130.905 082	21.18
		101	100.905 582	17.06			132	131.904 154	26.89
		102	101.904 350	31.55			134	133.905 395	10.44
		104	103.905 430	18.62			136	135.907 220	8.87
45 rhodium	Rh	103	102.905 504	100	55 caesium	Cs	133	132.905 447	100
46 palladium	Pd	102	101.905 608	1.02	56 barium	Ba	130	129.906 310	0.106
		104	103.904 035	11.14			132	131.905 056	0.101
		105	104.905 084	22.33			134	133.904 503	2.417
		106	105.903 483	27.33			135	134.905 683	6.592
		108	107.903 894	26.46			136	135.904 570	7.854
		110	109.905 152	11.72			137	136.905 821	11.232
47 silver	Ag	107	106.905 093	51.839			138	137.905 241	71.698
		109	108.904 756	48.161	57 lanthanum	La	138	137.907 107	0.090
48 cadmium	Cd	106	105.906 458	1.25			139	138.906 348	99.910
		108	107.904 183	0.89	58 cerium	Ce	136	135.907 144	0.185
		110	109.903 006	12.49			138	137.905 986	0.251
		111	110.904 182	12.80			140	139.905 434	88.450
		112	111.902 757	24.13			142	141.909 240	11.114
		113	112.904 401	12.22	59 praseodymium	Pr	141	140.907 648	100
		114	113.903 358	28.73	60 neodymium	Nd	142	141.907 719	27.2
		116	115.904 755	7.49			143	142.909 810	12.2
49 indium	In	113	112.904 061	4.29			144	143.910 083	23.8
		115	114.903 878	95.71			145	144.912 569	8.3
50 tin	Sn	112	111.904 821	0.97			146	145.913 112	17.2
		114	113.902 782	0.66			148	147.916 889	5.7
		115	114.903 346	0.34			150	149.920 887	5.6
		116	115.901 744	14.54	62 samarium	Sm	144	143.911 995	3.07
		117	116.902 954	7.68			147	146.914 893	14.99
		118	117.901 606	24.22			148	147.914 818	11.24
		119	118.903 309	8.59			149	148.917 180	13.82
		120	119.902 197	32.58			150	149.917 271	7.38
		122	121.903 440	4.63			152	151.919 728	26.75
		124	123.905 275	5.79			154	153.922 205	22.75
51 antimony	Sb	121	120.903 818	57.21	63 europium	Eu	151	150.919 846	47.81
		123	122.904 216	42.79			153	152.921 226	52.19
52 tellurium	Te	120	119.904 020	0.09	64 gadolinium	Gd	152	151.919 788	0.20
		122	121.903 047	2.55			154	153.920 862	2.18
		123	122.904 273	0.89			155	154.922 619	14.80
		124	123.902 819	4.74			156	155.922 120	20.47
		125	124.904 425	7.07			157	156.923 957	15.65
		126	125.903 306	18.84			158	157.924 101	24.84
		128	127.904 461	31.74			160	159.927 051	21.86
		130	129.906 223	34.08	65 terbium	Tb	159	158.925 343	100
53 iodine	I	127	126.904 468	100	66 dysprosium	Dy	156	155.924 278	0.06
54 xenon	Xe	124	123.905 896	0.09			158	157.924 405	0.10
		126	125.904 269	0.09			160	159.925 194	2.34
		128	127.903 530	1.92			161	160.926 930	18.91
		129	128.904 779	26.44			162	161.926 795	25.51
		130	129.903 508	4.08			163	162.928 728	24.90

Physical Data

PHYSICS

Z element	sym	A	m_a, M	NA
		164	163.929 171	28.18
67 holmium	Ho	165	164.930 319	100
68 erbium	Er	162	161.928 775	0.14
		164	163.929 197	1.61
		166	165.930 290	33.61
		167	166.932 045	22.93
		168	167.932 368	26.78
		170	169.935 460	14.93
69 thulium	Tm	169	168.934 211	100
70 ytterbium	Yb	168	167.933 894	0.13
		170	169.934 759	3.04
		171	170.936 322	14.28
		172	161.936 378	21.83
		173	172.938 207	16.13
		174	163.938 858	31.83
		176	175.942 568	12.76
71 lutetium	Lu	175	174.940 768	97.41
		176	175.942 682	2.59
72 hafnium	Hf	174	173.940 040	0.16
		176	175.941 402	5.26
		177	176.943 220	18.60
		178	177.943 698	27.28
		179	178.945 815	13.62
		180	179.946 549	35.08
73 tantalum	Ta	180	179.947 466	0.012
		181	180.947 996	99.988
74 tungsten	W	180	179.946 706	0.12
		182	181.948 206	26.50
		183	182.950 224	14.31
		184	183.950 933	30.64
		186	185.954 362	28.43
75 rhenium	Re	185	184.952 956	37.40
		187	186.955 751	62.60
76 osmium	Os	184	183.952 491	0.02

Z element	sym	A	m_a, M	NA
		186	185.953 838	1.59
		187	186.955 748	1.96
		188	187.955 836	13.24
		189	188.958 145	16.15
		190	189.956 445	26.26
		192	191.961 479	40.78
77 iridium	Ir	191	190.960 591	37.3
		193	192.962 924	62.7
78 platinum	Pt	190	189.959 930	0.014
		192	191.961 035	0.782
		194	193.962 664	32.967
		195	194.964 774	33.832
		196	195.964 935	25.242
		198	197.967 876	7.163
79 gold	Au	197	196.966 552	100
80 mercury	Hg	196	195.965 815	0.15
		198	197.966 752	9.97
		199	198.968 262	16.87
		200	199.968 309	23.10
		201	200.970 285	13.18
		202	201.970 626	29.86
		204	203.973 476	6.87
81 thallium	Tl	203	202.972 329	29.524
		205	204.974 412	70.476
82 lead	Pb	204	203.973 029	1.4
		206	205.974 449	24.1
		207	206.975 881	22.1
		208	207.976 636	52.4
83 bismuth	Bi	209	208.980 383	100
90 thorium	Th	232	232.038 050	100
92 uranium	U	234	234.040 946	0.005
		235	235.043 923	0.720
		238	238.050 783	99.275

Selected radioactive nuclides

m_a, M	atomic mass in u, molar mass in 10^{-3} kg/mol
$T_{1/2}$	half life (a = year, d = day, h = hour, min = minute, s = second)
decay mode	α-, β-, γ-decay, ε electron capture; • decay *not* accompanied by γ-decay
energy	for β-decay energies maximum value; emissions < 2% of total omitted

nuclide	m_a, M	$T_{1/2}$		decay mode	energy (MeV)
n	1.008 664 915 7	613.9	s	β^- •	0.7824
H-3	3.016 049	12.32	a	β^- •	0.0186
Be-10	10.013 534	$1.51 \cdot 10^6$	a	β^- •	0.5558
C-14	14.003 242	$5.70 \cdot 10^3$	a	β^- •	0.1565
Na-22	21.994 436	2.6019	a	$\beta^+ \varepsilon$ •	β^+: 0.545 / γ: 1.275
Na-24	23.990 963	14.9590	h	$\beta^- \gamma$	β^-: 1.393 / γ: 1.369; 2.754
P-32	31.973 907	14.263	d	β^- •	1.710

Physical Data

Nuclide	Mass	Half-life		Decay	β^- / γ energies (MeV)
Ar-41	40.964 501	109.61	min	$\beta^- \gamma$	β^-: 1.198 / γ: 1.293 (99%)
K-40	39.963 998	$1.261 \cdot 10^9$	a	$\beta^+ \varepsilon \beta^- \gamma$	β^-: 1.311 / γ: 1.460 (11%)
Fe-55	54.938 293	2.737	a	ε	
Co-60	59.933 817	5.2713	a	$\beta^- \gamma$	β^-: 0.318 / γ: 1.173; 1.332
Kr-85	84.912 527	10.776	a	$\beta^- \gamma$	β^-: 0.687
Rb-87	86.909 181	$4.923 \cdot 10^{10}$	a	$\beta^- \bullet$	0.283
Sr-89	88.907 451	50.53	d	$\beta^- \gamma$	β^-: 1.495
Sr-90	89.907 738	28.79	a	$\beta^- \bullet$	0.546
Tc-99 m	98.906 255	6.015	h	γ	0.140 (90%)
Ag-108	107.905 956	2.37	min	$\beta^+ \varepsilon \beta^-$	β^-: 1.649
Ag-110	109.906 107	24.6	s	$\beta^- \gamma$	β^-: 2.89 / γ: 0.658 (4.5%)
I-128	127.905 809	24.99	min	$\beta^+ \varepsilon \beta^- \gamma$	β^-: 2.12 / γ: 0.443 (13%)
I-131	130.906 125	8.02070	d	$\beta^- \gamma$	β^-: 0.606 / γ: 0.364 (82%); complex
Xe-135	134.907 227	9.14	h	$\beta^- \gamma$	β^-: 0.90 / γ: 0.250 (90%); 0.608 (3%)
Cs-137	136.907 090	30.1671	a	$\beta^- \gamma$	β^-: 1.176 (6%); 0.514 (94%) / γ: 0.662
Au-198	197.968 242	2.69517	d	$\beta^- \gamma$	β^-: 0.961 / γ: 0.412 (96%) (85%)
Pb-210	209.984 189	22.20	a	$\alpha \; \varepsilon \; \gamma$	β^-: 0.064 / γ: 0.047 (4%)
Bi-208	207.979 742	$3.68 \cdot 10^5$	a	$\varepsilon \; \gamma$	γ: 2.614
Bi-210	209.984 120	5.012	d	$\alpha \; \beta^-$	β^-: 1.162
Po-210	209.982 874	138.376	d	$\alpha \; \gamma$	α: 5.304
Rn-220	220.011 394	55.6	s	$\alpha \; \gamma$	α: 6.29
Rn-222	222.017 578	3.8235	d	$\alpha \; \gamma$	α: 5.49
Ra-226	226.025 410	$1.600 \cdot 10^3$	a	$\alpha \; \gamma$	α: 4.78 (94%); 4.60 (6%) / GRS*complex
Ac-227	227.027 752	21.772	a	$\alpha \; \beta^- \gamma$	β^-: 0.045
Th-230	230.033 134	$7.538 \cdot 10^4$	a	$\alpha \; \gamma$	α: 4.69 (76%); 4.62 (24%)
Th-232	232.038 055	$1.405 \cdot 10^{10}$	a	$\alpha \; \gamma$	α: 4.01 (78%); 3.95 (22%)
Pa-231	231.035 884	$3.276 \cdot 10^4$	a	$\alpha \; \gamma$	α: 5.0 (80%); 4.73 (8%) / GRS*complex
U-233	233.039 635	$1.592 \cdot 10^5$	a	$\alpha \; \gamma$	α: 4.82 (84%); 4.78 (13%) / GRS*complex
U-234	234.040 952	$2.455 \cdot 10^5$	a	$\alpha \; \gamma$	α: 4.77 (71%); 4.72 (28%) / GRS*complex
U-235	235.043 930	$7.04 \cdot 10^8$	a	$\alpha \; \gamma$	α: 4.58 (9%), 4.4 (75%) / GRS*complex
U-238	238.050 788	$4.468 \cdot 10^9$	a	$\alpha \; \gamma$	α: 4.20 (79%); 4.15 (21%)
U-239	239.054 293	23.45	min	$\beta^- \gamma$	β^-: 1.19 / γ: 0.044 (4%); 0.075 (49%)
Np-239	239.052 939	2.356	d	$\beta^- \gamma$	β^-: 0.330 (42%); 0.436 (45%) / GRS*complex
Pu-239	239.052 163	$2.411 \cdot 10^4$	a	$\alpha \; \gamma$	α: 5.16 (71%); 5.14 (17%) / GRS*complex
Am-241	241.056 829	432.2	a	$\alpha \; \gamma$	α: 5.49 (85%); 5.44 (13%) / GRS*complex

* GRS: γ-ray spectrum

Selected fusion reactions

$${}^1_1\text{H} + {}^1_1\text{H} \longrightarrow {}^2_1\text{H} + e^+ \quad (+ \quad 1.44\,\text{MeV})$$

$${}^1_1\text{H} + {}^2_1\text{H} \longrightarrow {}^3_2\text{He} \quad (+ \quad 5.49\,\text{MeV})$$

$${}^1_1\text{H} + {}^7_3\text{Li} \longrightarrow {}^4_2\text{He} + {}^4_2\text{He} \quad (+ \quad 17.3\,\text{MeV})$$

$${}^2_1\text{H} + {}^2_1\text{H} \longrightarrow {}^3_2\text{He} + n \quad (+ \quad 3.25\,\text{MeV})$$

$${}^2_1\text{H} + {}^2_1\text{H} \longrightarrow {}^3_1\text{H} + {}^1_1\text{H} \quad (+ \quad 4.0\,\text{MeV})$$

$${}^2_1\text{H} + {}^3_1\text{H} \longrightarrow {}^4_2\text{He} + n \quad (+ \quad 17.6\,\text{MeV})$$

$${}^2_1\text{H} + {}^3_2\text{He} \longrightarrow {}^4_2\text{He} + {}^1_1\text{H} \quad (+ \quad 18.3\,\text{MeV})$$

$${}^2_1\text{H} + {}^6_3\text{Li} \longrightarrow {}^4_2\text{He} + {}^4_2\text{He} \quad (+ \quad 22.4\,\text{MeV})$$

$${}^3_2\text{He} + {}^3_2\text{He} \longrightarrow {}^4_2\text{He} + {}^1_1\text{H} + {}^1_1\text{H} \quad (+ \quad 12.9\,\text{MeV})$$

$${}^3_1\text{H} + {}^3_1\text{H} \longrightarrow {}^4_2\text{He} + n + n \quad (+ \quad 11.3\,\text{MeV})$$

Physical Data

Binding energies

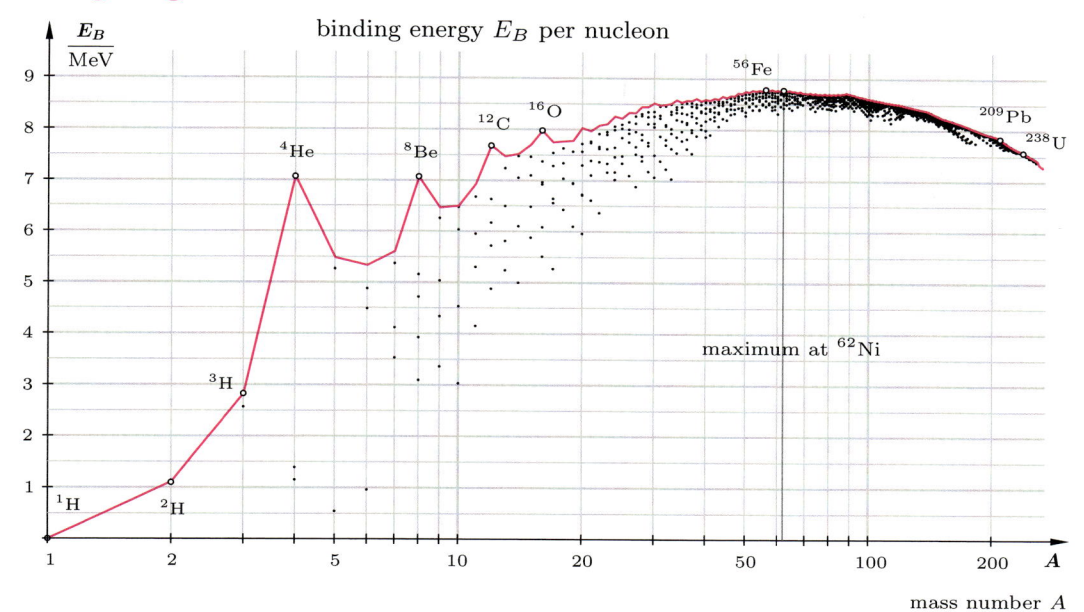

binding energy E_B per nucleon

Attenuation coefficients for γ-rays

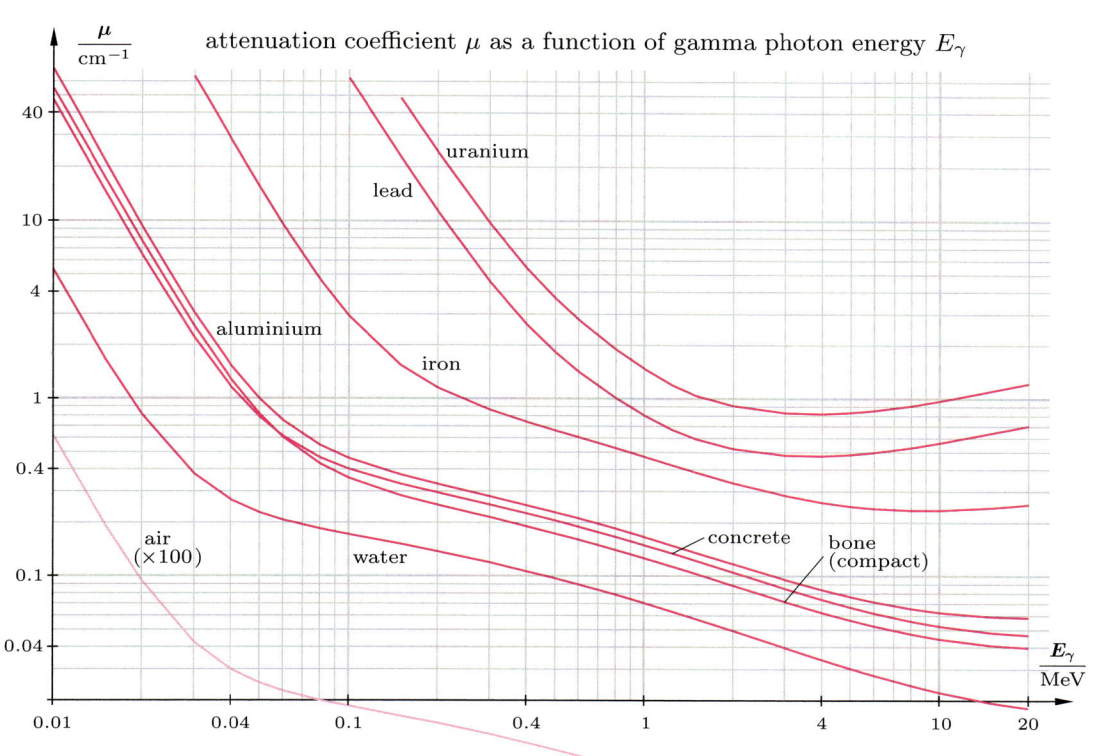

attenuation coefficient μ as a function of gamma photon energy E_γ

Physical Data

Radioactive decay chains

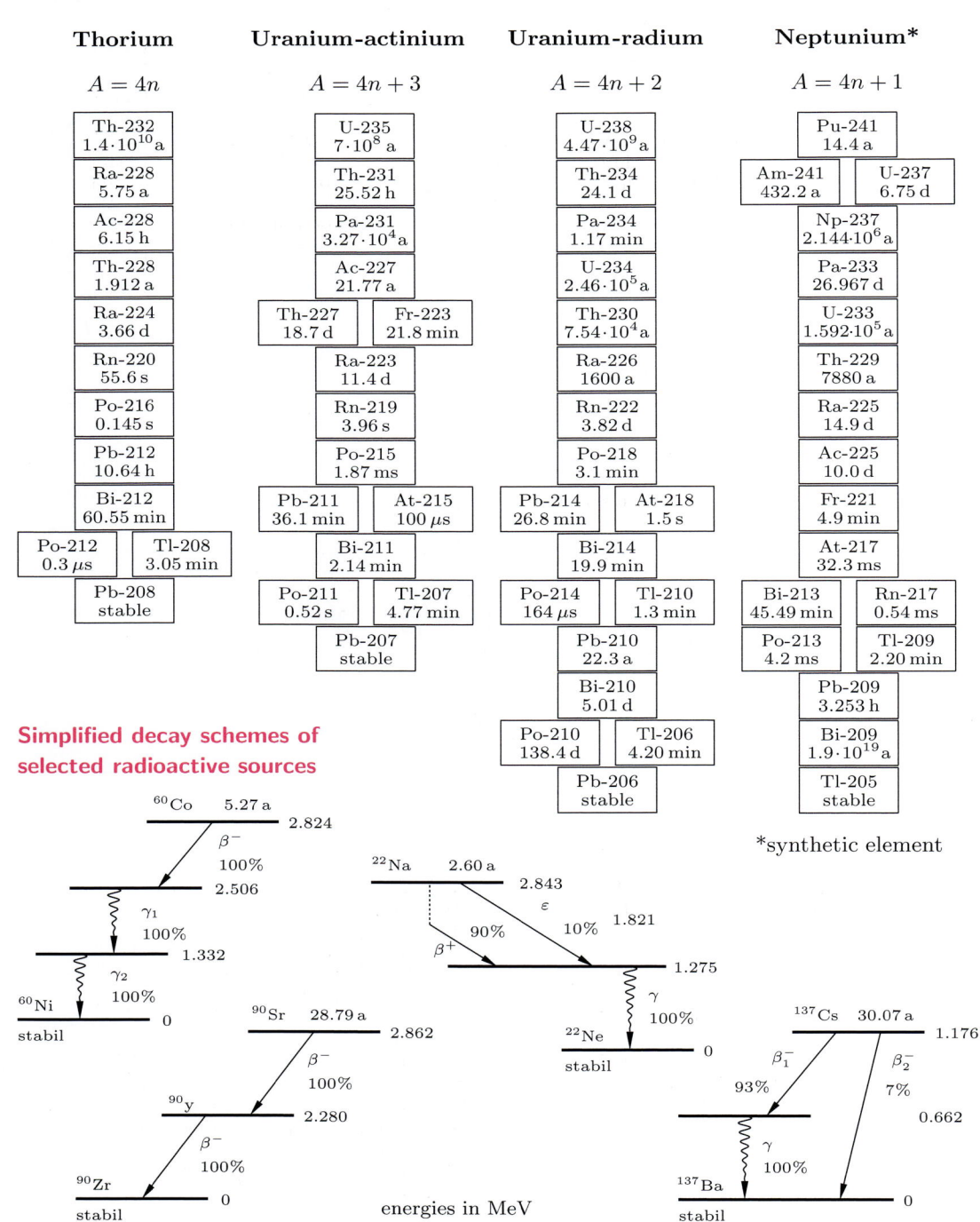

Thorium
$A = 4n$

Th-232	1.4·10¹⁰ a

Th-232 $1.4 \cdot 10^{10}$ a
Ra-228 5.75 a
Ac-228 6.15 h
Th-228 1.912 a
Ra-224 3.66 d
Rn-220 55.6 s
Po-216 0.145 s
Pb-212 10.64 h
Bi-212 60.55 min
— Po-212 0.3 μs / Tl-208 3.05 min
Pb-208 stable

Uranium-actinium
$A = 4n + 3$

U-235 $7 \cdot 10^{8}$ a
Th-231 25.52 h
Pa-231 $3.27 \cdot 10^{4}$ a
Ac-227 21.77 a
— Th-227 18.7 d / Fr-223 21.8 min
Ra-223 11.4 d
Rn-219 3.96 s
Po-215 1.87 ms
— Pb-211 36.1 min / At-215 100 μs
Bi-211 2.14 min
— Po-211 0.52 s / Tl-207 4.77 min
Pb-207 stable

Uranium-radium
$A = 4n + 2$

U-238 $4.47 \cdot 10^{9}$ a
Th-234 24.1 d
Pa-234 1.17 min
U-234 $2.46 \cdot 10^{5}$ a
Th-230 $7.54 \cdot 10^{4}$ a
Ra-226 1600 a
Rn-222 3.82 d
Po-218 3.1 min
— Pb-214 26.8 min / At-218 1.5 s
Bi-214 19.9 min
— Po-214 164 μs / Tl-210 1.3 min
Pb-210 22.3 a
Bi-210 5.01 d
— Po-210 138.4 d / Tl-206 4.20 min
Pb-206 stable

Neptunium*
$A = 4n + 1$

Pu-241 14.4 a
— Am-241 432.2 a / U-237 6.75 d
Np-237 $2.144 \cdot 10^{6}$ a
Pa-233 26.967 d
U-233 $1.592 \cdot 10^{5}$ a
Th-229 7880 a
Ra-225 14.9 d
Ac-225 10.0 d
Fr-221 4.9 min
At-217 32.3 ms
— Bi-213 45.49 min / Rn-217 0.54 ms
— Po-213 4.2 ms / Tl-209 2.20 min
Pb-209 3.253 h
Bi-209 $1.9 \cdot 10^{19}$ a
Tl-205 stable

*synthetic element

Simplified decay schemes of selected radioactive sources

^{60}Co 5.27 a — 2.824
β^- 100%
2.506
γ_1 100% — 1.332
γ_2 100%
^{60}Ni stabil — 0

^{90}Sr 28.79 a — 2.862
β^- 100%
^{90}Y — 2.280
β^- 100%
^{90}Zr stabil — 0

^{22}Na 2.60 a — 2.843
ε 10% / β^+ 90% — 1.821
1.275
γ 100%
^{22}Ne stabil — 0

^{137}Cs 30.07 a — 1.176
β_1^- 93% / β_2^- 7%
0.662
γ 100%
^{137}Ba stabil — 0

energies in MeV

Physical Data

Radiation weighting factors w_R

radiation type	energy range	w_R in Sv/Gy
γ-rays, X-rays	all energies	1
electrons, muons	all energies	1
neutrons	$< 10\,\text{keV}$	5
	$10\,\text{keV}$ to $100\,\text{keV}$	10
	$100\,\text{keV}$ to $2\,\text{MeV}$	20
	$2\,\text{MeV}$ to $20\,\text{MeV}$	10
	$> 20\,\text{MeV}$	5
protons	$> 2\,\text{MeV}$	5
α-particles		20

Tissue weighting factors w_T

tissue or organ	w_T
gonads	0.20
red bone marrow	0.12
colon	0.12
lungs	0.12
stomach	0.12
bladder	0.05
breasts	0.05
liver	0.05
oesophagus	0.05
thyroid	0.05
skin	0.01
bone surface	0.01
remainder of body	0.05

Selected fissile nuclides

selection criterion: half life > 1 year and fission cross section $\sigma_F >$ absorption cross section σ_A for thermal neutrons

abbreviations

- Z: atomic number
- sym: chemical symbol
- A: mass number
- DM: decay mode
- $T_{1/2}$: half life in years (a)
- σ_F: fission cross section in barn ($10^{-28}\,\text{m}^2$)
- σ_A: absorption cross section without fission in barn

Z	name	sym	A	DM	$T_{1/2}$	σ_F	σ_A
92	uranium	U	232	α	70	75.2	73
			233	α	$1.6 \cdot 10^5$	531	48
			235	α	$7.0 \cdot 10^8$	582	99
93	neptunium	Np	236	ε	$1.2 \cdot 10^5$	2500	
94	plutonium	Pu	239	α	$2.41 \cdot 10^4$	742	269
			241	β^-	14.4	1009	368
95	americum	Am	242 m	γ	141	6600	1400
96	curium	Cm	243	α	28.5	600	225
			245	α	8500	2020	345

Thermal neutron capture

nuclide		process	σ in $10^{-28}\,\text{m}^2$
H	1	(n, γ)	0.332
H	2	(n, γ)	$5.2 \cdot 10^{-4}$
He	3	(n, γ)	$5.4 \cdot 10^{-5}$
He	4	(n, γ)	0
Li	6	(n, α)	940
Be	9	(n, γ)	$8.6 \cdot 10^{-3}$
B	10	(n, α)	3837
C	12	(n, γ)	$3.4 \cdot 10^{-3}$
N	14	(n, p)	1.83
O	16	(n, γ)	$1.90 \cdot 10^{-4}$
Na	23	(n, γ)	0.40
Ar	40	(n, γ)	0.66
K	39	(n, γ)	2.10
Fe	54	(n, γ)	2.25
Co	59	(n, γ)	37.2
Ni	58	(n, γ)	4.6
Kr	80	(n, γ)	11.8
Rh	103	(n, γ)	146
Ag	107	(n, γ)	38
Ag	109	(n, γ)	93.5
Cd	113	(n, γ)	$2.073 \cdot 10^4$
In	115	(n, γ)	193
I	127	(n, α)	6.2
Xe	135	(n, γ)	$2.65 \cdot 10^6$
Cs	133	(n, γ)	29.4
Sm	149	(n, γ)	$4.1 \cdot 10^4$
Eu	151	(n, γ)	$9.2 \cdot 10^3$
Gd	157	(n, γ)	$2.54 \cdot 10^5$
Dy	164	(n, γ)	$2.52 \cdot 10^3$
Au	197	(n, γ)	99.8
Th	232	(n, γ)	7.48
U	238	(n, γ)	2.75

Physical Data

9.7 Geophysical data of Switzerland

Geodetic latitude and longitude, elevation, local acceleration of free fall

	geodetic latitude	geodetic longitude	elevation in m	acceleration of free fall in m/s²
Basel	47°33.5′	7°35.6′	270	9.80763
Bern	46°56.9′	7°27.1′	537	9.80597
Brig	46°19.0′	7°59.7′	715	9.80407
Chiasso	45°50.1′	9°02.0′	233	9.80577
Mte. Generoso	45°55.9′	9°01.3′	1701	9.80256
Chur	46°51.0′	9°32.3′	630	9.80453
Davos	46°48.7′	9°51.4′	1580	9.80273
Weissfluhgipfel	46°50.2′	9°47.7′	2843	9.80004
Fribourg	46°48.5′	7°09.8′	588	9.80571
Genève	46°12.4′	6°09.3′	374	9.80573
Gotthard Hospiz	46°33.4′	8°34.1′	2091	9.80193
Interlaken	46°41.2′	7°52.6′	570	9.80505
Jungfraujoch	46°32.8′	7°59.0′	3456	9.79901
Lausanne	46°31.4′	6°34.1′	392	9.80605
Luzern	47°03.4′	8°18.9′	445	9.80600
Martigny	46°06.1′	7°04.5′	473	9.80447
Mt. Ceneri	46°08.0′	8°54.5′	704	9.80512
Neuchâtel	47°00.1′	6°57.1′	486	9.80634
Olten	47°21.1′	7°54.2′	401	9.80688
Poschiavo	46°19.6′	10°03.6′	1016	9.80355
Pratteln	47°30.7′	7°42.4′	393	9.80731
St. Gallen	47°25.3′	9°22.0′	677	9.80590
Schaffhausen	47°42.0′	8°38.6′	435	9.80720
Zermatt	46°01.2′	7°44.8′	1616	9.80222
Zürich (Hönggerberg)	47°24.6′	8°30.5′	515	9.80648

source: Swiss Geodetic Commission, ETH-Hönggerberg, CH-8093 Zürich

Local geomagnetic field data (for 2006.5)

	D_G west	D_K west	I	B_H in µT
Basel	−0.64°	−0.54°	63.38°	21.238
Bern	−0.67°	−0.66°	62.81°	21.567
Brig	−0.44°	−0.03°	62.25°	21.892
Chiasso	−0.69°	0.48°	61.87°	22.119
Chur	−0.67°	0.86°	62.84°	21.570
Genève	−0.66°	−1.60°	62.07°	21.980
Neuchâtel	−0.66°	−1.02°	62.84°	21.547
Schaffhausen	−0.72°	0.16°	63.58°	21.134
Zürich	−0.74°	0.04°	63.30°	21.295

D_G declination with respect to geographical North

D_K declination with respect to map North of the Swiss national kilometric grid

I angle with respect to horizontal (inclination)

B_H horizontal component of the Earth's magnetic field; $[B_H] = $ T (tesla) $= $ V·s/m²

The declination currently decreases by approx. 0.11° per annum; the inclination and the horizontal components remain almost constant.

source: Institute of Geology and Hydrogeology, University of Neuchâtel

ASTRONOMY

Sources
- The Astronomical Almanac for the Year 2014
- NASA (various current Fact Sheets)
- selected websites known to be reliable

In cases of conflicting data, reference is made to the source judged more reliable by the author.

1 General

Astronomical units of distance

1 astronomical unit $= 1\,\text{au} = 1.495\,978\,707\,00 \cdot 10^{11}\,\text{m}$
$\approx$ mean Sun–Earth distance

1 light year $= 1\,\text{ly} =$ distance travelled by light in a year
speed of light ▶ inside back cover

1 parsec $= 1\,\text{pc} =$ distance of a point from which one astronomical unit would subtend an angle of one arc second $(1'')$

	au	ly	pc	m
1 au	1	$1.5813 \cdot 10^{-5}$	$4.8481 \cdot 10^{-6}$	$1.4960 \cdot 10^{11}$
1 ly	63 240	1	0.30659	$9.4605 \cdot 10^{15}$
1 pc	206 265	3.2616	1	$3.0857 \cdot 10^{16}$

Astronomical units of time

mean solar day	time interval between two successive transits of the so-called mean Sun
sidereal day	time interval between two successive transits of the vernal equinox
1 mean solar day	$= 1\,\text{d} = 24\,\text{h} = 86\,400\,\text{s} \approx 1.0027379$ sidereal days
1 sidereal day	$\approx 86\,164.090\,\text{s} \approx 0.99726957$ mean solar days
1 sidereal second	≈ 0.99726957 SI seconds
1 SI second	≈ 1.0027379 sidereal seconds
1 sidereal year (w.r.t. fixed stars)	$\approx 365.25636\,\text{d} \approx 3.1558150 \cdot 10^7\,\text{s}$
1 tropical year (w.r.t. vernal equinox ♈)	$\approx 365.24219\,\text{d} \approx 3.1556925 \cdot 10^7\,\text{s}$
1 Julian year	$= 365.25\,\text{d}$
1 calendar mean year (Gregorian calendar)	$= 365.2425\,\text{d}$
hour angle h of a celestial body	angle between the meridian plane and the hour plane of the object $(S \to W \to N \to E \to S,\ \text{in}\ °\ \text{or}\ \text{h},\ 15° = 1\,\text{h})$
sidereal time θ	hour angle of the vernal equinox

	General	
MATHEMATICS PHYSICS	**ASTRONOMY**	CHEMISTRY

apparent solar time — hour angle of the true Sun $\pm 12\,\text{h}$

mean solar time — hour angle of the mean Sun $\pm 12\,\text{h}$

equation of time — the value of the difference between apparent solar time and mean solar time

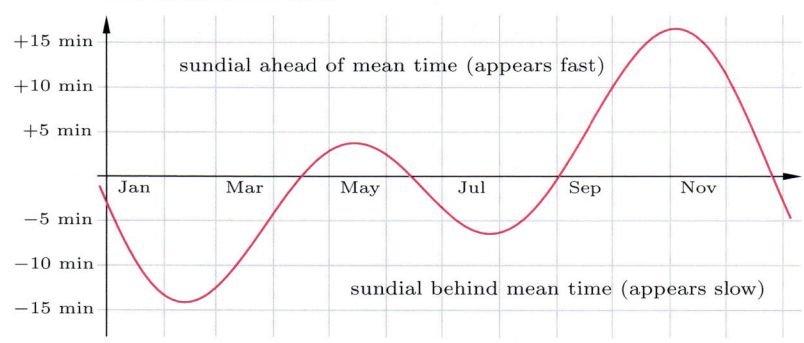

sundial ahead of mean time (appears fast)

sundial behind mean time (appears slow)

Physical, astronomical and civil time scales

TAI: International Atomic Time — Constant-rate time based on times kept by reference atomic clocks. p. 185 ◄ definition of the second

TT: Terrestrial Time — Constant-rate astronomical time, parallel to TAI:
$TT = TAI + 32.184\,\text{s}$.
Astronomical events are calculated and tabulated in terms of TT.

UT1: Universal Time — Conceptually mean solar time at Greenwich (0° longitude), in practice calculated mathematically from sidereal time.

UTC = Coordinated Universal Time (international standard for civil time) — A close approximation of UT1 using TAI offset by a whole number of seconds. UTC is always kept within 0.9 s of UT1 by the occasional insertion or removal of leap seconds.

CET: Central European Time — Standard time in Continental Europe, $CET = UTC + 1\,\text{h}$

CEST: Central European Summer time — corresponds to Eastern European Time, $CEST = CET + 1\,\text{h} = UTC + 2\,\text{h}$

corrections for irregularities in the Earth's rotation

start of the year	$\Delta T\,[\text{s}] =$ TT−UT1	$\Delta AT\,[\text{s}] =$ TAI−UTC	start of the year	$\Delta T\,[\text{s}] =$ TT−UT1	$\Delta AT\,[\text{s}] =$ TAI−UTC
1650	+124		2003	+64.47	+32.00
1700	+9	(changes	2004	+64.57	+32.00
1750	+13	only	2005	+64.69	+32.00
1800	+13.7	by leap	2006	+64.85	+33.00
1850	+7.1	seconds)	2007	+65.15	+33.00
1900	−2.72		2008	+65.43	+33.00
1950	+29.15		2009	+65.78	+34.00
1960	+33.15		2010	+66.07	+34.00
1970	+40.18		2011	+66.32	+34.00
1980	+50.54	+19.00	2012	+66.60	+34.00
1990	+56.86	+24.00	2013	+66.91	+35.00
2000	+63.83	+32.00	2014	+67.28	+35.00
2001	+64.09	+32.00	2015		
2002	+64.30	+32.00	2016		

General
ASTRONOMY

Celestial coordinate systems

coordinate system (Σ denotes fundamental plane)	spherical polar coordinates	Cartesian coordinates	axis directions

Horizontal coordinate system Σ: reference plane through observer's horizon
(ESO convention, azimuth w.r.t. South, left handed system)

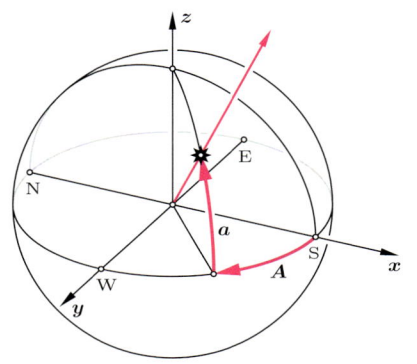

a: altitude	$x = r \cos h \cos a$	S
A: azimuth	$y = r \cos h \sin a$	W
r: distance	$z = r \sin h$	zenith

Equatorial coordinate system (left-handed)
$\overline{\Sigma}$: reference plane through Earth's equator, used with equatorial telescope mounts

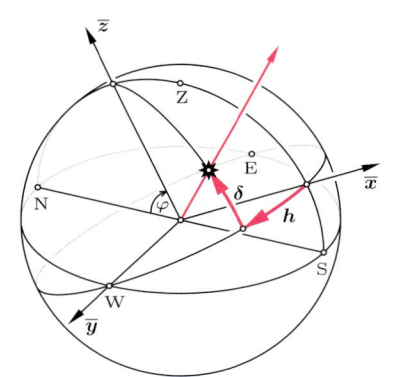

δ: declination	$\overline{x} = r \cos \delta \cos \sigma$	
h: hour angle	$\overline{y} = r \cos \delta \sin \sigma$	W
r: distance	$\overline{z} = r \sin \delta$	celestial pole
φ: observer's geographic latitude		

Equatorial coordinate system (right-handed) Σ^*: reference plane through Earth's equator

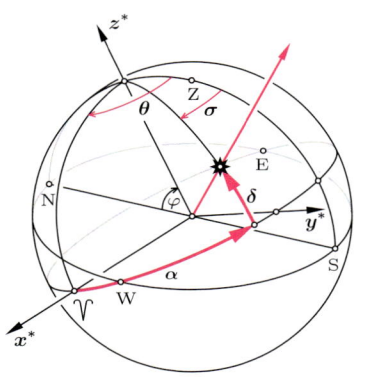

δ: declination	$x^* = r \cos \delta \cos \alpha$	vernal equinox
α: right ascension	$y^* = r \cos \delta \sin \alpha$	
r: distance	$z^* = r \sin \delta$	celestial pole
θ: sidereal time		
♈: vernal equinox		

coordinate conversions ▶ p. 208

General ASTRONOMY

Coordinate conversion

- $\Sigma \to \overline{\Sigma}$
$$\begin{cases} \tan h = \dfrac{\sin A}{\cos A \sin \varphi + \tan a \cos \varphi} \\ \sin \delta = \sin \varphi \sin a - \cos \varphi \cos a \cos A \end{cases}$$

- $\overline{\Sigma} \to \Sigma$
$$\begin{cases} \tan A = \dfrac{\sin h}{\cos h \sin \varphi - \tan \delta \cos \varphi} \\ \sin a = \sin \varphi \sin \delta + \cos \varphi \cos \delta \cos h \end{cases}$$

- $\overline{\Sigma} \leftrightarrow \Sigma^*$

hour angle h = sidereal time θ − right ascension α

Brightness of celestial bodies

	Stellar brightness is given in magnitudes.
apparent magnitude m	measure of brightness of a celestial body as observed from the Earth
absolute magnitude M	apparent magnitude of a celestial body as observed from a distance of $10\,\text{pc} \approx 32.6\,\text{ly}$
absolute magnitude for bodies in the Solar System	apparent magnitude of an object as it would appear if it were 1 au from both the observer and the Sun
	in the formulas below m und M denote the apparent magnitude and absolute magnitude respectively
relative magnitude	The relative brightness of two objects with respective illuminances E_1 and E_2 is given by $m_1 - m_2 = -2.5 \log_{10} \dfrac{E_1}{E_2}$.
relation between apparent and absolute magnitude	$m = M + 5 \log_{10} \dfrac{r}{10\,\text{pc}} = M + 5 \log_{10} \dfrac{r}{1\,\text{pc}} - 5$ r: distance of object
relation to other physical quantities	An object with a bolometric magnitude of 0.0 has a luminosity of $3.02 \cdot 10^{28}\,\text{W}$ (total radiant flux).
	The effective brightness in the visible range or in selected spectral ranges (e. g. UBV scale) is inherently lower than the brightness given by the magnitude. It depends on the particular spectral profile.

2 Earth and Its Satellites

Earth ⊕

radius
- equatorial $6.3781 \cdot 10^6$ m
- polar $6.3568 \cdot 10^6$ m
- equivalent spherical radius $6.3710 \cdot 10^6$ m

surface area $5.1007 \cdot 10^{14}$ m^2

volume $1.0832 \cdot 10^{21}$ m^3

mass $5.9722 \cdot 10^{24}$ kg

geocentric gravitational constant $3.986004418 \cdot 10^{14}$ m^3/s^2

mean density
- of the Earth $5.517 \cdot 10^3$ kg/m^3
- of the crust (depth 35 km) $2.60 \cdot 10^3$ kg/m^3
- of the core (radius $\approx$ 1200 km) $12.9 \cdot 10^3$ kg/m^3

escape velocity $11.19 \cdot 10^3$ m/s

solar constant (outside the atmosphere) $1.368 \cdot 10^3$ W/m^2 ▶ inside back cover

Geophysical data

acceleration of free fall (surface gravity)
- standard value 9.80665 m/s^2
- at the Equator 9.7803 m/s^2
- at 45° North latitude 9.8061 m/s^2
- at the North Pole 9.8322 m/s^2
- at a latitude of φ and elevation of h

$$(1 + k_1 \sin^2 \varphi + k_2 h) \cdot 9.7803 \text{ m/s}^2$$

$$k_1 = 5.3 \cdot 10^{-3}$$
$$k_2 = -3.15 \cdot 10^{-6} \text{ m}^{-1}$$

angular velocity of Earth's rotation $7.292 \cdot 10^{-5}$ /s

speed of a point on the Equator due to Earth's rotation 451 m/s

centripetal acceleration at the Equator $3.391 \cdot 10^{-2}$ m/s^2

Earth and Its Satellites

Moon ☾

angular radii	15′ 32.6″	mean value
	14′ 42″ to 16′ 46″	extreme values
distance from the Earth (in 10^8 m)	3.844	mean value
	3.564 to 4.067	extreme values
eccentricity of the lunar orbit	0.0549	mean value
orbital inclination (to ecliptic)	5° 08′ 43″	mean value

orbital periods
- sidereal (relative to fixed stars)   27.321662 d
- synodic (between identical phases)   29.530589 d
- tropical (between identical lunar equinoxes)   27.321582 d
- anomalistic (from perigee to perigee)   27.554550 d
- draconitic (between identical nodes)   27.212221 d

portion of the moon's surface visible from Earth (due to libration)	59%	
axial tilt (to ecliptic)	1° 32′ 34″	mean value
apparent magnitude of the full moon	−12.7	mean value

	absolute	relative (to Earth)
mean radius	$1.7374 \cdot 10^6$ m	0.27272
mass	$7.3458 \cdot 10^{22}$ kg	$0.0123 = \dfrac{1}{81.3}$
standard gravitational parameter	$4.9027779 \cdot 10^{12}$ m^3/s^2	
volumen	$2.197 \cdot 10^{19}$ m^3	0.0203
mean density	$3.350 \cdot 10^3$ kg/m^3	0.6051
equatorial surface gravity	1.622 m/s^2	$0.165 \approx \dfrac{1}{6}$
escape velocity	$2.38 \cdot 10^3$ m/s	

Selected artificial Earth satellites

name	launch date	orbit period	perigee	apogee	inclination	remarks
Sputnik I	04.10.1957	96.2 min	227 km	947 km	65.1°	1st satellite
Wostok I	12.04.1961	89.1 min	181 km	327 km	48.3°	1st manned space flight
Columbia	12.04.1981	89.9 min	274 km	277 km	60.3°	1st Space Shuttle
MIR	19.02.1986	92.2 min	378 km	389 km	51.1°	Russian space station
Hipparcos	08.08.1989	628.9 min	223 km	35 632 km	6.8°	astrometry
Hubble Space Telesc.	24.04.1990	96.7 min	506 km	610 km	28.5°	astronomy
ERS 2	21.04.1995	100.5 min	783 km	784 km	98.5°	remote sensing
Meteosat 7	02.09.1991	–	geostationary	0°	1.8°	Europ. weather sat.
Eutelsat W3	12.04.1999	–	geostationary	20° E	0.1°	telecommunication
Navstar	1978–1994	12 h	20 250 km		55.0°	GPS satellites (24)
ISS	1998–	95.5 min	402 km		51.6°	internat. space station

3 Sun ☉

angular radii	16′ 00″	mean value
	15′ 44″ to 16′ 16″	extreme values
distance from the Earth (in 10^{11} m)	1.496 ($\approx$ 1 au)	mean value
	1.471 to 1.521	extreme values
radius	$6.960 \cdot 10^8$ m	
surface area	$6.086 \cdot 10^{18}$ m^2	
volume	$1.4120 \cdot 10^{27}$ m^3	
mass ($m_\odot$)	$1.9884 \cdot 10^{30}$ kg	
solar mass parameter (heliocentric gravitational constant)	$1.32712442099 \cdot 10^{20}$ m^3/s^2	
mean density	$1.408 \cdot 10^3$ kg/m^3	
surface gravity	$2.740 \cdot 10^2$ m/s^2	
escape velocity (from surface)	$6.176 \cdot 10^5$ m/s	
axial tilt (to the ecliptic)	7° 15′	

sidereal rotation period (sun spots)
- at the solar equator 25.05 d $\triangleq$ 14.37°/d
- at 20° latitude 25.58 d $\triangleq$ 14.08°/d
- at 60° latitude 30.65 d $\triangleq$ 11.75°/d

effective surface temperature	5778 K

solar core (model)
- temperature $1.571 \cdot 10^7$ K
- density $1.622 \cdot 10^5$ kg/m^3
- pressure $2.477 \cdot 10^{16}$ Pa

luminosity (total radiant flux)	$3.846 \cdot 10^{26}$ W

total radiant intensity ▶ inside back cover
- at the surface $6.329 \cdot 10^7$ W/m^2
- at a distance of 1 au (solar constant) (outside the Earth's atmosphere) $1.368 \cdot 10^3$ W/m^2

apparent magnitude	−26.74
absolute magnitude	+4.83
spectral class	G2 V

4 Solar System

Planets, dwarf planets and small Solar System bodies (SSSB)

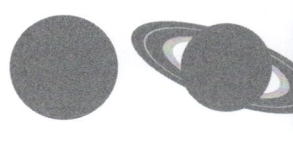

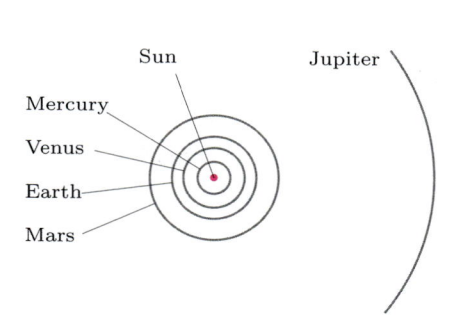

	planets					
	Mercury	Venus	Earth	Mars	Jupiter	Saturn
symbol / number	☿	♀	♁	♂	♃	♄
orbital semi-major axis	0.387099	0.72332	1.000015	1.52366	5.204	9.582
	57.9092	108.207	149.6001	227.936	778.5	1433
sidereal orbital period	87.969	224.701	365.256363	686.98	4332.59	10 747
sidereal orbital period	0.2408467	0.615197	1.00039	1.88089	11.8683	29.4577
numerical eccentricity	0.20563	0.00677	0.01670	0.09341	0.04851	0.05547
orbital inclination to ecliptic	7.0	3.4	–	1.9	1.3	2.5
equatorial radius	2.4397	6.0518	6.37814	3.3962	71.492	60.268
mass (without moons)	0.33010	4.8673	5.9722	0.64169	1898.5	568.46
standard gravitat. parameter	22.032	324.858592	398.6004418	42.8283752	126712.7625	37940.585
mean density	5.43	5.24	5.515	3.94	1.33	0.69
sidereal rotational period [1]	58.6462	−243.0185	0.99726963	1.02595676	0.41354	0.44401
axial tilt [2]	0	3.39471	23.45	25.2	3.1	26.7
surface gravity [3]	3.70	8.83	9.83	3.7	23.1	9.0
mean surface temperature	440	737	288	208	163	133
effective temperature [4]	443	232	254	210	110	81.1
atmospheric pressure	0	92	1	0.01	–	–
escape velocity	4.3	10.4	11.2	5.0	59.5	35.5
albedo	0.106	0.65	0.367	0.150	0.52	0.47
maximum angular diameter [5]	12.3	63.0	–	25.1	49.9	20.7
mean opposition magnitude [6]	−1.9	−4.6	–	−2.01	−2.7	+0.67
absolute magnitude [7]	−0.42	−4.4	−3.86	−1.52	−9.4	−8.88
number of known moons [8]	0	0	1	2	63	62

distances shown to scale

Solar System

ASTRONOMY

Sun

diameters shown to scale

	Uranus ♅	Neptune ♆	dwarf planets Ceres (1)	Pluto (134340)	Eris (136199)	sel. small Solar System bodies Pallas (2)	Eros (433)	Icarus (1566)	Apollo (1862)	Quaoar (50000)	units
	19.20	30.05	2.7668	39.48	67.66593	2.7717	1.4580	1.078	1.486	43.6	au
	2872	4495	413.91	5906	10122.67	414.78	218.1	161.3	222.3	6522	10^9 m
	30589	59800	1680	90588	$2.03\cdot10^5$	1687	643	409	622	$1.05\cdot10^5$	d
	84.0139	164.793	4.60	247.68	556.6	4.62	1.76	1.12	1.703	287	a
	0.04629	0.00899	0.080	0.244	0.44	0.23	0.223	0.827	0.57	0.035	°
	8.0	1.8	10.6	17.2	44.2	34.8	10.8	22.9	6.4	7.98	°
	25.559	24.764	0.4797	1.195	1.20	0.262	0.008	0.0007	0.0007	0.63	10^6 m
	86.818	102.45	0.939^a	14.560^a	16.695^a	0.205^a	7.2^b	2.9^c	5.1^c	2.5^a	10^{24} kg [9]
	5794.549	6836.527	0.0626	1	1.114	0.0137					10^{12} m^3 s^{-2}
	1.27	1.64	2.08	1.8	2.3	4.2	2.7	2	2	2	10^3 kg m^{-3}
	−0.71833	0.67125	0.3781	−6.3872	1.0800	0.33	0.2196	0.09471	0.1276		d
	97.8	28.3	4	122.5							°
	8.7	11.0	0.27	0.6	0.8	0.16				0.3	m s^{-2}
	78	73	167	48	43	162	227	242	222	50	K
	58.2	46.6		42.2							K
	—	—	0	0	0	0	0	0	0	0	bar
	21.3	23.5	0.51	1.1	1.4					0.7	km s^{-1}
	0.51	0.41	0.073	0.30	0.86	0.16	0.16	0.4	0.21	0.04	"
	4.1	2.4	0.840	0.110	0.088	0.34					"
	+5.52	+7.84	+6.9	+15.12		+7.9	+11.5	+12.2	+13.7		
	−7.19	−6.87	+3.34	−1.0	−1.12	+4.13	+11.16	+16.9	+16.25	+2.6	
	27	13	0	5	1	0	0	0	1	0	

Neptune

1) at the equator. Negative values signify rotation in the opposite direction to the orbital motion.
2) with respect to its orbital plane
3) without regard to its rotation
4) temperature of a black body that would emit the same total radiation
5) for an observer on Earth
6) Mercury and Venus: magnitude of maximum brightness
7) brightness as it would appear if it were 1 au from both the Sun and the Earth
8) known as of 2014
9) other units ^{a}: 10^{21} kg ^{b}: 10^{15} kg ^{c}: 10^{12} kg

Selected comets

	1P/Halley	8P/Tuttle	81P/Wild	166P/NEAT	C/1995 O1 (Hale-Bopp)	units
last/next perihelion passage	28.07.2061	27.01.2008	22.02.2010	20.05.2002	01.04.1997	
perihelion distance	0.586	1.027136	1.598059	8.564238	0.914142	au
orbital semi-major axis	17.8	5.701624	3.454448	13.912242	186	au
sidereal orbital period	75.3	13.6	6.42	51.9	2540	a
numerical eccentricity	0.967	0.819852	0.537391	0.384410	0.995086	
orbital inclination to ecliptic	162.3	54.9827	3.2375	15.3628	89.43	°
max. absolute magnitude [1]	+5.5	+7	+9	+5.5	−1.0	

[1] maximum brightness as it would appear if it were 1 au from both the Sun and the Earth.

5 Stars

Nearby fixed stars

name (designation)	coordinates ♈ 2000 RA α [h] [min]	dec δ	vis. magnitude m	M	type	distance [ly]	proper motion [″/a]	v_{rad} [km/s]
Proxima Cen	14 29.8	−62°41′	11.01	15.45	M5Ve	4.22	3.9	−16
α Cen B	14 39.7	−60°50′	1.35	5.70	K1V	4.39	3.7	−22
α Cen A	14 39.7	−60°50′	−0.01	4.34	G2V	4.39	3.7	−22
Barnards Pfeilstern	17 57.8	+04°40′	9.54	13.24	sdM4	5.94	10.4	−107
Wolf 359	10 56.6	+07°01′	13.45	16.68	M6	7.67	4.7	+13
Lalande 21185	11 03.3	+35°59′	7.49	10.46	M2V	8.31	4.8	−87
Sirius	06 45.2	−16°43′	-1.44	1.45	A0Vm	8.60	1.3	−8
Ross 154	18 49.8	−23°50′	10.37	13.00	M3.5Ve	9.69	0.7	−4
ε Eridani	03 32.9	−09°27′	3.72	6.18	K2V	10.50	1.0	+16
Lacaille 9352	23 05.8	−35°51′	7.35	9.76	M2/M3V	10.73	6.9	+10
Ross 128	11 47.7	+00°48′	11.12	13.50	M4.5V	10.89	1.4	−13
61 Cyg A	21 06.8	+38°44′	5.20	7.49	K5V	11.36	5.3	−64
Procyon	07 39.3	+05°14′	0.40	2.68	F5IV-V	11.41	1.3	−3
61 Cyg B	21 06.9	+38°44′	6.05	8.33	K7V	11.43	5.2	−64
SAO 31128	18 42.8	+59°37′	9.70	11.97	K5	11.47	2.3	−1
SAO 31129	18 42.8	+59°38′	8.94	11.18	K5	11.64	2.2	+6
SAO 36248	00 18.3	+44°01′	8.09	10.33	M1V	11.64	2.9	+14
ε Ind	22 03.3	−56°47′	4.69	6.89	K5V	11.83	4.7	−40
τ Cet	01 44.1	−15°56′	3.49	5.68	G8V	11.90	1.9	−16

$v_{rad} > 0$: radial velocity away from the sun

Stars

ASTRONOMY

The brightest fixed stars

name (Bayer designation)		coordinates ♈ 2000 RA α [h] [min]		dec δ	vis. magnitude m	M	type	distance [ly]	v_{rad} [km/s]
Sun					−26.74	+4.83	G 2	$1.58 \cdot 10^{-5}$	
Sirius	(α CMa)	6	45.2	−16°43′	−1.44	+1.45	A 1	8.60	−8
Canopus	(α Car)	6	23.9	−52°42′	−0.62	−5.53	F 0	313	+21
Toliman	(α Cen)	14	39.7	−60°50′	−0.01	+4.5	G 2	4.40	−22
Arcturus	(α Boo)	14	15.7	+19°11′	−0.05	−0.2	K 2	36.7	−5
Vega	(α Lyr)	18	36.9	+38°47′	+0.03	+0.58	A 0	25.3	−14
Capella	(α Aur)	5	16.7	+46°00′	+0.08	−0.05	G 5	42.2	+30
Rigel	(β Ori)	5	14.5	−8°12′	+0.18	−6.7	B 8	773	+21
Procyon	(α CMi)	7	39.3	+5°14′	+0.40	+2.68	F 5	11.4	−3
Achernar	(α Eri)	1	37.7	−57°14′	+0.50	−2.77	B 3	144	+16
Agena	(β Cen)	14	03.8	−60°22′	+0.60	−5.43	B 1	525	+6
Altair	(α Aql)	19	50.8	+8°52′	+0.76	+2.2	A 7	16.8	−26
Beteigeuse	(α Ori)	5	55.2	+7°24′	+0.58	−5.14	M 2	427	+21
Aldebaran	(α Tau)	4	35.9	+16°31′	+0.85	−0.63	K 5	65	+54
Spica	(α Vir)	13	25.2	−11°10′	+1.04	−3.55	B 1	262	+1
Antares	(α Sco)	16	29.4	−26°26′	+1.06	−5.28	M 1	604	−3

Stellar statistics

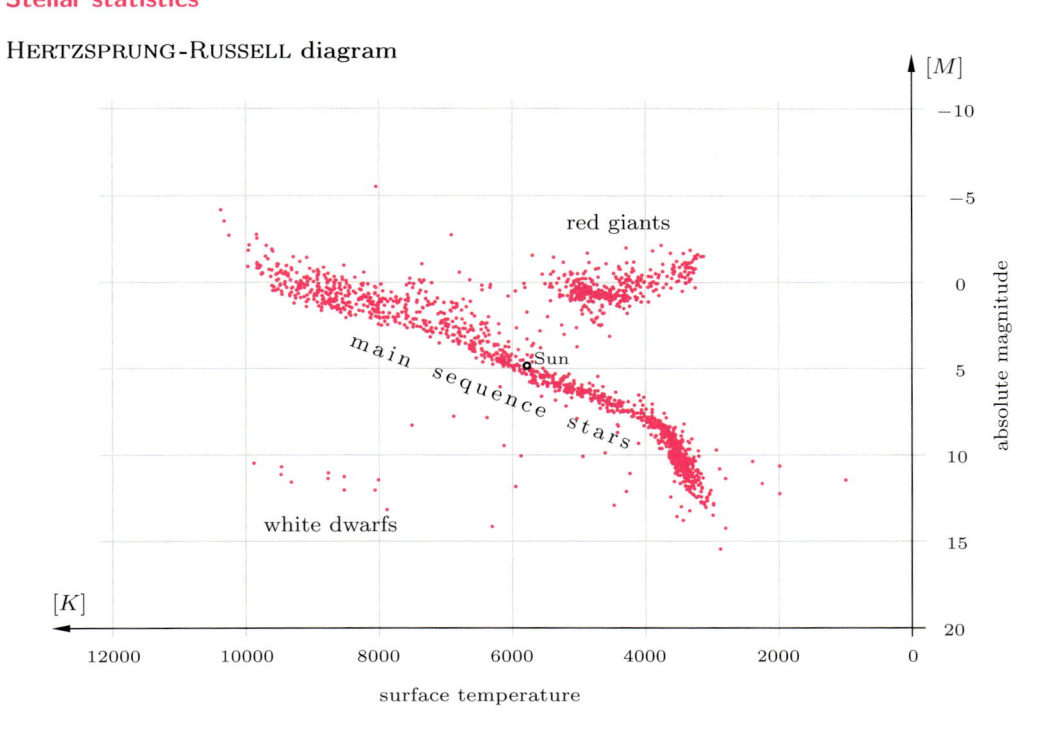

Hertzsprung-Russell diagram

6 Galaxies

Milky Way

approximate diameter	100 000 ly (30 kpc)
approximate disc thickness	6 500 ly (2 kpc)
approximate diameter	
• of core	16 000 ly (5 kpc)
• of halo	160 000 ly (50 kpc)
coordinates of Galactic Centre (Υ 2000)	RA = 17 h 45.5 min, dec = $-28°\,56'$
distance of the Sun	
• from the Galactic Centre	26 000 ly (9 kpc)
• from the central plane of the Milky Way	(26 ± 40) ly
Sun's orbital period about the Galactic Centre	$226 \cdot 10^6$ a
rotation velocity of galaxy near Sun	217 km/s
speed relative to neighbouring stars	19.4 km/s
mass	
• visible portion	$1.8 \cdot 10^{11}\ m_\odot$
• total	$6 \cdot 10^{11}\ m_\odot$
escape velocity from the Milky Way	
• from the Galactic Centre	700 km/s
• from the vicinity of the Sun	360 km/s
• from the edge of the Milky Way	240 km/s

Selected neighbouring galaxies

(in the so-called Local Group)

	right ascension α [h] [min]	declination δ °	visual magnitude m	visual magnitude M	distance in 10^6 ly	diameter in 10^3 ly	radial velocity in 10^3 ms^{-1}
(Milky Way)				-20.9		100	
Large Magellanic Cloud	5 24	-69.8	0.9	-17.7	0.168	32	313
Small Magellanic Cloud	0 52	-72.8	2.7	-16.2	0.197	18	175
Andromeda M 31	0 43	$+41.3$	4.4	-20.1	2.54	140	-298
M 32	0 43	$+40.9$	9	-15.4	2.49	6.3	-205
Triangulum Galaxy M 33	1 34	$+30.7$	6.3	-18.5	2.92	60	-179

7 Cosmos

Abundance of the chemical elements

(= no. of atoms / no. of Si atoms)

element		Earth[1]	Earth's crust[1]	Sun	Universe
hydrogen	(H)	0.045	0.013	28 000	40 000
helium	(He)	–	–	2 300	3 100
carbon	(C)	0.011	0.0013	7	3.5
nitrogen	(N)	0.0003	0.00002	1.8	8
oxygen	(O)	3.228	3.667	14	22
neon	(Ne)	–	–	2.1	8.5
magnesium	(Mg)	1.102	1.251	1	0.91
silicon	(Si)	1	1	1	1
sulphur	(S)	0.035	0.001	0.4	0.4
iron	(Fe)	0.997	0.15	0.9	0.6
nickel	(Ni)	0.054	0.003	0.05	0.04

1) W. F. McDonough: The Composition of the Earth's Core, 2005

Stellar densities near the Sun

estimated densities of all matter up to distances of approx. 250 ly from the Sun

category

- stars (excluding white dwarfs) $0.044\ m_\odot/\text{pc}^3 \approx 3.0 \cdot 10^{-21}\ \text{kg/m}^3 \;\widehat{=}\; 1.5\ \text{atoms/cm}^3$
- white dwarfs $0.02\ m_\odot/\text{pc}^3 \approx 1.4 \cdot 10^{-21}\ \text{kg/m}^3 \;\widehat{=}\; 0.7\ \text{atoms/cm}^3$
- interstellar gases $0.018\ m_\odot/\text{pc}^3 \approx 1.2 \cdot 10^{-21}\ \text{kg/m}^3 \;\widehat{=}\; 0.6\ \text{atoms/cm}^3$
- gas and dust clouds $0.0013\ m_\odot/\text{pc}^3 \approx 9 \cdot 10^{-23}\ \text{kg/m}^3 \;\widehat{=}\; 0.045\ \text{atoms/cm}^3$
- matter missing from observed gravitation $0.05\ m_\odot/\text{pc}^3 \approx 3 \cdot 10^{-21}\ \text{kg/m}^3 \;\widehat{=}\; 1.5\ \text{atoms/cm}^3$

Typical densities

	kg/m^3
interstellar gas	10^{-21}
red giants	10^{-3}
organic matter	10^3
Sun	$1.4 \cdot 10^3$
white dwarfs	10^9
neutron stars	10^{17}

Selected ages

human life on Earth	2 million years
Rigel (β Ori)	6 million years
Pleaides	50 million years
Hyades	600 million years
Earth	4.5 billion years
Sun	4.6 billion years
globular clusters	13 billion years
Universe	13.73 ± 0.1 billion years

CHEMISTRY

Table with the most important constants ▶ inside back cover

1 Definitions and Formulae

Stoichiometry

AVOGADRO constant	$N_A = 6.022\,141\,79(30) \cdot 10^{23}/\text{mol}$	p. 185 ◀ 1 Mol
atomic mass unit	$1\,\text{u} = 1.660\,538\,782\,(83) \cdot 10^{-24}\,\text{g}$	
rest mass of the electron	$m_e = m(\text{e}^-) = 9.109\,382\,15(45) \cdot 10^{-28}\,\text{g}$	
rest mass of the proton	$m_p = m(\text{p}^+) = 1.672\,621\,637(83) \cdot 10^{-24}\,\text{g}$	
rest mass of the neutron	$m_n = m(\text{n}) = 1.674\,927\,211(84) \cdot 10^{-24}\,\text{g}$	

variables and constants

n: amount of substance in mol
m: mass of an amount of substance in g
M: molar mass of a substance in $\text{g} \cdot \text{mol}^{-1}$
N: number of particles in an amount of substance
N_A: number of particles per mole in mol^{-1}
V: volume of an amount of substance in L
V_m: molar volume in $\text{L} \cdot \text{mol}^{-1}$
p: pressure
R: universal gas constant
k: BOLTZMANN constant
T: absolute temperature

amount of substance in a given mass	$n = \dfrac{m}{M}$
amount of substance in a given gas volume	$n = \dfrac{V}{V_m}$
amount of substance of a given number of particles	$n = \dfrac{N}{N_A}$
ideal gas law	$p \cdot V = n \cdot R \cdot T = N \cdot k \cdot T$

Definitions and Formulae

CHEMISTRY

Concentration specifications

amount concentration
(molar concentration)

$$c = \frac{n}{V} \quad (\text{in mol} \cdot \text{L}^{-1})$$

- notation $c(X)$ or $[X]$ means

amount concentration of substance X

mass concentration

$$c_m = \frac{m \,(\text{dissolved substance})}{V \,(\text{solution})} \quad (\text{in g} \cdot \text{L}^{-1})$$

mass fraction

$$w(A) = \frac{m(A)}{m_{\text{total}}} \quad (\cdot \, 100\%)$$

- mass per cent

If (A) is given in per cent
it is called mass per cent.

e. g. g of dissolved substance in 100 g of solution

volume fraction

$$\varphi(A) = \frac{V(A)}{V_{\text{total}}} \quad (\cdot \, 100\%)$$

- volume per cent

If $\varphi(A)$ is given in per cent
it is called volume per cent.

e. g. mL of dissolved substance in 100 mL of solution or mL of gas in 100 mL of a gas mixture

Chemical equilibrium

Law of mass action

equilibrium constant K
a, b, x and y: Stoichiometric coefficients
A and B: reactants, X and Y: products

reaction example:
$a\,\text{A} + b\,\text{B} \rightleftarrows x\,\text{X} + y\,\text{Y}$

in solution at concentration c

$$K_c = \frac{c^x(\text{X}) \cdot c^y(\text{Y})}{c^a(\text{A}) \cdot c^b(\text{B})}$$

in gas phase with partial pressure p

$$K_p = \frac{p^x(\text{X}) \cdot p^y(\text{Y})}{p^a(\text{A}) \cdot p^b(\text{B})}$$

Definitions and Formulae

CHEMISTRY

Acids and bases

pH of an aqueous solution

$$pH = -\log_{10} c(\mathrm{H_3O^+})$$

pOH of an aqueous solution

$$pOH = -\log_{10} c(\mathrm{OH^-})$$

ionic product/autoprotolysis of water
$2\,\mathrm{H_2O} \rightleftharpoons \mathrm{H_3O^+} + \mathrm{OH^-}$

$$c(\mathrm{H_3O^+}) \cdot c(\mathrm{OH^-}) = 10^{-14}$$
$$pH + pOH = 14 \quad (\text{at } 22\,^\circ\mathrm{C})$$

In the definitions below c_0 denotes the initial concentration of acid or base added.

pH of an aqueous solution of a monoprotic strong acid (approximation)

$$pH \approx -\log_{10} c_0 (\text{strong acid})$$

pOH and pH of an aqueous solution of a monoprotic strong base (approximation)

$$pOH \approx -\log_{10} c_0 (\text{strong base})$$
$$pH = 14 - pOH$$

pH of an aqueous solution of a monoprotic weak acid (approximation)

$$pH \approx \frac{1}{2}\left[pK_S - \log_{10} c_0 (\text{weak acid})\right]$$

- K_A: acidity constant

$$pK_A = -\log_{10} K_A$$

pOH and pH of an aqueous solution of a monoprotic weak base (approximation)

$$pOH \approx \frac{1}{2}\left[pK_B - \log_{10} c_0 (\text{weak base})\right]$$
$$pH = 14 - pOH$$

- K_B: basicity constant

$$pK_B = -\log_{10} K_B$$

▶ p. 248

pH of an aqueous solution of an acid and its conjugate base

HA: general formula of an acid
$\mathrm{A^-}$: general formula of its conjugate base

$$pH = pK_A + \log_{10} \frac{c(\mathrm{A^-})}{c(\mathrm{HA})}$$

(HENDERSON-HASSELBALCH equation for buffer solutions)

Electrochemistry, thermodynamics and reaction kinetics

Potential E at variable concentrations (NERNST equation)

E^0: potential at standard conditions
z: number of transferred electrons
R: universal gas constant
T: absolute temperature
F: FARADAY constant

$$E = E^0 + \frac{R \cdot T}{z \cdot F} \cdot \ln \frac{c(\mathrm{Ox})}{c(\mathrm{Red})} \qquad \text{p. 17} \blacktriangleleft \ln$$

$$E = E^0 + \frac{0.059\,\mathrm{V}}{z} \cdot \log_{10} \frac{c(\mathrm{Ox})}{c(\mathrm{Red})}$$

For the simplest half-cell reaction, Red $\rightleftharpoons$ Ox$+z\mathrm{e^-}$. Concentrations of other reactants in the solution (e. g. $\mathrm{OH^-}$ or $\mathrm{H^+}$) on the side of the reducing agent (Red) or the oxidizing agent (Ox) appear as factors (and coefficients as exponents) in the quotient.

Definitions and Formulae
CHEMISTRY

Internal energy change ΔU, first law of thermodynamics

Q: heat supplied to system
W: work done on system

$$\Delta U = Q + W$$

Enthalpy H

p: pressure, V: volume

$$H = U + p \cdot V$$

Enthalpy change ΔH

at constant pressure p, volume change ΔV and pressure-volume work $p \cdot \Delta V$

$$\Delta H = \Delta U + p \cdot \Delta V$$

Entropy change ΔS

ΔQ: heat exchanged in a reversible process
Ω: number of microstates

$$\Delta S = \frac{\Delta Q}{T} \qquad \text{thermal definition}$$

$$S = k \cdot \ln \Omega \qquad \text{statistical definition}$$

GIBBS free energy G (GIBBS energy)

T: absolute temperature

$$G = H - T \cdot S$$

GIBBS free energy change ΔG
(GIBBS-HELMHOLTZ equation)

$$\Delta G = \Delta H - T \cdot \Delta S$$

Maximum of entropy, minimum of GIBBS free energy, second law of thermodynamics

ΔS_T: total change of entropy
ΔS_Su: total change of entropy in the surroundings
ΔS_Sy: change of entropy in the system

$$\Delta S_\text{T} = \Delta S_\text{Su} + \Delta S_\text{Sy} \geqslant 0$$

The change of GIBBS free energy ΔG in a spontaneous process is $\Delta G \leqslant 0$.

Change of GIBBS free energy ΔG with an applied external potential

n: number of moles of electrons transferred
F: FARADAY constant
ΔE: electrical potential difference, voltage

$$\Delta G = -n \cdot F \cdot \Delta E$$

Equilibrium constant K and change of GIBBS free energy ΔG

R: universal gas constant

$$K = e^{\frac{-\Delta G}{R \cdot T}}$$

$$\Delta G = -R \cdot T \cdot \ln K$$

p. 52 ◀ e

Reaction rate constant (velocity constant) k and temperature T (ARRHENIUS equation)

A: frequency factor (measure of the number of favourable collisions)
E_A: activation energy

$$k = A \cdot e^{\frac{-E_A}{R \cdot T}}$$

2 Chemical Thermodynamics

Enthalpy of formation ΔH_f^0, Gibbs free energy of formation ΔG_f^0 and entropy S^0

Standard conditions. State of matter: gaseous g, liquid l, solid s or in aqueous solution aq.

Enthalpy of reaction $\Delta H_r^0 = \sum \nu_i \cdot \Delta H_f^0$, similarly for Gibbs free energy of reaction ΔG_r^0 and entropy of reaction ΔS_r^0. Stoichiometric coefficients ν_i negative for reactants, positive for products.

formula	state	ΔH_f^0 $\frac{\text{kJ}}{\text{mol}}$	ΔG_f^0 $\frac{\text{kJ}}{\text{mol}}$	S^0 $\frac{\text{J}}{\text{mol K}}$	formula	state	ΔH_f^0 $\frac{\text{kJ}}{\text{mol}}$	ΔG_f^0 $\frac{\text{kJ}}{\text{mol}}$	S^0 $\frac{\text{J}}{\text{mol K}}$
Ag	s	0	0	43	Fe^{3+}	aq	−49	−5	−316
Ag^+	aq	106	77	73	H	g	218	203	115
AgCl	s	−127	−110	96	H^+	aq	0	0	0
Al	s	0	0	28	H_2	g	0	0	131
Al_2O_3	s	−1676	−1582	61	HF	g	−271	−273	174
Br_2	l	0	0	152	HCl	g	−92	−95	187
Br_2	g	31	3	245	HCl	aq	−167	−131	56
C	g	717	671	158	HBr	g	−36	−53	199
C (graphite)	s	0	0	6	HI	g	26	2	206
C (diamond)	s	2	3	2	HNO_3	l	−174	−81	156
CO	g	−111	−137	198	HNO_3	g	−134	−74	267
CO_2	g	−393	−394	214	H_2O	l	−286	−237	70
Ca	s	0	0	41	H_2O	g	−242	−229	189
Ca^{2+}	aq	−543	−554	−53	H_2O_2	l	−188	−120	109
$CaCO_3$ (calcite)	s	−1207	−1129	93	H_2S	g	−21	−34	206
$CaCl_2$	s	−795	−749	105	H_2SO_4	l	−814	−690	157
$CaCl_2 \cdot 6\,H_2O$	s	−2607			H_2Se	g	30	16	219
CaO	s	−635	−604	40	H_2Te	g	100		
$Ca(OH)_2$	s	−987	−900	83	I_2	g	62	19	261
$CaSO_4$	s	−1434	−1322	107	I_2	s	0	0	116
$CaSO_4 \cdot \frac{1}{2} H_2O$	s	−1577	−1435	131	K	s	0	0	64
$CaSO_4 \cdot 2\,H_2O$	s	−2033	−1797	194	K^+	aq	−251	−282	103
Cl_2	g	0	0	223	KCl	s	−436	−408	83
Cl	g	121	105	165	Mg	s	0	0	33
Cl^-	aq	−167	−131	57	Mg^{2+}	aq	−467	−455	−138
Cu	s	0	0	33	$MgCl_2$	s	−642	−592	90
Cu^{2+}	aq	65	66	−100	MgO	s	−601	−570	27
CuO	s	−157	−130	43	$MgSO_4$	s	−1288	−1171	92
Cu_2O	s	−169	−146	93	$MgSO_4 \cdot 7\,H_2O$	s	−3388	−2872	372
CuS	s	−53	−54	66	N_2	g	0	0	192
$CuSO_4$	s	−771	−662	109	NH_3	g	−46	−16	192
$CuSO_4 \cdot 5\,H_2O$	s	−2280	−1880	300	NH_4^+	aq	−132	−79	113
Fe	s	0	0	27	NH_4Cl	s	−314	−203	95
Fe^{2+}	aq	−89	−79	−138	NH_4NO_3	s	−366	−184	151
Fe_2O_3	s	−824	−742	87	N_2O	g	82	104	220
Fe_3O_4	s	−1118	−1015	146	NO	g	90	87	211

Chemical Thermodynamics

formula	state	ΔH_f^0 $\frac{kJ}{mol}$	ΔG_f^0 $\frac{kJ}{mol}$	S^0 $\frac{J}{mol\,K}$
NO_2	g	33	51	240
NO_2^-	aq	−105	−32	123
NO_3^-	aq	−207	−111	146
Na	s	0	0	51
Na^+	aq	−240	−262	59
NaCl	s	−411	−384	72
Na_2CO_3	s	−1130	−1046	135
$Na_2CO_3 \cdot 10\,H_2O$	s	−4080	−3430	565
NaOH	s	−427	−381	64
Na_2SO_4	s	−1384	−1267	149
$Na_2SO_4 \cdot 10\,H_2O$	s	−4324	−3644	593
O_2	g	0	0	205
O_3	g	143	163	239
OH^-	aq	−230	−157	−11
S_8	s	0	0	32
SO_2	g	−297	−300	248
SO_4^{2-}	aq	−909	−745	20
Se	g	227	187	177
Se	s	0	0	42
Te	g	197	157	183
Te	s	0	0	50
Zn	s	0	0	42
ZnO	s	−348	−318	44
Zn^{2+}	aq	−154	−147	−112
methane	g	−75	−51	186
ethane	g	−85	−33	230
propane	g	−104	−24	270
butane	g	−126	−17	310
pentane	g	−146	−8	349
hexane	l	−167	0	388
heptane	l	−188	8	428
octane	l	−209	16	467
nonane	l	−228	26	506
decane	l	−250	33	545
cyclohexane	l	−156	27	204
cyclohexane	g	−123	32	298
ethene (ethylene)	g	52	68	220
ethine (acetylene)	g	227	209	201
cyclohexene	l	−39		
cyclohexene	g	−5	107	311
1,3-cyclohexadiene	g	108		
benzene	l	49	125	173
benzene	g	83	130	269
Z-1,2-dichlorethene	l	−28	22	199
E-1,2-dichlorethene	l	−23	27	196
fluoromethane	g	−234	−210	223
chloromethane	g	−86	−63	235
bromoethane	l	−92	−28	199
bromoethane	g	−65	−27	287
1,2-dibromoethane	l	−81		
1,2-dibromoethane	g	−39	−11	330
iodoethane	l	−40	15	212
methanol	l	−239	−166	127
methanol	g	−201	−163	240
methanol	aq	−246	−175	133
ethanol	l	−278	−175	161
ethanol	g	−235	−168	283
ethanol	aq	−288	−182	149
methanal (formaldehyde)	g	−116	−110	219
ethanal (acetaldehyde)	g	−166	−133	264
propanone (acetone)	g	−218	−153	295
methanoic acid (formic acid)	l	−425	−362	129
(formic acid)	g	−379	−351	249
not ionized	aq	−426	−373	163
ionized	aq	−426	−351	92
ethanoic acid (acetic acid)	l	−485	−390	160
(acetic acid)	g	−435	−377	283
not ionized	aq	−486	−397	178
octadecanoic acid (stearic acid)	s	−949		
urea	s	−333	−198	105
glycine	s	−529	−369	104
glucose	s	−1274	−910	212

Chemical Thermodynamics

Bond enthalpy

Enthalpy of reaction

$$\Delta H_r^0 = \sum (\text{bond enthalpy products}) - \sum (\text{bond enthalpy reactants})$$

average values of molecules in gas phase (thermodynamically negatively defined) in kJ·mol^{-1}

Single bonds

C–H	−413	Si–H	−323	N–Cl	−200	O–H	−463	S–Br	−218	Br–F	−237
C–C	−348	Si–Si	−226	N–Br	−243	O–O	−146	S–S	−266	Br–Cl	−218
C–N	−293	Si–C	−301			O–F	−190			Br–Br	−193
C–O	−358	Si–O	−368	H–H	−436	O–Cl	−203	F–F	−155		
C–F	−485			H–F	−567	O–I	−234			I–Cl	−208
C–Cl	−328	N–H	−391	H–Cl	−431			Cl–F	−253	I–Br	−175
C–Br	−276	N–N	−163	H–Br	−366	S–H	−339	Cl–Cl	−242	I–I	−151
C–I	−240	N–O	−201	H–I	−299	S–F	−327				
C–S	−259	N–F	−272			S–Cl	−253				

Multiple bonds

C=C	−614	C=O	−745	N=N	−418	O=O	−495
C≡C	−839	C=O in CO$_2$	−803	N≡N	−941		
C=N	−615					S=O	−323
C≡N	−891	C≡O in CO	−1072			S=S	−418

Bond length

average values in molecules in picometres [pm]

H–H	74	I–I	268	Br–H	141	C–N	148	C≡C	120
N≡N	110	C–H	109	I–H	161	C=N	122	C–C in benzene	139
O=O	121	N–H	101	O–O	148	C≡N	116		
F–F	142	O–H	96	C–O	143			B–B	177
Cl–Cl	199	F–H	92	C=O	123	C–C	154	Si–Si	230
Br–Br	228	Cl–H	127			C=C	134		

Lattice and hydration enthalpy

Enthalpy of dissolution $H_{\text{dissolution}}$ of salts: $H_{\text{dissolution}} = H_{\text{hydration}} - H_{\text{lattice}}$

lattice enthalpy H_{lattice} of selected salts in kJ·mol^{-1}, thermodynamically negatively defined

salt	H_{lattice}	salt	H_{lattice}	salt	H_{lattice}	salt	H_{lattice}	salt	H_{lattice}
LiF	−1019	CsCl	−623	K$_2$S	−1979	CaS	−3084	LiNO$_3$	−848
LiCl	−838	Li$_2$O	−2799	Rb$_2$S	−1929	BaS	−2707	NaNO$_3$	−755
LiBr	−798	Na$_2$O	−2481	MgO	−3929	Cu$_2$S	−2786	NH$_4$NO$_3$	−661
LiI	−742	K$_2$O	−2238	CaO	−3477	CaF$_2$	−2611	NaOH	−887
NaCl	−766	Rb$_2$O	−2163	SrO	−3217	CaCl$_2$	−2146	Al$_2$O$_3$	−15100
KCl	−703	Li$_2$S	−2464	BaO	−3042	CaBr$_2$	−2025		
RbCl	−665	Na$_2$S	−2192	MgS	−3347	CaI$_2$	−1920		

Chemical Thermodynamics

hydration enthalpy $H_\text{hydration}$ of selected ions in kJ·mol^{-1}

ion	$H_\text{hydration}$	ion	$H_\text{hydration}$	ion	$H_\text{hydration}$	ion	$H_\text{hydration}$
Li$^+$	-508	Mg^{2+}	-1908	Co^{2+}	-2020	F$^-$	-510
Na$^+$	-398	Ca^{2+}	-1577	Ni^{2+}	-2100	Cl$^-$	-376
K$^+$	-314	Sr^{2+}	-1431	Cu^{2+}	-2110	Br$^-$	-342
Rb$^+$	-289	Ba^{2+}	-1289			I$^-$	-298
Cs$^+$	-256	Zn^{2+}	-2056	Al^{3+}	-4602	OH$^-$	-364
Ag$^+$	-468	Cd^{2+}	-1791	Fe^{3+}	-4485	CN$^-$	-349
NH$_4^+$	-293	Hg^{2+}	-1820			NO$_3^-$	-255
H$_3$O$^+$	-1048	Fe^{2+}	-1958				

Solubility product of salts with low solubility

$$M_aX_b\,(s) \rightleftarrows a\,M^{+m}(aq) + b\,X^{-n}(aq) \qquad K_L = c^a(M^{+m}) \cdot c^b(X^{-n}) \qquad pK_L = -\log_{10} K_L$$

K_L: solubility product, pK_L: negative decimal logarithm (common logarithm) of the solubility product
M^{+m}: (metal) cation with the charge $+m$ and the index a in the formula unit
X^{-n}: (non metal) anion with the charge $-n$ and the index b in the formula unit

formula	pK_L	formula	pK_L	formula	pK_L	formula	pK_L	formula	pK_L
Ag$_2$CO$_3$	11.2	BaSO$_4$	10.0	Cu$_2$S	46.7	Mg(OH)$_2$	11.2	PbCrO$_4$	13.7
Ag$_2$S	48.8	Ca(OH)$_2$	5.4	CuBr	7.4	MgC$_2$O$_4$	4.1	PbI$_2$	8.1
AgBr	12.3	CaC$_2$O$_4$	8.6	CuC$_2$O$_4$	7.5	MgNH$_4$PO$_4$	12.6	PbS	27.5
AgCl	9.7	CaCO$_3$	8.3	CuI	11.3	Mn(OH)$_2$	13.4	PbSO$_4$	7.8
AgI	16.1	CaF$_2$	10.4	CuS	36.1	MnS	14.9	Zn(OH)$_2$	13.7
AgOH	7.8	CaSO$_4$	4.6	Fe(OH)$_2$	13.8	Ni(OH)$_2$	15.3	ZnC$_2$O$_4$	8.9
Al(OH)$_3$	32.3	Cd(OH)$_2$	13.9	Fe(OH)$_3$	38.6	NiS	23.9	ZnCO$_3$	10.2
BaC$_2$O$_4$	6.8	CdS	28.4	FeC$_2$O$_4$	6.7	PbBr$_2$	5.7	ZnS	24.7
BaCO$_3$	8.1	CoS	25.5	FeS	18.1	PbCl$_2$	4.8		
BaF$_2$	5.8	Cu(OH)$_2$	19.8	HgS	52.4	PbCO$_3$	13.1		

Solubility as a function of temperature

Gases in water

solids in water ▶ p. 226

Maximum volume of gas V in mL reduced to standard conditions (273.15 K) dissolved in 1 L of water at temperature ϑ and standard pressure

ϑ [°C]	H$_2$	N$_2$	O$_2$	Cl$_2$	CO$_2$	CH$_4$	NH$_3$	HCl
0	21.5	23.5	48.9	4610	1713	55.6	1 170 000	507 000
10	19.6	18.6	38.0	3150	1194	41.8	898 000	474 000
20	18.2	15.5	31.0	2300	878	33.1	698 000	442 000
30	17.0	13.4	26.1	1800	665	27.6	534 000	412 000
40	16.4	11.8	24.0	1440	530	23.7	421 000	386 000
50	16.0	10.9	20.9	1230	436	21.3	343 000	362 000
60		10.2	19.5	1020	359	19.5	314 000	339 000
70		9.77	18.3	862		18.3	256 000	
80		9.58	17.6	683		17.7	203 000	
90		9.50	17.2	390		17.4	150 000	

Solids in water

Maximum mass m of a substance dissolved in g per 100 g water at temperature ϑ

ϑ [°C]	NaCl	NH$_4$Cl	KCl	KNO$_3$	Ca(OH)$_2$	CaSO$_4 \cdot$ 2 H$_2$O	saccharose	urea
0	35.6	29.7	28.2	13.3	0.172	0.176	179	66.7
10	35.7	33.5	31.3	21.5			190	82.4
20	35.9	37.4	34.4	31.5	0.164	0.204	204	108
30	36.2	41.4	37.3	45.6			220	134
40	36.4	46.0	40.3	63.9	0.132	0.212	238	165
50	36.7	50.4	43.1	85.7			260	205
60	37.1	55.3	45.6	110	0.110	0.205	287	251
70	37.5	60.2	48.3	138			321	
80	38.5	65.6	51.0	168	0.087	0.197	362	400
90	38.7	73.1	53.4	202			416	
100	39.2	77.3	56.2	245	0.069	0.162	487	733

3 Atomic Structure

Energy of ionization

values in MJ/mol

	1	2	3	4	5	6	7	...							
1 H	1.31														
2 He	2.37	5.25													
3 Li	0.52	7.29	11.9												
4 Be	0.90	1.76	14.9	21.0											
5 B	0.80	2.43	3.66	25.1	32.8										
6 C	1.09	2.35	4.62	6.22	37.8	47.3									
7 N	1.40	2.86	4.58	7.48	9.44	53.3	64.3								
8 O	1.31	3.39	5.30	7.47	11.0	13.3	71.3	84.0							
9 F	1.68	3.38	6.05	8.40	11.0	15.1	17.8	92.0	106						
10 Ne	2.08	3.96	6.13	9.37	12.2	15.2	20.0	23.1	116	131					
11 Na	0.49	4.56	6.91	9.54	13.3	16.6	20.2	25.5	28.9	142	159				
12 Mg	0.73	1.45	7.73	10.5	13.6	18.0	21.7	25.7	31.6	35.5	170	189			
13 Al	0.58	1.81	2.74	11.6	14.9	18.4	23.2	27.5	31.8	38.4	42.6	202	222		
14 Si	0.78	1.57	3.23	4.35	16.1	19.8	23.8	29.2	33.9	39.0	45.9	50.6	235	258	
15 P	1.01	1.90	2.91	4.96	6.27	21.2	25.4	29.8	35.9	41.0	46.3	54.0	59.0	272	296
16 S	1.00	2.25	3.36	4.56	7.01	8.49	27.1	31.6	36.6	43.1	48.7	54.5	62.9	68.2	311
17 Cl	1.25	2.30	3.82	5.16	6.54	9.36	11.0	33.6	38.6	44.0	51.0	57.1	63.4	72.4	78.0
18 Ar	1.52	2.66	3.93	5.77	7.24	8.78	12.0	13.9	40.7	46.2	52.0	59.6	66.2	72.9	82.8
19 K	0.41	3.05	4.41	5.88	7.98	9.65	11.4	15.0	17.0	48.5	54.4	60.7	68.9	75.9	83.2
20 Ca	0.59	1.15	4.91	6.47	8.14	10.5	12.3	14.2	18.2	20.4	57.0	63.3	70.0	78.7	86.3
	1	2	3	4	5	6	7	8	9	10	11	12	13	14	15

Atomic Structure

Energy levels of electrons in the atom

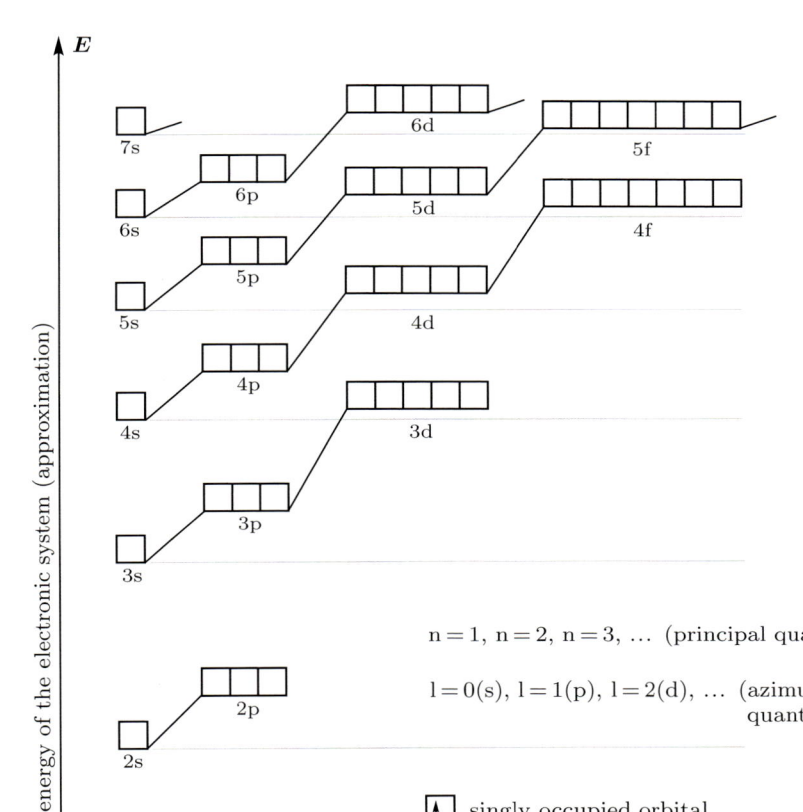

n = 1, n = 2, n = 3, ... (principal quantum number)

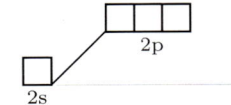

l = 0(s), l = 1(p), l = 2(d), ... (azimuthal (or orbital) quantum number)

| ↑ | singly occupied orbital |

| ↑↓ | doubly occupied orbital |

The two arrows symbolize two electrons with anti-parallel spin

337				
353	381			
88.6	397	427		
93.4	99.4	445	476	
94.0	105	112	495	528
16	17	18	19	20

4 Elements

Properties of the elements

atomic number Z	name	symbol	molar mass (atomic mass) in g·mol^{-1}	melting point in °C	boiling point in °C	density at 25 °C, 101.3 kPa in g·cm^{-3} *gases g·L^{-1}
1	hydrogen	H (H$_2$)	1.00794(7)	−259	−253	*0.082
2	helium	He	4.002602(2)	−272	−269	*0.164
3	lithium	Li	6.941(2)	180	1342	0.534
4	beryllium	Be	9.012182(3)	1287	2471	1.85
5	boron	B	10.811(7)	2075	4000	2.34
6	carbon	C (graphite)	12.0107(8)	3550	4827	2.26
		C (diamond)	12.0107(8)	3650		3.51
7	nitrogen	N (N$_2$)	14.0067(2)	−210	−196	*1.15
8	oxygen	O (O$_2$)	15.9994(3)	−219	−183	*1.31
		O (O$_3$, ozone)	15.9994(3)	−193	−111	*1.96
9	fluorine	F (F$_2$)	18.9984032(5)	−220	−188	*1.55
10	neon	Ne	20.1797(6)	−249	−246	*0.825
11	sodium	Na	22.98976928(2)	98	883	0.97
12	magnesium	Mg	24.3050(6)	650	1090	1.74
13	aluminium	Al	26.9815386(8)	660	2519	2.70
14	silicon	Si	28.0855(3)	1414	3265	2.33
15	phosphorus	P (P$_4$, white)	30.973762(2)	44	280	1.82
		P (P$_x$, red)	30.973762(2)	—	590 subl.	2.16
16	sulfur (sulphur)	S (S$_8$, α rhomb.)	32.065(5)	115	444	2.07
		S (S$_8$, β monocl.)	32.065(5)	115	444	2.07
		S (S$_n$, amorph.)	32.065(5)	ca. 120	444	1.92
17	chlorine	Cl (Cl$_2$)	35.453(2)	−101	−34	*2.90
18	argon	Ar	39.948(1)	−189	−186	*1.63
19	potassium	K	39.0983(1)	63	759	0.89
20	calcium	Ca	40.078(4)	842	1484	1.54
21	scandium	Sc	44.955912(6)	1541	2836	2.99
22	titanium	Ti	47.867(1)	1670	3287	4.51
23	vanadium	V	50.9415(1)	1910	3407	6.0
24	chromium	Cr	51.9961(6)	1907	2671	7.15
25	manganese	Mn	54.938045(5)	1246	2061	7.3
26	iron	Fe	55.845(2)	1538	2861	7.87
27	cobalt	Co	58.933195(5)	1495	2927	8.86
28	nickel	Ni	58.6934(4)	1455	2913	8.90
29	copper	Cu	63.546(3)	1085	2562	8.96
30	zinc	Zn	65.38(2)	420	907	7.14
31	gallium	Ga	69.723(1)	30	2204	5.91
32	germanium	Ge	72.64(1)	938	2833	5.32
33	arsenic	As	74.92160(2)	—	613 subl.	5.75
34	selenium	Se	78.96(3)	220	685	4.81
35	bromine	Br (Br$_2$)	79.904(1)	−7	59	3.10
36	krypton	Kr	83.798(2)	−157	−153	*3.43
37	rubidium	Rb	85.4678(3)	39	688	1.53
38	strontium	Sr	87.62(1)	777	1382	2.64
39	yttrium	Y	88.90585(2)	1522	3345	4.47
40	zirkonium	Zr	91.224(2)	1854	4409	6.52
41	niobium	Nb	92.90638(2)	2477	4744	8.57
42	molybdenum	Mo	95.96(2)	2622	4639	10.2

Elements

43	technetium	Tc	–	2157	4265	11
44	ruthenium	Ru	101.07(2)	2333	4150	12.1
45	rhodium	Rh	102.90550(2)	1963	3695	12.4
46	palladium	Pd	106.42(1)	1554	2970	12.0
47	silver	Ag	107.8682(2)	962	2162	10.5
48	cadmium	Cd	112.411(8)	321	767	8.69
49	indium	In	114.818(3)	157	2072	7.31
50	tin	Sn	118.710(7)	232	2602	7.26
51	antimony	Sb	121.760(1)	630	1750	6.69
52	tellurium	Te	127.60(3)	449	988	6.24
53	iodine	I (I_2)	126.90447(3)	114	184	4.93
54	xenon	Xe	131.293(6)	−112	−108	*5.37
55	caesium	Cs	132.9054519(2)	29	671	1.93
56	barium	Ba	137.327(7)	727	1897	3.62
57	lanthanum	La	138.90547(7)	918	3464	6.15
58	cerium	Ce	140.116(1)	798	3453	6.77
59	praseodymium	Pr	140.90765(2)	931	3520	6.77
60	neodymium	Nd	144.242(3)	1021	3074	7.01
61	promethium	Pm	–	1042	3000	7.26
62	samarium	Sm	150.36(2)	1074	1794	7.52
63	europium	Eu	151.964(1)	822	1529	5.24
64	gadolinium	Gd	157.25(3)	1313	3273	8.23
65	terbium	Tb	158.92535(2)	1356	3230	8.23
66	dysprosium	Dy	162.500(1)	1412	2566	8.55
67	holmium	Ho	164.93032(2)	1474	2780	8.80
68	erbium	Er	167.259(3)	1529	2868	9.07
69	thulium	Tm	168.93421(2)	1545	1950	9.32
70	ytterbium	Yb	173.054(5)	819	1196	6.90
71	lutetium	Lu	174.9668(1)	1663	3402	9.84
72	hafnium	Hf	178.49(2)	2233	4603	13.3
73	tantalum	Ta	180.94788(2)	3007	5458	16.4
74	tungsten	W	183.84(1)	3414	5555	19.3
75	rhenium	Re	186.207(1)	3186	5596	20.8
76	osmium	Os	190.23(3)	3033	5012	22.59
77	iridium	Ir	192.217(3)	2446	4428	22.56
78	platinum	Pt	195.084(9)	1768	3825	21.5
79	gold	Au	196.966569(4)	1064	2856	19.3
80	mercury	Hg	200.59(2)	−39	357	13.53
81	thallium	Tl	204.3833(2)	304	1473	11.8
82	lead	Pb	207.2(1)	327	1749	11.3
83	bismuth	Bi	208.98040(1)	271	1564	9.79
84	polonium	Po	–	254	962	9.20
85	astatine	At	–	302	337	–
86	radon	Rn	–	−71	−62	*9.07
87	francium	Fr	–	27	677	–
88	radium	Ra	–	700	1140	5
89	actinium	Ac	–	1051	3198	10
90	thorium	Th	232.03806(2)	1750	4788	11.7
91	protactinium	Pa	231.03588(2)	1572	–	15.4
92	uranium	U	238.02891(3)	1135	4131	19.1
93	neptunium	Np	–	640	3902	20.2
94	plutonium	Pu	–	640	3228	19.7
95	americium	Am	–	994	2607	–
96	curium	Cm	–	1340	–	–

Periodic table of the elements ▶ inside back cover

Elements

MATHEMATICS   PHYSICS   ASTRONOMY   **CHEMISTRY**

Atomic radii and ionic radii

values in picometres ($1\,\text{pm} = 10^{-12}\,\text{m}$)

H^+ 0.0013

H 30

H^- > 130 (very variable)

● cations
○ atoms
○ anions

Li^+ 60 Be^{2+} 31

Li 152   Be 112   B 88   C 77   N 70   O 66   F 64

O^{2-} 140 F^- 136

Na^+ 95 Mg^{2+} 65 Al^{3+} 54

Na 186   Mg 160   Al 125   Si 117   P 110   S 104   Cl 99

S^{2-} 184 Cl^- 181

K^+ 133 Ca^{2+} 97 Sc^{3+} 81 Cu^+ 96 Zn^{2+} 74 Ga^{3+} 62 Ge^{4+} 53

K 231   Ca 197   Sc 160   Cu 128   Zn 133   Ga 122   Ge 122   As 121   Se 117   Br 114

Se^{2-} 184 Br^- 195

Rb^+ 148 Sr^{2+} 113 Y^{3+} 93 Ag^+ 126 Cd^{2+} 97 In^{3+} 81 Sn^{4+} 71

Rb 244   Sr 215   Y 180   Ag 144   Cd 149   In 162   Sn 140   Sb 141   Te 137   I 133

Te^{2-} 221 I^- 216

Cs^+ 169 Ba^{2+} 135 La^{3+} 115 Au^+ 137 Hg^{2+} 110 Tl^{3+} 95 Pb^{4+} 84

Cs 262   Ba 217   La 188   Au 144   Hg 150   Tl 171   Pb 175   Bi 146   Po 140   At 140

5 Inorganic Chemistry

Physical properties of inorganic compounds

see also: Properties of the elements
(at standard pressure 1013 hPa, s = sublimation, d = decomposition, density at 20°C)

substance	formula	melting point/°C	boiling point/°C	density /g·cm^{-3}
water	H_2O	0	100	1
deuterium oxide (heavy water)	^2H_2O or D_2O	4	101	1.1
tritium oxide	^3H_2O or T_2O	4.5	102	
hydrogen peroxide	H_2O_2	0	158	1.4
hydrogen sulfide	H_2S	−83	−62	
ammonia	NH_3	−78	−33	1.4
phosphine	PH_3	−133	−88	
hydrazine	H_2NNH_2	2	114	1.01
hydrogen fluoride	HF	−83	19	
hydrogen chloride	HCl	−114	−85	
hydrogen bromide	HBr	−87	−67	
methane	CH_4	−183	−162	
carbon dioxide	CO_2		−78s	
carbon monoxide	CO	−205	−190	
silane	SiH_4	−185	−112	
sulfur dioxide	SO_2	−73	−10	
oxygen difluoride	OF_2	−234	−145	
phosphoric acid	H_3PO_4	42	213d	1.87
sulfuric acid	H_2SO_4	10	340d	1.84
nitric acid	HNO_3	−41	86	1.51
lithium fluoride	LiF	870	1670	2.3
lithium chloride	LiCl	610	1350	2.1
lithium bromide	LiBr	550	1265	3.5
lithium iodide	LiI	450	1171	3.5
lithium oxide	Li_2O	> 1700	< 1000s	2
lithium hydroxide	LiOH	450	924	1.46
sodium fluoride	NaF	992	1700	2.2
sodium chloride	NaCl	801	1465	2.2
sodium bromide	NaBr	747	1390	3.2
sodium iodide	NaI	660	1300	3.7
sodium hydride	NaH	800d		0.9
sodium hydroxide	NaOH	322	1388	2.13
potassium fluoride	KF	852	1505	2.49
potassium chloride	KCl	773	1413	1.98
potassium bromide	KBr	732	1380	2.75
potassium iodide	KI	450	1171	3.5
potassium hydroxide	KOH	360	1320	2.04
beryllium oxide	BeO	2530	3900	3

▶ continued overleaf

Inorganic Chemistry

substance	formula	melting point/°C	boiling point/°C	density g·cm^{-3}
magnesium chloride	$MgCl_2$	708	1412	2.3
magnesium oxide	MgO	2800	3600	3.6
calcium chloride	$CaCl_2$	772	> 1600	2.1
calcium oxide	CaO	2570	2850	3.3
calcium carbonate	$CaCO_3$	900d		2.7
aluminium oxide	Al_2O_3	2050	2980	3.94
silicon dioxide	SiO_2	1713	> 2200	2.2–2.7
copper (II) chloride	$CuCl_2$	630		3.39
copper (I) chloride	$CuCl$	426	1490d	4.14
copper (II) oxide	CuO	1026d		6.4
copper (I) oxide	Cu_2O	1230	1800d	6
copper (II) sulfide	CuS	220d		4.6
copper (II) sulfate	$CuSO_4$	650d		3.6
iron (II) oxide	FeO	1380		5.7
iron (III) oxide	Fe_2O_3	1560d		5.2
iron (II,III) oxide	Fe_3O_4	1538d		5.2
tungsten (VI) oxide	WO_3	1473	> 1750	7.16

Formation constants of metal complexes

$$M + z\,L \rightleftarrows [ML_z] \qquad K_F = \frac{c([ML_z])}{c(M) \cdot c^z(L)} \qquad pK_F = -\log_{10} K_F$$

M: metal cation (or atom), L: ligand, z: number of ligands bound, K_F: formation constant

complex	pK_F	complex	pK_F	complex	pK_F
$[Ag(CN)_2]^-$	−20.8	$[Co(NH_3)_6]^{3+}$	−35.1	$[HgI_4]^{2-}$	−30.5
$[AgCl_2]^-$	−5.4	$[CuCl_4]^{2-}$	−5.6	$[Ni(CN)_4(H_2O)_2]^{2-}$	−22
$[Ag(NH_3)_2]^+$	−7.1	$[Cu(H_2O)_2(NH_3)_2]^{2+}$	−8.0	$[Ni(NH_3)_6]^{2+}$	−8.7
$[Ag(SCN)_2]^-$	−9.8	$[Cu(NH_3)_4]^{2+}$	−13.3	$[Ni(H_2NC_2H_4NH_2)_3]^{2+}$	−18.3
$[Ag(S_2O_3)_2]^{3-}$	−13.5	$[Cu(H_2NC_2H_4NH_2)_3]^{2+}$	−21.0	$[Ni(edta)]^{2-}$	−18.6
$[AlF_6]^{3-}$	−19.8	$[Fe(CN)_6]^{4-}$	−24	$[PbI_4]^{2-}$	−6.2
$[Al(OH)_4]^-$	−32	$[Fe(CN)_6]^{3-}$	−31	$[Pb(OH)_4]^{2-}$	−14.6
$[Au(CN)_2]^-$	−21	$[FeCl(H_2O)_5]^{2+}$	−0.47	$[SnF_3(H_2O)]^-$	−9.92
$[Cd(CN)_4]^{2-}$	−18.6	$[FeF(H_2O)_5]^{2+}$	−9.16	$[Zn(CN)_4]^{2-}$	−16.9
$[Cd(NH_3)_4]^{2+}$	−7.12	$[Fe(SCN)(H_2O)_5]^{2+}$	−5.94	$[Zn(NH_3)_4]^{2+}$	−9.6
$[Cd(H_2NC_2H_4NH_2)_3]^{2+}$	−12.3	$[Hg(CN)_4]^{2-}$	−41.5	$[Zn(H_2NC_2H_4NH_2)_3]^{2+}$	−12.9
$[Co(Cl)_4]^{2-}$	−6.6	$[HgCl_4]^{2-}$	−15.1	$[Zn(OH)_4]^{2-}$	−15.8
$[Co(NH_3)_6]^{2+}$	−4.7	$[Hg(NH_3)_4]^{2+}$	−19.3		

6 Organic Chemistry

Functional groups

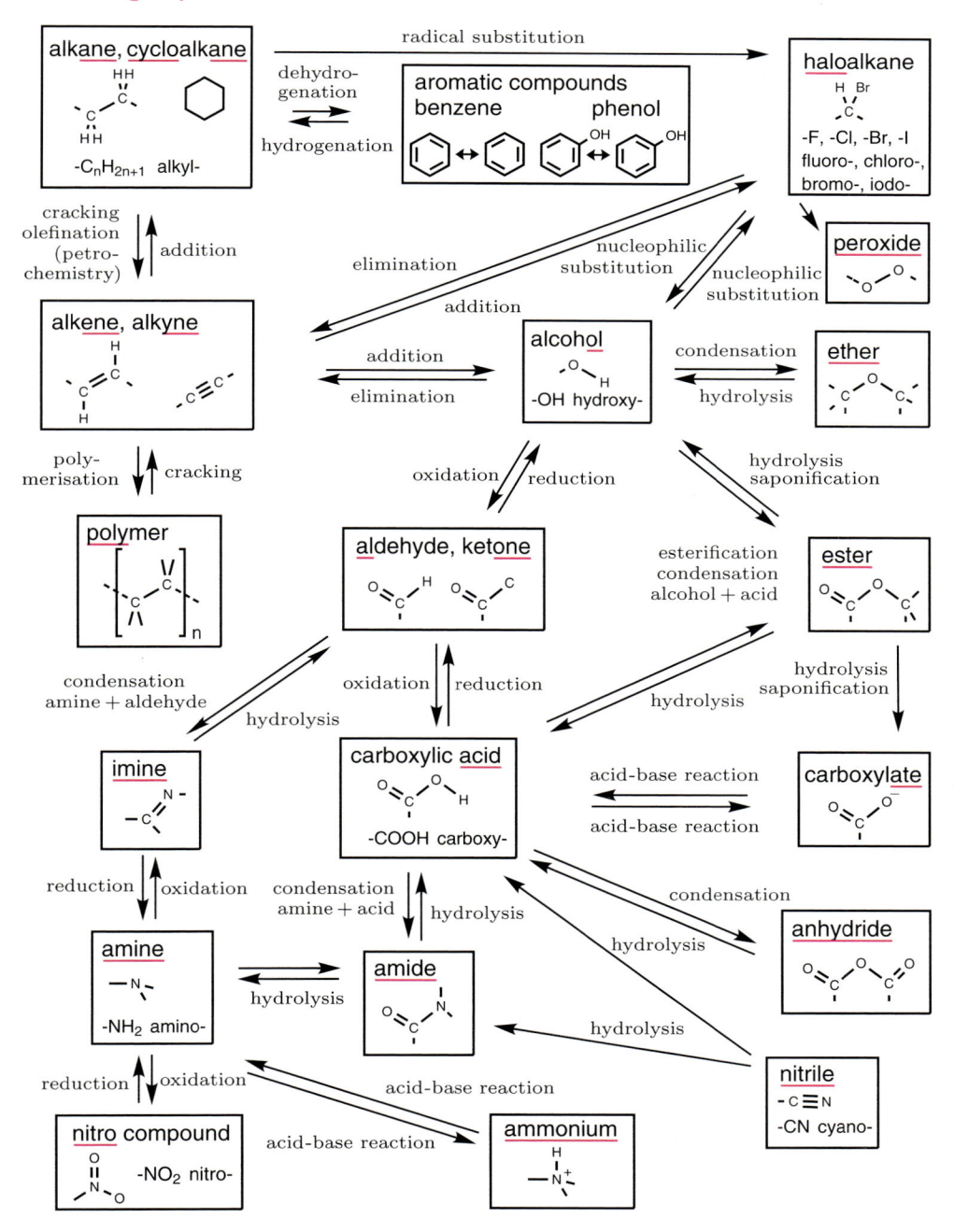

alkane, cycloalkane -C$_n$H$_{2n+1}$ alkyl-

— radical substitution → **haloalkane** -F, -Cl, -Br, -I fluoro-, chloro-, bromo-, iodo-

alkane ⇌ (dehydrogenation / hydrogenation) **aromatic compounds** benzene, phenol

alkane ⇌ (cracking, olefination (petrochemistry) / addition) **alkene, alkyne**

alkene ⇌ (polymerisation / cracking) **polymer**

alkene ⇌ (addition / elimination) **alcohol** -OH hydroxy-

haloalkane ⇌ (nucleophilic substitution) alcohol

haloalkane → (elimination) alkene

alcohol ⇌ (condensation / hydrolysis) **ether**

haloalkane → (nucleophilic substitution) **peroxide**

alcohol ⇌ (oxidation / reduction) **aldehyde, ketone**

aldehyde, ketone ⇌ (oxidation / reduction) **carboxylic acid** -COOH carboxy-

carboxylic acid + alcohol ⇌ (esterification, condensation / hydrolysis, saponification) **ester**

ester → (hydrolysis, saponification) alcohol

carboxylic acid ⇌ (acid-base reaction / acid-base reaction) **carboxylate**

carboxylic acid ⇌ (condensation / hydrolysis) **anhydride**

aldehyde + amine ⇌ (condensation amine + aldehyde / hydrolysis) **imine**

imine ⇌ (reduction / oxidation) **amine** -NH$_2$ amino-

amine + acid ⇌ (condensation amine + acid / hydrolysis) **amide**

amide → (hydrolysis) amine

nitrile → (hydrolysis) carboxylic acid / amide

nitrile -CN cyano-

amine ⇌ (reduction / oxidation) **nitro compound** -NO$_2$ nitro-

amine ⇌ (acid-base reaction / acid-base reaction) **ammonium**

233

Organic Chemistry

Physical properties of organic compounds

(at standard pressure 1013 hPa, s = sublimation, d = decomposition, density at 20°C)

substance	formula	melting point/°C	boiling point/°C	density /g·cm^{-3}
methane	CH_4	−183	−162	
ethane	C_2H_6	−183	−89	
propane	C_3H_8	−188	−42	
butane	C_4H_{10}	−138	0	
pentane	C_5H_{12}	−130	36	0.621
hexane	C_6H_{14}	−95	69	0.655
heptane	C_7H_{16}	−91	98	0.68
octane	C_8H_{18}	−57	126	0.698
nonane	C_9H_{20}	−54	151	0.714
decane	$C_{10}H_{22}$	−30	174	0.726
undecane	$C_{11}H_{24}$	−26	196	0.737
dodecane	$C_{12}H_{26}$	−10	216	0.745
tridecane	$C_{13}H_{28}$	−6	235	
tetradecane	$C_{14}H_{30}$	6	254	
pentadecane	$C_{15}H_{32}$	10	271	
hexadecane	$C_{16}H_{34}$	18	280	
heptadecane	$C_{17}H_{36}$	23	303	
octadecane	$C_{18}H_{38}$	28	316	
nonadecane	$C_{19}H_{40}$	32	330	
icosane	$C_{20}H_{42}$	37	343	
2-methylpropane (isobutane)	C_4H_{10}	−160	−12	0.551
2-methylbutane (isopentane)	C_5H_{12}	−160	28	0.615
2,2-dimethylpropane (neopentane)	C_5H_{12}	−17	10	0.585
2-methylpentane	C_6H_{14}	−154	60	0.649
3-methylpentane	C_6H_{14}	−163	63	0.66
2,2-dimethylbutane	C_6H_{14}	−100	50	0.644
2,3-dimethylbutane	C_6H_{14}	−129	58	0.657
2,2,4-trimethylpentane (isooctane)	C_8H_{18}	−107	99	0.692
cyclopropane	C_3H_6	−127	−33	
cyclobutane	C_4H_8	−91	13	0.689
cyclopentane	C_5H_{10}	−94	49	0.74
cyclohexane	C_6H_{12}	7	81	0.774
ethene	C_2H_4	−169	−104	
propene	C_3H_6	−185	−48	
but-1-ene	C_4H_8	−185	−6	
Z-but-2-ene	C_4H_8	−139	4	
E-but-2-ene	C_4H_8	−106	1	
pent-1-ene	C_5H_{10}	−165	30	0.635
Z-pent-2-ene	C_5H_{10}	−151	36.9	0.65
E-pent-2-ene	C_5H_{10}	−140	36.4	0.643
hex-1-ene	C_6H_{12}	−140	64	0.668
Z-hex-2-ene	C_6H_{12}	−141	68.9	0.683
E-hex-2-ene	C_6H_{12}	−133	67.9	0.673
Z-hex-3-ene	C_6H_{12}	−138	66.5	0.675
E-hex-3-ene	C_6H_{12}	−113	67.1	0.672
cyclopentene	C_5H_8	−135	44	0.767
cyclohexene	C_6H_{10}	−104	83	0.806
propadiene (allene)	C_3H_4	−136	−35	

Organic Chemistry

1,2-butadiene	C_4H_6	−136	11	
1,3-butadiene	C_4H_6	−109	−4	
2-methyl-1,3-butadiene (isoprene)	C_5H_8	−146	34	0.676
ethyne	C_2H_2	−81	−84	
propyne	C_3H_4	−103	−23	
but-1-yne	C_4H_6	−126	8	
but-2-yne	C_4H_6	−32	27	0.686
pent-1-yne	C_5H_8	−106	40	0.689
pent-2-yne	C_5H_8	−109	56	0.706
hex-1-yne	C_6H_{10}	−132	71	0.71
benzene	C_6H_6	6	80	0.874
methylbenzene (toluene)	$C_6H_5CH_3$	−95	111	0.862
ethylbenzene	$C_6H_5C_2H_5$	−95	136	0.863
1,2-dimethylbenzene (o-xylene)	$C_6H_4(CH_3)_2$	−25	144	0.876
1,3-dimethylbenzene (m-xylene)	$C_6H_4(CH_3)_2$	−48	139	0.86
1,4-dimethylbenzene (p-xylene)	$C_6H_4(CH_3)_2$	−13	138	0.857
1,3,5-trimethylbenzene (mesitylene)	$C_6H_3(CH_3)_3$	−6	205	0.857
naphtalene	$C_{10}H_8$	80	218	1.14
anthracene	$C_{14}H_{10}$	216	340	1.24
phenanthrene	$C_{14}H_{10}$	101	340	1.18
iodomethane (methyl iodide)	CH_3I	−67	42	2.265
diiodomethane (methylene iodide)	CH_2I_2	6	182	3.308
triiodomethane (iodoform)	CHI_3	119	−218	4.178
tetraiodomethane	CI_4		s130−40	4.23
bromomethane (methyl bromide)	CH_3Br	−94	4	1.662
dibromomethane (methylene bromide)	CH_2Br_2	−53	97	2.484
tribromomethane (bromoform)	$CHBr_3$	8	150	2.876
tetrabromomethane	CBr_4	91	190	3.42
chloromethane (methyl chloride)	CH_3Cl	−98	−24	
dichloromethane (methyl chloride)	CH_2Cl_2	−95	40	1.421
trichloromethane (chloroform)	$CHCl_3$	−64	62	1.443
tetrachloromethane	CCl_4	−23	77	1.457
fluoromethane (methyl fluoride)	CH_3F	−142	−78	
difluoromethane	CH_2F_2	−136	−52	
trifluoromethane (Halon 1300)	CHF_3	−160	−84	
tetrafluoromethane	CF_4	−187	−128	
trifluorochloromethane (Freon 13)	HCF_3	−181	−81	
difluorochloromethane (Freon 22)	$HCClF_2$	−147	−41	1.49
fluorodichloromethane (Freon 21)	$HCCl_2F$	−135	9	1.405
difluorodichloromethane (Freon 12, R-12)	CCl_2F_2	−158	−30	1.75
pentafluoroethane (Halon 2500)	C_2HF_5	−103	−49	1.19
1,1,1-trichloroethane	$C_2H_3Cl_3$	−30	74	1.339
trichloroethene	C_2HCl_3	−73	87	1.464
chlorobenzene	C_6H_5Cl	−45	132	1.106
1,2-dichlorobenzene	$C_6H_4Cl_2$	−18	179	1.30
1,4-dichlorobenzene	$C_6H_4Cl_2$	53	174	1.23
methanol	CH_3OH	−98	65	0.787
ethanol	C_2H_5OH	−114	78.3	0.785
propan-1-ol	C_3H_7OH	−126	97	0.799
propan-2-ol	C_3H_7OH	−89	82	0.781
butan-1-ol	C_4H_9OH	−89	118	0.799
butan-2-ol	C_4H_9OH	−115	100	0.702

Organic Chemistry

substance	formula	melting point/°C	boiling point/°C	density g·cm^{-3}
2-methylpropan-1-ol (isobutyl alcohol)	C_4H_9OH	−108	108	0.798
2-methylpropan-2-ol (tert.-butyl alcohol)	C_4H_9OH	26	83	0.781
pentan-1-ol	$C_5H_{11}OH$	−78	138	0.811
hexan-1-ol	$C_6H_{13}OH$	−45	157	0.816
decan-1-ol	$C_{10}H_{21}OH$	7	230	0.83
cyclohexanol	$C_6H_{11}OH$	24	161	0.95
ethanediol (ethylene glykol)	$C_2H_4(OH)_2$	−16	197	1.11
propanetriol (glycerine)	$C_3H_5(OH)_3$	18	290d	1.26
phenol	C_6H_5OH	51	182	1.132
methylamine (methanamine)	H_2NCH_3	−94	−6	0.656
dimethylamine	$HN(CH_3)_2$	−92	7	0.65
trimethylamine	$N(CH_3)_3$	−117	3	0.627
ethylamine	$H_2NC_2H_5$	−81	17	0.677
aminobenzene (aniline)	$C_6H_5NH_2$	−6	184	1.02
methanal (formaldehyde)	CH_2O	−117	−19	
ethanal	CH_3CHO	−123	20	0.784
propanal	C_2H_5CHO	−81	49	0.8
propenal (acrolein)	C_2H_3CHO	−88	52	0.83
hydroxyethanal (glycolaldehyde)	$HOCH_2CHO$	97		1.37
ethanedial (glyoxal)	OHCCHO	15	50	1.37
benzaldehyde	C_6H_5CHO	−26	178	1.04
glucose	$C_6H_{12}O_6$	146	d	1.56
sucrose (saccharose)	$C_{12}H_{22}O_{11}$	185	$>160d$	1.57
propanone (acetone)	CH_3COCH_3	−95	56	0.785
butanone	$CH_3COC_2H_5$	−86	80	0.8
cyclohexanone	$C_6H_{10}O$	−26	156	0.95
methanoic acid (formic acid)	HCOOH	8	101	1.214
ethanoic acid (acetic acid)	CH_3COOH	17	118	1.044
propanoic acid (propionic acid)	C_2H_5COOH	−21	141	0.988
butanoic acid (butyric acid)	C_3H_7COOH	−5	163	0.988
hydroxyethanoic acid (glycolic acid)	$HOCH_2COOH$	80	100d	
aminoethanoic acid (glycine)	H_2NCH_2COOH	262d		
2-hydroxypropanoic acid (lactic acid)	$H_3CCH(OH)COOH$	17 (RS) 53 (R or S)	122 (RS)	1.21
ethanedicarbonic acid (oxalic acid)	HOOCCOOH	190d		1.90
ascorbic acid	$C_6H_8O_6$	191d		1.65
benzoic acid	C_6H_5COOH	122	249	1.266
methyl methanoate	$HCOOCH_3$	−99	32	0.974
ethyl methanoate	$HCOOC_2H_5$	−81	55	0.897
methyl ethanoate	$H_3CCOOCH_3$	−98	57	0.933
ethyl ethanoate	$H_3CCOOC_2H_5$	−84	70	0.917
methanamide (formamide)	$HCONH_2$	3	106	1.134
dimethyl formamide	$HCON(CH_3)_2$	−61	153	0.95
ethaneamide (acetamide)	CH_3CONH_2	82	221	0.999
ethanoyl chloride (acetyl chloride)	CH_3COCl	−112	52	1.104
ethanoic anhydride (acetic anhydride)	$(H_3CCO)_2O$	−73	136	1.082
ethanenitrile (acetonitrile)	H_3CCN	−46	82	0.777
urea	$(NH_2)_2CO$	133	d	1.32
dimethyl ether	H_3COCH_3	−142	−25	
diethyl ether	$H_5C_2OC_2H_5$	−116	35	0.71

7 Biochemistry

Fatty acids, fats and oils

hexadecanoic acid (palmitic acid)

octadecanoic acid (stearic acid)

Z-9-octadecenoic acid (oleic acid)

Z,Z-9,12-octadecadienoic acid (linolic acid)
essential, as other polyinsaturated fatty acids

triglyceride (example of a fat or oil molecule)

Carbohydrates

Monosaccharides

D-glucose
open chain form

β-D-glucopyranose
ring form

D-fructose
open chain form

β-D-fructofuranose
ring form

Biochemistry

Amino acids – constituents of proteins

with lipophilic side chains

glycine	alanine	valine*	leucine*	isoleucine*	methionine*	proline	phenylalanine*
Gly G	Ala A	Val V	Leu L	Ile I	Met M	Pro P	Phe F
$pH_I = 6.0$	$pH_I = 6.0$	$pH_I = 6.0$	$pH_I = 6.0$	$pH_I = 6.0$	$pH_I = 5.7$	$pH_I = 6.3$	$pH_I = 5.5$

with hydrophilic side chains

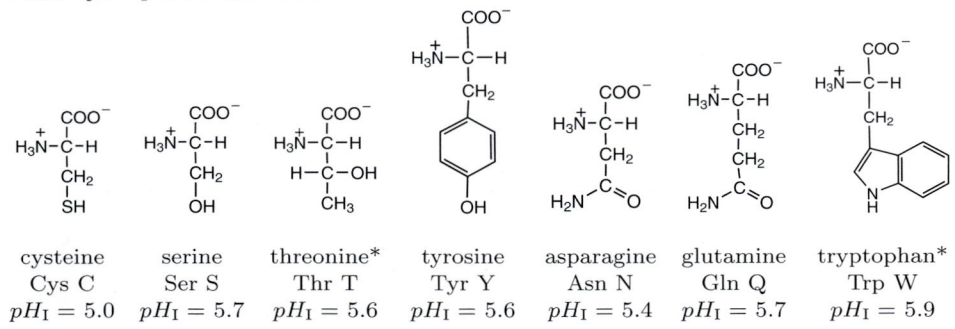

cysteine	serine	threonine*	tyrosine	asparagine	glutamine	tryptophan*
Cys C	Ser S	Thr T	Tyr Y	Asn N	Gln Q	Trp W
$pH_I = 5.0$	$pH_I = 5.7$	$pH_I = 5.6$	$pH_I = 5.6$	$pH_I = 5.4$	$pH_I = 5.7$	$pH_I = 5.9$

with hydrophilic acidic side chains

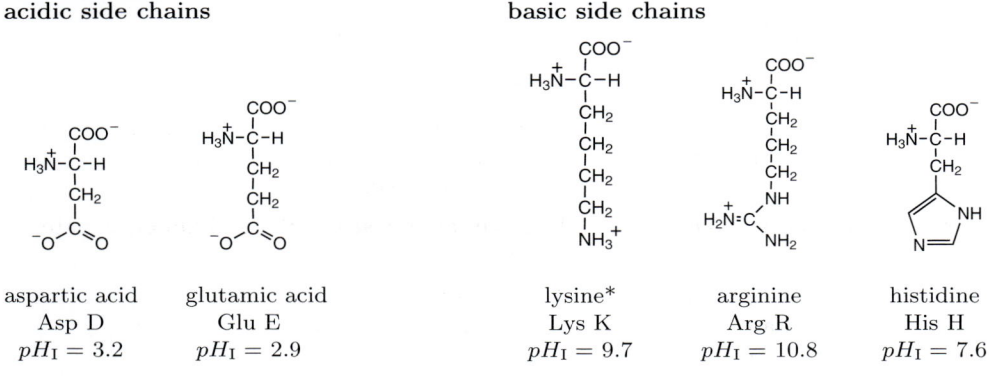

aspartic acid	glutamic acid
Asp D	Glu E
$pH_I = 3.2$	$pH_I = 2.9$

with hydrophilic basic side chains

lysine*	arginine	histidine
Lys K	Arg R	His H
$pH_I = 9.7$	$pH_I = 10.8$	$pH_I = 7.6$

The illustrations depict the prevalent forms of the ions at pH 7. At the isoelectric pH, at pH_I, they carry equal amounts of positive and of negative charge and appear electrically neutral from outside. The amino acids marked with * are essential amino acids and must be supplied by diet.

Energy values of nutrients and foods

values in kJ·g^{-1}. They can vary a little for nutrients due to variable composition and vary much for food (up to 20%).

Nutrients

carbohydrates	17	fats	39	proteins	17

Food

butter, margarine, cream	30	hard cheese	16	bread	10
beer	2	fruits	1.5–6	fish	3–13
beef	5–14	hamburger	16	potatoes	3.5
corn	15	cooking oil	39	pork	5–26
mushrooms	1	whole milk	3	rice	15
potato crisps, chips	24	green vegetables	1	salt	0
roasted peanuts	24	hazelnuts	26	wine	3
water	0	quark	3–7		

Food additives

E-numbers	Funktion	Examples
E100–E199	colourants	E120 carmine, E140 chlorophylls, E150 caramel colour, E162 betanin (beetroot red), E174 silver
E200–E299	preservatives, antioxidants	E210 benzoic acid, E220 sulfurous acid, E236 formic acid, E260 acetic acid
E300–E399	antioxidants, acids	E300 ascorbic acid (vit. C), E306 tocopherol (vit. E), E322 lecithin, E330 citric acid
E400–E499	gelling agents, emulsifiers, thickeners	E400 alginic acid, E406 agar-agar, E412 guar gum, E414 gum arabic, E460 cellulose
E500–E599	anticaking agents, acidity regulators	E500 sodium carbonate (soda), E503 ammonium carbonate, E507 hydrochloric acid, E524 sodium hydroxide
E600–E699	flavour enhancers	E620 glutaminic acid, E621 sodium glutamate, E640 glycine
E900–E999	glazing agents, propellants, sweeteners	E901 bees wax, E905 paraffin, E941 nitrogen, E942 dinitrogen monoxide, E954 saccharin
>E1100	gelling agents, thickeners and humectants	E1103 invertase, E1105 lysozyme, E1200 polydextrose, E1404 oxidized starch

More food additives as flavors, enzymes, gum bases, surface treatment agents etc. are found in more extensive lists e.g. on the Internet.

Biochemistry

Nucleotides and nucleic acids

DNA and RNA

- nucleobases

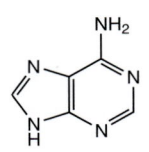

adenine A

guanine G

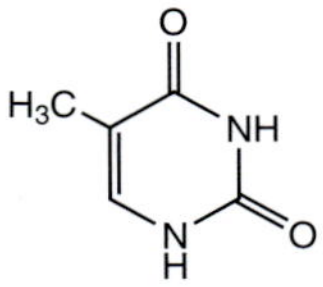

thymine T
without H₃C-: uracil U

cytosine C

- nucleotides

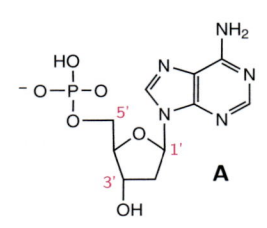

A

2'-desoxyadenosine-
5'-monophosphate

G

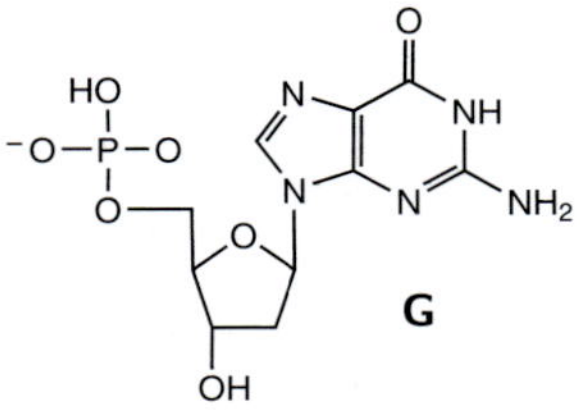

2'-desoxyguanosine-
5'-monophosphate

T

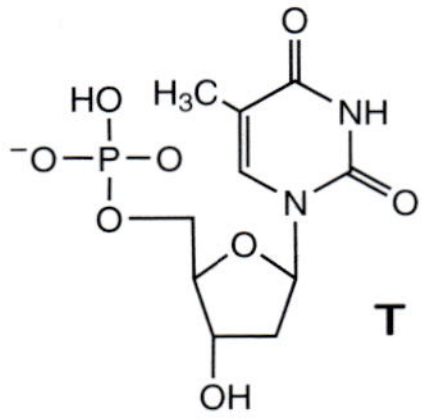

2'-desoxythymidine-
5'-monophosphate

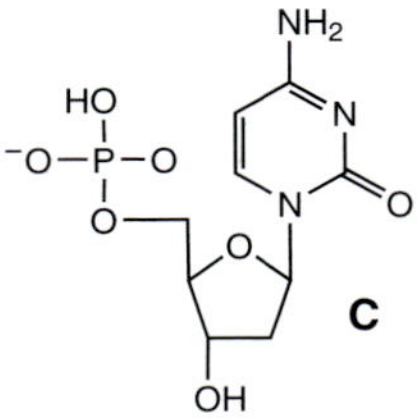

C

2'-desoxycytidine-
5'-monophosphate

Selected ribonucleotides

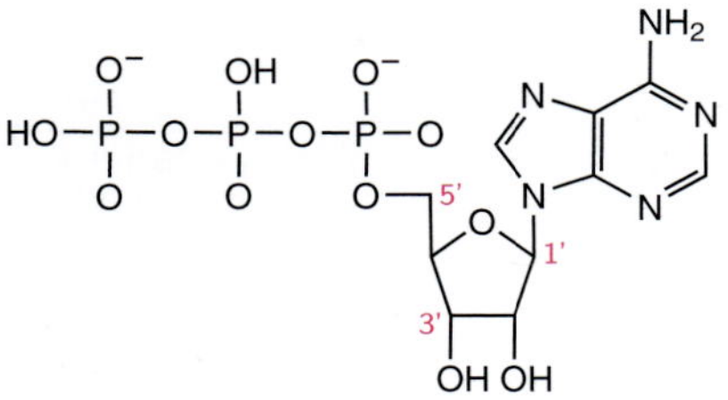

adenosine-5'-triphosphate ATP:
the most important short-term
energy storage in cells

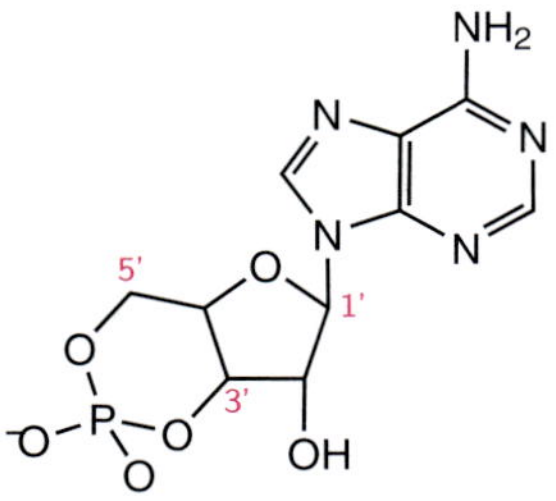

cyclic adenosine-5',3'-monophosphate cAMP:
intracellular second messenger transferring
the effect of some hormones in the blood

Biochemistry
CHEMISTRY

NADH ⇌ NAD$^+$ + H$^+$ + 2e$^-$

nicotinamide adenine dinucleotide NADH or nicotinamide adenine dinucleotide phosphate NADPH (with a phosphate group linked to C-2') transporting e$^-$ in biochemical reactions

Nucleotide chains and base pairing in DNA

DNA, RNA and polypetide/protein: flow of genetic information

replication: Both strands of the double helix DNA are read from 3' to 5' and from both a complementary DNA is synthesized from 5' to 3'.

transcription, e. g. synthesis of an mRNA: The non-coding antisense strand (template) is read from 3' to 5' and the mRNA is synthesized from 5' to 3'.

antisense strand (template) of the double helix DNA at transcription

sense strand (coding) of the double helix DNA at transcription

mRNA

tRNA

translation (synthesis of a protein): The ribosome reads the mRNA from 5' to 3' and synthesizes the polypeptide chain progressively from the H_2N end to the COOH end. On the ribosome the aminoacyl-tRNA with the anticoden binds on the codon (base triplet) of the mRNA.

Biochemistry
CHEMISTRY

Genetic code

The position of an amino acid in a protein (primary structure) is coded by the sequence of three nucleotides in the mRNA (triplet or codon).

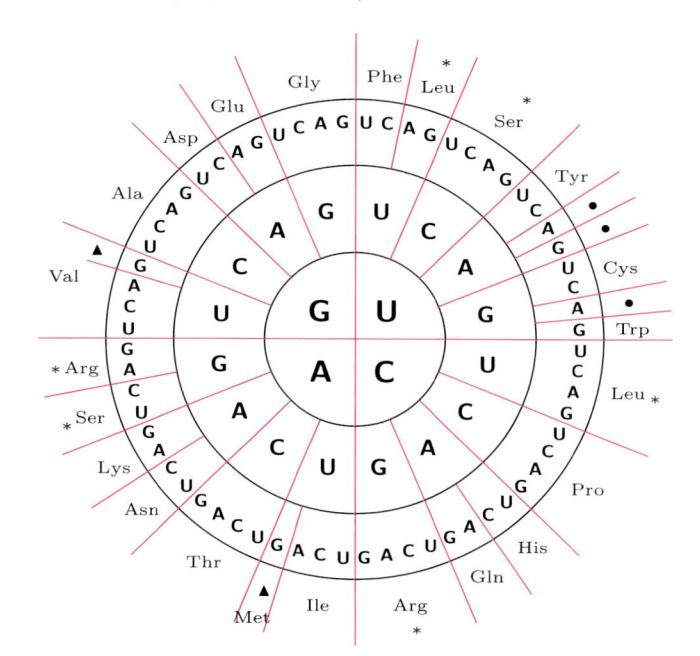

G = guanine
C = cytosine
A = adenine
U = uracil
(T = thymine)

In the figure the codons are read from the inner circle (5') to the outer circle (3'). They specify the base sequences of the mRNA codons assigned to the amino acids outside the circle.

- * amino acid appearing twice
- • stop (termination) codons ⇒ end of chain
- ▲ start (initiation) codons at the beginning of a translation always insert Met (rarely Val); codons in the middle of messenger insert the amino acids corresponding to their genetic codes.

243

8 Instrumental Analysis

Spectrum of visible light described by the RGB/CMY colour model

wavelength interval	colour at light emission	complementary colour at light absorption
400–420 nm	magenta	green
420–470 nm	blue	yellow
470–500 nm	cyan	red
500–560 nm	green	magenta
560–590 nm	yellow	blue
590–610 nm	orange	blue-cyan
610–700 nm	red	cyan

UV-VIS-spectrometry

Coloured substances absorb visible light (VIS). We observe the colour resulting from the remaining spectrum. Usually this is the so-called complementary colour. Substances can also absorb ultra-violet light UV, but they are not coloured in this case. The energy of the absorbed electromagnetic radiation excites electrons from the highest occupied to the lowest unoccupied energy level of the corresponding molecule or the complex.

In complexes of transition metals the electrons change between d-orbitals of different energy levels, caused by geometrically different orbital-ligand-repulsion.

In organic molecules transition takes place mostly between π molecular orbitals. There are three possibilities:
- No absorption above 220 nm: molecules with single bonds and without aromatic systems, π systems or conjugated double bonds → colourless substances
- Absorption between 220 nm and 400 nm, no absorption above 400 nm: molecules with small aromatic or π systems and with few conjugated double bonds
  → colourless but UV-absorbing substances
- Absorption above 400 nm: molecules with larger aromatic or π systems and with more conjugated double bonds, especially with heteroatoms (n-electrons)
  → coloured substances

Beer-Lambert law

Relation between the concentration c of an absorbing coloured substance and the absorption A

absorption (extinction) A_λ of light at wavelength λ: $\quad A_\lambda = \log_{10} \dfrac{I_0}{I} = \varepsilon_\lambda \cdot c \cdot d$

I: intensity of transmitted light
I_0: intensity of incident light
c: concentration of the absorbing substance in solution
ε_λ: molar absorption coefficient (extinction coefficient) at wavelength λ
d: path length

Instrumental Analysis

Infrared spectrometry

Electromagnetic radiation energy in the IR range makes groups of bonded atoms vibrate and oscillate. Oscillating in the direction of the bond is called stretching, transverse to the bond bending. IR spectrometry allows not only finding functional groups but also differentiating and identifying different substances in the so-called fingerprint-region (1500−600 cm^{-1}). The energy of the absorbed IR radiation is proportional to the spectroscopic wavenumber $\tilde{\nu}$ in cm^{-1}. The wavelength is then $\lambda = 1/\tilde{\nu}$ (in cm!).

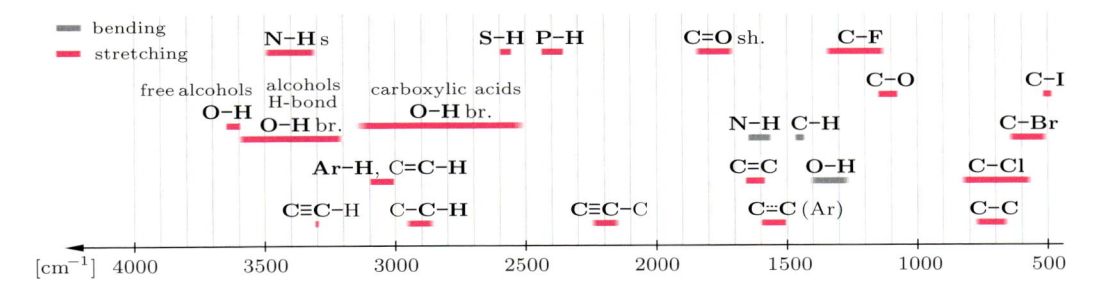

^{1}H Nuclear magnetic resonance spectrometry (^{1}H NMR)

The spin of the ^{1}H nucleus aligns itself parallel to an external magnetic field. Radio waves can invert the spin (nuclear resonance) so that the alignment becomes anti-parallel. The nuclear resonance is affected by the chemical neighbourhood of the ^{1}H atom and the strength of the applied external magnetic field.

The **chemical shift** δ measures this effect in ppm (parts per million). The strongly shielded ^{1}H-atoms in tetramethylsilane $Si(CH_3)_4$ serve as a reference (0 ppm). The weaker the shielding, e.g. near electronegative atoms, the larger the chemical shift.

A **coupling** is observed between spins of vicinal ^{1}H atoms and, as a consequence, information about the number and the distribution of the ^{1}H atoms can be deduced.

The **integral** of the signals indicates the proportion of chemically identical ^{1}H atoms responsible for the signal.

The **signal width** shows the exchange rate of the ^{1}H atoms with the solvent, hence their acidity.

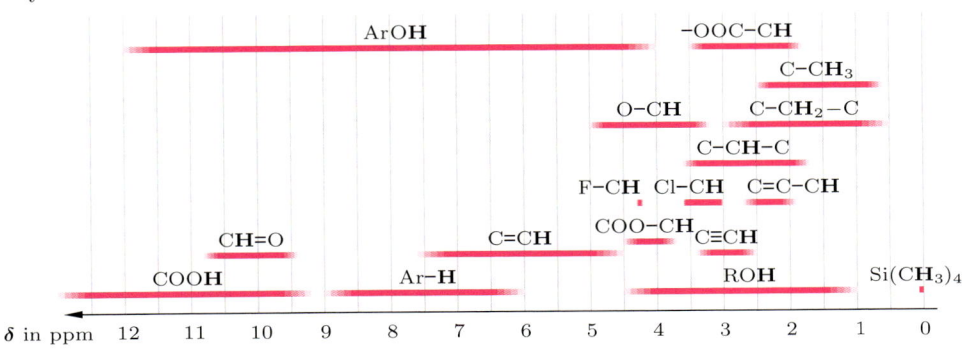

^{13}C Nuclear magnetic resonance spectrometry (^{13}C NMR)

The spin of the ^{13}C nucleus aligns itself parallel to an external magnetic field. Radio waves can invert the spin (nuclear resonance) so that the alignment becomes anti-parallel. The nuclear resonance is affected by the chemical neighbourhood of the ^{13}C atom and the strength of the applied external magnetic field.

The **chemical shift δ** measures this effect in ppm (parts per million). The strongly shielded ^{13}C atoms in tetramethylsilane Si(CH$_3$)$_4$ serve as a reference (0 ppm). The weaker the shielding, e. g. near electronegative atoms, the larger the chemical shift.

Decoupling: The coupling with the magnetically active ^{1}H atoms can be neutralized. There are also coupled spectra. They indicate the number of ^{1}H atoms bonded to a C atom.

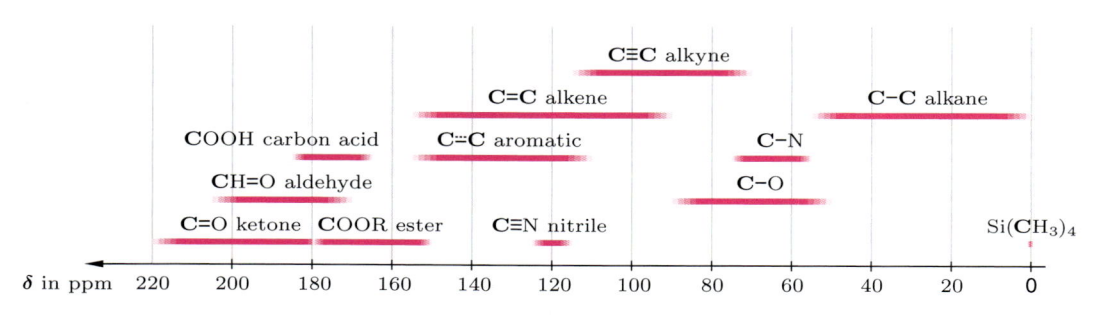

					C≡C alkyne					
				C=C alkene				C–C alkane		
	COOH carbon acid		C≃C aromatic			C–N				
	CH=O aldehyde					C–O				
	C=O ketone	COOR ester		C≡N nitrile					Si(CH$_3$)$_4$	
δ in ppm	220	200	180	160	140	120	100	80	60	40	20	0

Mass spectrometry

In mass spectrometry particles of substances are ionized and accelerated in an electric field. The resulting deviation depends on the inertia of the mass and the charge of the particle, from which the mass-to-charge ratio of the particle can be calculated. The following signals are important for the analysis: The molecular ion M, sometimes the ion $M+1$ (with an additional mass of 1 u after addition of H$^+$) and fragment ions from the disintegration. The isotope pattern of polyisotopic elements such as Cl, Br or I also appears in the mass distribution of the fragments.

Instrumental Analysis
CHEMISTRY

Qualitative analysis of substances, ions and functional groups (selected methods)

Na, Li, Ca, Sr, Cu (basically all elements, likewise in compounds)	flame colour	halogen alkanes (halogen = F, Cl, Br, I)	BEILSTEIN test: heating with a copper wire gives a green flame colour
$Cl^-_{(aq)}$, $Br^-_{(aq)}$, $I^-_{(aq)}$	precipitation of $AgCl_{(s)}$, $AgBr_{(s)}$, $AgI_{(s)}$ with $AgNO_{3(aq)}$	alkenes, alkynes	addition of bromine Br_2 (in the dark)
$SO_4^{2-}{}_{(aq)}$	precipitation of $BaSO_{4(s)}$ with $BaCl_{(aq)}$	C in organic substances	$CO_{2(aq)}$ from combustion or $C_{(s)}$ (carbon black) from incomplete combustion
$CO_3^{2-}{}_{(aq)}$	formation of CO_2 after addition of hydrochloric acid, precipitation of $CaCO_{3(s)}$ with $Ca(OH)_{2(aq)}$, or $BaCO_{3(s)}$ with $BaCl_{(aq)}$	aromatic compounds (e.g. on thin layer chromatography)	UV-absorption (together with other methods)
$O_{2(g)}$	glowing splint test	starch	blue-black complex with iodide/iodine-solution
$H_{2(g)}$	combustion of oxyhydrogen (knallgas)	amino acids/proteins	biuret test: blue-violet complex with Cu^{2+}-ions xanthoproteic reaction
$CO_{2(g)}$	precipitation of $CaCO_{3(s)}$ with $Ca(OH)_{2(aq)}$ or $BaCO_{3(s)}$ with $Ba(OH)_{2(aq)}$ candle test	reducing sugars, e.g. glucose	FEHLING (reduction of Cu^{2+}) or TOLLENS reaction (reduction of Ag^+) or reduction of Mn(VII)
$I_{2(aq)}$ ($+ I^-_{(aq)} \rightarrow I^-_{3(aq)}$)	blue-black complex with starch	nitrate, water hardness, glucose and a lot of other substances and ions	highly selective test strips

9 Acids and Bases

Table of acids and bases

pK_S	acid		base		pK_B
*−10	$HClO_4$	perchloric acid	ClO_4^-	perchlorate	*24
*−10	HI	hydrogen iodide	I^-	iodide	*24
*−9	HBr	hydrogen bromide	Br^-	bromide	*23
*−6	HCl	hydrogen chloride	Cl^-	chloride	*20
*−3	H_2SO_4	sulfuric acid	HSO_4^-	hydrogen sulfate	*17
−1.3	HNO_3	nitric acid	NO_3^-	nitrate	15.3
**	H_3O^+	hydroxonium	H_2O	water	**
0	$HClO_3$	chloric acid	ClO_3^-	chlorate	14.0
1.9	H_2SO_3	sulfurous acid	HSO_3^-	hydrogen sulfite	12.1
1.9	HSO_4^-	hydrogen sulfate	SO_4^{2-}	sulfate	12.1
2.1	H_3PO_4	phosphoric acid	$H_2PO_4^-$	dihydrogen phosphate	11.9
2.2	$[Fe(H_2O)_6]^{3+}$	hexaaqua iron (III)	$[FeOH(H_2O)_5]^{2+}$	pentaaquahydroxy-Fe	11.8
3.1	H_3Cit	citric acid	H_2Cit^-	dihydrogen citrate	10.9
3.3	HNO_2	nitrous acid	NO_2^-	nitrite	10.7
3.8	HCOOH	formic acid	$HCOO^-$	formate	10.2
4.0	$H_2C_6H_6O_6$	ascorbic acid (vit. C)	$HC_6H_6O_6^-$	hydrogen ascorbate	10.0
4.2	C_6H_5COOH	benzoic acid	$C_6H_5COO^-$	benzoate	9.8
4.8	CH_3COOH	acetic acid	H_3CCOO^-	acetate	9.2
4.8	H_2Cit^-	dihydrogen citrate	$HCit^{2-}$	hydrogen citrate	9.2
5.0	$[Al(H_2O)_6]^{3+}$	hexaaqua Al (III)	$[AlOH(H_2O)_5]^{2+}$	pentaaquahydroxy-Al	9.0
6.4	$HCit^{2-}$	hydrogen citrate	Cit^{3-}	citrate	7.6
*6.4	H_2CO_3	carbonic acid	HCO_3^-	hydrogen carbonate	*7.6
7.1	H_2S	hydrogen sulfide	HS^-	hydrosulfide	6.9
7.2	HSO_3^-	hydrogen sulfite	SO_3^{2-}	sulfite	6.8
7.2	$H_2PO_4^-$	dihydrogen phosphate	HPO_4^{2-}	hydrogen phosphate	6.8
9.2	NH_4^+	ammonium	NH_3	ammonia	4.8
9.2	HCN	hydrogen cyanide	CN^-	cyanide	4.8
10.0	C_6H_5OH	phenol	$C_6H_5O^-$	phenolate	4
10.4	HCO_3^-	hydrogen carbonate	CO_3^{2-}	carbonate	3.6
11.6	H_2O_2	hydrogen peroxide	HO_2^-	hydroperoxide	2.4
11.8	$HC_6H_6O_6^-$	hydrogen ascorbate	$C_6H_6O_6^{2-}$	ascorbate	2.2
12.3	HPO_4^{2-}	hydrogen phosphate	PO_4^{3-}	phosphate	1.7
12.9	HS^-	hydrosulfide	S^{2-}	sulfide	1.1
**	H_2O	water	OH^-	hydroxide	**
*16	C_2H_5OH	ethanol	$C_2H_5O^-$	ethanolate	*−2
*19	CH_3COCH_3	acetone	$CH_3COCH_2^-$	acetonate	*−5
*23	NH_3	ammonia	NH_2^-	dihydrogennitride	*−9
*24	OH^-	hydroxide	O^{2-}	oxide	*−10
*34	CH_4	methane	CH_3^-	trihydrogencarbide	*−20
*40	H_2	hydrogen	H^-	hydride	*−26

acid-base pairs in water at standard conditions 25 °C, 1013 hPa and concentration 1 mol·L^{-1}

acid strength $pK_A = -\log_{10} K_A$, base strength $pK_B = -\log_{10} K_B$ p. 220 ◀

* approximate values

** Water in aqueous solutions has no standard concentration, consequently no strengths are indicated.

front cover ◀ transition range of pH-indicators

10 Redox Reactions

Table of reducing and oxidizing agents with standard electrode potentials

standard reduction potential in V	reducing agent	oxidizing agent	
-3.04	Li	Li^+	$+1\,e^-$
-2.93	K	K^+	$+1\,e^-$
-2.87	Ca	Ca^{2+}	$+2\,e^-$
-2.71	Na	Na^+	$+1\,e^-$
-2.37	Mg	Mg^{2+}	$+2\,e^-$
-1.66	Al	Al^{3+}	$+3\,e^-$
-1.18	Mn	Mn^{2+}	$+2\,e^-$
-0.83	$H_2 + 2\,OH^-$	$2\,H_2O \qquad pH\ 14\ (2)$	$+2\,e^-$
-0.76	Zn	Zn^{2+}	$+2\,e^-$
-0.74	Cr	Cr^{3+}	$+3\,e^-$
*-0.58	$CH_3CHO + H_2O$	$CH_3COOH + 2\,H^+$	$+2\,e^-$
-0.48	$HS^- + OH^-$	$S + H_2O$	$+2\,e^-$
-0.45	Fe	Fe^{2+}	$+2\,e^-$
*-0.41	$H_2 + 2\,OH^-$	$2\,H_2O \qquad pH\ 7\ (2)$	$+2\,e^-$
*-0.34	2 cysteine	cystine (disulfide) $+ 2\,H^+$	$+2\,e^-$
*-0.32	NADH	$NAD^+ + H^+$	$+2\,e^-$
*-0.32	NADPH	$NADP^+ + H^+$	$+2\,e^-$
-0.26	Ni	Ni^{2+}	$+2\,e^-$
*-0.20	CH_3CH_2OH	$CH_3CHO + 2\,H^+$	$+2\,e^-$
*-0.19	lactate $CH_3CHOHCOO^-$	pyruvate $CH_3COCOO^- + 2\,H^+$	$+2\,e^-$
-0.14	Sn	Sn^{2+}	$+2\,e^-$
-0.13	Pb	Pb^{2+}	$+2\,e^-$
*-0.08	$Cu_2O + 2\,OH^- + H_2O$	$2\,Cu(OH)_2$	$+2\,e^-$
-0.04	Fe	Fe^{3+}	$+3\,e^-$
0	H_2	$2\,H^+ \qquad pH\ 0\ (2)$	$+2\,e^-$
*0.06	$H_2C_6H_6O_6$ (Vit. C)	$C_6H_6O_6 + 2\,H^+$	$+2\,e^-$
*0.07	cytochrome b (+2)	cytochrome b (+3)	$+1\,e^-$
0.14	H_2S	$S + 2\,H^+$	$+2\,e^-$
0.15	Cu^+	Cu^{2+}	$+1\,e^-$
*0.22	cytochrome c (+2)	cytochrome c (+3)	$+1\,e^-$
0.34	Cu	Cu^{2+}	$+2\,e^-$
0.40	$4\,OH^- \qquad pH\ 14\ (1)$	$O_2 + 2\,H_2O$	$+4\,e^-$
0.40	$S_2O_3^{2-} + 3\,H_2O$	$2\,H_2SO_3 + 2\,H^+$	$+4\,e^-$
0.42	$Cl_2 + 4\,OH^-$	$2\,ClO^- + 2\,H_2O$	$+2\,e^-$
*0.49	$Ni(OH)_2(s) + OH^-$	$NiOOH(s) + H_2O$	$+1\,e^-$
0.54	$2\,I^-$	I_2	$+2\,e^-$
0.60	$MnO_2 + 4\,OH^-$	$MnO_4^- + 2\,H_2O$	$+3\,e^-$
0.60	$2\,S + 3\,H_2O$	$S_2O_3^{2-} + 6\,H^+$	$+4\,e^-$
*0.74	$2\,MnOOH\,(s) + 2\,OH^-$	$2\,MnO_2(s) + 2\,H_2O(l)$	$+2\,e^-$
0.77	Fe^{2+}	Fe^{3+}	$+1\,e^-$
0.80	Ag	Ag^+	$+1\,e^-$
0.81	$Cl^- + 2\,OH^-$	$ClO^- + H_2O$	$+2\,e^-$
*0.82	$2\,H_2O \qquad pH\ 7\ (1)$	$O_2 + 4\,H^+$	$+4\,e^-$
0.85	Hg	Hg^{2+}	$+2\,e^-$
0.96	$NO + 2\,H_2O$	$HNO_3 + 3\,H^+$	$+3\,e^-$

Redox Reactions

standard reduction potential in V	reducing agent	oxidizing agent	
1.07	$2\,Br^-$	Br_2	$+2\,e^-$
1.18	Pt	Pt^{2+}	$+2\,e^-$
1.22	$Mn^{2+} + 2\,H_2O$	$MnO_2 + 4\,H^+$	$+2\,e^-$
1.23	$2\,H_2O \qquad pH\ 0\ (1)$	$O_2 + 4\,H^+$	$+4\,e^-$
1.36	$2\,Cr^{3+} + 7\,H_2O$	$Cr_2O_7^{2-} + 14\,H^+$	$+6\,e^-$
1.36	$2\,Cl^-$	Cl_2	$+2\,e^-$
1.45	$Cl^- + 3\,H_2O$	$ClO_3^- + 6\,H^+$	$+6\,e^-$
1.46	$Pb^{2+} + 2\,H_2O$	$PbO_2 + 4\,H^+$	$+2\,e^-$
1.50	Au	Au^{3+}	$+3\,e^-$
1.51	$Mn^{2+} + 4\,H_2O$	$MnO_4^- + 8\,H^+$	$+5\,e^-$
*1.68	$PbSO_4(s) + 2\,H_2O$	$PbO_2(s) + SO_4^{2-} + 4\,H^+$	$+2\,e^-$
1.78	$2\,H_2O$	$H_2O_2 + 2\,H^+$	$+2\,e^-$
2.01	$2\,SO_4^{2-}$	$S_2O_8^{2-}$	$+2\,e^-$
2.08	$H_2O + O_2$	$O_3 + 2\,H^+$	$+2\,e^-$
2.87	$2\,F^-$	F_2	$+2\,e^-$

Redox pairs in water at standard conditions 25 °C, 1013 hPa and concentration $1\ mol \cdot L^{-1}$.
Exceptions: oxidation (1) or reduction (2) of water and reactions in galvanic cells and biochemistry (*, $E°'$). p. 237 ◀ Biochemistry

Index

A

ABEL-RUFFINI 24
ABELian group 25
absolute
— error 64, 184
— frequency 116
— magnitude 208
— value (in $\mathbb{C}$) 19
— value (in $\mathbb{R}$) 15
absorbed dose 183
absorption 11
acceleration 156
— average $\sim$ 155
— instantaneous $\sim$ 155
— of free fall 204, 209
acid 220, 248
— strength 248
acid-base
— pair 250
— reaction 233
acidity constant 220
acoustics 166
activation energy 221
activity 183
actuarial life tables 152
acute 104
addition (Chemistry) 233
addition law 118
additive
— food $\sim$ 239
additivity 28
adjacency matrix 49
adjacent 46
affine
— linear function 22
— transformation 55
— transformation (plane) 111
— transformation (space) 112
affinity 111
alcohol 233
aldehyde 233
algebra
— σ-algebra 117
algebraic structure 25
algorithm
— EUCLID's $\sim$ 36
— GAUSS 135
— systematic doubling 140
alkane 233
alkene 233
alkyne 233
altitude 86, 93

amide 233
amine 233
amino acid 238, 242, 243
ammonium 233
amount
— concentration 219
— of substance 170
ampere (unit) 185
amplitude 160
analysis of curves 65
angle
— bisector 86, 87
— of elevation 156
— of intersection 101, 107
— radian measure 91
Ångström 185
angular
— acceleration 162
— displacement 162
— impulse 161
— momentum 161, 163
— velocity 155, 162
anhydride 233
antibaryon 195
antiderivative 71
antiparticle 195
antisense strand 242
antisymmetric 12
aphelion 160
APOLLONIUS 85
apparent
— magnitude 208
— power 179
approximation 64, 81, 136
— by normal distribution 123
— error 64
— function 66
arc length 75, 92
arccosine function 59
arcsine function 58
arctangent function 59
area
— integral 75
— law (KEPLER) 160
— of upper base 93
— surface of revolution 75
— under curve 72
argument 13
arithmetic
— mean 16, 39, 81, 115, 116
— progression 39
— sequence 39

aromatic compounds 233
ARRHENIUS equation 221
associativity 9, 11, 13, 25
astroid 68
astronomical unit 205
asymptote 59, 66, 78
— (hyperbola) 109
— horizontal $\sim$ 57
— oblique $\sim$ 57
— vertical $\sim$ 57
asymptotic function 66
atm 186
atomic
— mass (radioactive nuclide) 199
— mass (stable nuclides) 196
— mass unit 218
— radius 230
— structure 226
ATP 240
attenuation coefficient 201
attribute 124
autoprotolysis (water) 220
average rate of change 62
AVOGADRO constant 218
axioms of KOLMOGOROV 117
azimuthal quantum number 227

B

ballistic trajectory 156
bar 186
barometric formula 164
barycentric formula 134
baryon 195
base 248
— (Chemistry) 220
— pairing 241
— sequence 243
— strength 248
— triplet 242
— unit (Physics) 185
basicity constant 220
basis 26
— canonical $\sim$ 27
— standard $\sim$ 27
— vector 28
BAYES 119
BEER-LAMBERT law 244
behaviour at infinity 57
BERNOULLI 81, 165
BERNOULLI-L'HOPITAL 61
biconditional 9

Index

bijective 13
binary logarithm 17
binding energy 201
BINET-CAUCHY identity 105
binomial
— coefficient 20, 42
— distribution 121, 150
— expansion 20
— product 20
— test 126
— theorem 43
Biochemistry 237
BIOT-SAVART law 177
bisection 138
bisector 86
bivariate data 116
black body 182
BOHR model of the hydrogen atom 182
boiling point 191, 228
bond
— enthalpy 224
— length 224
boson 196
bottom quark 195
bounded 51
— function 54
box plot 115
brachistochrone 69
BRAHMAGUPTA 90
brightness 208
BROGLIE 182
buffer solutions 220
buoyancy 164

C

calculus 51
— fundamental theorem 71
— mean value theorem 64
calorie 186
cAMP 240
candela 185
canonical basis 27
capacitance 174
capacitor discharge 175
carat 186
carbohydrate 237
carboxylate 233
carboxylic acid 233
CARDANO 23
cardinality (set) 12, 14
cardioid 68
CARNOT 172
carrying capacity 67
Cartesian
— form 18

— product 12
casus irreducibilis 23
catenary 69
CAUCHY-SCHWARZ inequality 81, 104
CAVALIERI 92
ceiling function 15
Celsius 170, 186
central angle 85, 90
Central European Time 206
centre of mass 76, 86, 106, 161
centrifugal force 159
centripetal
— acceleration 156
— force 159
centroid 86
CEVA 84
chain rule 63
change of base 17
characteristic
— equation 41, 82
— polynomial 32
charm quark 195
CHEBYSHEV 121
chemical equilibrium 219
chi-squared distribution 123, 151
Chinese
— postman problem 50
— remainder theorem 37
chord 85, 92
chromatic number 50
circle 92, 102
— theorem 85
circuit 46
circular frequency 160, 166
circumcentre 86
circumference 92
circumradius 86–88
circumsphere 95
class 116
closed
— curve 76
— path 46
code, genetic 243
codomain 13
codon 242
coefficient
— attenuation $\sim$ 201
— matrix 34
— of binomials 20
— of friction 157, 189
— of linear expansion 190
— of rolling resistance 157
— of variation 115
— of volume expansion 191

cofactor 31
collinear vectors 103
collision
— elastic 159
— inelastic 159
column
— space 28
— vector 28
combination 45
combinatorics 44
comet 214
common
— divisor 35
— logarithm 17
— multiple 35
commutative group 25
commutativity 9, 11
comparison test 53
complement 11
complementary colour 244
complete graph 47
complex
— conjugate 19
— number 14, 18
— plane 18
component
— scalar $\sim$ 107
— vector $\sim$ 107
composition 13
— functional $\sim$ 13
— of two functions 54
compound pendulum 160
compressibility 188
compression 164
concave 65
concentration
— of substance 219
condensation 170, 233
— point 191
conditional probability 119
conductance, electrical 176
conductivity, electrical 176
cone 94
confidence interval 126
— for expected value 128
congruence
— modulo 37
— theorem 88
congruent modulo 37
conic section 108, 109
conjunction 9
connected graph 47
conservation of
— angular momentum 161
— energy 158
— momentum 157

252

Index

constant
— factor rule 63
— of integration 71
continued fraction 52
continuity 61
— equation 165
continuously differentiable 62
contradiction 10
contrapositive 9
contrary hypothesis 125
convergence criterion 51, 53
converse 9
convex 65, 89
coordinate
— Cartesian ∼s 113, 114
— cylindrical polar ∼s 114
— equation of the plane 106
— polar ∼s 113
— spherical polar ∼s 114
— transformation 113
Coordinated Universal Time 206
coplanar vectors 103
coriolis force 159
correlation coefficient 116
cosecant 97
cosine 97
— function 59
— rule 87
— rule for angles 100
— rule for sides 100
cotangent 97
COULOMB 173
covariance 116
CRAMER's rule 33
critical
— density 191
— pressure 191
— temperature 191
— value 151, 152
cross
— product 104
— sectional area 75
cube 93, 95
curie (unit) 186
current density, electric 175
curvature 65
curve
— JORDAN ∼ 76
— plane ∼ 66
cycle 46
cyclic
— adenosine-5',3'-monophosphate 240
— group 25, 38
— quadrilateral 90

cycloalkane 233
cycloid 68
cylinder 93
cylindrical polar coordinate 114

D

damped oscillation 82
data
— bivariate ∼ 116
— univariate ∼ 115
DE LA VALLÉE POUSSIN 36
DE MOIVRE 18
DE MORGAN 9, 11
decay
— chain 202
— exponential ∼ 82
— radioactive ∼ 122, 199
decomposition 12
definite integral 70
degree of freedom 123
dehydrogenation 233
delay law, radioactivity 183
density (of)
— (mass) 157
— chemical elements 228
— common gases 187
— common solids 187
— critical ∼ 191
— liquids 187
dependent variable 13
derangement 45
derivative 62
— function 63
— higher order ∼ 63
— of a power series 77
— of elementary function 65
— of the inverse function 63
— partial ∼ 63
— rules of differentiation 63
DESCARTES 21, 24
determinant 31
DFT 143
diagonal
— matrix 30
— number of ∼s 91
diagonalizable matrix 30
dielectric constant 195
difference
— quotient 62
— sequence 38
— set 11
differentiable 62
differential equation 81, 142
differentiation 62
diffraction 168
dimension 26

dipole moment
— electric ∼ 173
— magnetic ∼ 177
direct
— proof 10
— proportionality 15
direction
— cosine 114
— field 142
— vector 67, 106
directrix 109, 110
DIRICHLET 36
discontinuity 66
discret FOURIER transform 143
discriminant 22, 23
disjoint 11, 117
disjunction 9
displacement vector 106
distance
— line–line 108
— plane–plane 108
— point–line 107
— point–plane 108
— point–point 107
distribution
— POISSON ∼ 122
— binomial ∼ 121
— chi-squared ∼ 123, 151
— hypergeometric ∼ 122
— in tests 123
— normal ∼ 123
— of random variable 119
— prime numbers 36
distributivity 9, 11, 25
division
— harmonic ∼ 83
— of a line segment 101
divisor 36, 37
— greatest common ∼ 35, 36
DNA 240, 241
dodecahedron 95
domain 13, 54
— of validity 81
dome 96
DOPPLER effect
— acoustic 169
— optical 169
— relativistic 181
dose equivalent 183
dot product 104
double
— helix 241
— right circular cone 110
down quark 195
drag 165
— coefficient 189

dual graph 49
dwarf planets 212
dynamic lift 165

E
e 52
E-numbers 239
Earth 209
eccentricity 109, 110, 160, 212
edge 46
— length 95
effective
— dose 183
— value 179
efficiency 158
— Carnot $\sim$ 172
eigenbasis 32
eigenspace 32
eigenvalue 32
eigenvector 32
elastic
— force 157
— modulus 187
elasticity 164
electric
— current 175
— dipole moment 173
— displacement 173
— field 173
electrochemistry 220
electromagnetic wave 166
electron 195, 218
— energy 182
— volt 186
element
— chemical $\sim$ 228
— identity $\sim$ 25
— inverse $\sim$ 25
elementary
— event 117
— particle 195
elimination 233
— algorithm (GAUSS) 135
— conditional $\sim$ 10
— of biconditional operator 10
— of material conditional operator 10
ellipse 108–110
ellipsoid 96
emf 178
emissivity 190
energy 158
— GIBBS $\sim$ 221
— charged capacitor 175
— charged particle 174
— current-carrying coil 179

— density 164
— density (electric field) 175
— density (flux) 166
— density (magnetic field) 179
— internal $\sim$ 221
— kinetic $\sim$ 158
— kinetic $\sim$, relativistic 181
— level of electron in atom 227
— nutrient/food 239
— of ionization 226
— photon $\sim$ 182
— potential $\sim$ 158, 161
— rotational $\sim$ 163
— stretched spring 158
— total relativistic 181
enthalpy 221
— bond $\sim$ 224
— free $\sim$ 221
— free bond $\sim$ 222
— hydration $\sim$ 224
— lattice $\sim$ 224
— of dissolution (salt) 224
— of formation ΔH_f^0 222
— of reaction ΔH_r^0 222, 224
entropy 171
— S^0 222
— change 221
— of reaction ΔS_r^0 222
equality (of)
— functions 13, 54
— sets 11
equation (of)
— NERNST 220
— 4th degree 24
— a circle 102
— a plane 106
— ARRHENIUS $\sim$ 221
— buffer 220
— characteristic $\sim$ 82
— continuity $\sim$ 165
— cubic $\sim$ 23
— degree n 22
— differential $\sim$ 81
— GIBBS-HELMHOLTZ 221
— HENDERSON-HASSELBALCH $\sim$ 220
— higher degree 24
— linear differential $\sim$ 82
— monic form 22, 23
— quadratic $\sim$ 22
— quartic $\sim$ 24
— reduced form 23
— SCHRÖDINGER $\sim$ 182
— time 206
equilateral triangle 88
equilibrium

— chemical 219
— constant 219, 221
— criteria 162
equivalence 9
— class 12
— relation 12
error
— absolute $\sim$ 64
— bound 64
— propagation 64
— relative $\sim$ 64
ester 233
estimation (parameters) 124
ether 233
EUCLID 88
EUCLID's algorithm 36
EULER method 142
EULER's
— formula 18, 49
— identity 18
— line 86
— number 52
— polyhedron formula 95
— totient function 37
EULERian circuit 48
EULER-FERMAT 37
EULER-MASCHERONI constant 52
even function 54
event 117
excircle
— radius 87
— tangent 86
existential quantifier 10
expansion
— binomial $\sim$ 20
expectation 120
expected value 120
explanatory variable 132
explicit definition 38
exponent 56
exponential
— decay 82
— form ($\mathbb{C}$) 18
— function 52, 58
— growth 67, 82
exposure 183
exradius 88
extension 66
exterification 233
exterior
— angle 86
— point 83
extinction 244
extrema 65

Index

F

face 49
factor
— rule 71
— theorem 21
factorials 42
factorization 20
Fahrenheit 186
FARADAY 178
fat 237
fatty acid 237
FERMAT 37
FERRARI 24
FIBONACCI numbers 41
field 14, 25, 38
— electric $\sim$ 173
— magnetic $\sim$ 177
finite group 25
fixed
— point 111
— star 214, 215
floor function 15
flux
— density (magnetic) 177
— electric $\sim$ 173
— magnetic $\sim$ 178
focal
— length 167
— parameter 109
focus 109, 110
folium of DESCARTES 69
food
— additive 239
— energy 239
foot 185
force 157, 181
— external $\sim$ 161
— inner $\sim$ 161
— magnetic $\sim$ 177
— resultant $\sim$ 157
formation constant
— metal complex 232
formula (of)
— barometric $\sim$ 164
— BRAHMAGUPTA 90
— CARDANO 23
— EULER 18, 49
— EULER's polyhedron $\sim$ 95
— HERON 87
— polyhedron $\sim$ 95
— reduction $\sim$ 99
— STIRLING 81
— VIETA 23, 24
four colour theorem 50
FOURIER
— series 80
— transform 143
fraction
— continued $\sim$ 52
free
— bond enthalpy ΔG_f^0 222
— electrons (concentration) 195
— enthalpy 221
— fall 204, 209
freezing point 191
frequency 155, 160
— absolute 116
— relative 116
friction 189
frustrum 94
function 13, 38, 54
— affine linear $\sim$ 22
— approximation $\sim$ 66
— arccosine 59
— arcsine 58
— arctangent 59
— asymptotic $\sim$ 66
— ceiling $\sim$ 15
— cosine 59
— derivative $\sim$ 63
— exponential $\sim$ 58
— floor $\sim$ 15
— growth $\sim$ 67
— hyperbolic $\sim$ 60
— hyperbolic cosine 60
— hyperbolic sine 60
— hyperbolic tangent 60
— identity $\sim$ 54
— in two variables 63
— integrable $\sim$ 70
— inverse hyperbolic $\sim$ 60
— inverse hyperbolic cosine 60
— inverse hyperbolic sine 60
— inverse hyperbolic tangent 60
— inverse trigonometric $\sim$ 58
— linear $\sim$ 22
— logarithmic $\sim$ 58
— natural exponential $\sim$ 58
— partial derivative 63
— polynomial $\sim$ 57
— power $\sim$ 56
— quadratic $\sim$ 22
— rational $\sim$ 57
— real $\sim$ 54
— series expansions 77
— signum $\sim$ 15
— sine 58
— special limit 62
— tangent 59
— totient 37
— trigonometric $\sim$ 58
— value 54
functional
— group 233
— value 13
fundamental theorem
— of algebra 21
— of arithmetic 36
— of calculus 71
fusion reaction 200

G

gallon 185
galvanic cell 250
gas
— law of ideal $\sim$ 218
— mean translational kinetic energy 171
GAUSS 21, 36, 178
— (unit) 186
— linear least squares 136
GAUSSian
— function 123
— quadrature 140
gcd 35, 36
generatrix 110
genetic code 243
genetics
— antisense strand (template) 242
— flow of genetic information 242
— replication (DNA) 242
— ribosome 242
— sense strand (coding) 242
— transcription (in mRNA) 242
— translation 242
geocentric gravitational constant 209
geomagnetic field data 204
geometric
— mean 16, 40, 81
— mean theorem 88
— progression 40
— sequence 40
— series 40, 53
geophysical data 204
GIBBS-HELMHOLTZ 221
gluon 196
golden ratio 83
GRAM-SCHMIDT 108
graph 46, 47
— edge-labelled 48
— of a function 54
— theory 46
— vertex-labelled 48
grating
— diffraction $\sim$ 168

gravitational
— constant 160
— field 158
— force 157, 161
— potential 161
graviton 196
great circle 100
greatest common divisor 35
group 25, 111
— ABELian $\sim$ 25
— commutative $\sim$ 25
— cyclic $\sim$ 25, 38
— finite $\sim$ 25
— order 25
growth
— bounded $\sim$ 67
— exponential $\sim$ 67, 82
— function 67

H

HADAMARD 36
hadron 195
HAGEN-POISEUILLE 165
half life 183, 199
half-angle substitution 99
half-value layer 183
haloalkane 233
HAMILTONian cycle 48
handshaking lemma 48
harmonic
— division 83
— mean 16
— oscillator 160
— series 52
— wave 166
heat capacity (molar) 170
heat of
— condensation 170
— fusion 170, 190
— vaporization 170, 191
heating value 170
height 93
HEISENBERG uncertainty
 principle 182
HELMHOLTZ coil pair 178
HERON's formula 87
HERTZSPRUNG-RUSSELL
 diagram 215
HESSE
— normal form (plane) 106
— standard form 101
higher order derivative 63
histogram 116
hole 95
homogeneity 28
homogeneous

— differential equation 82
— dilation 55
HOOKE's law 157
— for continuous media 164
horizontal
— asymptote 57, 66
— scaling 55
— translation 55
HORNER's method 133
hour angle 205
hull, linear 26
hydration enthalpy 224
hydrogenation 233
hydrolysis 233
hydrophilic 238
hydrostatic pressure 164
hyperbola 56, 108–110
hyperbolic
— cosine function 60
— function 60
— sine function 60
— spiral 68
— tangent function 60
hypergeometric distribution 122
hypothesis testing 125

I

i 18
icosahedron 95
ideal gas law 171, 218
idempotence 11
identity
— element 25
— EULER's $\sim$ 18
— mapping 13
— matrix 30
— transformation 30
— trigonometric functions 97
illuminance 168
image 13, 54
imaginary
— number 18
— part 18
— unit 18
imine 233
impedance 179, 180
implication 9
impulse 157
inch 185
incident 46
incircle 86
inclination 101
inclusion 11
inclusion-exclusion principle 45
indefinite integral 71
independent

— events 119
— variable 13
index of refraction 193
induced electromotive force 178
inductance 178
induction (proof) 10
inequality (of)
— AM-GM 81
— among means 16
— BERNOULLI 81
— CAUCHY-SCHWARZ $\sim$ 81, 104
— CHEBYSHEV 121
— triangle $\sim$ 15, 19, 81, 86
inference 124
infinite series 52
inflection point 65
inhomogeneous differential
 equation 82
initial
— condition 142
— phase 160
— value problem 142
injective 13, 54
inner product 104
inorganic chemistry 231
inradius 86–88
inscribed angle theorem 85
insphere 95
instantaneous rate of change 62
integer 14
integrable 70
integral
— definite $\sim$ 70
— function 71
— improper $\sim$ 72
— indefinite $\sim$ 71
integrand 71
integration 70
— by parts 71
intensity level (sound) 169
interaction
— electromagnetic $\sim$ 196
— strong $\sim$ 196
— weak $\sim$ 196
intercept
— form of a line 101
— form of a plane 106
— theorem 84
interior
— angle 86
— point 83
intermediate value theorem 62
interpolation
— polynomial $\sim$ 134
— with cubic splines 134
interquartile range 115

Index

intersecting chord 85
intersection 11
interval (musical) 188
invariant 111
inverse
— element 25
— function 14, 54
— hyperbolic cosine function 60
— hyperbolic function 60
— hyperbolic sine function 60
— hyperbolic tangent function 60
— image 13
— mapping 54
— matrix 30, 32
— proportionality 15
— square law 168
— trigonometric function 58
invertible
— function 54
— matrix 30, 31
involute of a circle 69
ion
— hydration enthalpy 225
ionic
— product water 220
— radius 230
ionization
— energy 226
ISA model 164
isoelectric 238
isometry 111
isomorphic graphs 47

J

JORDAN curve 76
JOULE heating 176

K

Kelvin 185, 186
KEPLER's
— Fassregel 140
— law 160
ker 28
kernel 28, 32
ketone 233
kilogram 185
kinetic
— energy 158
— friction 157
— reaction 220
— theory 171
KIRCHHOFF's laws 176
knot 185
KOLMOGOROV 117
kWh 186

L

LAGRANGE's identity 105
lateral surface area 93
lattice enthalpy 224
law (of)
— absorption 11
— addition $\sim$ 118
— AMPÈRE-MAXWELL 178
— area (KEPLER) 160
— associativity 11
— BEER-LAMBERT 244
— BIOT-SAVART 177
— commutativity 11
— COULOMB's $\sim$ 173
— decay 183
— distributivity 11, 25
— exponents 17
— FARADAY, induction 178
— GAUSS, electric flux 173
— GAUSS, magnetic flux 178
— HAGEN-POISEUILLE 165
— HOOKE 157, 164
— ideal gas 218
— idempotence 11
— illumination 168
— induction 178
— KEPLER 160
— KIRCHHOFF's laws 176
— logarithms 17
— mass action 219
— MAXWELL-AMPÈRE 178
— motion, NEWTON's 2nd $\sim$ 157
— motion, NEWTON's 3rd $\sim$ 157
— OHM 175
— PLANCK 182
— reflexion 167
— roots 17
— SNELL's $\sim$ 167
— STEFAN-BOLTZMANN $\sim$ 182
— thermodynamics 170, 172
— total probability 119
— WIEN's displacement $\sim$ 182
lcm 36
least
— common multiple 35
— squares approximation 136
LEIBNIZ 53
lens system 167
lepton 195
level
— for current 180
— for power 180
— for voltage 180
— of significance 125
life table 153
ligand 232

light
— absorption 244
— emission 244
— year 205
limit
— of function 61
— of integration 70
— of special sequence 52
— point 61
line
— equation 101
— in space 106
— in the plane 101
linear
— algebra 27
— combination 26, 27, 41, 103
— correlation 116
— differential equation 82
— equation 33
— expansion 170
— hull 26
— regression 116, 137
— span 26
— transformation 28, 29
— velocity 162
linearly dependent 81
lipophilic 238
local
— maximum 65
— minimum 65
— rate of change 62
locus 109
logarithm 17
— binary $\sim$ 17
— change of base 17
— common $\sim$ 17
— natural $\sim$ 17
logarithmic
— function 58
— spiral 68
logic 9
logistic differential equation 81
loop 46
LORENTZ
— force 177
— transformation 181
LUCAS numbers 41
luminance 168
luminous flux 168

M

MACLAURIN series 77
magnitude 104
— stellar brightness $\sim$ 208
mapping 13
— identity $\sim$ 13

257

mass 157
— atomic ∼ 196, 199
— concentration 219
— defect 183
— molar ∼ 228
— number 183
— per cent 219
— relativistic ∼ 181
— spectrometry 246
material conditional 9
mathematical induction 14
matrix 27
— addition 29
— adjacency ∼ 49
— antisymmetric ∼ 30
— coefficient ∼ 28, 34
— cofactor 31
— column space 28
— column vector 28
— diagonal ∼ 30
— diagonalizable ∼ 30, 32
— dimension 28
— elements 28
— identity ∼ 30
— inverse ∼ 30, 32
— invertible ∼ 30
— kernel 28
— multiplication 28, 29
— rank 30
— row echelon form 30
— row operations 30
— row space 28
— row vector 28
— similar ∼ 30
— singular ∼ 30
— skew symmetric ∼ 30
— square ∼ 30
— submatrix 31
— symmetric ∼ 30
— trace 29
MAXWELL-AMPERE 178
mean
— arithmetic ∼ 16, 39, 81
— geometric ∼ 16, 40, 81
— harmonic ∼ 16
— quadratic ∼ 16
— value theorem (differential calculus) 64
— value theorem (integration) 70
— weighted arithmetic ∼ 16
median 86, 87, 115
melting point 190, 228
MENELAUS 84
mesons 195
metal complex 232

method
— RUNGE-KUTTA ∼ 142
metre 185
midpoint 86
— of line segment 106
midsegment 90
mile 185
Milky Way 216
mirror (spherical) 167
mod 15, 37
moduli of roots 21
modulo 15, 37
modulus 15, 144
— of complex number 19
modus
— ponens 10
— tollens 10
Mol 218
molar
— concentration 219
— heat capacity 191
— mass 170, 228
— volume 218
mole 185
moment of inertia 76, 162
momentum 157
— relativistic 181
monosaccharide 237
monotonically
— decreasing 51, 54, 65
— increasing 51, 54, 65
monotonicity 65, 72
Moon 210
motion
— linear ∼ 155
— parabolic ∼ 156
— straight-line ∼ 156
— uniform circular ∼ 155
— uniform linear ∼ 155
— uniformly accelerated ∼ 155, 156
multinomial 43
multiple
— least common ∼ 35, 36
multiplication
— matrix ∼ 29
— matrix-vector ∼ 28
— principle 44
— scalar ∼ 26
muon 195, 196
musical interval 188
mutually exclusive 117

N

n-gon 91
NADH 241

NADPH 241
natural
— exponential function 58
— logarithm 17
— number 14
negation 9
NERNST equation 220
net of regular polyhedron 95
neutrino 195
neutron 195, 196, 218
NEWTON-COTES formula 140
NEWTON-RAPHSON method 138
nicotinamide adenine dinucleotide 241
nitrile 233
nitro compound 233
norm 104
normal 67
— distribution 123
— line 66
— stress 164
nuclear radius 183
nucleic acid 240
nucleobase 240
nucleotide 240
nuclide
— fissile ∼ 203
— radioactive ∼ 199
— stable ∼ 196
null
— hypothesis 125
— sequence 51, 53
— space 28
number
— complex ∼ 14, 18
— imaginary ∼ 18
— natural ∼ 14
— prime ∼ 36
— rational ∼ 14
— real ∼ 14, 15
— theory 35
numerical analysis 133
nutrient
— energy 239

O

oblique asymptote 57, 66
obtuse 104
octahedron 95
odd function 54
oersted (unit) 186
OHM's law 175
oil 237
one-to-one correspondence 13
optical power 167
optics 166

Index

orbital quantum number 227
order 13
— of a group 25
organic Chemistry 233
orthocentre 86
orthogonal 107
— decomposition 107
— projection 112, 113
orthogonalization procedure 108
oscillation
— damped ∼ 82
— forced ∼ 82
osculating circle 66, 67
oxidation 233
oxidizing agent 249

P

π 92, 154
paired
— data 130
— samples 130
PAPPUS-GULDIN theorem 96
parabola 22, 56, 108–110
parallel 102
parallelepiped 93
parallelogram 89
parameter representation 67
parametric equation 67
parsec 205
partial
— derivative 63, 142
— order 13
partite graph 50
partition 12, 119
— of an interval 70
PASCAL's triangle 43
path 46
pendulum
— compound ∼ 160
— physical ∼ 160, 163
— simple ∼ 160
pentagon 91
peptide 242
perihelion 160
period 155, 160
periodic 59
— function 54
permeability 195
permutation 45
peroxide 233
perpendicular 102
— bisector 86
— vector 107
pH
— aqueous solution 220
— connection with pOH 220

phase shift 180
phenol 233
photoelectric emission 182
photometry 168
photon 196
physical pendulum 160, 163
pint 185
pion 196
pK_B 220
pK_A 220
planar
— curve segment 76
— graph 47
PLANCK 182
plane 106
— curve 66
— graph 47
PLATONic solids 95
polar
— coordinates 113, 207
— equation 67
— form 18
— line 107
pole 66, 107
polygon 91
polyhedron 95
polymer 233
polymerisation 233
polynomial 21, 133
— TAYLOR ∼ 77, 78
— characteristic ∼ 32
— function 21, 57
— root 21
— zero 21
polypeptide 242
polytropic atmosphere 164
position vector 102, 106
potential 220
— chemical ∼ 170
— electric ∼ 174
— energy 158, 161
pound 186
pound-force 186
power 16, 158, 163
— complex numbers 18
— electric ∼ 176
— factor 179
— function 52, 56
— of a point 107
— of binomial 20
— series 77
— set 12
pressure
— critical ∼ 191
— hydrostatic ∼ 164
— partial ∼ 219

— standard ∼ 164
primary structure 243
prime 36
— number 36, 146
— number distribution 36
principal quantum number 227
prism 93
prismatoid 94
PRNG 144
probability 117
— addition law 118
— density function 120
— of elementary event 117
— space 118
product
— Cartesian ∼ 12
— complex numbers 18
— cross ∼ 104
— dot ∼ 104
— inner ∼ 104
— matrix-vector ∼ 28
— rule (differentiation) 63
— rule (probability) 119
— scalar ∼ 104
— scalar triple ∼ 105
— set 12
— vector ∼ 104
— vector triple ∼ 105
progression
— arithmetic ∼ 39
— geometric ∼ 40
projection rule 87
proof
— by contradiction 10
— by induction 10
— direct ∼ 10
— mathematical induction 14
propagation error 64
proportionality 15
proposition 9
— contrapositive ∼ 9
— converse ∼ 9
propositional logic 9
protein 238, 242, 243
proton 195, 218
PS 186
pyramid 93
Pythagorean triples and
    quadruples 148

Q

quadratic
— equation 22
— function 22
— mean 16
quadrature, GAUSS 140

259

quadrilateral 89
— bicenctric 90
— cyclic $\sim$ 90
— tangential $\sim$ 90
quantifier 10
quark 195
quartile 115
quotient
— complex numbers 18
— sequence 38
quotient rule 63

R

radian measure 91
radiation weighting factor 203
radioactive decay 199
— chain 202
radius
— of convergence 77
— of curvature 66, 156, 167
random number 154
— generation 144
random variable 119
— continuous $\sim$ 120
— discrete $\sim$ 119
— variance 121
range 13, 54
rank 30
rank-nullity theorem 34
rate of change 62
ratio
— golden $\sim$ 83
— test 53
rational
— function 57
— number 14
reaction
— kinetics 220
— rate constant 221
reactive power 179
real
— function 54
— gas 171
— number 14, 15
— part 18
— power 179
realization of random variable 119
rectangle 89
rectangular
— function 80
— solid 93
recurrence equation 41
recursion formula 38
redox reaction 249
reducing agent 249

reductio ad absurdum 10
reduction 233
— formula 98
reflection 112
— about the x-axis 55
— about the y-axis 55
reflexive 12
refractive index 167
refrigerant 192
regression line 137
regular polyhedra 95
relation 12
— divisibility 35
— equivalence 12
— order 13
— partial order 13
— subset 11
relative
— error 64
— frequency 116
relatively prime 35, 145
remainder 15
removable discontinuity 66
replication 242
residual 136
residue class 38
resistance (electrical) 175
resistivity
— electrical $\sim$ 194, 195
— specific $\sim$ 175
resonance 82
— frequency 180
response variable 132
rest energy 181
reversible process 171
revolution 96
rhomboid 89
rhombus 90
ribonucleotide 240
ribosome 242
RIEMANN sum 70
right-angled triangle 88, 97
right-handed system 105
RNA 240
roentgen (unit) 186
rolling resistance 157
root 16, 21, 65
— function 56
— integer $\sim$ 21
— multiple $\sim$ 21
— of unity 19
— square $\sim$ 15
— test 53
rotation
— in space 112
— in the plane 112

— matrix 112
rotational energy 163
row
— operation 30
— space 28
— vector 28
rule (of)
— BERNOULLI-L'HÔPITAL 61
— associativity 9
— chain $\sim$ 63
— commutativity 9
— constant factor $\sim$ 63
— contraposition 10
— cosine 87
— cosine for angles 100
— cosine for sides 100
— CRAMER's $\sim$ 33
— differentiation 63
— distributivity 9
— factor $\sim$ 71
— integration 71
— product $\sim$ 63
— product (combinatorics) 44
— product (probability) 119
— projection $\sim$ 87
— quotient $\sim$ 63
— SARRUS 31
— sine 87
— sine (spherical) 100
— sine-cosine 100
— sum $\sim$ 63, 71
— tangent 87
— transitivity 10
RUNGE-KUTTA 142

S

saddle point 65
salt, enthalpy of dissolution 224
sample 124
saponification 233
SARRUS 31
satellite 210
saturated vapour pressure 191
saturation level 67
sawtooth function 80
scalar 26, 27
— component 103, 107
— multiplication 26, 27, 29
— product 104
— triple product 105
scaling 55
scatter diagram 116
SCHRÖDINGER equation 182
secant 64, 85, 97
second 185
second-order curves 108

Index

sector 92
segment 92
selection 44
self induction 178
semiperimeter 86
sense strand 242
separable differential equation 81
sequence 38
— arithmetic $\sim$ 39
— difference $\sim$ 38, 40
— explicit definition 38
— geometric $\sim$ 40
— of partial sums 39, 51, 52
— of real numbers 51
— of the squared natural numbers 39
— quotient $\sim$ 38
— recursion formula 38
— sum $\sim$ 39
series 39, 51
— absolutely convergent $\sim$ 52, 53
— convergence criteria 53
— convergent $\sim$ 52, 53
— expansion 77, 79
— geometric $\sim$ 40, 53
— harmonic $\sim$ 52
— infinite $\sim$ 52, 53
— MACLAURIN $\sim$ 77
— TAYLOR $\sim$ 77, 78
set 11
— cardinality 12
— complement 11
— difference 11
— intersection 11
— number of subsets 45
— partition 12
— power $\sim$ 12
— product 12
— symmetric difference 11
— union 11
sgn 15
shear 111
— strain 165
SI units 185
side chains 238
sidereal
— day 205
— time 205
σ-algebra 117
sign function 15
similar matrix 30
similarity
— theorems 88
— transformation 111

simple
— event 117
— path 46
— pendulum 160
sine 97
— function 58
— rule 87
— rule (spherical) 100
sine-cosine rule 100
— polar 100
singular
— matrix 30
— point 65
sinusoidal
— alternating current 179
— alternating voltage 179
skew symmetric matrix 30
slant height 93
slope 66, 101
— -intercept form 101
— of secant 62
— of tangent 62
small Solar System body 212
SNELL's law 167
solar
— constant 209
— day 205
Solar System 212
solid of revolution 75, 96
solubility 225
sound
— intensity 169
— pressure amplitude 166
— wave 166, 188
space
— column $\sim$ 28
— diagonal 93
— of solutions 32
— row $\sim$ 28
— vector $\sim$ 26, 27
span, linear 26
specific heat 170, 190, 191
spectrometry 246
spectrum of visible light 244
speed 156
sphere 96
spherical
— cap 96
— excess 100
— mirror 167
— polar coordinate 114
— sector 96
— segment 96
— triangle 100
— trigonometry 100
— zone 96

spin
— anti-parallel 227
— parallel 227
spiral 68
— hyperbolic $\sim$ 68
— logarithmic $\sim$ 68
— ARCHIMEDES 68
spontaneous (process) 221
square 89
— matrix 30
— root 15
squared residuals 137
standard
— basis 27
— deviation 115, 116, 184
— electrode potential 249
— form 18, 22
— gravitational parameter 161, 210
— normal distribution (table) 149
— pressure 164
standing wave 169
static friction 157
statistical
— inference 124
— population 124
— quantities 115
— test 123, 126
statistics, descriptive 115
STEFAN-BOLTZMANN law 182
STIRLING 42, 81
stoichiometry 218
STOKES 165
strange quark 195
strictly monotonically
— decreasing 54
— increasing 54
submatrix 31
subsets 11
subspace 26
substitution
— nucleophilic $\sim$ 233
— radical $\sim$ 233
sum (of)
— complex numbers 18
— cubes of natural numbers 40
— exterior angles 91
— infinite geometric series 40
— interior angles 91
— linear transformations 29
— natural numbers 40
— powers 40
— sequence 39
— squares of natural numbers 40

261

sum rule
— (differentiation) 63
— (integration) 71
Sun 211
superposition principle
    34, 41, 82
surface
— area 93
— gravity 209
— of revolution 75
— tension 164, 188
surjective 13
switch-on transient current
    through inductor 179
symmetric 12
— about y-axis 54
— difference 11
— inversion through origin 54
— matrix 30
system
— homogeneous $\sim$ 34
— inhomogeneous $\sim$ 34
— of linear equations 33

T

t-distribution 151
t-Test
— for regression line 132
tangent 64, 67, 85, 97, 109
— function 59
— line 66
— rule 87
— -secant theorem 85
— to the circle 102
tangential quadrilateral 90
tau 195
TAYLOR
— polynomial 77, 78
— series 77, 78
temperature
— absolute $\sim$ 170
— Celsius $\sim$ 170
— centigrade 170
— coefficient 194
— critical $\sim$ 191
tensile strength 188
test (of)
— STUDENT's t-$\sim$ 128
— WILCOXON-MANN-WHITNEY 152
— chi-squared $\sim$ 129
— difference of expected values 130
— normal distribution 128
— slope of regression line 132
tetrahedron 93, 95, 106

THALES' theorem 85
theorem (of)
— THALES' $\sim$ 85
— ABEL-RUFFINI 24
— BAYES 119
— binomial $\sim$ 43
— CEVA's $\sim$ 84
— Chinese remainder $\sim$ 37
— circle 85
— congruence $\sim$s 88
— DE MORGAN 9, 11
— DIRAC 49
— EULER 48
— EULER-FERMAT 37
— factor $\sim$ 21
— four colour $\sim$ 50
— fundamental $\sim$ (algebra) 21
— fundamental $\sim$ (arithmetic) 36
— fundamental $\sim$ (calculus) 71
— geometric mean 88
— HUYGENS-STEINER 163
— identity $\sim$ 21
— inscribed angle 85
— intercept $\sim$ 84
— intermediate value $\sim$ 62
— limits of functions 61
— limits of sequences 51
— mean value $\sim$ 64, 70
— MENELAUS' $\sim$ 84
— of intersecting chords 85
— PAPPUS-GULDIN 96
— PTOLEMY 90
— PYTHAGORAS 88
— rank-nullity 34
— rational root $\sim$ 21
— similarity $\sim$s 88
— STEINER 163
— tangent-secant $\sim$ 85
— TAYLOR's $\sim$ (remainder term) 77
— unique factorization 36
thermal
— conductivity 172, 190, 191
— radiation 172
— transmittance 190
thermodynamics 220
— 1st law 170, 221
— 2nd law 172, 221
thin lens 167
time scale 206
top quark 195
torque 161
— electric dipole 174
— planar current loop 177
Torr 186

torus 96
total
— degree of a graph 48
— moment 161
— probability 119
totient function 37
tour 46
tr 29
trace 29
tractrix 69
trail 46
transcription 242
transformation
— affine 111
— in space 114
— in the plane 113
— linear $\sim$ 28
transformer 180
transitive 12
transitivity 10, 11
translation 112, 242
— horizontal $\sim$ 55
— vertical $\sim$ 55
transpose 29
trapezoid 90
trapezoidal rule 140
travelling salesman problem 50
tree 47
triangle 86, 88
— angle bisector 87
— equilateral 88
— inequality 15, 19, 81, 86, 104
— isosceles right-angled 88
— median 87
— right-angled 88
— spherical 100
triangular function 80
triglyceride 237
trigonometric function 58
trigonometry 97
— spherical $\sim$ 100
trinomial 43
triple point 193
trochoid 68
tropical year 205
TUKEY-ANSCOMBE plot 132
turbulent flow 165
type I error 126
type II error 126, 131

U

uncertainty principle
    (HEISENBERG) 182
undamped oscillation 82
uniaxial stress 164
union 11

Index

unique factorization theorem 36
unit
— astronomical $\sim$ 205
— fraction 56
— imaginary $\sim$ 18
— SI $\sim$ 185
— vector 106
univariate data 115
universal quantifier 10
up quark 195

V

valency 48
vaporization 170
vapour pressure 191, 192
variable
— dependent $\sim$ 13
— explanatory 132
— independent $\sim$ 13
— response 132
variance 115, 121
vector 26, 27, 102
— addition 27
— collinear $\sim$s 103
— column $\sim$ 28
— component 103, 107
— coplanar $\sim$s 103
— eigenvector 32
— of constants 34
— of unknowns 34
— product 104
— projection $\sim$ 104
— space $\mathbb{R}^n$ 27
— space (real) 26
— triple product 105
velocity
— addition (relativistic) 181
— average $\sim$ 155
— constant 221
— instantaneous $\sim$ 155
vertex 22, 46
— -labelled graph 48
— equations 109
vertical
— asymptote 57, 66
— scaling 55
— translation 55
VIETA 23, 24
viscosity
— dynamic $\sim$ 189
voltage 174
volume
— expansion 170
— flow 165
— of solid 93
— per cent 219
— solid of revolution 75

W

W boson 196
walk 46
water
— autoprotolysis 220
— ionic product 220
wave 166
— electromagnetic $\sim$ 166
— harmonic $\sim$ 166
— number 166
— standing $\sim$ 169
wavelength 166
— spectral lines 194
weight 157
weighted
— arithmetic mean 16
— graph 48
WICHMANN-HILL 145
WIEN's displacement law 182
WILCOXON 129
work 158, 163
— of compression 164

Y

yard 185
year 205
YOUNG's modulus 164

Z

Z boson 196
zero 21, 65
— absence of $\sim$ divisors 15
— multiple $\sim$ 21

Selected units and conversion factors

(equals signs in this table denote definitions)

Length			
	1 Å (Ångström)	$= 10^{-10}$ m	
	1 inch (inch)	$= 2.540 \cdot 10^{-2}$ m	
	1 foot	$= 12$ in	$= 0.3048$ m
	1 yard	$= 3$ ft	$= 0.9144$ m
	1 mile	$= 5280$ ft	$= 1609.344$ m
Volume			
	1 gallon (US)	$= 3.785\,411\,784 \cdot 10^{-3}$ m^3	
	1 pint (UK)	$= 0.568\,261\,25 \cdot 10^{-3}$ m^3	
Speed			
	1 knot	$= 1.852$ km/h	≈ 0.5144 m/s
Mass			
	1 pound	$= 0.453\,592\,37$ kg	
	1 ct (metric carat)	$= 0.2 \cdot 10^{-3}$ kg	
Force			
	1 lbf (pound-force)	$= 4.448\,221\,615\,260\,5$ N	
Energy			
	1 cal$_{IT}$ (international Steam Table calorie)	$= 4.1868$ J	
	1 kWh (kilowatt-hour)	$= 3.6 \cdot 10^6$ J	
	1 eV (elektron volt)	$\approx 1.602\,176\,487 \cdot 10^{-19}$ J	
Power			
	1 hp(M) (metric horsepower)	$= 75$ kp·m/s	$= 735.498\,75$ W
Pressure			
	1 bar	$= 10^5$ N/m^2	$= 10^5$ Pa
	1 atm (standard atmosphere)	$= 101\,325$ Pa	$= 1.013\,25$ bar
	1 Torr	$= \frac{1}{760}$ atm ≈ 1.333 mbar ≈ 1 mm Hg	
Dosimetry			
	1 Ci (curie)	$= 3.7 \cdot 10^{10}$ Bq	
	1 R (roentgen)	$= 2.58 \cdot 10^{-4}$ C/kg	
	1 rad (radiation absorbed dose)	$= 0.01$ Gy	
	1 rem (roentgen equivalent in man)	$= 0.01$ Sv	

Metric prefixes

prefix	code	power of ten	prefix	code	power of ten
deca	da	10^1	deci	d	10^{-1}
hecto	h	10^2	centi	c	10^{-2}
kilo	k	10^3	milli	m	10^{-3}
mega	M	10^6	micro	μ	10^{-6}
giga	G	10^9	nano	n	10^{-9}
tera	T	10^{12}	pico	p	10^{-12}
peta	P	10^{15}	femto	f	10^{-15}
exa	E	10^{18}	atto	a	10^{-18}
zetta	Z	10^{21}	zepto	z	10^{-21}
yotta	Y	10^{24}	yocto	y	10^{-24}